logic

BASIC BOOKS, INC., Publishers

New York / London

logic:

a comprehensive introduction

Samuel D. Guttenplan   Martin Tamny

SECOND PRINTING

©1971 by Samuel D. Guttenplan and Martin Tamny

Library of Congress Catalog Card Number: 77-58447

SBN 465-04160-4

Manufactured in the United States of America

FOR

dora

AND

myrna

preface

The writing of a text for courses in logic presents problems that do not arise for courses in other university subjects. This is so because of the seeming diversity of topics collected under the rubric of logic. Some approaches emphasize the formal side of logic to the almost complete exclusion of informal reasoning, philosophy of language, and scientific method. Other approaches tend to place special emphasis on the informal aspects of the subject to the detriment of formal matters. Any balanced treatment would require a text that not only contains sufficient material to deal adequately with all areas but one which unites this material by means of an underlying theme.

The writing of such a text has been our goal. To this end we have included chapters on the main topics in formal logic not excepting a rigorous treatment of formal systems, on the syllogistic, on logic and language, on the logic of science, and the logic of philosophic arguments. The underlying theme which we have used to draw these apparently diverse topics together is the tripartite distinction of the syntactic, semantic, and pragmatic aspects of language as applied to logical discourse.

In that logic is an ongoing enterprise we have sought to overcome the appearance of dealing with a dead subject (a common impression left by many texts) by including discussions of the history of logic and introductory material on frontier research. This latter material is represented by sections on truth trees (semantic tableaux), modal logic, many-valued logic, and electronic interpretations of logic. In addition, there is an introductory treatment of Gödel's proof based on a restricted language of self-reference.

logic: a comprehensive introduction. . . . .

The comprehensive nature of the book allows for a considerable degree of flexibility in the design of courses keyed to it. The instructor will almost certainly find that there is more material in the text than could possibly be covered in a one semester course. Although we are sure that each instructor will want to utilize this book in his own way we offer the following as suggested syllabi for one semester courses:

Introduction to Logic	Chapters 1, 2, 3, 6
Introduction to Formal Logic	Chapters 1, 3, 4, 6
Logic and Methodology	Chapters 1, 2, 3, 6, 7, 8
Symbolic Logic	Chapters 1, 3, 4, 5 (Some additional material can be supplied through the reading of articles on completeness proofs.)

In conclusion we would like to express thanks to our instructors Daniel J. Bronstein, Kaikhosrov D. Irani, Richard C. Jeffrey, and Isaac Levi who are largely responsible for our interest in logic. We would also like to thank the publisher's reader whose identity is unknown to us but whose helpful comments did much to improve this book. Thanks are also due to the hundreds of students who have passed (and otherwise) through our classrooms and who by their questions and reactions have made it possible for us to write this book.

Finally special thanks to Myrna Tamny who besides producing the congenial atmosphere in which this book was written, also copied out large sections of the manuscript in preparation for the final typescript.

Fall 1971
New York, N.Y.

S. D. GUTTENPLAN
M. TAMNY

contents

3 propositional logic

4 predicate logic   149

8 philosophical arguments   353

logic

introduction

1.1 WHAT IS LOGIC?

Almost everyone agrees that logic has something to do with thinking, though the difficulty enters when one tries to specify this relationship more exactly. However, of all the possible ways in which logic is related to thinking two rather general ways present themselves as first approximations. First, it is possible that logic is concerned with describing the ways in which we do carry on our thinking and second, logic may tell us how we ought to think. Both these positions have certain merits, and neither is completely correct, but we will have to examine them more closely.

1.1.1 Does logic describe how we think?

Logic surely does describe the way we sometimes think, but it does not describe the way we usually think. We usually think in a rather haphazard way tending in some general direction but often stopping here and there and going off in various new directions, sometimes to return to the old, sometimes not. Writers like Joyce, and more recently Burroughs, have attempted to capture this "natural" thought in their "stream of consciousness" styles. It should be seen that if there is any discipline whose primary business is the description and explanation of how we think it is surely psychology and not logic.

1.1.2 Does logic tell us how we ought to think?

Does logic prescribe? Here as before the answer is sometimes. There are situations where logic does indeed tell us how to think, when we are, for instance, trying to solve some puzzle. But surely if a person were to always think by using some explicit set of rules of logic his thinking would be enormously inefficient.

When we are trying to solve a puzzle we are concerned with the logical rules that might help us but we do not use logical rules in every step of our reasoning. Human beings are capable of making conceptual jumps that save large numbers of steps as compared, say, with computers, which do operate by the stepwise use of some finite number of explicit rules.[1] This idea of a *conceptual leap* is familiar to anyone who has ever tried to work on a mathematical puzzle; for a while one is not sure as to how to proceed and then the answer is suddenly "seen."

We may best be able to show how these two elements of description and prescription operate together in logic by considering an example. One morning Professor E came down to a breakfast of a cereal, which, for reasons known only to advertising executives, is square in shape. As he was pouring the milk over his cereal it suddenly flashed upon him that $E = mc^2$. The actual "flow" of thought could be described as "milk (m) . . . cereal square (c^2) . . . gives energy (E)." Of course Professor E had been thinking about the relation between mass and energy for months before. But he had been unable to reach any sort of acceptable conclusion. Now he felt sure that he had. Several weeks later Professor E reads a paper in which he states that $E = mc^2$. A fellow physicist in the audience then asks the good professor how he arrived at this marvelous conclusion. Does Professor E now recount the story about his milk and cereal? Obviously not, though he may have if his questioner were a psychologist and the context somewhat different. But what our physicist is asking for is not an actual account of the "stream" of thought that terminated in $E = mc^2$, but rather a justification for the claim that $E = mc^2$. What Professor E must do is provide an argument in support of his claim. This he may do by first presenting certain assertions whose truth is

---

[1] The great speed of computers lies in their ability to carry out these large numbers of steps in relatively short periods of time, not in the fact that the computer's mode of operation is more efficient than human thought.

agreed on by both the professor and his questioner. He may then proceed by showing that given these assertions the truth of $E = mc^2$ follows according to the rules of logic, i.e., that having accepted these assertions one is committed to accepting that $E = mc^2$. This procedure is of the right sort to justify the truth of his assertion whereas a description of the milk and cereal incident is obviously irrelevant to the truth or falsity of the professor's claim.

What then does the preceding example tell us about the nature of logic? First, it shows how logic gives us a model against which we can judge the correctness of the form of a given justification. Second, it indicates that logic tells us the way we ought to construct our justifications, i.e., it tells us what form a justification should take.

Though logic prescribes how we ought to construct our justifications (in the sense of the form of the justifications and not what facts to base our justifications on), we can still understand how logic is sometimes descriptive and this is because we do on occasion use rules of logic to actually construct our justifications. In any case, the form of justification we arrive at (whether by conceptual jumps or by explicit use of logical rules) must be compared to the "correct" forms which logic delimits. Thus, the primary role of logic is prescriptive, or normative, in that it establishes standards, or "norms," against which we can compare our own justifications and in accordance with which we can construct them.

1.2 ARGUMENTS

In section 1.1 we have described logic as providing a means of evaluating the justifications of claims. In logic we generally call these justifications *arguments*. By the term *argument* we do not mean a disagreement amongst people that can be heated or mild, ill-timed, or "just what he deserved." Instead we are using the term *argument* to describe attempts to justify the claim of truth for a given assertion by reference to the truth of other assertions that support or are evidence for the claim. Arguments in our sense are then convincing or unconvincing, good or bad, sound or unsound, etc.

The identification of arguments is not so simple a task as one might suspect. The first thing one must do is identify the claim being made and then note those assertions being offered in support of the claim. It is sometimes difficult to distinguish between a claim and an argument. Consider the statement,

1. Today is Tuesday because yesterday was Monday.

Is it a claim or an argument? If 1 is an argument the claim it contains would be

    2. Today is Tuesday.

which would be supported by the assertion

    3. Yesterday was Monday.

If, on the other hand, 1 is a claim rather than an argument it would require some other assertion in its support, such as, say,

    4. The day after Monday is always Tuesday.

The only thing that would enable us to tell whether 1 was an argument or a claim would be the context. If someone asserted 1 and then said "I say that because the day after Monday is always Tuesday" it would be clear that 1 was a claim and not an argument.

It is useful when writing an argument to write the supporting statements and the claim being supported on separate lines. Thus if it is determined that 1 above is an argument it should be rewritten as,

    Yesterday was Monday.
    ∴ Today is Tuesday.

Such words as "therefore," "because," and "since" are usually present in an argument, but their presence, as we have seen, does not assure us that we are dealing with an argument.

Those assertions in an argument that are offered as supporting ones are termed *premises,* whereas the assertion they are taken to support is termed the *conclusion* of the argument.

Arguments are *deductive* or *inductive* according to whether the truth of the premises leads with certainty to the truth of the conclusion or leads with some degree of probability to the truth of the conclusion. This distinction is here greatly oversimplified, and in a sense this entire book can be viewed as an attempt to differentiate and trace the connections between inductive and deductive arguments.

1.3   ARGUMENT FORMS AND VALIDITY

We all have some notion of what constitutes a good or bad argument. It is part of the business of logic to clarify this notion and make it as exact as possible. We will now attempt to clarify the notion of a "good" deductive argument and in so doing also clarify the notion of a "bad" deductive argument. Our consideration of inductive arguments will have to wait until Chapter 7.

Let us proceed by taking a paradigm case of what appears to be a good deductive argument. This we can do by offering the reader two premises and letting him draw the conclusion that he feels necessarily follows.

> All *A* are *B*.
> All *B* are *C*.
> ∴ ?

The reader surely has concluded that, All *A* are *C*. We may then tentatively take the following argument as our paradigm of a "good" deductive argument,

> All *A* are *B*.
> All *B* are *C*.
> ∴ All *A* are *C*.

The first thing to be noticed about our paradigm is that it does not seem to be about anything. What, after all, does "All *A* are *C*" assert? It surely is not making an assertion about the letters *A* and *B*. But if this is the case there seem to be good grounds for asserting that our paradigm is not an argument at all. This is so because, if the reader will recall, an argument consists of a claim and a list of assertions which is used to justify the claim. However, the sentence "All *A* are *B*" is not a claim in that one cannot tell whether it is true or false and thus the paradigm under consideration is only an argument in superficial appearance. If it itself is not an argument, how can we turn it into one? This can be done by replacing *A, B,* and *C* with class names. A class is any group of things having some property in common, and a class name is merely a word that has a given class as its referent. Thus "men" is a class name designating the class of individual men. If we then replace *A* in our paradigm with the class name "men" and B with the class name "mammals" and C with the class name "air breathers" we have,

> All men are mammals.
> All mammals are air breathers.
> ∴ All men are air breathers.

which is indeed an argument. Let us then call such things as

> All A are B.
> All B are C.
> ∴ All A are C.

which exhibit the form of an argument but not its content, i.e., which give its structure but not what it is about, *argument forms*, or *argument types*.

We have seen that our notion of "good argument" concerns the form of the argument and not its content. Thus every argument having the argument form above is a "good argument." It should also be noted that "All A are B" is not a statement, because it is not about anything and is neither true nor false. "All A are B" can, however, be turned into a statement by replacing A and B in it by class names. The resultant statement would then be either true or false.[2] Let us then call things of the sort "All A are B" *statement forms*. When we speak of the possibility of a statement form being true or false we mean thereby that it becomes either true or false depending on the particular class names substituted for the capital letters it contains.

We will establish a convention to be used in speaking of the truth or falsity of the premises of an argument. When all the statements constituting the premises are true the premises will be said to be true. When one or more of the statements constituting the premises are false the premises will be said to be false. Given this convention it is clear that the premises of an argument are either true or false but not both. We can now see that there are four possible combinations of truth and falsehood of the premises and conclusion. The premises and conclusion can both be true; the premises may be true and the conclusion false; the premises may be false and the conclusion true; and finally both the premises and conclusion may be false. It is possible, however,

---

[2] It may be that strictly speaking this is not the case. It could be argued that the substitution of certain combinations of class names for A and B lead to nonsense and, therefore, not to statements that are true or false. An example might be "All days of the week are green things." A discussion of this matter will be found in Chapter 6.

for a given argument form not to allow all these four possibilities. That is, given a particular argument form there may exist no class names that can be substituted for the capital letters that will yield, e.g., an argument with true premises and a false conclusion. Indeed we will find that it is just this fact that characterizes our good arguments.

Let us attempt to find various class names which when substituted for A, B, and C in our paradigm argument form yield the four possibilities indicated above.

1. If we allow A to be "squares," B to be "rectangles," and C to be "parallelograms," we will have the case of true premises and true conclusion.

> All squares are rectangles. **T**
> All rectangles are parallelograms. **T**
> ∴ All squares are parallelograms. **T**

2. If we allow A to be "squares," B to be "circles," and C to be "parallelograms" we will have the case of false premises and true conclusion.

> All squares are circles. **F**
> All circles are parallelograms. **F**
> ∴ All squares are parallelograms. **T**

3. If we allow A to be "triangles," B to be "circles," and C to be "parallelograms" we will have the case of false premises and a false conclusion.

> All triangles are circles. **F**
> All circles are parallelograms. **F**
> ∴ All triangles are parallelograms. **F**

We have seen, so far, that our paradigm case of a good argument form can have true premises and a true conclusion, false premises and a true conclusion, and false premises and a false conclusion. There is one more possibility to consider: Can such an argument form have true premises and a false conclusion? The answer is no! Though methods to prove that this is the case will be introduced in the next chapter it would be useful for the reader to try and find substitution instances of A, B, and C that will make the premises true and the conclusion false.

The fact that a good argument cannot have true premises and a false conclusion can be used as the defining characteristic of such arguments. We may indeed now drop the vague term *good argument* and replace it with the precise term *valid argument.* An argument is said to be *valid* if it is impossible for its premises to be true and its conclusion false. Any argument in which it is possible to have true premises and a false conclusion is said to be *invalid.*

It is to be noted that the question of validity is not concerned with the actual truth or falsity of statements but rather with their possible truth or falsity in relation to each other. Thus one can be confronted with an argument with true premises and a true conclusion that is still invalid because what is crucial is whether it is *possible* for the premises to be true and the conclusion false.

> It is August 19.
> ∴ It is a Monday.

is such an argument. On August 19, 1968, both its premise and conclusion were true, but it was not a valid argument because it was (and is) possible for its premise to be true while its conclusion is false. On August 19, 1969, e.g., its premise is, in fact, true and its conclusion false. We must not then ask whether the premises are true and the conclusion false but rather whether it is possible for the premises to be true and the conclusion false. If the premises are in fact true and the conclusion false the argument is, of course, invalid, because the actual occurrence of a situation proves that such a situation is possible.

The foregoing will enable us to exhibit the invalidity of some argument forms. Consider the following argument form.

> All *A* are *B*.
> All *C* are *B*.
> ∴ All *A* are *C*.

It is possible to construct an argument of this form that has true premises and a true conclusion, e.g.,

> All squares are figures. **T**
> All parallelograms are figures. **T**
> ∴ All squares are parallelograms. **T**

The existence of this argument indicates nothing about the validity of the above argument form. But if we could find an argument with true premises and a false conclusion that had the form above we would show the argument form invalid. If we allow A to be "men," B to be "mortal," and C to be "women" we will have the desired argument.

> All men are mortal. **T**
> All women are mortal. **T**
> ∴ All men are women. **F**

The existence of this argument shows that our original argument form is invalid and therefore that any argument of the form

> All A are B.
> All C are B.
> ∴ All A are C.

is invalid, because we have shown that it is possible for an argument of this form to have true premises and a false conclusion.

EXERCISE

1 Construct an argument for each of the following argument forms that will demonstrate the argument forms, invalidity.

a.   All A are B.
     All B are C.
     ∴ All B are A.

b.   All B are A.
     All B are C.
     ∴ All C are A.

c.   All C are B.
     All A are B.
     ∴ All C are A.

The method that you have been asked to use in the above set of exercises is called the method of analogy. This method of testing the validity of arguments is lacking in several respects. It is true that if you can construct an argument with true premises and false conclusion that has the same form as a given argument then the given argument is invalid despite the truth or falsity of its premises and conclusion. But what if we are unable to construct an obviously invalid analogue to our given argument? Does this show that our given argument is valid? It does not. Our failure to construct the analogue may be owing to one of two reasons: it may be that the argument is valid, or it may be that we are simply not clever enough to construct the obviously invalid analogue. Thus, though the method can show the invalidity of an argument, it cannot show its validity. It is, so to speak, a negative test because it at best shows the invalidity of a given argument.

The sort of method we would like to have for testing the validity of arguments would be one that will allow us in every case to decide without question whether the argument is valid or invalid. The ideal method of testing for validity or invalidity would then be mechanical in the sense that anyone could successfully apply the test by following an explicit set of rules. It should be obvious that one of the major tasks of logic is to seek such a method.

1.4   SENTENCES AND PROPOSITIONS

In section 1.3 we spoke of the truth and falsity of statements, but did not make clear what we mean by the term *statement*. In this connection we would like to now raise the question of what it is that is said to be true or false in logic. What are we to call that thing that can serve as the premise or the conclusion of an argument? More importantly, what properties does it have?

We may start with the one property with which we are by now familiar, namely that this "thing" is either true or false, but not both and then proceed by considering several sorts of things that are said to be true or false. Included in this group would be beliefs, judgments, sentences, assertions, propositions. First, it might be argued that when we say that a certain belief or judgment is true what we mean is that a sentence, statement, assertion, or proposition is believed or judged to be true. That is to say, when we speak of beliefs and judgments as being true or false we do so only derivatively; that truth and falsity are predicated on sentences, statements, assertions, or propositions and only of judgments and beliefs because they are about sentences, statements, assertions, and propositions. But if this is so might it not also be the case that, though we speak of the truth or falsity of sentences, statements, assertions, and propositions, some of these are only derivatively true or false?

Let us make the following distinctions between *sentences, sentence tokens,* and *propositions.* A sentence token is an actual physical inscription of a sentence. Thus below we have two sentence tokens, i.e., two inscriptions of the sentence "It is raining."

It is raining.
It is raining.

There are two sentence tokens above, but how many sentences are there? The answer is one; the one English sentence "It is raining." Now, consider the following list:

It is raining.
It is raining.
Es regnet.[3]

How many sentence tokens and how many sentences have we here? We have three sentence tokens since there are three inscriptions, and we also have two sentences, the English sentence "It is raining" and the German sentence "Es regnet." When one looks at the three sentence tokens or two sentences above, one gets the feeling that there is *one* something or other there. After all, the two sentences above have the "same meaning." In attempting to explain this we generally speak of there being one *proposition* above. One writes a proposition by writing a sentence token that "expresses" a sentence, the "meaning" of which is the proposition. We have tried to indicate that this is an oversimplification of matters through the use of quotation marks. Propositions as the things that are true or false cannot, of course, be the meanings of sentences. For it is not the meaning of a sentence that is true or false but rather what is meant by it, i.e., what is asserted when one uses it. That these are not the same thing can be seen by considering the sentence, "That is mine." Two people may use this same sentence to assert different things. Thus I point at the book and say "That is mine" and you point at the same book and say "That is mine." We are surely asserting different things, for what one of us says is true while what the other says is false. But we are both, after all, using the same sentence, which has but one meaning which might be paraphrased, "The thing pointed to by the utterer of this sentence belongs to the utterer of this sentence." So a proposition is what one asserts when using a sentence rather than what the sentence means. Propositions are not in any specific language whereas the sentences

[3] The German sentence meaning "It is raining."

associated with them are in specific languages, e.g., English or German.

Are sentences true or false or is what they mean (assert) true or false? Consider the sentence

It is raining.

Is it true or false? Perhaps the reader looked out of the window and replied true if it was raining and false if it was not. But what makes the reader think that this sentence is about the meteorological conditions at the time and place he is reading it. Generally a sentence in the present tense refers to the time when it is written or uttered. But then it must be written or uttered, i.e., used, in order to assert something; if it is merely an example of a sentence it is hard to see how it could be either true or false.[4] When one encounters the sentence "It is raining" without also encountering the act of its utterance or its being written one does not know the time and place to which it refers and therefore its truth or falsity cannot be determined. If in addition we are told that the sentence is not meant as an assertion then it is not just that we cannot determine the sentence's truth or falsity, but rather that it is neither true nor false. The notion of an assertion is then a critical one, and it is perhaps the same as our notion of proposition.

Our point, that sentences are said to be true or false derivatively in that they are true or false only in that what they are used to assert is true or false, can perhaps be strengthened by noting that certain grammatical distinctions are irrelevant to logical issues. Consider, e.g., the distinction between declarative, interrogative, and imperative sentences. It is in general true that we use declarative sentences when making assertions, interrogative sentences when asking questions, and imperative sentences when making commands. But clearly we can assert, question, and command without using the respective kinds of sentences.

A teacher is giving a command, albeit nicely, when he says, "Would you please hand in your examinations now?" despite his use of an interrogative sentence. The same teacher might use the declarative sentence "I expect your papers to be handed in on time" to give a command. Similarly one can use declarative sentences to ask questions, e.g., by saying "This is the 14th Street station" to the conductor and waiting to see if he agrees or disagrees. Have we not all encountered rhetorical questions that are really assertions?

[4] Of course, one can imagine what such a sentence would express if it were used.

In sum, then, the item that can function as either a premise or conclusion of an argument is not a sentence token or a sentence but a proposition. There are, of course, similarities between the notion of a declarative sentence and a proposition, but we will emphasize the fact that a proposition is either true or false (but not both, of course) whereas sentences may be used in nonpropositional ways.

1.5   SYNTACTICS, SEMANTICS, AND PRAGMATICS

In our preliminary discussion we have only briefly outlined the main elements of logic viz. argument, proposition, validity, and truth and indicated their interconnections. In the remainder of the book we will fill in the detail and develop ways to evaluate deductive and inductive arguments. It may be useful for the reader if we discuss here a distinction that we will return to again and again in later chapters. In the study of language one hears of a division into semantic, syntactic, and pragmatic aspects or studies. In essence, this (and any other) introduction to logic consists of material that bears on each of these, and it will be helpful to briefly define these and indicate the way in which these linguistic terms enter into the organization of logic. The study of syntax (or grammar, an often used synonym) is the study of the forms and order of linguistic elements. As the reader can appreciate even in our brief discussion, logic itself is the study of form—argument forms. Chapters 2, 3, 4, and 5 will present different systems of *formal logic,* and they will represent the syntactical aspects.

Semantics is, in linguistic contexts, concerned with the relation of linguistic elements (or sentence tokens) to facts or elements in the world. In more ordinary terms, semantics is the study of the meaning of linguistic terms (words, sentence tokens, punctuation marks, etc.). In developing the formal apparatus of Chapters 2, 3, 4, and 5 we will continually be defining new symbols and will in this sense depend on semantical relations. Also, we will base several of the methods of evaluating arguments on semantic factors. Finally, some general semantic considerations will be discussed in Chapter 6.

In the previous discussion of the term *proposition* we noticed that the context of utterance was often necessary to determine what was being asserted. That is, when we are given the sentence,

The weather is fine.

we cannot be sure whether it is true or false unless we know the circumstances under which it was uttered or written. Concern with the circumstances or context of linguistic elements is known as *pragmatics,* and in parts of Chapters 6, 7, and 8 we will present what might be called the pragmatics of logic. That is, we will be considering the uses of arguments (in philosophy and science) and the dependence of various types of nonformal arguments on context. We feel that the use of this linguistic trio can be profitably applied to logic and we will amplify this throughout the book.

the syllogistic

2.1 DEVELOPMENT OF THE SYLLOGISTIC

In this chapter we will be examining a certain branch, or perhaps better, a fragment of logic. It is the topic known variously as Aristotle's logic, syllogistic, or categorical logic, and as we shall see shortly, there are good grounds for all these names. The reader should keep all of the points of the introductory chapter in mind as he learns the terminology and procedures of this branch of logic, as a main object of this chapter will be the clarification and specification of these concepts. Thus while the ideas of argument, truth, validity, et al. were spoken of rather generally in Chapter 1, here they will be fleshed out and given a thoroughly concrete treatment.

This logic was first detailed by Aristotle (384-322 B.C.) in a work known as the *Prior Analytics,* but really reached its present form through changes after Aristotle's death. Elements of Stoic philosophy (third century B.C.) added much to its development and, in large part, this development was completed by the end of the fourteenth century. As is generally well known the medieval scholastic writers devoted considerable time to the syllogistic, and this will be evident in the large number of Latin phrases and devices that cling to the syllogistic logic. The reader may wonder why a subject whose development was largely closed in 1400 is still relevant to a modern course in logic. The answer is, of course, that the syllogistic utilizes most of the significant general ideas of logic such as argument, validity, and inference and because of this will serve as a useful introduction to the more modern branches of logic. The limitations of the Aristotelian logic, however, will become obvious and will be discussed at the end of this chapter and the beginning of the next.

Without claiming any special historical accuracy let us imagine how the idea of the syllogistic might have been developed by Aristotle. First keep in mind the goal that motivated its development. What we want (and presumably what Aristotle wanted) is a method of evaluating an argument; that is, a method of deciding whether the premises lead validly to the conclusion. Further, it would be very useful if the method we develop would allow us to make the decision about validity without possibility of error and without spending a large amount of wasted effort. In Chapter 1 we did have a method of evaluation. It consisted of attempting to construct an argument of similar structure to the one we were evaluating; this second argument, however, was to contain true premises and an obviously false conclusion. Thus, to use this method to evaluate:

A. 1. Some dogs are mammals.
   2. Some mammals are carnivores.
   ∴ Some dogs are carnivores.

We construct a very similar argument such as:

A'. 1. Some dogs are mammals.
    2. Some mammals are cats.
    ∴ Some dogs are cats.

Now as can be seen A' is of precisely the same structure as A.[1] (As we will shortly see, this structure is known as *logical form*.) However in A' the premises are incontrovertibly true and the conclusion just as obviously false. This shows, of course, that in an argument of form A the conclusion does not invariably follow from premises 1 and 2 and so we call the argument A' a *counterexample*; this method of searching for counterexamples is known as the method of *logical analogy*, because A' is an analogue of A. Now, despite the

---

[1] The reader should note that reference to sameness of structure applies to the grammatical structure of the sentences used to express the propositions in each argument. In general, discussions about the structure of propositions will be based on judgments about the grammatical structure of sentences used to assert them.

fact that this is an interesting and quite common procedure of evaluation (we often use counterexamples in informal argumentation without ever thinking about the logical theory involved in its use), it fails to meet our expectations about certainty and efficiency. To begin with it is often hard to think of a counterexample, and thus we cannot avoid trial and error work, which even after considerable effort may not provide us with an evaluation. Also, the truth of the premises and the falsehood of the conclusions are not always so certain as in the above example. And finally, if we should be presented with a valid argument our method cannot prove it so. This is because we could never be sure that our inability to find a counterexample was owing to the validity of the argument and not to the possibility that we had overlooked a counterexample through carelessness or lack of ingenuity. The development of the syllogistic is an attempt to overcome the shortcomings of the method of logical analogy and substitute a procedure that will give a definite yes or no answer to the question "Is this a valid argument?"

The way in which this was achieved by Aristotle involved limitations on logical form or structure. It is obvious that validity is a property of the form of an argument and not the content of each of the premises (see Chapter 1 and the above example of logical analogy for further reference). Thus, if we limit the number and variations of the form of an argument we could test the form directly for this property and in this way evaluate all arguments, which are representive of the basic forms. This, in outline, is precisely what is done in Aristotelian logic.

2.2 BASIC ELEMENTS OF THE SYLLOGISTIC: CATEGORICAL PROPOSITIONS

The first step in achieving the desired limitation on form is the careful specification of the form that each premise or conclusion may take. If we were to allow our premises to assume any form whatever, then at this stage it would not be clear how we would be able to definitely and efficiently test the argument as we would have an infinite number of such forms. What we will do, then, is to limit our premises and conclusions to one of the four following proposition types:

1. All x's are y's.
2. No x's are y's.

    3. Some x's are y's.
    4. Some x's are not y's.

The syllogistic will be a complete exploration of valid inferences involving propositions of the above type, known as *categorical propositions*. This is, of course, why many people call this logic the *categorical logic*. Now the reader is probably well aware of the fact that many arguments contain premises and conclusions that will not fit into any of these four forms, and this is an obvious shortcoming. However, as we have noted, the Aristotelian logic gives up this wide scope in an attempt to formulate a precise evaluation procedure, and it is to this task we will turn our efforts in the remaining pages of the chapter. Inasmuch as the whole of this logic will depend on these four proposition types it becomes imperative that we understand exactly what the categorical propositions assert. As a preliminary, though, the reader should observe several things. First, the above four proposition types are not really complete propositions. They are indefinite and rather like patterns or formulas for ordinary propositions because they have unknowns (or variables) for subjects and predicates, and this is why we called them *proposition types*. Consider proposition type 1. If by 1 we mean

    a. All dogs are mammals.

then, of course, it will be true; but, if we mean

    b. All children are males.

then it will be false. This fact is perfectly acceptable, however, because we are interested in the form of each premise or conclusion, not in the specific subject matter and 1 through 4 as stated are only concerned with form. It is as if we wrote blanks in place of x and y in each proposition and filled them in later.

    Second, each of these proposition types seems to be an assertion about the relationship between one class or group of things and another. They differ in the degree and way in which they relate these groups, but each proposition contains two such groups and the English copulative "are" between them. These facts will play a significant role in our later discussion of their interrelationships, but for the present we are concerned with the precise meaning of each of the four categorical propositions considered separately.

The reader may think that their meaning is fairly obvious and without any ambiguity or vagueness, but this is not so.

2.2.1   Some *x*'s are *y*'s

Let us begin with the third proposition type:

Some *x*'s are *y*'s.

of which typical examples would be

   a. Some numbers are even numbers.
   b. Some flowers are annuals.
   c. Some automobiles are dangerous vehicles.

Because each of these asserts that the first class of objects is, in part, included in the second, this proposition is called *affirmative,* and because this inclusion is only partial it is also known as *particular.* Thus the third proposition type can be completely described as a *particular affirmative* categorical. Suppose, however, that you were in a certain college course in which there was one girl and someone in the class were to say:

Some members of this class are girls.

Would this be a correct description of this situation? In fact in c above how many cars would have to be dangerous before c would be true? Just how many is "some"? The answer to this question is very important as any ambiguity here would lead to a possible imprecision in our evaluation work. However, the answer to the question is the not surprising one that the meaning of "some" varies from one context to another, and most people would not want to say that the above statement about members of the class being girls was wrong just because there was only one girl in the class. What we will do, therefore, is to *stipulate* that 3, the particular affirmative proposition, will be true *when and only when there is at least one* x *which is a* y. This leaves us with the rather peculiar consequence that when every member of *x* is *y* it will still be true that some *x* is *y*; but this will create no problem in the logic. The reader should keep in mind, however, that the above stipulation renders the particular affirmative proposition precise though slightly at variance with the ordinary use of "some." We sacrifice the vagueness of ordinary language for the needed precision of formal logic.

It may be helpful to diagram the meaning of this and other propositions by using a representation for each of the classes involved. Thus if we consider b above

Some flowers are annuals.

then this could be represented by Figure 2-1, using F for "flowers" and A for "annuals."

FIGURE 2-1.

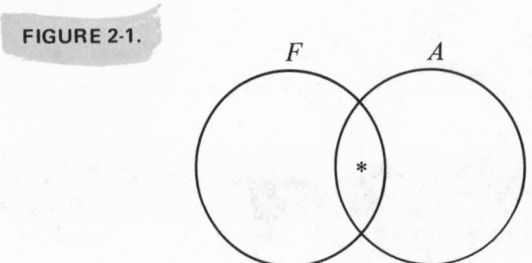

This use of circles to represent classes is known as a *Venn diagram* after the nineteenth-century English mathematician. The fact that there is an asterisk in the area where the two circles meet represents the fact that there is at least one object in this class; and the existence of at least one flower that is also an annual is precisely what the particular affirmative categorical proposition asserts.

2.2.2   Some *x*'s are not *y*'s

This fourth proposition type, which has

a. Some flowers are not annuals.
b. Some airships are not objects heavier than air.
c. Some politicians are not elected officials.

as instances, is also particular in that it contains the word "some." Thus, we know that it can be read as:

At least one x is not a y.

However, instead of class inclusion as in the previous proposition it involves an assertion of *not belonging or being a member of* and is thus not affirmative but *negative*. The diagram for this categorical proposition can be drawn in a similar way to the particular affirmative. Thus

b. Some airships are not objects heavier than air.

is represented as Figure 2-2.

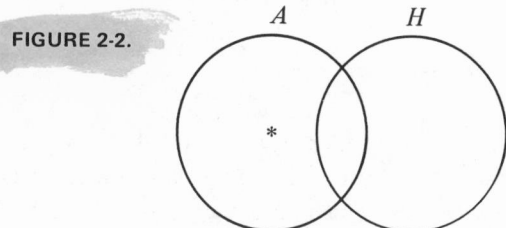

FIGURE 2-2.

In this case we put the asterisk which again (and always) means "at least one" in the area of the class of "airships" which is outside that of the class of "objects heavier than air." In effect we are saying:

There is at least one "airship" which is not a member of the class "objects heavier than air."

and this is precisely what the negative particular proposition asserts.

2.2.3 All x's are y's

The first proposition type is affirmative in that it asserts the total inclusion of the class of x's in the class of y's. It is, moreover, universal in that it does include all the members of the subject class in the predicate class. Examples of this universal affirmative proposition would be:

a. All dogs are mammals.
b. All fish are swimmers.
c. All radios are electric appliances.

There is no question of vagueness as the word "all" is precise enough. Later we shall deal with several synonyms of "all," such as "every" and "any." The diagram, however, presents a small problem; this is so because we cannot use our asterisk symbol, which means "at least one," to denote "all." The standard form of our diagram is shown as Figure 2-3.

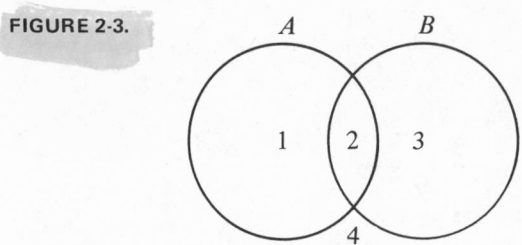

FIGURE 2-3.

The reader can see that it consists of four areas: (1) the *A* class which is not *B*; (3) the *B* class which is not *A*; (2) the class of both *A* and *B*; and (4) the area we have not considered yet, which is neither *A* nor *B*. Each of the previous propositions was accommodated in this diagram by the appropriate placing of an asterisk in either area 1 or 3. The universal affirmative proposition, however, says that:

All *A* are *B*.

Now, in a slightly different way we could say this as:

There are no *A*'s that are not *B*'s.

If we use a series of lines to mean "there is nothing in the lined area" then we could diagram the proposition as shown in Figure 2-4.

This diagram says that no *A* can exist outside of the class *B* and a moment's thought should show that this is precisely what is meant by "All *A*

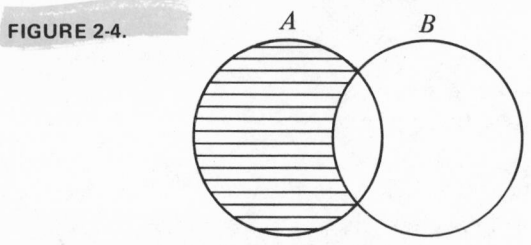

FIGURE 2-4.

are *B*." Thus, by using the lines as a second element in the diagram we are able to handle the universal affirmative proposition.

2.2.4 No *x*'s are *y*'s

The second proposition, the last we will consider, is quite obviously negative, and because it makes a statement about the whole class of *x*'s (albeit a negative one) it is universal. Instances of the universal negative are:

   a. No men are perfect creatures.
   b. No books are useless things.
   c. No horses are crustaceans.

As with the universal affirmative there is little room here for misunderstanding the exact meaning of the proposition. Also, using the technique of lines we can devise a method for diagramming this proposition. "No *A* are *B*" asserts that there are no objects in the class or section that is both *A* and *B*. (See Figure 2-5.)

FIGURE 2-5.

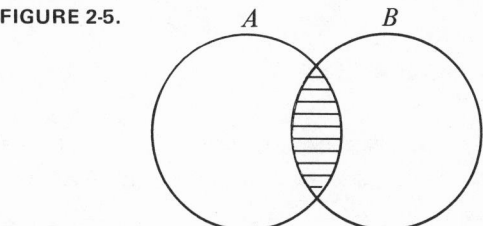

We are now finished with the preliminary discussion of the four categorical propositions and by the use of examples and diagrams we have attempted to exhibit the complete and precise sense of each of them. There is, however, one issue that we have left untouched. Suppose that someone were to assert a particular affirmative proposition, say,

Some flowers are annuals.

Would the assertion of this proposition commit the speaker to the fact of the existence of at least one flower? The answer is certainly yes. Further, he would equally commit himself to the fact of there being at least one annual.

23

These consequences are obvious in the Venn diagram, because the asterisk (see Figure 2-1) is the schematic picture of an existing object which is both a flower and an annual (of course, there may be more than one). To summarize, any particular affirmative proposition—some A are B—carries with it the implicit assertion of the existence of at least one member in both the subject (A) and predicate (B) classes. All this may seem so obvious as to require no special emphasis but let us turn to the universal affirmative proposition. When someone says,

> All dogs are mammals.

is he likewise committing himself to asserting the existence of "dogs" and "mammals?" The answer again seems to be yes, but we must look a little more closely. Figure 2-4 does not carry any such commitment. It contains only a series of lines whose purpose it is to *deny* membership to the class represented by the left-most area of the diagram. The reader may then think that this is a defect of the diagram and that ordinary usage does commit us to the existence of both dogs and mammals. But suppose the proposition under discussion were either of the following:

1. All unicorns are fictitious animals.
2. All rigid bodies are perfectly elastic bodies.

Both 1 and 2 are true and fairly ordinary propositions (2 is a statement that might be made in an elementary physics text) and yet no one would want the assertion of either of them to imply the existence of such things as "unicorns," "fictitious animals," or "perfectly elastic bodies." Thus, though many uses of universal affirmative sentences are existence-committing in ordinary conversation, still others are meant to be true assertions without such commitment. It is, or course, very important that we specify which meaning is to be reflected in our universal affirmative categorical proposition. The categoricals must have no vagueness or ambiguity because the goal of this chapter will be the evaluation of arguments involving categoricals and such evaluation might be jeopardized by lack of precision. The whole question of whether terms imply existence is known as the problem of *existential import*. Since ordinary language sanctions both the existential and the nonexistential positions we must again *stipulate* which version we will adopt. We will save the final decision for the next sections but the reader should recognize the three options open to us: (1) We may deny existential import to both subject and predicate terms. (2) We may assume the existential import of both terms. (3) We may assume existence in the subject but not the predicate term. This last option is indicated by the fact that the universal and particular negative propositions are often used in such a way that they imply the existence of only the members of the subject class. Thus, in the proposition

No UFO's are flying saucers.

it is quite clear that the speaker believes there are unidentified flying objects but wants, certainly, to deny that they are explainable as "flying saucers." Which of the options we choose will await further exposition of the interrelationships of the categorical propositions.

2.2.5 Some terminology

The syllogistic logic is often associated with a large number of terms (many in Latin) and devices that are supposed to be helpful in organizing the various arguments and relationships of propositions. They do serve this purpose, but they also can mislead the student as to the real issues of this or any logic. We have tried to keep these to a minimum and will now introduce the more useful items. We have spoken of universal, particular, negative and affirmative propositions. The universal or particular scope of a proposition is known as its *quantity* while the negative or affirmative property is known as the *quality* of the proposition. Thus, the proposition

Some flowers are annuals.

would have a *quantity* particular and a *quality* affirmative, whereas

Some politicians are not elected officials.

would have a quantity particular and a quality negative.

The second useful bit of terminology consists in the assigning of letters to each of the four propositions so that we can refer to them with a minimum of space. The basis for the assignment are the two Latin words *affirmo* ("I affirm") and *nego* ("I deny"). The first two vowels of *affirmo* are the *A* and *I*; the *A* becomes the label for the universal affirmative while the *I* is used for the particular affirmative. Similarly, the *E* of *nego* represents the universal negative and the *O*, the particular negative. This information is summarized in Table 2-1 and to the right of the proposition we have written the symbolic representative that we will employ in the remainder of this chapter. The efficacy of this device will be obvious when we have to deal with a large number of premises. Notice that we write the proposition type (*A*, *E*, *I*, or *O*) in the center flanked by first the appropriate letter for the subject term and last by the predicate term letter—both lower case.

TABLE 2-1.

1. *A* proposition: All *x*'s are *y*'s.	*xAy*
2. *I* proposition: Some *x*'s are *y*'s.	*xIy*
3. *E* proposition: No *x*'s are *y*'s.	*xEy*
4. *O* proposition: Some *x*'s are not *y*'s.	*xOy*

We indicated above that we could use "appropriate" letters for the subject and predicate terms and thus, given

Some flowers are annuals.

we could write:

fIa

The last point in this section concerns a property known as *distribution*. A term (subject or predicate) will be *distributed* when the assertion of which it is a part concerns the whole of its membership. Thus in the *A* proposition

All dogs are mammals.

a statement is being made about each and every member of the class dogs, namely, that they· are mammals. However, this same proposition does not make an assertion about each and every member of the class mammals. The possibility that there may be other mammals—mammals that are not dogs—is an obvious part of this proposition, and we say, therefore, that the subject term of an *A* proposition is *distributed* whereas the predicate term is *undistributed*.

In the *I* proposition

Some flowers are annuals.

no assertion is being made about either the whole class of flowers or the whole class of annuals, and so we say that neither the subject nor the predicate term of an *I* proposition is distributed.

The *E* proposition requires some closer thought. If we say

No herbivores are meat-eaters.

then it is obvious that we are saying something about each and every herbivore—namely, that it is not a meat-eater. This means that the subject term is distributed. However, we are also saying something about each and every meat-eater; we are saying that there are no herbivores among the entire class of meat-eaters. This means that the *E* proposition distributes both the subject and predicate terms.

Last, we turn to the *O* proposition. Since

Some politicians are not elected officials.

begins by speaking of only "some" members of the class of politicians the *O* proposition does not distribute the subject term. Still, it says of the whole class "elected officials" that there are some politicians which are not in it and thus in an indirect way it asserts something about the whole predicate class. This can be seen if the reader will consider the assertion, "Some books are not books on my shelf." How much of the shelf would one have to examine to decide on the truth of this proposition? Obviously, one would have to examine the whole shelf, and this is the basis for our considering the predicate of the *O* proposition distributed. The *O* proposition, then, distributes the predicate term but not the subject. The results of our discussion of distribution can be listed as in Table 2-2.

TABLE 2-2.

	Subject	Predicate
A	distributed	undistributed
E	distributed	distributed
I	undistributed	undistributed
O	undistributed	distributed

EXERCISE

1 The reader should be able to determine the type of each of the following categoricals and state their quantity, quality, subject, and predicate terms and which terms are distributed:
   a. Some sons of distinguished families are neither intelligent nor sensitive human beings.
   b. Some paintings by even the most famous artists are not the sort of paintings one would want in one's home.
   c. All European scholars in the medieval period are considered members of the Church by modern historians.
   d. Some philanthropes are not persons of compassion so much as wealthy men seeking a way to lessen their taxes.
   e. No persons who have ever suffered through some emotionally trying episode are the sort of people who would turn their backs on a friend's difficulties.

2.3 THE SQUARE OF OPPOSITION AND SOME MORE ON EXISTENTIAL IMPORT

The next step in the development of the syllogistic requires that we examine the logical relationships that hold between the four categorical propositions. Each of the propositions makes assertions about the relation between two classes and if we imagine these assertions to be about the *same* two classes we get the following four propositions:

   1. All UFO's are flying saucers.
   2. Some UFO's are flying saucers.
   3. No UFO's are flying saucers.
   4. Some UFO's are not flying saucers.

These propositions are clearly related to one another in that one seems incompatible with another, one implies another, and so on. In fact these would seem to be the four different positions one could take with respect to the membership of the subject class to the predicate class. We will work out and label the relationships between these four in a diagram that is traditionally known as the *square of opposition* (see Figure 2-6). In it we place the four categorical propositions in such a way that it is clear which ones contradict, imply, or are compatible with which others. (The appropriate Venn diagrams are reproduced below the names of the propositions.)

The first logical relation to consider is the one known as *contradiction*. This relation will hold between any two propositions that always have opposite truth value. That is, if proposition *P* is the contradictory of proposition *S* then when *P* is false, *S* must be true, and when *P* is true, *S* must be false. In the square of opposition the *A* is said to be the contradictory of the *O* and the *E*, of the *I*. This is clearly supported by the diagrams because in the *A* we have the declaration that the left-most area is without members while in the *O* this area is shown as containing at least one member. The same situation is apparent with respect to the diagrams for the *E* and the *I* propositions. Now, it might have seemed more reasonable to some to hold *A* and *E* as contradictories (and *I* and *O*). This is a persuasive intuition because we are aware of the fact that given a person, say Jones, who maintains,

All UFO's are flying saucers.

another person, say Smith, will often take issue with Jones by saying,

No, you are wrong. No UFO's are flying saucers.

FIGURE 2-6.

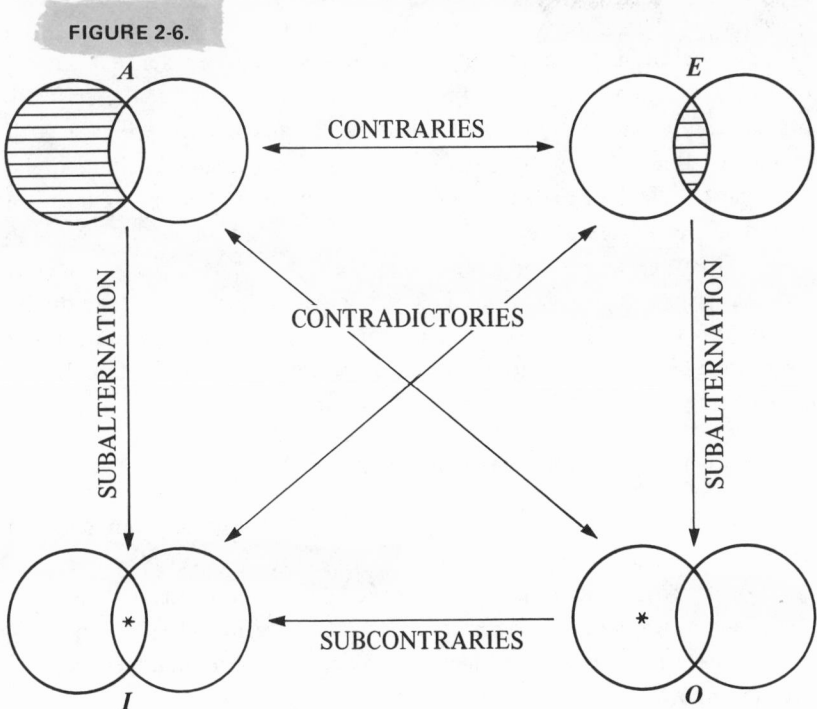

29

However, close examination will show that these propositions are not contradictory (i.e., having opposite truth value) because they could both be false. Thus, suppose there are one or two UFO's that are flying saucers and the others are either hoaxes or are explainable as illusions. In this case both the *A* and the *E* propositions will be false. Still, they could never be true at the same time and because of this we call *A* and *E* contraries. A contrary pair of propositions can both be false, but cannot both be true. This is somewhat different from the contradictory where both propositions cannot together be either true or false at the same time.

There is one problem in this contrary relationship that we have discussed before and must now resolve—that of *existential import.* We must consider what would happen to the contrary relation between *A* and *E* if we adopt any of the existential options outlined at the end of section 2.2.4. If the assertion of neither the *A* nor the *E* implies the existence of either "UFO's" or "flying saucers," in accordance with option 1, then the *A* and the *E* could both be true. This is so as a result of the fact that both *A* and *E* will be saying that the empty class is a member of the empty class, an assertion that is trivially true. Thus, the withholding of existential import (option 1) results in the loss of any contrary relationship. The contradictory relationships between *A-O* and *E-I* remain even in the case where *A* and *E* do not imply existence of subject or predicate. Even though this first option seems to rule out the perfectly ordinary notion of contrariness, it will turn out later that we will have good reason to adopt it. However, for the moment, let us shelve this option and continue to construct the square of opposition with some form of existential import. We could use either option 2 or option 3. The second option would commit the speaker of an *A* or *E* proposition to maintaining the existence of members in both the subject and predicate classes. As was mentioned briefly before, this form of existential commitment is too strong because it debars us from using *A* or *E* propositions in situations where they are ordinarily and meaningfully employed. Thus, we might want to say

No real human beings are immortal creatures.

even though we do not intend the above assertion to imply our belief in "immortal creatures." For this reason the third option—existential import of the subject class—is the one we will use temporarily. Eventually, considerations such as we used to reject option 2 will be brought to bear on option 3, but for the present we will complete the square of opposition under the third type of import.

First, we notice that the contrary relationship holds under the subject existential presupposition. This is so because, in that there is at least one "UFO," it cannot be both "a flying saucer" and "not a flying saucer." This means that the *A* and the *E* cannot both be true—though, as before, they may both be false. However, the Venn diagrams in Figure 2-6 below the *A* and the *E* sentences do not express these propositions with the subject existential presupposition; they contain the "no existence" lines but would not, by themselves, indicate membership in either class. To revise the diagram to reflect the existential presupposition we must add an appropriate asterisk to each. (See Figure 2-7.)

FIGURE 2-7.

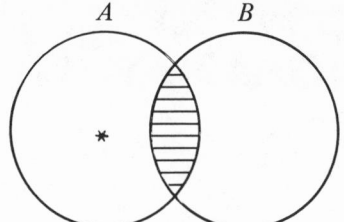 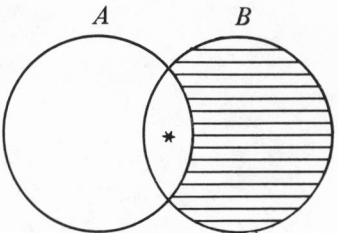

We put the asterisk in the central area of the *A* diagram because this is the nonempty part of the subject class. In doing this, we, of course, presuppose the existence of at least one member of the predicate class, and this is as we should have expected inasmuch as the members of the subject class will be members of the predicate class by virtue of the *A* proposition itself. In the *E* proposition, because our existential presupposition only includes the subject class, we can indicate this by placing an asterisk in the left-most area of the diagram for the *E* proposition. Thus, we preserve the contrary relationship between the *E* and the *A* propositions (both cannot be true because one has an asterisk where the other has lines) and still avoid making too strong an existential presupposition.

With our option 3 presupposition and the revised diagram in mind let us finish the square of opposition. The *A* proposition now clearly implies the *I* proposition. That is, the truth of the *A* assertion guarantees the truth of the corresponding *I* proposition. Also, the same implication relation holds between the *E* and the *O*. This relationship is known as *subalternation.*

Finally, it can be seen that the *I* (say, "Some UFO's are flying saucers") and the *O* ("Some UFO's are not flying saucers") can both be true but, under ordinary circumstances, cannot both be false. It is important here to be aware of the difference between a true proposition committing one to the existence of some members of a class and existential presupposition. When the *I* proposition is true than it follows that there is at least one member of the subject class that is a member of the predicate class, but when it is false or possibly false we are only committed (under option 3) to the existence of a member of the subject class that may or may not be a member of the predicate class. Thus both the *I* and the *O* may both be false without such presupposition but cannot both be false with it. Since we are now working with the subject class presupposition the latter relationship—the *subcontrary* relation—will hold. This completes the square and with it we have a primitive form of a valid inference table, though in this case the inferences are from one premise to a conclusion. By inference table it is meant that we can infer the truth or falsity of a number of the four propositions from the given truth or falsity of any one proposition; thus if we know that it is true that all *A* are *B* we can infer

1. It is true that Some *A* are *B*.
2. It is false that No *A* are *B*.
3. It is false that Some *A* are not *B*.

We get these three conclusions from one-step arguments known as *immediate inferences.*

EXERCISES

1 Each of the following is a categorical proposition that is assumed true. Using the square of opposition determine the truth or falsity of the three other corresponding categoricals for each of the given propositions.

a. Some mice are short-tailed animals.

b. No drugs are completely harmless substances.

c. Some plants are not green things.

d. All gardens are laborious projects.

2 Do the same with the following categoricals except assume that they are false.

a. No misogynists are married men.

b. All animals that swim are fish.

c. Some dogs are herbivores.

d. Some children are not youngsters.

3 Draw Venn diagrams for the following propositions according to each of the instructions below:
1. Diagram an *A* proposition with existential presupposition.
2. Diagram an *E* proposition with no existential presupposition.
3. Diagram an *O* proposition with no existential presupposition.
4. Diagram an *O* proposition with existential presupposition.

2.4 IMMEDIATE INFERENCE

The one-step arguments of the square of opposition are not the only immediate inferences that can be employed with categorical propositions. By utilizing three procedures known as *conversion, contraposition,* and *obversion* we can completely explore the one-step consequences of all categorical propositions.

2.4.1 Conversion

When a proposition is converted the subject and predicate terms are switched without change in any other part of the proposition. This procedure changes the meaning of the proposition, but in some cases the resulting new proposition is a valid consequence of the original. Given the proposition

1. Some flowers are annuals.

the converse (result of conversion) is

1'. Some annuals are flowers.

Now the second proposition, 1', is true when the first is and thus, the conversion of an *I* proposition results in a new *I* proposition which is a valid

FIGURE 2-8.

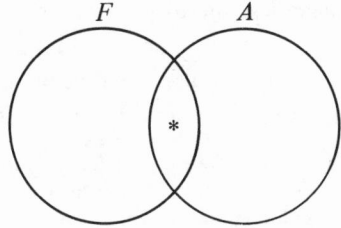

consequence of the original.[2] To see this is so consider the diagram for proposition 1 in Figure 2-8. If we were to draw the diagram for the converse, 1′, then it would appear identical to that in Figure 2-8, and thus we can convert an *I* proposition validly. Next we will convert an *A* proposition:

  2. All dogs are mammals.
  2′. All mammals are dogs.

In this case it is clear that we cannot validly infer 2′ from 2 because 2 is true and 2′ is false. This is shown conclusively by Figure 2-9. The left-hand diagram is 2 and the right-hand diagram is 2′. The incompatibility of these two means that we cannot convert *A* propositions.

FIGURE 2-9.

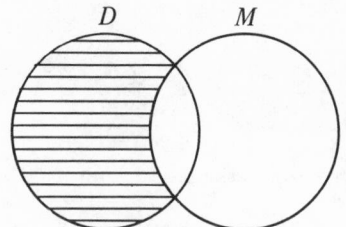 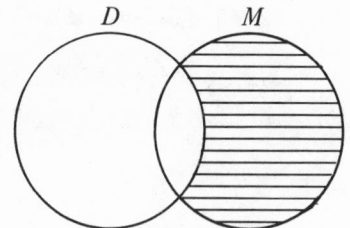

Before proceeding to determine the validity of the *E* and *O* conversions let us briefly consider the evaluation tests we have so far informally employed. We have first drawn diagrams for the original proposition and compared them with diagrams for the converse. Second, we have asked ourselves whether the original proposition could be true while its converse was false. To see why both of these methods work as tests for the validity of an immediate inference and to see that both are basically the same we need only recall the definition of validity discussed in Chapter 1. An inference is valid when the truth of its premise(s) guarantees the truth of the conclusion. In other words a test that shows that one statement cannot be false when a second one is true (i.e., the conclusion cannot be false when the premise is true) is a test of the validity of the inference from one statement to the other. The Venn

---

[2] Strictly speaking 1 and 1′ are not different propositions but different sentences that express the same proposition. This is a consequence of the fact that the conversion of a sentence expressing an *I* proposition results in a new sentence that expresses the same proposition.

diagrams are merely schematic representations of the conditions of truth of categorical propositions. When we show that the diagram for an *I* proposition is the same as the diagram for its converse we are showing that if one is true the other one must be true and hence the *I* converse is a valid consequence of the original *I* proposition. The *A* converse has a different diagram from the original *A* and thus the *A* conversion is invalid. This is seen even without a diagram because the true *A* statement, "All dogs are mammals," became by conversion the false statement, "All mammals are dogs."

Continuing now, the *O* proposition,

3. Some mammals are not dogs.

becomes by conversion

3'. Some dogs are not mammals.

As is obvious this second statement is false whereas the former one is true, and thus conversion does not hold with an *O* proposition. The Venn diagram for 3 (see Figure 2-10) and 3' also shows that the two have different truth conditions and one does not validly follow from the other.

FIGURE 2-10.

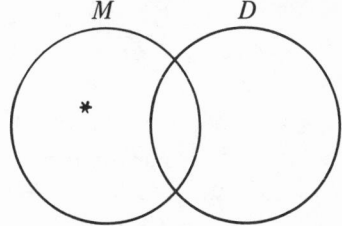 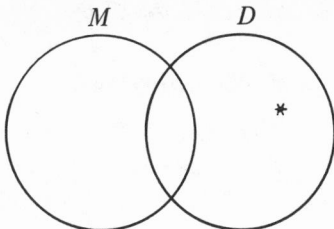

Next consider the *E* statement:

4. No men are immortal creatures.

Its converse is

4'. No immortal creatures are men.

It is clear that when 4 is true 4' will be true, and this is borne out by the Venn diagram (see Figure 2-11).

FIGURE 2-11.

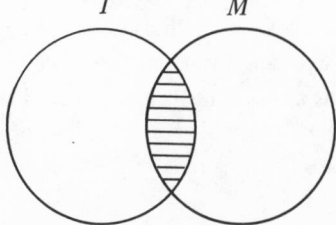
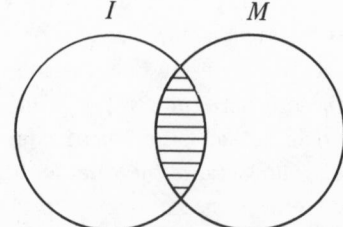

Both propositions have the same diagram and thus a conversion is a valid inference procedure with an *E* proposition.

Though the *A* proposition cannot be converted we can combine one of the results of the square of opposition with conversion in the following manner. We first derive an *I* proposition from the *A* by subalternation and then we validly can convert the *I.* This procedure is known as *conversion by limitation,* because we first limit the *A* sentence by subalternation. It is interesting to note that the process of conversion is symmetrical in that the converse of an *E* or an *I* can itself be converted to yield the original *E* or *I.* Thus, if we converted "No *A* are *B*" we would get "No *B* are *A*," which when converted again (and this is valid in that the converse of an *E* is also an *E*) becomes "No *A* are *B*"—the original proposition. However, this property of symmetry does not hold for conversion by limitation.

2.4.2 Obversion

The second immediate inferential process is obversion, and it is somewhat more complex than conversion. The first notion required to understand this procedure is that of *class complement.* When we have a term in one of our categorical propositions we have a word that designates some class of objects. That is, the use of the term *flowers* designates a large collection or class of objects which are alike in being flowers. Another way of looking at this is to say that the term *flowers* separates everything in the world into two classes—the flowers and everything else. It does so because the act of considering the class of flowers requires us to put all and only flowers into it and we thereby must recognize the boundary of *flower* and *other than flower.* This latter class—the class of nonflowers—is known as the *complement* of the class of flowers. The process of obversion requires us to (1) change the quality of the proposition under consideration without changing the quantity and (2) replace the predicate term with its complement. This second step is sometimes misleadingly called *negating the predicate term*. To see how this procedure is carried out we will begin with the obversion of the *A* proposition:

    1. All baseballs are spheres.

Step 1 requires us to change the quality of the proposition, and we must do so without changing the quantity. Since 1 is universal affirmative we must write the universal negative proposition

    1'. No baseballs are spheres.

Step 2 asks us to write the complement of the predicate term in place of the predicate term. This gives us

    1". No baseballs are nonspheres.

which is the obversion of 1. The issue now is this: Is the obversion of 1 a valid consequence of 1? A careful reading of 1 and 1" would seem to support a yes answer, but let us turn to the diagram. The diagram for 1" requires us to indicate that it is impossible for there to be a baseball in the class of nonspheres. In the Venn diagram this is shown by cross-hatching the area that represents being a baseball and a nonsphere. This gives us Figure 2-12, which is precisely what the diagram for 1 would be. Notice that the right-hand circle in Figure 2-12 is labeled "sphere" even though we are diagramming a proposition containing the term nonsphere. This is necessary since the identity of any two Venn diagrams is significant only when the class terms of each match and are on the same side of the diagram.

FIGURE 2-12.

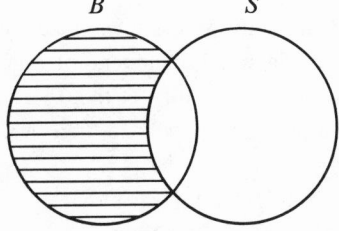

Obversion, when performed on the remaining three categorical propositions gives the results shown in Table 2-3.

TABLE 2-3.

Proposition	Obverse
I: Some flowers are annuals.	Some flowers are not nonannuals.
E: No carnivores are trees.	All carnivores are nontrees.
O: Some horses are not gentle animals.	Some horses are nongentle animals.

The obverse of the *I* assertion contains the rather peculiar phrase "not
nonannuals." In diagramming this, the double negative becomes an affirmative and thus, the obverse of the *I* is equivalent to the original *I*. The
underlying reason for the translation of "not non-*A*" as simply "*A*" is
connected with the notion of complement. Non-*A* is the complementary class
of *A,* and when we say that a certain object is not a member of the
complement of a class, we are, in effect, saying that it is a member of the
original class. That is, the complement of the complement of class *M* is *M*
itself.

The obverse of the *E* statement is shown equivalent to the original *E* by
actually drawing the diagram for both (see Figure 2-13.)

FIGURE 2-13.

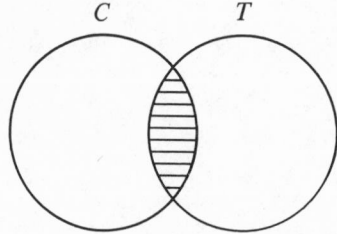 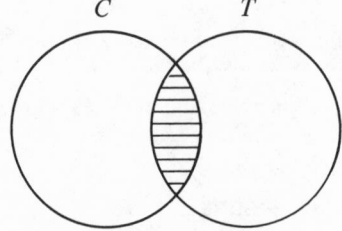

The obverse of *E* has the same diagram as the *E* in that it says that all
members of the subject class are members of the complement of the
predicate. In essence, this comes to the fact that there can be no members of
the class "trees" in the class "carnivores" and the *E* is shown equivalent to its
obverse.

The last obversion in our previous list is that of the *O* proposition. It is
"Some horses are nongentle animals." Now, it is quite clear that since the

only difference between this assertion and the original *O* proposition is that one has "not" where the other has "non," the two have the same meaning and diagram (see Figure 2-14).

FIGURE 2-14.

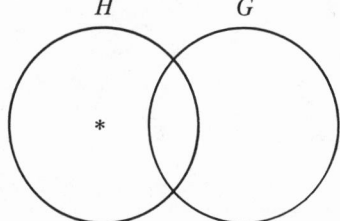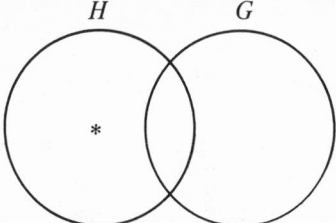

The reader may, therefore, wonder why we do not use "not" as the method of indicating class complementarity. The reason is that the notion of a complement is concerned with changing the term. This is done by using the "non" and results in a new term without effect on the basic quality of a sentence. This latter is indicated by the inclusiveness or exclusiveness of the copulative expression (i.e., "Some _____ are _____" or "Some _____ are not _____"). The obverse of an *O* proposition must have a different quality and the same quantity. If we were to use "not" instead of "non," then confusion would arise as to the quality of a proposition, and it would become difficult to say whether a certain proposition was affirmative with a complementary term or negative with a noncomplementary term (i.e., whether it was an *I* or an *O*). This ambiguity is not so problematical at this stage, but later on it would result in difficulties in the evaluation of arguments.

2.4.3 Contraposition

The final process of immediate inference is known as *contraposition,* and it requires that the subject and predicate terms be reversed and replaced by their complements. Thus the *A* proposition "All dogs are mammals" has the following contrapositive:

1. All nonmammals are nondogs.

It is possible to intuitively see that 1 is a valid consequence of the original *A* assertion, but there is a more direct way of determining the validity of contraposition.[3] To see how this works we must first recognize that the process of contraposition is really describable in terms of the previous two forms of inference. That is, instead of our speaking of contraposition as a one-step inference we could consider it a three-step process as follows. First, obvert the proposition, then convert this result and finally obvert the result of the second step. In terms of the *A* proposition

> All dogs are mammals.

this would appear as follows: step 1, the obverse of *A,*

> No dogs are nonmammals.

step 2, the converse of 1,

> No nonmammals are dogs.

step 3, the obverse of 2,

> All nonmammals are nondogs.

Step 3 is precisely the same as the previously described contrapositive of *A,* and because each step is valid the contrapositive of *A* is a valid consequence of *A* itself. Of course, the reason each step above is valid is because obversion always is valid and conversion is valid for *E* propositions (step 2 is an *E* proposition). Carrying out the above process for the other categorical propositions results in the validity of contraposition for the *O* statement but not for the *E* and *I.* That this is so follows from the fact that the obverse of an *E* is an *A* proposition, which when converted, as in step 2, leads to an invalid consequence. In a similar manner the obversion of the *I* proposition yields an *O,* and this cannot validly be converted. However, the *O* proposition itself can be contraposited validly as follows:

> *O.* Some horses are not gentle animals.
> 1. Some horses are nongentle animals.
> 2. Some nongentle animals are horses.
> 3. Some nongentle animals are not nonhorses.

[3]The diagrams for the contrapositive are not always easy to determine as they involve two complementary classes.

The final result is a valid consequence of the *O* proposition inasmuch as step 1 is an *I* statement and is *validly converted* to give step 2. Also, it is possible to carry out a contraposition by limitation on the *E* statement in much the same way we described conversion by limitation earlier. That is, we first deduce the *O* proposition from the *E* by the rule of subalternation from the square of opposition (see section 2.3) and then contraposit the *O*. The result of this contraposition by limitation resembles the conversion by limitation in that they are only one-way valid inferences. Thus, the process of contraposition by limitation cannot be carried out on the resultant proposition as a means of getting the original proposition. This fact is, however, not surprising in that subalternation is a one-way inference.

EXERCISES

1 Give the converse of each of the following:
   a. No conductors are mutes.
   b. Some international intrigues are newsworthy stories.
   c. No actors are politicians.

2 Give the obverse of each of the following:
   a. All persons who have short tempers are difficult individuals.
   b. Some writers are conformists.
   c. No protesters are fascists.

3 Give the contrapositive of each of the following:
   a. Some athletes are not professionals.
   b. All dignitaries are stuffed shirts.
   c. All women are mystics.

4 In each pair below the second proposition was derived from the first by one or more uses of the immediate inferences. Determine which inferences might have been used and whether the second proposition does follow validly from the first:
   a. No octopi are quadrupeds.
      Some quadrupeds are nonoctopi.
   b. All planets are nonsolar bodies.
      All solar bodies are nonplanets.
   c. Some crocodiles are gregarious creatures.
      Some nongregarious creatures are not crocodiles.
   d. No philosophers are sophists.
      All sophists are nonphilosophers.

5 Draw the Venn diagram for each of the propositions in exercise 4 and check your answers there by comparing the diagram for the first proposition with that of the second.

2.5   SYLLOGISM I

We have now thoroughly examined the implications of the four categorical propositions and can say whether a certain proposition is an *A*, *E*, *I*, *O*, follows from one, or is, in some way, incompatible with them. However, the original task of the chapter is not yet begun. Earlier, we spoke of developing a method to evaluate any argument which involved the categorical propositions; at this point we have really only considered one-premise arguments. In order to expand our procedures to allow evaluation of arguments of any length we must develop these procedures for all two-premise arguments. After doing this it will be a simple matter to show that the use of immediate inference and chains of two-premise arguments will provide us with a means of testing validity for a categorical argument of any length. These two-premise arguments are known as *syllogisms,* and the title of this chapter is derived from this term.

The first important point to recognize about two-premise arguments, where each premise and the conclusion are categoricals, is that the structure of these categoricals is not arbitrary. That is, not any two premises coupled with a conclusion make an argument into a syllogism. In fact, the reader should note that the premises of a syllogism will have to share a term (either subject or predicate) and that the conclusion will have to relate the two classes in the premises which are not so shared. These restrictions are not something that we add arbitrarily—they are the necessary consequences of formulating a possibly valid two-premise categorical argument. Let us make these restrictions clearer by an example. First consider an arbitrary two-premise argument:

All dogs are mammals.
Some flowers are annuals.
∴ All trees are plants.

The reason this cannot count as a syllogism is that it is not an argument at all but merely a list of three categorical propositions. However, if we demand that the premises have at least one term in common and that the conclusion relate the unshared terms of the premises then we get a syllogism such as

All mammals are warm-blooded creatures.
All dogs are mammals.
∴ All dogs are warm-blooded creatures.

The above argument qualifies as a syllogism because it is a two-premise argument and not a listing of just any categorical propositions. The fact that it is an argument, of course, is merely a consequence of the arrangement of the terms which it contains. However, the reader must not confuse the fact that this argument is in correct syllogistic form with the additional question of whether it is valid. The above argument certainly seems valid but we most certainly could have syllogisms that are invalid. The procedures for separating the valid from the invalid syllogism is our main task, but first we will define a few notions that will allow us to describe any syllogism. Using the notation discussed in section 2.2.5, the above syllogism could be written as:

A. m A w   Major premise
    d A m   Minor premise
    d A w   Conclusion

The first premise is known as the *major premise* and the second as the *minor premise*. The term that is shared in the premises (and that forms a "link" between the premises) is known as the *middle term* and, in the above case, is the word "mammals." The term in the major premise that is not the middle term is the *major term* and the nonmiddle term in the minor premise is the *minor term*. Finally, we require that the predicate term of the conclusion be the major term. This means, of course, that the structure of the conclusion determines the order of the premises; if the predicate of the conclusion should be C then C would be the major term and the premise containing C would be the major premise. We adopt this convention because we want our notation to yield an unambiguous description of all syllogisms, and because the order of premises is immaterial to the validity of an argument the syllogism under discussion might have been written

B. d A m
    m A w
    d A w

To avoid confusion we shall speak of a syllogism with the major term as predicate of the conclusion as a *standard-form syllogism;* this will aid our attempts to apply concise descriptions to all syllogisms. Note that one cannot put any syllogism into standard form by switching the order of terms in the conclusion (i.e., converting them) as this would change the argument, whereas changing the order of the premises does not alter the original argument. However, we can convert a conclusion without changing the validity of the argument if the conclusion is either an *E* or an *I* proposition.

Having determined the placement of the various terms in a standard-form syllogism we must next decide how many different forms such a syllogism can take. That is, in our initial example

$$\begin{array}{c} \text{m } A \text{ w} \\ \underline{\text{d } A \text{ m}} \\ \text{d } A \text{ w} \end{array}$$

we had three *A* propositions, and it is clear that this need not have been so. Each of the premises and the conclusion might have been an *I, E,* or *O* proposition instead of the *A* they were. Also, there is no reason that the middle term must occur as the subject of the major premise and as the predicate of the minor premise. The middle term is required to occur in two places in the premises, but there are four ways in which this requirement could be fulfilled. Besides the above-mentioned configuration, the middle term could be repeated as the subject of both major and minor premises, as the predicate of both, or as predicate of the major premise and the subject of the minor. It will be helpful in the remainder of this chapter to assign names to these possible forms so that we can unambiguously refer to them. We will call a three-letter code for each syllogism the *mood* of the syllogism, and we will take the code to consist of the following: *first letter*—major premise; *second letter*—minor premise; and *third letter*—conclusion (in each case these letters must, of course, be *A, E, I, O*). Thus the mood of a syllogism such as:

All *A* are *B*.
Some *B* are not *C*.
∴ Some *C* are not *A*.

will be characterized as *AOO*.

Next we will adopt a convention with regard to the location of the middle term. Its position will determine the *figure* of a syllogism and by previous discussion the reader should realize that there are four figures. The table below contains the numerical code which we will use. In this table we have indicated the position of the middle terms with respect to the major and minor terms; no conclusion is included since it does not affect the figure of any syllogism and, by the same token, we have not specified the type of premises the syllogism contains. Again, this latter fact would be basic to determining the mood but need not occur in a table of figures. The assignment of figures is by convention and we have adopted the standard list in this regard. (See Table 2-3.)

TABLE 2-3.

B	A	A	B	B	A	A	B
C	B	C	B	B	C	B	C
Figure 1		Figure 2		Figure 3		Figure 4	

It can now be seen that the figure of the syllogism above (mood AOO) is 4. Thus, we could completely and unambiguously describe this syllogism as $AOO4$, and anyone could use this code to write out the form of the original syllogism. The last point to consider in this section concerns the number of possible forms of the syllogism, i.e., how many distinct syllogisms there are. The answer to this question is easily given when we first ask how many different moods of syllogism there are. Since each premise and the conclusion may be A, E, I, or O there will be 4^3, or 64 moods. However, inasmuch as each mood could occur in one of four figures the total number of possible syllogisms will be 64 X 4 or 256. It is extremely important to recognize that, *though there are 256 syllogisms, this number is not necessarily the number of valid syllogisms.* We have yet to work out a procedure for evaluating syllogisms and when we do we will come to realize that only a small fraction of the 256 forms are valid argument forms (less than 10 per cent). The reader may have already noticed that though $AOO4$ is one of the 256 syllogisms, it is not a valid syllogism.

EXERCISE

1 Put into proper syllogistic form and give the mood and figure of each of the following:
   a. All picotees are carnations because some carnations are dark-edged flowers and all picotees are dark-edged flowers.

b. Since some women are lissome, some lissome persons are desirable because some women are desirable.

c. All airplanes are objects heavier than air and no objects heavier than air are things that can support themselves without engines, so some objects heavier than air are things that can support themselves without engines.

d. No ghosts are real objects because all ghosts are illusions and no real objects are illusions.

e. No lectures on physical chemistry are fascinating so some lectures on physical chemistry are impossible things to follow as no things that are impossible to follow are fascinating.

2.6 SYLLOGISM II: AN EVALUATION PROCEDURE

We will now develop a method of testing a syllogism for validity that will involve the use of Venn diagrams. In order to fully appreciate the working of this procedure the reader is asked to recall some basic facts about validity. An argument was said to be valid when its form was such that the truth of the premises necessarily conferred truth on the conclusion. Another way of saying this would be: In a valid argument it is impossible that the premises be true and the conclusion false. The Venn diagrams for each proposition contain a schematic representation of the truth of the proposition, and by properly constructing the diagrams for the two premises we should be able to tell by inspection whether it is possible for the conclusion to be false. It is as if we picture the truth of the premises and see if their truth could be consistent with the falsity of the conclusion; if the conclusion could be false then the argument is invalid as validity only arises from the truth of the premises making it impossible for the conclusion to be false.

In drawing our Venn diagrams we must first recognize that the two diagrams for the premises will always share one circle (or part of one circle) in common—the middle-term circle. Thus if we had the syllogism

b A c
a A b
——————
a A c AAA1

we could fill in a diagram for both the major and minor premises on the same diagram. (See Figure 2-15.)

FIGURE 2-15.

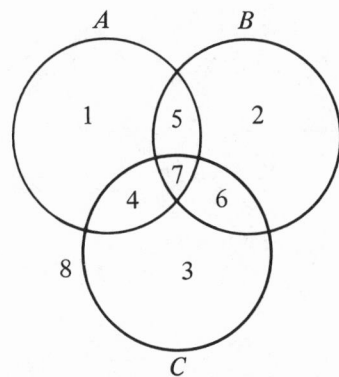

This diagram will also allow us to answer the question as to what the truth of the premises indicates about the truth or falsity of the conclusion. The procedure can be outlined as follows: (1) Use the previous method of diagramming to fill in for the major premise. (2) Repeat (1) with minor premise. (3) Inspect for possibility of truth or falsity of the conclusion. As the reader probably realizes it is necessary that each pair of terms be considered separately when carrying out steps 1 and 2, and this will mean that some care must be taken in using Figure 2-15. Step 1 for the syllogism *AAA*1 listed above is shown as Figure 2-16.

FIGURE 2-16.

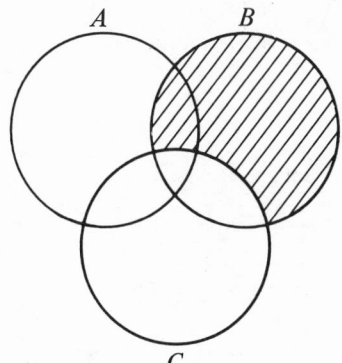

In step 1 we consider the areas representing *B* and *C* while ignoring any other lines. This necessitates our cross-lining areas 2 and 5 (see Figure 2-15). The second step requires that we diagram *aAb* on the diagram in Figure 2-16 (i.e., the one that already has step 1 completed). This gives us Figure 2-17.

FIGURE 2-17.

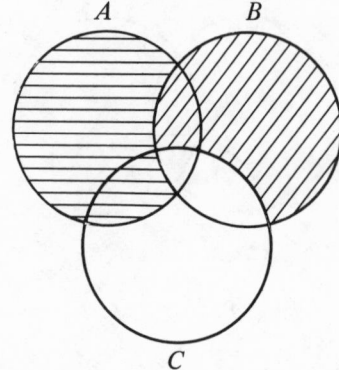

Here we have cross-lined areas 1 and 4 (see Figure 2-15). The final step involves no new construction; we simply inspect Figure 2-17 and see whether or not it renders the conclusion necessarily true. Just before doing this it is a good idea to ask yourself what the diagram would look like if the truth of the conclusion were contained in it. Since the conclusion is *aAc,* it would require that 1 and 5 in Figure 2-15 be empty. Examination shows that this is the case in Figure 2-17 and so we know that it is impossible to diagram the major and minor premises of *AAA*1 without at the same time fulfilling the conditions for the truth of the conclusion. This means, of course, that it is impossible for the conclusion to be false if the premises are true. Thus *AAA*1 is valid.

As a second example consider the *AOO*4 syllogism, which was discussed above. The result of step 1 is shown in Figure 2-18.

FIGURE 2-18.

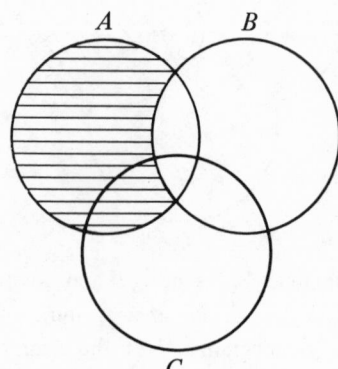

Next, we have to add the minor premise to this diagram. However, the minor premise calls for there being at least one member in the areas of *B* which are not *C*; on our diagram this would be areas 2 and 5. The problem is that we must put the asterisk down in such a way that this one individual could be in either area 2 or 5. This problem did not arise previously because with only two circles there are no extra lines which could cause confusion. The solution is to put the asterisk on the line so that we are saying it is either in area 2 or 5. Remember an asterisk on a line does not mean that each area has at least one member but merely that both together have at least one member. Thus step 2 yields Figure 2-19. The final step now requires us to inspect Figure 2-19 and see if

FIGURE 2-19.

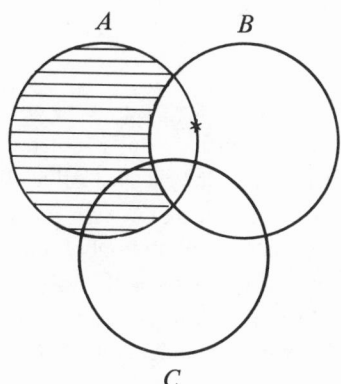

it contains the conclusion (i.e., contains the conditions for making the conclusion true). In order for the conclusion (which is *cOa*) to be true we should expect areas 3 and 6 to be nonempty, i.e., to contain at least one member. A glance at Figure 2-19 shows that nothing whatever has been done to areas 3 and 6. This means two things: First, the truth of the conclusion is not necessitated by the premises so the argument is invalid, and second, though the argument is invalid, it is possible for the conclusion to be true, though its truth would not be a result of the premises. It is extremely important to keep these two factors distinct because there is a temptation to think that Figure 2-19 makes *AOO*4 valid because the conclusion is not shown as necessarily false. *This is incorrect.* A diagram shows validity only when the conclusion is necessarily true and since Figure 2-19 leaves the truth or falsity of *cOa* open this is sufficient to invalidate *AOO*4.

49

As a last example we will consider *AAI*1. The diagram for this is found in Figure 2-20.

FIGURE 2-20.

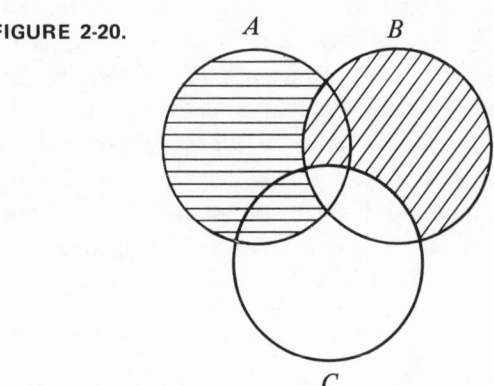

The conclusion (*cIa*) would require the diagram to contain an asterisk in the area that is both *C* and *A*. Inasmuch as this is not the case the argument is invalid. However, the reader may have realized that the *AAA*1 syllogism is valid, and so it seems peculiar that the same two premises can validly imply "All *C* are *A*" whereas, they cannot validly imply "some *C* are *A*"; *it certainly* seems that this latter proposition should be derivable from "all *B* are *A*" and "all *C* are *B*." (We say "certainly" because *cIa* follows from *cAa* by the subalternation step in the square of opposition.) The reason that *AAI*1 is invalid in Figure 2-20 is that universal premises do not include asterisks in their diagrams while the particular conclusion requires an asterisk. If, however, we diagram the premises with existential presupposition (and thus with asterisks) then we would get a result as in Figure 2-21.

FIGURE 2-21.

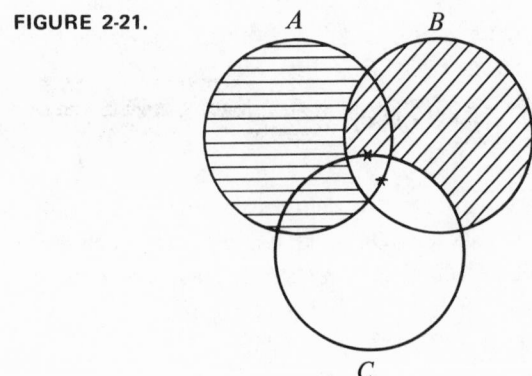

As can be seen the *AAI*1 in Figure 2-21 is valid. This result requires us to recognize that the question of existential import has important consequences for validity. As a general rule syllogisms such as *AAI*1 are said to be invalid unless special mention is made about the premises. This uncertainty reflects the intrinsic problem which is generated by the notion of existential commitments. The ancient and medieval logicians were prepared to allow syllogisms such as *AAI*1 to be valid but considerations arising out of modern logical notions and set theory have made the other position more attractive. There is no need for us to stipulate one way or the other at this point so long as the reader himself is aware of the possibilities and their consequences.

Before we go on to consider an alternative method of evaluation let us briefly examine some of the general aspects of the Venn diagram method. Methods such as the Venn diagram and others, which will be discussed in the next chapter, are most often described as *model theoretic* evaluative procedures. That is, they depend on the use of some model of the argument as a means to evaluating it. In the case of the Venn diagrams this model is quite evident (though it is schematic). The finished diagram of any syllogism is really a representation (model) of the premises as jointly true. Examination of this model reveals whether or not the conclusion is included, and it is on this examination that our decision about validity rests. The reader may get a clearer understanding of this if he considers the following analogy. Suppose you were given a set of driving instructions such as

1. Drive 10 miles west to town *A*.
2. At town *A* turn north and continue 15 miles to the Big River.
3. Drive east along the Big River to Eastville which is 7 miles along the river.

Now, these three instructions (premises) purport to be an adequate set of directions for getting from where you are to Eastville. How would one test their validity? (The word "validity" is used somewhat differently here than it would be in describing a syllogism. However, its use here should illuminate its more strictly logical use.) Well, you could follow each of them and find out whether you did, in fact, reach Eastville. Instead of this, however, you could trace out 1-3 above on a map and determine whether they were valid instructions. This procedure involves the use of a model (the road map) which contains the premises (the instructions) and which will indicate their adequacy. The Venn diagram for any particular syllogism is much like the map and our test for validity is analogous to the examination of a map to test a set of instructions.

EXERCISES

1 Using the Venn diagrams evaluate the syllogisms which you constructed from the arguments on page 46. Be careful to say whether they are valid with or without existential presupposition.

2 Evaluate each of the following with Venn diagrams and make sure to indicate any existential presuppositions you make.
   a. No megalosauri are creatures living in Alaska because all megalosauri are extinct animals and no extinct animals are creatures living in Alaska.
   b. All prudes are persons difficult to get along with, so no ecdysiasts are prudes since no ecdysiasts are persons difficult to get along with.
   c. No olympic gold medal winners are poor athletes and some poor athletes are brilliant students, therefore some brilliant students are not olympic gold medal winners.
   d. All men are imperfect creatures, thus some men are irrational beings because all irrational beings are imperfect creatures.
   e. No hemidemisemiquavers are easy notes to play on the French horn and no short notes are easy to play on the French horn, so all hemidemisemiquavers are short notes.

2.7   EVALUATION BY RULES

The Venn diagram method of testing for validity is not the only one that has been devised for the Aristotelian logic. The reader probably realizes that the underlying reason why an argument is invalid is that its form is defective in some way. The construction of Venn diagrams exposed these defects in form by plotting the truth conditions of the premises and discovering whether these automatically included the conditions necessary for the truth of the conclusion. The evaluation procedure of this section, however, will distinguish invalidating defects in the argument directly and will not require any representations of the truth conditions of the premises. We will present five rules of form which will determine whether or not a syllogism is valid. That is, if a given syllogism were to satisfy all of these rules then it would be valid, while if it violated any one of these rules then it would be invalid. A demonstration of the effectiveness of these rules and a short discussion of their genesis will follow their exposition.

2.7.1 Syllogistic rules

1. The middle term of a valid syllogism must be distributed at least once.
2. In a valid syllogism if a term is distributed in the conclusion that term must be distributed in the premises.
3. A valid syllogism must not have two negative premises.
4. In a valid syllogism if the conclusion is negative then there must be a negative premise and if a premise is negative the conclusion must also be negative.
5. A valid syllogism cannot have universal premises and a particular conclusion.

The application of the first rule is quite straightforward. Any syllogism will have its middle term occurring at two places in the premises and rule 1 requires that at least one of these premises distribute the middle term (check section 2.2.5 for a review of distribution). A syllogism that has its middle term undistributed in both places will be invalid and will be said to commit the *fallacy of an undistributed middle.*

The best procedure for applying the second rule is to first examine the conclusion. It may distribute one, both, or neither term. If a term is distributed then rule 2 requires that this same term be distributed in its occurrence in a premise. Of course, if one or both terms are not distributed in the conclusion then rule 2 requires nothing about their distribution in a premise. Now, since rule 2 could be violated in two different ways we will have two fallacies. If the major term (predicate of the conclusion) violates rule 2 we call it the *fallacy of an illicit major term,* and if the minor term (subject of the conclusion) is in violation of rule 2 then the syllogism is said to commit the *fallacy of an illicit minor.* Rule 2 is violated when at least one of these fallacies is committed though it is possible for an invalid syllogism to have *both* an illicit major and minor.

The third and fourth rules require no special discussion and their violation is not usually given any special name. However, rule 5 does require a brief discussion. Suppose we were to have a syllogism that satisfied rules 1-4 but violated rule 5—*AAI*1, e.g. As we saw in the previous section this syllogism is invalid when we do not assume any form of existential import but is valid (by

Venn diagrams) when we presuppose the existence of members of the subject classes of the premises. Since we want our rules to mirror the results we get with Venn diagrams (two different procedures should validate the same arguments) we must recognize a certain flexibility with rule 5. Unlike the other four rules this rule may or may not be used depending on whether we allow existential presupposition. Of course, if a syllogism violates rule 5 and one of the other rules it will be invalid regardless of any existential point of view.

These rules were chosen in such a way that a violation of any one of them (subject to the discussion of rule 5 above) will invalidate a syllogism while the satisfaction of all of them guarantees the validity of a syllogism. The best way to test our rules is to show that they validate all and only those syllogisms that the Venn diagrams validate. This is easily done since there are only 15 valid syllogistic forms (24 if we add existential presupposition). The rules themselves, however, make no reference to the truth conditions of any premise or conclusion, and we will call such a method *proof theoretic* as opposed to the Venn method, which is *model theoretic*. The importance of these concepts will be more apparent in Chapters 3, 4, and 5. The reader should note that the rule method, like the Venn diagram, is mechanical and effective. This is so because there are only a finite number of rules that can be applied by straightforward inspection procedures after which a definite yes or no answer is given to the question: Is this syllogism valid?

The rules are gotten by examining the valid syllogisms and abstracting from them certain general principles (later our rules) which hold for all and only those syllogisms that are in this group. It is interesting to note that our five rules, though not the only rules, are special in that they are the minimum number of rules that could make up an evaluation procedure. If we drop any one of them we will not be able to correctly evaluate all syllogisms. Some books include various additional rules which we feel unnecessary. For example, the rule to the effect that a valid first figure syllogism must have a negative major premise if it has a negative conclusion. Now, this is certainly true, but it can be "proven" by means of our rules as follows:

If a first figure syllogism were to have an affirmative major premise and a negative conclusion then the conclusion would always distribute its predicate term (the major), and the affirmative major premise would never distribute its predicate term (also, the major in the first figure). This would mean that a first figure syllogism with an affirmative major and negative conclusion would always violate rule 2 (illicit major) and could not be valid. (An alternative method of proof of this rule from rules 1-5 would be to list all of the cases of syllogisms of the first figure with negative conclusions and affirmative major premises and show them invalid by our rules. There would be 32 cases.)

EXERCISES

1 Evaluate the syllogisms on page 46 and page 52 using the rules of the syllogism instead of the Venn diagrams but check to see that both methods give the same result.

2 Evaluate the following by first putting them into correct form and then applying the rules of the syllogism. Indicate whether there are any that violate only rule 5.
   a. Some protesters are college students and some college students are not well-informed persons, so some protesters are not well-informed persons.
   b. All metals are electrical conductors, so some liquids are electrical conductors for some liquids are metals.
   c. All novels by Dickens are social commentaries and some social commentaries are not works that have lasting interest, so some novels by Dickens are not works that have lasting interest.
   d. No hard-hit line drives are easy chances and some easy chances are sources of errors, so some sources of errors are hard-hit line drives.
   e. Some trips to Europe by senators are junkets and no trips to Europe by senators are necessary excursions, so some necessary excursions are junkets.

3 List all the valid syllogisms in which the middle term is distributed in both places.

4 What is the maximum number of rules that a syllogism can violate simultaneously?

5 The rules we have presented are sufficient to evaluate any syllogistic argument but they are not the only rules that hold for valid syllogisms. Below are a number of statements that are true of valid syllogisms. In each case present an argument using only the first four rules to support the truth of the statement. (This can be done by considering the various cases which are described by the statement in question.)
   a. In the first figure the minor premise is affirmative.
   b. If the major term is the predicate of the major premise, then the minor premise must be affirmative.
   c. If one premise is particular the conclusion is particular.
   d. In the second figure the conclusion is negative.
   e. In the first figure the major premise is universal.

2.8   TRANSLATION OF NONSTANDARD FORMS

The logic we have worked out so far is perhaps most notable for its limitations. It is a complete logic of categorical propositions (subject to one addition in the next section), but there are only four of these and they are not a very general sample of the sorts of premises that one might use in ordinary arguments. Though there is no way we can make the syllogistic an entirely general logic it can be expanded by the recognition of numerous propositions which are really *A, E, I,* or *O* propositions expressed in somewhat different language. Also, there are a number of arguments that are translatable into syllogistic form even though superficial examination would classify them as nonsyllogistic. This section will systematically consider such variant forms and the reader should do the exercises at the end of this section so that he will develop facility in translation of nonstandard forms. We will begin with propositions that are variant in certain respects, first those with nonstandard terms.

2.8.1   Nonstandard terms

In our original specification we insisted that the subject and predicate terms of a categorical proposition be the names of some class of objects such as "flowers," "flying saucers," etc. However, if we are given a proposition such as

Some marigolds are yellow.

it seems reasonable to translate this into the standard form *I* proposition:

Some marigolds are yellow things.

Thus, an adjective can easily become an object-class name (and hence, a term) by supplying some object or noun-like word.

2.8.2   Nonstandard quantity indicators

The next group of variations concerns the quantity words that occur in the categorical propositions. The following words are synonymous with "all" and any proposition in which they occur can be rewritten as an *A* proposition:

Each A is *B.*
Any A's are *B*'s.
Every A is a *B.*

Besides these directly interchangeable expressions there are a number of ordinary language forms which are commonly used to assert *A* propositions. Consider the following two statements:

1. A whale is a mammal.
2. Worms are hermaphrodites.

Both these are evidently universal affirmative assertions and may be rewritten as *A* propositions. The reader, however, should be aware of the fact that the use of "all" in propositions with the form of 1 and 2 is not always justified. Thus, if instead of 1 and 2 above, we were presented with:

3. A sailboat is damaged.
4. Children are present.

we would not translate these as *A* propositions but as *I* propositions, viz.,

3'. Some sailboats are damaged things.
4'. Some children are persons who are present.

(note the translation of the predicates of these two propositions as per section 2.8.1). The appropriate categorical equivalents of assertions such as 1-4 is a matter of context and judgment and cannot be specified in advance. An alternate way of expressing universal affirmative propositions uses the standard quantity word "all" but a nonstandard word order. The proposition

Trees are all living organisms.

has precisely the same meaning as

All trees are living organisms.

The final nonstandard *A* proposition we will consider involves the words "only" and "none but." The assertions

Only citizens are voters.
None but the brave deserve the fair.

are both affirmative universal, but one must be careful about the order in which the terms are written in the standard translation. The first proposition does not mean "all citizens are voters" but "all voters are citizens." This is so because the word "only" has the effect of making the term that immediately follows it the predicate. The second proposition (which is from the Dryden poem, *Alexander's Feast*) can be rendered accurately though less beautifully as

All fair persons are persons deserved by brave persons.

Thus, the phrase "none but" is a somewhat archaic but perfectly acceptable way of saying "only." As with assertions that have no quantifier expressions (see above 1-4) one must be cautious in translating the word "only." As a general rule it is fair to say that "Only *A* are *B*" means "All *B* are *A*," but the proposition "The only countries that are peaceful are small" is *not* translatable as "All small countries are peaceful countries." The correct *A* proposition is "All peaceful countries are small countries." In this case the use of the definite article "the" in front of the quantifier "only" reversed the order of terms. So much for the nonstandard *A* proposition quantifiers.

The *I* proposition is stipulated as "Some (at least one) *A* is *B*," and there are numerous ordinary language statements that are written as *I* statements. The following is a partial list:

Most *A* are *B*.
Many *A* are *B*.
A few *A* are *B*.
Several *A* are *B*.
One, two . . . *A* are *B*.

In translating these statements into *I* form we are not, of course, reflecting the exact meaning of each of them as we did in the case of nonstandard *A* propositions. Obviously, "Many *A* are *B*" means something different from "Some *A* are *B*." Still, this latter assertion is part of the former and for the purpose of syllogistic evaluation it will do; it could never happen that "Many *A* are *B*" was true while "Some *A* are *B*" was false since "some" means merely "at least one." The alternate methods of expressing the quantity for the *I* proposition are clearly applicable to the *O* proposition. Thus, e.g., "Many *A* are not *B*" becomes "Some *A* are not *B*." In addition to the above group there are two types of propositions that are *I* or *O* propositions and that have variant quantifiers. Consider the following:

There are impossible problems.
Not all politicians are dishonest.

The first assertion can be translated as the *I* proposition "Some problems are impossible problems" while the second becomes the *O* proposition "Some politicians are not dishonest." The negative *E* proposition also has a number of alternate forms. All the following are accurately rendered by the corresponding *E* assertions:

There are no small elephants.
No small things are elephants.
None of the trees are bare.
No trees are bare things.

The reader may sometimes encounter a proposition such as "All *A* are not *B*." This form is highly ambiguous and, depending on context, may mean "not all *A* are *B*" or "no *A* are *B*." This ambiguity can be illustrated by the following examples:

All children are not allowed to smoke.
All students are not athletes.

The first is the *E* proposition and the second the *O*. These last forms should not provide too much difficulty, however, as they are awkward expressions and are not often encountered.

We have so far considered various nonstandard ways of stating the quantity of categorical propositions. Before discussing matters besides the quantity of such propositions we will analyze an interesting and somewhat complex quantifier known as an *exceptive* quantifier. It might occur as "almost all," "all but," "all except," etc. in a statement such as

All members except those in their first year are voting members.

This assertion cannot be translated into an *A* or *I* assertion alone. In fact, it may be considered a compound of the following two categoricals:

Some members are voting members.
Some members are not voting members.

That is, the exceptive proposition contains both a denial that "All *A* are *B*" and an affirmation that "Some *A* are *B*." Since, in a syllogism, both forms cannot be used (this would mean three premises, as the exceptive would be one of the original two) we must write out two syllogisms with each part of the exceptive as a premise in each syllogism. If evaluation of both shows that one is valid then the original argument with the exceptive premise is valid. This is so because this original argument actually contains both syllogisms.

2.8.3 Nonstandard verbs

The connective or copulative "are," which we stipulated as the standard categorical verb, is not the only way of expressing class inclusion or exclusion. We may come across an assertion such as

Everybody dislikes a snob.

Now this statement is clearly a universal affirmation assertion, and it can be rendered as a standard categorical by

All persons are persons who dislike snobs.

In general any verb can be transformed into a noun expression with the standard copula by a construction such as the one above. The second group of variations we include under this heading really involves more than a nonstandard verb—though this is part of their structure. Consider the statement

The college student is always dissatisfied.

This statement can be translated into categorical form by the use of a device known as *parameters*. This entails the choosing of some term that can serve, when suitably qualified, as both the subject and predicate term of a categorical. Now the statement above *does not simply mean* either that all college students are dissatisfied or that some college students are dissatisfied. However, we can capture its meaning quite precisely by introducing time as a parameter as in the following:

All times are times when there are dissatisfied college students.

The particular parameter that is chosen will depend on the argument in which the nonstandard premise occurs. This is so because the ultimate objective of any translation is the construction of an evaluable syllogism. Thus, the choice of parameters is governed by the necessity of having three terms in the syllogism. It may happen that a particular proposition lends itself to two alternative standard translations but only one of these allows the construction of a syllogism and it is, of course, this latter translation that should be employed.

The last nonstandard proposition we will discuss is quite common and is nonstandard because of an alteration in both the copulative and subject terms. This form is exemplified by such propositions as

John is tall.
The old desk upstairs is broken.

Both these statements are alike in having singular verbs and subject terms that are specific and contain one member; not surprisingly they are known as *singular* propositions. Now since the subject term of a singular proposition is a unit (one member) class the reader may feel that the above are particular propositions. However, a little further consideration shows that these propositions can be better handled as universal propositions. This is so because the predicate term ("tall" in the first or "broken" in the second) describes every member of the subject class even though there is only one such member. Keeping this in mind we may rewrite the singular propositions as:

All members of the class "John" are tall.
All members of the class "desks upstairs" are broken.

These formulations may sound awkward but they do capture the intent of the original propositions.

2.8.4 Summary

Having finished our systematic description of the more common nonstandard categoricals we have considerably enlarged the scope of our logic. That is, there are now many more arguments that can be evaluated with either the syllogistic rules or the Venn diagrams. Before closing this section, however, it may be useful to describe a way in which the immediate inferences can be employed in the construction and evaluation of syllogisms.

The following argument contains five terms and would not appear to be a syllogism.

> All persons who are good in mathematics are intelligent.
> Some athletes are unintelligent.
> ∴ Some athletes are poor in mathematics.

The five terms are (1) athletes, (2) persons who are unintelligent, (3) persons who are intelligent, (4) persons who are good in mathematics, and (5) persons who are poor in mathematics. However, terms 2 and 3 and terms 4 and 5 appear to be related; they are, in fact, complementary classes (we can assume that "unintelligent" is "nonintelligent" and that "poor" is "nongood"). This suggests a way in which we can use the immediate inferences of either obversion or contraposition (both involve the use of class complements) to "reduce" the number of terms above. In this case it is most efficient to obvert the minor premise and the conclusion as this gives us the following *AOO*2 syllogism:

> All G are I.
> Some A are not I.
> ∴ Some A are not G.   *AOO*2

Either Venn diagrams or the application of the rules would show this to be a valid syllogistic argument. In this way we may use the immediate inferences to reduce the number of terms and arrive at standard form arguments, but the inference used must be valid for the type of proposition it is used on. In our example we used two applications of obversion, and this inference yields valid consequences when applied to any categorical proposition. However, any attempt to reduce the number of terms by, say, converting an A proposition, will result in an argument not equivalent to the original. Of course, the reason this is a defect is that we are trying to evaluate the original argument and not some other.

EXERCISES

1 Translate each of the following into standard categorical form:
   a. There are times when nothing goes right.
   b. Lithium is a metal.

  c. Baboons live in socially organized units.
  d. Time flies.
  e. A penny saved is a penny earned.
  f. Mark likes toys.
  g. Insanity is often hereditary.
  h. Not every baseball game is interesting.
  i. Julia always goes to sleep early.
  j. Some medieval buildings are exquisite.
  k. Anyone who works as hard as Martin deserves success.
  l. There are no issues of *Scientific American* in the high school library.
  m. Only persons who have known hunger are good judges of the new welfare laws.
  n. At no time did Jim lose control of the situation.
  o. Each member of the class is required to do the algebra problem.
  p. All college teachers except lecturers are eligible for tenure.
  q. A few people left the party early.
  r. Books have covers.
  s. All horses except thoroughbreds are gentle.
  t. There are no simple ways to translate propositions into standard form.

2 Put each of the following arguments into syllogistic form by using the notions of section 2.8 including the use of immediate inference to reduce the number of terms. Having done this evaluate each syllogism by both the Venn diagram and the rule methods.

  a. Some boors are teachers since no pedants are nonboors and some pedants are teachers.
  b. Some poets are intellectual and all poets are nonshrewd businessmen, so some shrewd businessmen are unintellectual.
  c. No inebriates are teetotalers, so some people are not inebriates since some people are teetotalers.
  d. There are no mediocre symphonies by Beethoven. However, since all of the symphonies written in 1831 were mediocre, none of Beethoven's symphonies was written in 1831.
  e. No quarks have ever been observed and some real things have been observed so some quarks are unreal.

2.9 SORITES

At this point we have a logic that completely develops the implications of one and two premise categorical arguments. However, our original goal was the development of a logic that could express and evaluate categorical arguments of any length. It might be thought that the extension of our two-premise syllogisms to be categorical arguments of indefinite length will require considerable revision of our procedures, but it is, in fact, not very involved. Consider the following three-premise arguments

1. aAb
2. cAa
3. dEb
$\therefore dEc$

Even in symbolic form one can recognize the validity of the argument but a little ingenuity will allow us to use our syllogistic methods to evaluate it. First we should note that the initial pair of premises implies another categorical proposition by our previous syllogism $AAA1$. Thus, we can write:

A. 1. aAb
2. cAa
$\therefore cAb$

Next, we can use the conclusion of this premise together with premise 3 to derive the conclusion of our original argument (dEc) by $AEE2$.

B. cAb
3. dEb
$\therefore dEc$

Combining A and B above we get a chain of two syllogisms connected by the sharing of the conclusion of one as the major premise of the other; this chain is known as a *sorites* (from the Greek word meaning "heap"). Written out in full we get

1. aAb
2. cAa
$\therefore cAb$
3. dEb
$\therefore dEc$

The reader should, of course, note that a sorites is valid only when all the syllogisms that make it up are valid.

To see how the sorites can be used in an argument of a less formal nature consider the following:

1. A cat is a quadruped.
2. A quadruped is an animal.
3. An animal is a substance.

∴ A cat is a substance.

This sorites consists of *AAA*1 with the unwritten conclusion, "All cats are animals," followed by a second *AAA*1 syllogism that has the conclusion of the first as its major premise.

EXERCISE

1 Below are examples of valid sorites. Use the methods of section 2.9 to arrange the arguments as a series of ordinary syllogisms and evaluate each. State whether the original sorites is valid.
   a. Everyone who is sane can do logic. No lunatics are fit to serve on a jury but none of your sons can do logic; therefore, none of your sons is fit to serve on a jury.[4]
   b. The only books in this library that I do not recommend for reading, are unhealthy in tone. The bound books are all well written. All the romances are healthy in tone. I do not recommend you to read any of the unbound books. Therefore, all the romances in this library are well written.
   c. No one whose soul is not sensitive can be a Don Juan. There are no profound scholars who are not great lovers of music. Only profound scholars can be dons at Oxford. No insensitive souls are great lovers of music. Therefore, all Oxford dons are Don Juans.
   d. All the candidates for office are men. Only persons over thirty-five are candidates. Everyone over thirty-five is middle-aged. No one who is middle-aged can run the mile in under four minutes. Therefore, none of the candidates can run the mile in under four minutes.

2.9.1 Enthymemes

In the construction of sorites it was often necessary to supply an additional premise to complete the chain. Thus, we added "All *C* are *B*" in

[4] The first three sorites are from Lewis Carroll's *Symbolic Logic.*

the first example and then used it to continue the sorites. However, this premise was not added gratuitously but was itself implied by the first two premises. Sometimes, though, an argument is used with an implicit understanding that one of its premises has been surpressed. Thus, a speaker may argue

> Every citizen is entitled to his constitutional rights so John is entitled to his rights.

Now, as it stands this argument would be translated into categorical form as

$$\frac{\text{All } C \text{ are } R.}{\therefore \text{ All } J \text{ are } R.}$$

where C is "citizens," R is "persons entitled to their rights," and J is "persons identical to John." This is, first of all, not a syllogism and is certainly not a valid immediate inference. However, the speaker in the above argument probably intended his argument to include the premise,

> John is a citizen.

and this would have made the argument into the following valid syllogism:

$$\frac{\begin{array}{l}\text{All } C \text{ are } R.\\ \text{All } J \text{ are } C.\end{array}}{\therefore \text{ All } J \text{ are } R. \qquad AAA1}$$

When we come across a situation in which a premise is left unsaid (i.e., is a "suppressed" premise) we describe the argument as an *enthymeme* (a word derived from the Greek which refers to the fact that an enthymeme contains the "spirit" of the complete argument). One usually encounters enthymemes in situations where the context of utterance makes the explicit presentation of a premise (or conclusion) pedantic or even redundant. In the above example, if everyone being addressed by the speaker was aware that John was a citizen, then his point is made much more effectively by leaving this premise out. In effect, this omission amplifies the importance of the major premise and strengthens the rhetorical appeal of the argument. When the enthymeme has a suppressed major premise it will be said to be *first order;* a suppressed minor premise results in a *second-order* enthymeme; and a suppressed conclusion is *third order.*

EXERCISE

1 The reader should supply the missing proposition in each of the following syllogisms and then evaluate it.
   a. We cannot play tennis this morning because it rained hard early in the morning.
   b. Absence makes the heart grow fonder, so you must be very fond of Joan by now.
   c. Yon Cassius has a lean and hungry look. . . . Such men are dangerous.
   d. Everyone at the party tonight is in college so they were all high school graduates.
   e. Benjamin cannot be a doctor because he is not listed in the AMA directory.

propositional logic

3.1 THE ELEMENTS OF PROPOSITIONAL LOGIC

In the syllogistic (see Chapter 2) it was possible to work out evaluation procedures as we did because of the restrictions we placed on the argument forms and elements of the arguments. Thus, by these restrictions we worked out effective, mechanical decision procedures to replace the rather hit-or-miss methods of intuitive evaluation. However, if the overall goal of logic, which we set in the introduction, is kept in mind, the reader will appreciate the insufficiency of the syllogistic. The general aim of logic is the developing of methods to evaluate any argument that can be expressed in common parlance by methods that are more precise and effective than ordinary intuition (remember, however, that this "intuition" is not discarded so much as organized, since at bottom any decision procedure requires intuitive acceptance of some sort). Now, though the number of arguments that can be handled by the syllogistic is infinite, the number of argument types is limited to at most 256, and it is not hard to think of argument types that cannot be evaluated by the Aristotelian methods. For example, consider the following two-premise arguments:

A. If it rains on Thursday, the game will be postponed.

It is most certainly going to rain.

∴ The game will have to be postponed.

B. Either the maid or the guest took the book as they were the only persons to have access to the library on Tuesday.

The maid, however, did not have the book.

∴ The guest must have taken it.

Now, though these arguments, in some respects, superficially resemble syllogisms, they are not translatable into syllogistic form. Still, they embody two very common argument forms, and we would not have much of a logic if we could not evaluate them. It will be the purpose of this chapter to outline procedures that will allow us to do just that, and to thereby increase the scope of our logic.

It might be suggested that the best way to proceed would be to introduce supplementary propositions to the original set of four. Thus, we could consider new groups of propositions derived from such arguments as A and B above and any other arguments that seem incompatible with any of the syllogistic forms. The patchwork nature of this alternative is obvious, and it will not be employed. However, the insight of this course is that the way to incorporate more argument forms into logic is to drop some or all of the restrictions on the forms that premises and conclusions can take. In doing this we, of course, have to abandon all the procedures developed in the last chapter, but, as we shall shortly see, new procedures will arise directly out of our present discussion.

Suppose we decide to drop most of the restrictions on statements employed in arguments; what are the minimal number of restrictions we can have? Well, if we turn to Chapter 1, we realize that any premise or conclusion of an argument must be a proposition. All other conditions on the form of argument statements were introduced in the syllogistic so let us see how far we can get with a logic of propositions. As was explained in Chapter 1 the primary subject matter for logic is in the field of arguments—arguments that employ sentences as premises and conclusions. However, not all sentences are propositional. The sentences

1. Please shut the door!
2. Where do you want to go this evening?

are not propositional and, briefly, this means that any talk of their being true or false is somehow irrelevant or misguided. Imagine being seriously asked whether 1 or 2 above were true or false. However, for many sentences it is a very relevant question. Thus,

3. There is a foreign film at the Scala.
4. The earth is approximately 8,000 miles in diameter.

are both the sorts of sentences of which it makes sense to say they are either true or false, and this is what is meant by our calling them *propositional*.[1] The reader should not confuse the fact that these sentences are either true or false with the fact that they may not be known to be true or false with any degree of certainty. Thus

5. There is a planet the size of earth in the nearest galaxy to our own.

is propositional even though it is not even probably known true or false. It is, however, a truth "candidate" (i.e., either true or false) whereas sentences 1 and 2 above are not even this. The upshot of this discussion is that the propositional logic of this chapter will have propositions as elements, and the only piece of information that we have about such elements is that they are truth candidates. As a last preliminary let us inquire into the form of these propositions. Since we have placed no special restrictions on the basic propositions in this logic we can know nothing in advance about the form of these propositions. They may resemble 3, 4, 5, or such propositions as

6. All dogs are mammals.
7. Jim is six feet tall and his brother is six feet one inch.

Proposition 6 is the universal affirmative categorical proposition, which for the purposes of this logic is merely one amongst many propositions. Proposition 7, though, is different from 3-6 in that it seems to be made up of two individual propositions connected by "and." These two propositions could be written as

[1] In this discussion we are only focusing on the notion of a proposition and the true-false dichotomy. There are, of course, other aspects of the difference between "proposition," "sentence," etc., and these were touched on in Chapter 1.

7a. Jim is six feet tall.
7b. Jim's brother is six feet one inch tall.

Now each of these cannot be broken down into simpler complete propositions. When we have such a simple proposition we will call it *atomic* as opposed to such propositions as 7, which is made up of atomic propositions and is called *molecular*. If we let the letter *P* stand for 7a and *Q* stand for 7b, then 7 itself could be written as

    7′. *P* and *Q*.

In conclusion of this first section, then, we may summarize

    1. The basic units of this logic are propositions that are candidates for being true or false and may in fact be known to be one or the other.

    2. We cannot in advance say anything about the form of these propositions except that they may be *atomic* or *molecular.*

    3. We may, for ease, refer to any proposition in this logic by an upper case italicized letter, e.g., *P, Q,* etc. The letters may stand for atomic or molecular propositions, but we can always write more and more complex propositions by connecting two or more propositions as in (7′). Section 3.2 will explore the ideas behind these molecular propositions.

3.2   MOLECULAR PROPOSITIONS, CONNECTIVES, AND TRUTH: PART I

When we join two atomic propositions by a word such as "and" we, of course, get a longer proposition. Thus

    1. The forecast is for rain.
    2. It is now 73 degrees.

when joined become,

    3. The forecast is for rain, and it is now 73 degrees.

Notice, moreover, that 3 is a proposition—though molecular—and as such it is a truth candidate. Further, the truth of 3 seems to depend on the truth of both 1 and 2. What this means is quite straightforward; if anyone were to want to check the truth of 3 he would first have to check the truth of 1 and 2. Because of this we say that the truth of 3 is a function of the truth of 1 and 2 and since the use of "and" results in this truth-functional dependence, we say that "and" is a *truth-functional connective* (or operator).

Suppose we are given two atomic propositions, P and Q, and are told nothing about the truth or subject matter of either; what can we say about P, Q, and the molecular proposition "P and Q" (which we will write as P & Q from now on using the ampersand to stand for the English word "and"). First we know that P must be either true or false and that Q must be either true or false and that depending on the values of P and Q the molecular proposition P & Q will be either true or false. See Table 3-1 for a tabular rendering of this information. The **T**'s and **F**'s listed below the proposition letter merely indicate

TABLE 3-1.

P	Q	P & Q
T	T	T or F*
F	F	T or F*

*Depending on the values of P and Q.

possible values. Next ask yourself how many possible different ways could the value under P and the value under Q come out. That is, it could be that (1) P was true, Q was true, (2) P was true, Q was false, (3) P was false, Q was true, or (4) both P and Q are false. In case 1 we would say that P & Q was true but in 2-4 that P & Q was false. (See Table 3-2.)

TABLE 3-2.

Row	P	Q	P & Q
1	T	T	T
2	T	F	F
3	F	T	F
4	F	F	F

In Table 3-2 it is important to read across each of the rows. Thus in case 1 the proposition P is true and the proposition Q is true and the molecular proposition P & Q is true as a result of the values of P and Q. In case 2, P is true but Q is false and since $P \& Q$ certainly requires the truth of *both* its parts in order for it to be true, we assign it the value **F**. In 3, P is **F** and Q is **T** and by similar reasoning to 2 $P \& Q$ is assigned the value **F**. In 4, of course, both P and Q are **F** and $P \& Q$ will again get the value **F**. In sum, a result of Table 3-2 is that anyone looking at it can tell that in order for a compound with the "&" connective to be true both of its parts must be true. In fact, this is part of what is meant by the ordinary English word "and," and we have merely recorded this meaning in our truth table under $P \& Q$. The proposition $P \& Q$ is called a *conjunction*, and its component parts are called *conjuncts*. Notice that we are able to work out this information without going into any detail as to the actual propositions P and Q. If we knew what P and Q were we would not have to talk about the four possible cases. Instead we might know that, as a matter of fact, 3 were the case. Still the truth table is very informative in the respect that it covers all possible cases and can actually define a connective.

This will become clearer if we consider other connectives. Again using weather as an example, a newsman might say

> It will either be completely overcast and cloudy tomorrow or will shower all day.

If P were "it will be overcast and cloudy tomorrow" and Q were "it will shower all day" then the proposition could be written as

> P or Q.

As before we will use a special symbol for the English word "or." In this case the wedge, "v," is most often used to replace "or." The truth value of the new symbolic formula

> $P \lor Q$

will depend on the truth values of its component parts. Since "or" means something different from "and" the truth table of "or" will be different from that of the "and" as found in Table 3-2. (See Table 3-3.)

It should be noted that the first part of the truth table will always be the same since there are only four different ways in which the truth or falsity of two propositions could occur, and these are given by 1-4 of either Table 3-2 or Table 3-3. However, the truth table under $P \lor Q$ differs, as expected, from that

TABLE 3-3.

Row	P	Q	P v Q
1	T	T	T
2	T	F	T
3	F	T	T
4	F	F	F

in Table 3-2. Thus in case 1, where both *P* and *Q* are **T** the value of *P* v *Q* will be **T**. In case 2 where *P* is **T** and *Q* is **F** the compound *P* v *Q* is **T** because in an "or" proposition it is enough for one of the components to be true to make the whole proposition true. Thus, if the *P* v *Q* were the newsman's prediction and it did not rain at all (making *Q* false) but was cloudy and completely overcast (making *P* true) then we would have no hesitation in saying that the forecast was correct. This is why both cases 2 and 3 confer a **T** on *P* v *Q*. In case 4, however, both *P* and *Q* are **F** and so *P* v *Q* receives a truth value of **F**. It is as if it neither rained nor was overcast in which case we would not hesitate to say that the forecast was incorrect. Molecular propositions constructed with the v are known as *disjunctions* and in propositions such as *P* v *Q* the atomic propositions *P* and *Q* are called *disjuncts*.

There is, though, one small but very important point to be made about the relationship between the symbolic connectives **v** and **&** and their literal counterparts. There is a strong temptation to say that the symbols are merely names for the connectives in English or that they mean the same thing as the English connectives. Certainly, the overall purpose of formal logic is capturing the precise meaning of ordinary language arguments and connectives. Still, we can only say that this has been accomplished when the **v** could replace the "or" in all contexts without confusion. We saw in Chapter 2 that the word "some" has a vagueness about it which led to our stipulation that "some" in the syllogistic was to mean "at least one." If there are cases where the meaning of **v** as given in Table 3-3 does not match its use in some ordinary but common context of "or" then we must realize that **v** is not the same as "or." What we shall say instead will become obvious shortly. First let us consider a case where the "or" diverges from **v** as it is defined in Table 3-3. If a patron were to read the statement

The price of dinner includes dessert or beverage.

he would, in almost every case, not be justified in assuming that he was entitled to both a dessert and a beverage. That is, it would be inconsistent with the above proposition to demand both a dessert and beverage. However, in Table 3-3, the proposition $P \vee Q$ is true in case 1 where both P and Q are true. This forces us to admit that the proposition [above] embodies a sense of "or" which is inconsistent with that of "$P \vee Q$." What we must say is that there are two sorts of "or" which differ in that one is true when both disjuncts are true and the other is false when both are true. In all other cases they will have the same values. The first type is known as *inclusive* disjunction and the second as *exclusive* disjunction.[2] See Table 3-4 for exclusive disjunction and its symbolic representative.

TABLE 3-4.

P	Q	P + Q
T	T	F
T	F	T
F	T	T
F	F	F

As a matter of fact, the $\vee$ type of "or" is more common and will be employed most often in this text, but it should be realized that the English word "or" requires two symbols with slightly different truth values to represent it. As so often happens, the translation into symbolic form requires us to recognize a potentially confusing ambiguity in the English word.

While discussing the ambiguity surrounding the use of the connective "or" we should point out that the "and" is not completely free from imprecision. In describing the truth table for the & we never considered whether the order of the conjuncts made a difference to the truth of the conjunction. However, in the assertion "Jill got married and had a baby" the order of the two conjoined propositions makes all the difference. We did not feel it necessary to provide a special symbol for this use of "and" because it is, in fact, an abbreviated form of "and then." This latter expression contains the notion of temporal sequence and is nontruth-functional (further discussion of nontruth-functional connectives will follow shortly).

Another connective that belongs in any discussion of alternate versions of "and" is "but." In the statement

---

[2] Languages such as Latin include separate words for these two senses and it is the Latin *vel* which is the source of the v for inclusive disjunction.

John is intelligent but lazy.

there are two aspects to the connective—one that is synonymous with "and" and one that is nontruth-functional. This is made clear by the recognition of the fact that the statement asserts

John is intelligent *and* lazy.

Also, however, the "but" in the first statement carries with it the implication that it is both unusual to find the properties of intelligence and laziness together and that the "laziness" detracts from the "intelligence." This aspect of the meaning of "but" cannot be captured by the "and" in the second statement and is nontruth-functional. In future situations the reader will find it sufficient to use the & for "but."

The third connective we shall consider is very central to propositional logic but somewhat variant from the previous three. This is the logical operator "not" which shall be symbolically written with the tilde sign, $\sim$. Recall the proposition

There is a foreign film at the Scala.

It may be that someone wants to deny or negate the statement (if, e.g., he believes that the film has changed, etc.). One way of doing so would be to assert the proposition

It is not the case that there is a foreign film at the Scala.

This new statement, in fact, is the result of negating the original atomic proposition and if we call the first P, then the second will be

It is not the case that P.

or

$\sim P$

This new connective is like the other three in that it can create a molecular proposition from an atomic one; still, it differs in the respect that it operates on only one proposition letter. The &, v, and + all required flanking letters to make any sense but the ~ is a one-place, or *monadic,* connective; the others are, obviously, *diadic* connectives. Since the ~ operates on one proposition its truth table will be somewhat simpler than the others. (See Table 3-5.)

TABLE 3-5.

P	~P
T	F
F	T

The proposition P can be either true or false. If P is T then its negation, ~P, will be F, and if P is F then its negation, ~P, will be T. In general, the negation sign works like a truth value reverser so that if there were two propositions that differed only in that one had a ~ in front of it then they would have opposite truth values. This is true no matter how many rows there are in the truth tables of the two propositions. For example, suppose someone were to negate the molecular proposition:

P & Q

The truth table for this formula is given in Table 3-2.

TABLE 3-2.

P	Q	P & Q
T	T	T
T	F	F
F	T	F
F	F	F

Now the denial of P & Q will be written as ~(P & Q) and its truth table can be calculated using Table 3-5 (see Table 3-6).

TABLE 3-6.

(1)	(2)	(3)	(4)
P	*Q*	(*P* & *Q*)	~(*P* & *Q*)
T	T	T	F
T	F	F	T
F	T	F	T
F	F	F	T

Column 4 is derived from column 3 by using the principle of truth reversal, which is the basis of negation. Notice that we use parentheses around *P* & *Q*. This is because we do not want any confusion to arise between the negation of *P* & *Q*, written as

$$\sim(P \& Q)$$

and another proposition

$$\sim P \& Q$$

which is read as

It is not the case that *P*, and *Q*.

In ~*P* & *Q* only the first letter is negated. See Table 3-7 for its truth table. In this table we use the truth value of ~*P* and the truth value of *Q* to give us the truth value of the compound ~*P* & *Q*, and this differs from that of ~(*P* & *Q*). We will have more to say about parentheses, but they basically play the same role as parentheses in ordinary algebra where they prevent unnecessary confusion. Thus, we all know that − (6 + 4) is an entirely different number from − 6 + 4. (The first is, of course, −10 and the second is −2.)

TABLE 3-7.

P	*Q*	~*P*	~*P* & *Q*
T	T	F	F
T	F	F	F
F	T	T	T
F	F	T	F

It should be obvious to the reader that the use of the negation operator and the other three diadic operators will give us a number of truth tables like Table 3-7 but with somewhat different truth columns.

EXERCISE

1 It would be a helpful exercise for the reader to write out the truth tables for
   a. $\sim(P + Q)$
   b. $\sim(P \lor Q)$
   c. $\sim P \& \sim Q$
   d. $\sim(P \lor \sim Q)$
   e. $\sim(P \& \sim Q)$
   f. $\sim(\sim P \& \sim Q)$

3.3 MOLECULAR PROPOSITIONS, CONNECTIVES, AND TRUTH: PART II

In section 3.2 we developed the notion of a truth table from the fairly straightforward notion that each proposition may have the value true or false. Then we used these truth tables to succinctly spell out the truth-functional meaning of various ordinary connectives in English. This is, of course, preliminary to developing techniques for evaluating arguments involving these connectives, and it thus becomes important to have a complete listing of all such connectives and their truth tables. However, there are many connectives ("unless," "if . . . then," "because," "but," "only if," etc.) and we cannot be sure that the fairly random procedure of taking them as they occur will provide us with a thorough list. A more rigorous way of completing the task would be to ask ourselves the question: "How many different truth tables could we write for a molecular proposition based on two atomic propositions, P, and Q?" If we knew the answer to this question and if we had a list of these connectives we could check off the list of connectives in English against this complete list. Of course, it must be remembered that this list will be a complete list of only truth-functional diadic connectives, i.e., those where the truth of the component propositions determines the truth of the compound. As an aside, note that a connective phrase such as "in order to" is *nontruth-functional.* Think of the compound

John ran to the station *in order to* catch the eight o'clock train.

The overall truth of this assertion does not depend on the truth of either "John ran to the station" or "John caught the eight o'clock train" because the compound can be true whether or not he caught the train, and likewise could be false whether or not he caught the train or ran to the station. The connective "in order to" expresses a relationship that could never be expressed in a truth table in the way that "and" was expressed in Table 3-2.

To return to the main issue, can we answer the question above? We know from our previous truth table work that any two atomic propositions will have four possible joint values. Thus, any compound made from these will, itself, have four distinct cases, each of which will be either **T** or **F**. If ∅ is a connective of whose meaning we know nothing we can still agree on the truth table (see Table 3-8).

TABLE 3-8.

P	*Q*	*P ∅ Q*
T	T	T or F
T	F	T or F
F	T	T or F
F	F	T or F

Our previous question then reduces to "How many different ∅'s are there?" where each ∅ is considered to be defined by a list of four truth values as per Table 3-8. The answer to this question is given rather simply by a little knowledge of permutations. The table for any compound will have four items in it and each of the items will take either the value **T** or **F**. Since we are asking the question "How many ways can you take two things four at a time?" we can then calculate that there are 4^2, or 16, distinct truth tables for a compound of two atomic propositions and each of the 16 will potentially represent a connective. Of course, we expect to find the tables for v, +, &, and ~ in various positions among these 16. Moreover, when we have written out the full table we can systematically examine each row and determine which connective it represents in ordinary language.

The list of the 16 possible truth-functional compounds is given in Table 3-9. What we have done is to begin with the column that has all **T**'s and end with the all **F** column while including, as systematically as possible, all the other combinations. The reader, at this point, may find the idea of a proposition with all **T**'s or all **F**'s rather confusing, but the significance of columns 1 and 16 will be discussed later. However, the reader should see that the following

TABLE 3-9.

P	Q	(1) ?	(2) P∨Q	(3) P	(4) P&Q	(5) Q	(6) ~(P+Q)	(7) ?	(8) ?	(9) ?	(10) ?	(11) P+Q	(12) ~Q	(13) ~(P&Q)	(14) ~P	(15) ~(P∨Q)	(16) ?
T	T	T	T	T	T	T	T	T	T	F	F	F	F	F	F	F	F
T	F	T	T	T	F	F	F	T	F	T	F	T	T	T	F	F	F
F	T	T	T	F	F	T	F	F	T	F	T	T	F	T	T	F	F
F	F	T	F	F	F	F	T	T	T	F	F	F	T	T	T	T	F

81

list of columns have already been worked out in our earlier discussion and can be appropriately labeled:

    4. $P \& Q$
    2. $P \vee Q$
  11. $P + Q$

That is, the above three columns are, in fact, the separate truth tables which we worked out in previous cases for the connectives &, v, +. Also, in section 3.2 we computed truth tables for a number of other compounds involving the negation sign, ~. A glance at Table 3-9 will show that the monadic connective generates the truth tables for the following:

  13. $\sim(P \& Q)$
  15. $\sim(P \vee Q)$
   6. $\sim(P + Q)$

This is so because the truth tables for 13, 15, and 6 contain a **T** for an **F** and an **F** for a **T** in each row of 4, 2, and 11, respectively.

Next look at columns 3, 5, and 12. Columns 3 and 5 match the values of the original P and Q, respectively. We will say, then, that the connective defined by column 3 is logically equivalent to P and that defined by 5 is logically equivalent to Q. Logical equivalence (which will be discussed further) is, for now, the name of the relationship that exists when two propositions (of any length) have the same truth value for any given truth values of their constituent atomic propositions. By this definition, then, the proposition heading column 14 is logically equivalent to $\sim P$ and column 12 to $\sim Q$.

Up to this point we have found some significance for all the columns but 7, 8, 9, 10, 1, and 16. It should be obvious from the exercise at the end of the previous section that we could write out a symbolic sentence using only P, Q, ~, &, v, and + which was logically equivalent to each of these. Thus, there would seem to be no need to examine any further ordinary language connectives in order to fulfill our goal of writing a complete truth table for all possible two-component molecular compounds. This is a very important statement for it tells us, in effect, that *any molecular proposition compounded from any connectives other than those already discussed will be logically equivalent to some proposition compounded from P, Q, v, ~, &, +.*

This fact, however, does not mean that it is unimportant to discover whether there are any other ordinary language connectives that are logically equivalent to the above. Remember, the purpose of this chapter is to develop techniques that can be used to evaluate any propositional argument in English. Since there may be any number of subtly different connectives in these arguments we must learn how to best translate them into symbolic form. In doing so we will, of course, discover where each of them is equivalent to some other proposition involving only the connectives so far considered. Still, we can continue the examination of ordinary language connectives sure in the knowledge that we have considered all possible compound propositions or at least propositions logically equivalent to all such compounds, and this thoroughness was the purpose of Table 3-9.

EXERCISES

1 Write out propositions, using connectives so far considered, that will have truth tables logically equivalent to columns 7, 8, 9, 10, 1, and 16 of Table 3-9.

2 Do we need all four connectives to write molecular propositions which will be logically equivalent to the sixteen different compounds in Table 3-9?

3.4 SOME ADDITIONAL CONNECTIVES

The most common connective in ordinary, nonformal argumentation which we have not yet considered is the "If . . . then" as it might occur in:

If the weather is suitable *then* we will play tennis on Thursday.

This connective (or better "connective phrase") is known as the *conditional*; it is sometimes called *implication* but we have reason for not using this name (see section 3.7.1). It is clear that the truth of a compound such as the above depends on the truth of its component propositions and that this type of proposition is used to assert some sort of a dependency relation of the second proposition on the first (hence, the name *conditional*). Allowing P to stand for "the weather is suitable" and Q for "we will play tennis on Thursday" we will symbolize the above

$$P \supset Q$$

read "If P then Q." The "⊃" sign for the conditional is known as the *horseshoe* and should not be confused with the similar sign meaning "class inclusion" in set theory. Using our previous models we will now work out a truth table that will attempt to capture the meaning of this conditional relation in our formal apparatus. (See Table 3-10.)

TABLE 3-10.

Row	P	Q	$P \supset Q$
1	T	T	?
2	T	F	?
3	F	T	?
4	F	F	?

It is clear that anyone who asserts "If the weather is suitable then we will play tennis on Thursday" intends that the truth of the first utterance, P, guarantees or ensures the truth of the second. Thus, we will say that in case 1 the compound sentence $P \supset Q$ will be true and in case 2 it will be false. The naturalness of settling cases 1 and 2 in this way can be seen clearly if the reader will recall the original meaning of P and Q above. We say that $P \supset Q$ is true when it is the case that the weather is suitable, P, and tennis is played on Thursday, Q. In case 2 the weather is suitable and yet tennis is not played. This clearly violates the assertion that if the weather is suitable tennis will be played on Thursday and we thus say, in this case, that $P \supset Q$ is false. Before considering cases 3 and 4, however, we must note one thing: case 1 for $P \supset Q$ is true but we do not ordinarily say that it is true just because both P and Q happen to be true. On the contrary, we ordinarily use the "If . . . then" only in cases where there is believed to be some special connection between P and Q (this may be, e.g., *causal connection*). Having noted this we shall continue to construct the table.

In case 3 the antecedent statement P is false and the consequent Q is true. One's first reaction to this case is that the circumstances it describes are such that no one would assert the conditional proposition $P \supset Q$ in this context. This is certainly true, and it is true because as we noted above the assertion of the conditional usually means that the speaker believes there is a special connection between the antecedent and consequent whereas this case, 3, seems to imply that there is no connection between them. However, it is important to keep in mind that we are not trying to decide whether we would ordinarily assert $P \supset Q$ in case 3 but whether $P \supset Q$ is true or false in case 3. Suppose someone had asserted

If the weather is suitable then we will play tennis on Thursday.

and further suppose that it turned out that the weather was *not* suitable but that the game was played indoors. These facts would not make the statement false since nothing about it rules out the possibility that the game could be played in spite of the weather. However, if these facts were known to the utterer of the statement he would most likely never have asserted it. By calling $P \supset Q$ true when P is false and Q is true we are effectively considering the truth of the conditional proposition and not the aptness of its assertion. Still, the reader may ask "Since in usual cases the lack of grounds for the assertion of a proposition are grounds for its falsehood, why not in this case?" First, the conditional proposition is usually asserted on the basis of some connection known or believed to exist between P and Q. This is precisely the source of our discomfort in calling $P \supset Q$ true in case 3. However, we do use the "If . . . then" connective in a way that does not necessarily imply a special connection between P and Q. Consider this situation: An award is to be given for writing a history essay; all juniors and seniors are considered eligible. Now suppose someone were to say to a student:

If you are a senior then you are eligible.

It is clear that the statement remains true even in the event that the student is a junior (making P false and Q true). It is this sense of the conditional that we wish to capture in the symbolic form $P \supset Q$, and it is often called the *material* conditional to indicate that there need be no special relationship (such as "cause and effect") between P and Q. In fact, the relationship of P and Q in the above statement is best described as *conventional*, meaning that there is a convention or agreement that connects P and Q and not some causal law. It should be noted that the proposition, though true, is still somehow inappropriate for the case where P is false and Q is true.

The last case to consider, 4, is the situation in which both the antecedent and the consequent are false. In this case $P \supset Q$ is true. Thus, to return to the proposition

If the weather is suitable then we will play tennis on Thursday.

if it turned out that the weather was unsuitable and that tennis was not played on Thursday then we would have no hesitation in saying that the original proposition was true. This consideration of cases 1-4 indicates that the truth table for the material conditional will be as shown in Table 3-11.

TABLE 3-11.

Row	P	Q	$P \supset Q$
1	T	T	T
2	T	F	F
3	F	T	T
4	F	F	T

If we check the master table for all two-proposition compounds we will see that the truth table in Table 3-11 makes the material conditional $P \supset Q$ equivalent to the following proposition

$$\sim P \vee Q$$

At this point the reader is probably wondering why we have chosen to interpret the "If . . . then" as the material conditional. If you followed the discussion of this section carefully you realize that there is a genuine and fairly widespread use of the "If . . . then" as a material conditional but this is not our sole reason. First, the material conditional can be used to express any other sense of the "If . . . then." That is, if we want to express a causally necessary relation between P and Q we will be able to do so by utilizing two material conditional statements (this will be discussed next).[3] Second, our interpretation of the "If . . . then" relation will lend itself perfectly (and in an intuitively natural way) to constructing the evaluation procedure for propositional logic (see section 3.7). These reasons, then, justify our interpretation of $P \supset Q$ even if this interpretation requires us to use one sense of the ordinary "If . . . then" at the expense of others.

We mentioned above that we can use the material conditional to capture the rather stronger sense of "If . . . then" which obtains in certain causal situations. Consider the proposition

---

[3]The discussion of this relation will be an analysis of necessary and sufficient conditions and will not be an analysis of the concept of "cause" itself.

If you put blue litmus paper in acid then it will turn red.

When this is proposed as a chemical test for acidity it is obvious that the material conditional is inadequate. This is so because if the proposition were treated as $P \supset Q$ then it would be true when (1) the blue paper were not put in acid and (2) it did turn red, i.e., when P was false and Q was true. However, if litmus paper turned red in or out of acid it would not be a very good chemical test for acidity. In order to better express the proposition symbolically we must realize that it is really a shortened version of the proposition

> If you put blue litmus paper in acid then it turns red, and only if it is put in acid does it turn red.

Thus we can express the proposition completely if we can conjoin two propositions—one of which is $P \supset Q$ and the other Q only if P. This latter proposition can be written as $Q \supset P$. To see that this is so consider this statement:

1. You can vote only if you are a citizen.

The "only if" has the force of making this proposition the same as:

2. If you can vote then you are a citizen.

It cannot be translated as:

3. If you are a citizen then you can vote.

Because it is perfectly consistent with 1 that someone who is a citizen cannot vote because of residency requirements, while a citizen who cannot vote clearly renders 3 false. On the basis of this we can now write

> If you put blue litmus paper in acid then it turns red, and only if it is put in acid does it turn red.

as

$P \supset Q$ and $Q \supset P$ or $(P \supset Q) \,\&\, (Q \supset P)$

We will call this the *biconditional* relationship, and it is usually expressed in English by the phrase, "if and only if." An examination of the truth table for the above will show that the only circumstance that would make it true is when P and Q have the same truth value. Because of this fact the biconditional can be taken as defining an equivalence and may be written with the $\equiv$ symbol as

$$P \equiv Q$$

Keep in mind, though, that since the equivalence is understood as a biconditional and each conditional is a material conditional it will be known as *material equivalence*. Earlier, we spoke of two propositions being "logically" equivalent when they had the same truth table. The distinction between material and logical equivalence is that logical equivalence is a material equivalence that could not be false. Thus $P \equiv Q$ could be false depending on the truth tables for P and Q; however,

$$(P \supset Q) \equiv (\sim P \vee Q)$$

is a logical equivalence in that regardless of the truth values of P and Q the equivalence will hold (this is because the truth table for $P \supset Q$ is precisely the same as the truth table for $\sim P \vee Q$). In later development of the propositional logic we will make considerable use of this sort of logical equivalence.

As a final note on the conditional we should mention several apparent synonyms. These will be given on the left in Table 3-12 and their translation with the horseshoe will appear on the right. Notice that each of these requires the reversal of the order of P and Q in the symbolic form. Still, another connective that belongs in a discussion of the "If . . . then" is "unless." When someone says, "I am not going out unless Peter comes home first" he is, in effect, saying that either he is not going out or Peter is coming home first. This is $\sim P \vee Q$ and so $\sim P$ unless Q translates directly into $P \supset Q$ as per the logical equivalence considered above.

TABLE 3-12.

P provided that Q	$Q \supset P$
P on the condition that Q	$Q \supset P$
P when Q	$Q \supset P$

EXERCISES

1 Construct two propositions that have the same truth table as ~P v Q.

2 Translate each of the following into symbolic form and write the truth table for each:
  a. John cannot be both lazy and incompetent.
  b. Unless I did not hear the weather correctly, we will have rain tomorrow.
  c. Edith would have come home sooner if the train was on time.
  d. It is not the case that Julius has a four handicap in golf.
  e. I will live in Europe for at least a year, provided that I have enough money.
  f. Phyllis can type 60 words a minute unless she is interrupted continually.
  g. If you cannot symbolize this statement, you do not understand section 3.4.
  h. Derek has neither milk nor lemon with his tea.
  i. Navy will beat Army only if the weather is suitable for passing.
  j. Your father will not allow you to either use the car or come home late.
  k. You cannot win if you do not play.
  l. Jonathan's two guests were Bill and Joe.
  m. Clouds will yield rain if and only if glaciation takes place.
  n. Edward can fulfill his humanities requirements with English or History.

3.5 TAUTOLOGIES, CONTRADICTIONS, AND CONTINGENT PROPOSITIONS

At this point we have completed our discussion of the connectives and their representations in truth tables. The propositional apparatus that we now have is sufficient to express symbolically all truth-functional propositions that are compounded from one or two atomic propositions. Yet the reader will recall that we have not touched on columns 1 or 16 of our comprehensive Table 3-9. Column 1 represents a truth-functional compound that never has the value F and column 16 can be considered its negation. If we had to write a proposition that had this table we could use

P v ~P

or

$$Q \vee \sim Q$$

Both these propositions can never have an **F** in their truth columns just as

$$\sim(P \vee \sim P)$$

and

$$\sim(Q \vee \sim Q)$$

will always have **F**'s in their columns. Now, while 1 and 16 do not represent any common English connective they will be very significant for evaluating arguments. We shall call any proposition that has all **T**'s in its truth column a *tautology* and its negation, or any other proposition that happens to have all **F**'s in its truth column, a *contradiction*. Any proposition that is neither a tautology nor a contradiction we will call *contingent*; this last name is used because propositions such as 2-15 (see Table 3-9) can be either true or false, contingent on the values of their components, whereas 1 and 16 are always true and false, respectively, regardless of their components truth values. If we pause for a moment to consider what sort of propositions 1 and 16 would be in ordinary language, we would get the following sorts of examples:

Either the tree is 16 feet tall or the tree is not 16 feet tall. *Tautology*
It is not the case either that the tree is 16 feet tall or is not 16 feet tall. *Contradiction*

First note that the contradiction, which we wrote as $\sim(P \vee \sim P)$ is really the same as $P \ \& \sim P$ or

The tree is 16 feet tall and the tree is not 16 feet tall.

This latter proposition is the more usually used form of a self-contradictory assertion and it is obviously (work out the truth table) logically equivalent to $\sim(P \vee \sim P)$. This equivalence and others will play an important role in the later development of the propositional logic.

Next consider the falsity of the contradiction. One might be tempted to say that an English sentence such as the contradiction example above could conceivably be true—say if the tree were to vary in its height from morning to evening by as little as .001 inches every day. Would not the tree then be both 16 feet tall and not 16 feet tall over a certain period of time and would not the sentence be true? The answer, of course, is that the rules we have used for translation into symbolic form demand that a proposition take on one of two values, **T** or **F**. If we were to allow the simultaneous truth of P and $\sim P$ then our logic would not be the two-valued propositional logic. As a matter of fact we do sometimes use the form of the contradiction in ordinary language to express a borderline or extremely small variation so that we might say of the tree that it is both 16 and not 16 feet tall if it grows from morning to evening. Still, our use of such a locution is little more than an assertion of the fact that it would be very difficult to say whether the tree were a certain height unless we were to pin down the time of measurement. Once we do so, we realize that no tree could be both 16 feet tall and not 16 feet tall at the same time. The peculiar fact that we recognize about a *genuine* contradiction as opposed to an *apparent* one (i.e., one where the opposite cases both apply because of some ambiguity or imprecision in their formulation) is that there is no possible situation or state of affairs that could make it true. In part, our avoidance of self-contradictions in everyday arguments is based on this fact, namely, that a genuine contradiction can never assert anything that could conceivably be true and if employed makes the intelligibility of our argument marginal.

The same issues that surround contradictions also arise in connection with tautologies. First, there are cases in ordinary language where the form of a tautology is used to make an assertion that is not a genuine tautology. Thus,

John will either be very successful in life or he will not.

is the sort of assertion which we do not usually accept as tautologically true. In fact, one might claim that it is false, if you believed that great success and lack of success are not exclusive alternatives. Still, when the senses of any proposition and its negation are precisely set, then a statement compounded out of the proposition and its negation flanking the v will be a tautology and will, therefore, be true in every case. However, there is a striking analogy between the contradiction and the tautology with respect to their application to factual situations or states of affairs. If someone were to assert the tautology above:

Either the tree is 16 feet tall or the tree is not 16 feet tall.

what would he really be saying about the tree? A moment's thought should convince the reader that this proposition, though true, is trivially so; i.e., its truth arises from the logical connectives and not from any correspondence between the proposition and the facts in the world. It tells us nothing at all about the tree but it does say a great deal about the logical connectives, and we will shortly use this as a means to evaluate arguments. Before we can do this, however, we must extend our truth table apparatus so that we can decide whether any proposition of any length is a tautology, a contradiction, or is contingent. The situation at this point is that we can write truth tables for any formula with two component propositions. The next section will detail the mechanics of writing a truth table for a proposition with more than two components.

3.6 TRUTH TABLE CONSTRUCTION FOR FORMULAS WITH MORE THAN TWO PROPOSITION LETTERS

This section will be the last one preliminary to developing our evaluation procedures. What we are going to do here is to extend our method of constructing truth tables in such a way that we will be able to decide whether any compound proposition is a tautology, a contradiction, or a contingent assertion. Actually, this extension will require no new concepts, merely the rethinking of the material in the last few sections. It will be remembered that the basis for all previous truth tables for two-proposition compounds was deciding how many possible situations of truth and falsity could arise with two propositions. That is, two propositions could be jointly true or false in four different ways; and we listed these in a column (see Tables 3-2 through 3-8). The governing principle, then, for constructing a truth table for a compound was deciding whether the compound was true or false in each of these four cases. Now, if we had three proposition letters in a formula, say,

$P \vee (Q \& R)$

then the first step in constructing its truth table will be the listing of all the possible joint true-false situations for P, Q, and R. Since we have two options

(T or F) for three items (P, Q, R) we know that there will be 2^3, or 8, rows in our truth table. The reader will find these listed in Table 3-13. Also, we now adopt the general rule that given any compound proposition with, say n *different* proposition letters, the number of rows in the truth table will be 2^n; remember, though, this applies to different letters so that, e.g., $\sim P$ is not an additional proposition but a compound of P. Next, in writing the table for $P \vee (Q \& R)$ we should be aware that since it is composed of two parts, our truth table for it must be built up from tables for each of its parts. That is, $P \vee (Q \& R)$ is really like any two-proposition compound—$A \vee B$—only B itself is a compound, namely, $Q \& R$. Thus, we can most efficiently write the table for $P \vee (Q \& R)$ by first writing that for $Q \& R$ and then using this table and the table for P to get that for $P \vee (Q \& R)$. This stepwise procedure has been carried out in columns 4 and 5 of our Table 3-13 and column 5 is the truth table for $P \vee (Q \& R)$.

TABLE 3-13.

(1) P	(2) Q	(3) R	(4) $Q \& R$	(5) $P \vee (Q \& R)$
T	T	T	T	T
T	T	F	F	T
T	F	T	F	T
T	F	F	F	T
F	T	T	T	T
F	T	F	F	F
F	F	T	F	F
F	F	F	F	F

Notice that though the number of rows in the truth table is given by the formula 2^n it is not always so obvious how to efficiently write these 2^n possible situations. A good rule of thumb to follow (as in Table 3-13) is to write one-half T's and one-half F's for the first proposition letter, then one-quarter T's, one-quarter F's for the second proposition letter, and continue this sort of halving procedure until the last letter (in Table 3-13 this is R) has a column consisting of alternating T's and F's. This mechanical procedure will always result in a complete list and is much more effective than a haphazard search for the list of combinations.

When a truth table for a compound is completed it is a simple matter to decide whether the given compound is tautologous, contradictory, or contingent. Simply inspect the column under the compound: (1) If it has all **T**'s then the compound is a tautology. (2) If it has all **F**'s then the compound is a contradiction. (3) If it is neither (1) or (2) (even if it is mostly **T** or **F**) then it is contingent. Table 3-13 clearly shows that $P \vee (Q \,\&\, R)$ is contingent.

As a further example consider the compound proposition

$$P \supset [(Q \,\&\, S) \vee P]$$

First we must write out the 2^3, or 8, possible truth situations (see Table 3-14). Next, we write out the truth table for $(Q \,\&\, S)$; this appears as column 4 in Table 3-14. Using this column as the truth table for $(Q \,\&\, S)$ and the column under P we write another table (column 5) for $(Q \,\&\, S) \vee P$. Finally, we use column 5 and P again to write out the table for $P \supset [(Q \,\&\, S) \vee P]$. Keep in mind that in each step the determining factor in our writing the truth table is the particular connective involved. This table now tells us that $P \supset [(Q \,\&\, S) \vee P]$ is a tautology since it has **T**'s in its table for all eight cases of the joint values of P, Q, and S.

TABLE 3-14.

(1) P	(2) Q	(3) S	(4) Q & S	(5) (Q & S) v P	(6) P ⊃ [(Q & S) v P]
T	T	T	T	T	T
T	T	F	F	T	T
T	F	T	F	T	T
T	F	F	F	T	T
F	T	T	T	T	T
F	T	F	F	F	T
F	F	T	F	F	T
F	F	F	F	F	T

The most important part of being able to write truth tables for any proposition is the ability to build up successive truth tables for the constituent units of the whole proposition. In this way the truth table will end with the column that represents the truth column of the whole proposition. As can be seen by the previous examples this last column is determined by the main connective of the proposition. Thus, in the previous example the main connective was the $\supset$ which followed the first occurrence of P and the last column on the right is the truth table for this connective and for

$P \supset [(Q \& S) \vee P]$. It is not usually too difficult to determine which is the main connective as it is indicated by the use of parentheses and brackets. Thus, in

$$[Q \& (S \supset (P \& {\sim}Q))] \supset S$$

the brackets tell us that this proposition is of the form $A \supset B$ where A is $Q \& (S \supset (P \& {\sim}Q))$ and B is S and its main connective is the $\supset$ before the last S. Further, A is a proposition whose main connective is & and which is basically of the form $C \& D$ where C is Q and D is $S \supset (P \& {\sim}Q)$. By proceeding in this way until we come to the atomic propositions P, Q, S we are successively determining the main connective of first the whole formula and then its component parts. The truth table requires the same pairing operation but successively builds up components until the last truth column is the column appropriate to the main connective.

EXERCISES

1 Below each of the following ordinary language statements are symbolic propositions. Use truth tables to decide whether, in each case, the symbolic proposition is logically equivalent to the statement above it.

a. If Carol can do well on the first quiz and if her teacher is fair then she will either get an A or a B.

$$(P \& Q) \supset (R \vee S)$$

b. If Robert arrives with Leon or with Timothy, and Tony arrives with Bert then there will be one too many boys.

$${\sim}[(P \vee Q) \& R] \vee S$$

c. Myrna is good-looking but she is also intelligent and unless Harry is a poor judge of women he will ask her out.

$$[(P \& Q) \& R] \vee S$$

d. Michael was either going home or to Cathy's house, and if he did not go home then if he did not have trouble with the car, he went to Cathy's house.

$${\sim}({\sim}H \& {\sim}C) \& [H \vee (C \supset T)]$$

e. The Emmet party will either stay in the executive suite or in rooms 40 and 41 but as the executive suite is occupied they cannot stay there and if they cannot stay there they will occupy room 40.

$$\{ [E \lor (R \,\&\, S)] \,\&\, \sim\!E \} \,\&\, (E \supset R)$$

2 Use truth tables to decide whether each of the following is a tautology, a contradiction, or is contingent:

a. $(A \,\&\, B) \equiv (B \supset \sim\!B)$
b. $P \,\&\, [(Q \lor R) \supset (\sim\!P \supset P)]$
c. $P \supset (Q \supset P)$
d. $P \supset [P \supset (Q \lor \sim\!P)]$
e. $[P \supset (P \,\&\, Q)] \lor P$
f. $(P \supset Q) \,\&\, (P \,\&\, \sim\!Q)$

3.7 AN EVALUATION PROCEDURE USING TRUTH TABLES

We are now ready to formulate our procedure for testing the validity of any propositional argument. To understand precisely how it works the reader should recall the definition of validity we discussed in Chapters 1 and 2, namely, that an argument will be said to be valid when it is impossible for all the premises to be true and the conclusion false. On the basis of our interpretation of material implication this is like saying that a proposition formed out of the premises and conclusion of an argument in the following way:

$$(\text{Premise}_1 \,\&\, \text{Premise}_2) \supset \text{Conclusion}.$$

can never be false. That is, jointly true premises and a false conclusion would make the proposition false but this eventuality could only arise if the argument itself were invalid. Thus, if we test the proposition by a truth table and find it tautologous we will have proven the impossibility of the truth of the premises and the falsity of the conclusion and, in this way, we will have proven the argument valid. To see more concretely how this test works let us evaluate the following two arguments:

A. $P \supset Q$
   $\dfrac{\sim\!Q}{\therefore \sim\!P}$

First, we must form a proposition from the premises and conclusion of this argument as per the proposition above. For future reference we will call the proposition that consists of the conjunction of the premises as antecedent, and the conclusion as consequent of the conditional, the *argument proposition.* Thus, the argument proposition of A will be

$$[(P \supset Q) \& (\sim Q)] \supset \sim P$$

Its truth table is shown as Table 3-15.

TABLE 3-15.

(1) P	(2) Q	(3) $\sim Q$	(4) $\sim P$	(5) $P \supset Q$	(6) $(P \supset Q) \& \sim Q$	(7) $[(P \supset Q) \& (\sim Q)] \supset \sim P$
T	T	F	F	T	F	T
T	F	T	F	F	F	T
F	T	F	T	T	F	T
F	F	T	T	T	T	T

Since by column 7 of Table 3-15 the argument proposition of A is a tautology, the original argument is valid.

B. $P \supset Q$
   $Q \supset R$
   _____
   $\therefore P \supset R$

The argument proposition for this is

$$[(P \supset Q) \& (Q \supset R)] \supset (P \supset R)$$

and its truth table is shown as Table 3-16. The reader can clearly see that the result in Table 3-16, column 8, shows the original argument valid.

Of course, we want our evaluation procedure to work on ordinary language arguments as well as symbolic arguments. That it is adequate to this is seen by considering the following argument:

C. Ralph and Paul are coming to the party on Wednesday.
   However, Paul will not come unless Sarah treats him in a civil manner.
   _____
   $\therefore$ Either Sarah treats him in a civil manner or Ned will not bring his wife.

97

TABLE 3-16.

(1) P	(2) Q	(3) R	(4) P ⊃ Q	(5) Q ⊃ R	(6) P ⊃ R	(7) [(P ⊃ Q) & (Q ⊃ R)]	(8) [(P ⊃ Q) & (Q ⊃ R)] ⊃ (P ⊃ R)
T	T	T	T	T	T	T	T
T	T	F	T	F	F	F	T
T	F	T	F	T	T	F	T
T	F	F	F	T	F	F	T
F	T	T	T	T	T	T	T
F	T	F	T	F	T	F	T
F	F	T	T	T	T	T	T
F	F	F	T	T	T	T	T

The first step in evaluating this argument is the translation of its two premises and conclusion from the English to the symbolic language. Using the techniques discussed in sections 3.1-3.5 this results in the following argument form:

$$R \,\&\, P$$
$$\sim P \vee S$$
$$\overline{\therefore S \vee N}$$

Next, we formulate the argument proposition for this argument form and construct a truth table for it. Both the argument proposition and its truth table are found in Table 3-17, column 10. Since, the argument proposition is tautologous the argument is valid. Notice, though, the size of Table 3-17. Since C has four proposition letters the table has 2^4, or 16, rows.

The final example will be:

D. If Lowell wins the first prize, his mother will be proud of him.
  Either his mother will be proud of him or Nancy will win the second prize.
  If Nancy wins the second prize then Lowell will win the first prize.
  ∴ Lowell will win the first prize.

The reader, by now, should be able to follow the construction of both argument propositions and truth tables. Also, he should be able to decide the validity of this argument by inspecting Table 3-18.[4]

[4]In constructing Table 3-18 we shortened our work considerably by writing the truth column for the argument proposition without the intermediate steps of writing the column for the conjunction of the premises. This can be done when it shortens the length of the table and when one is quite sure that no error is being allowed by carelessness.

TABLE 3-17.

(1) N	(2) P	(3) R	(4) S	(5) ~P	(6) R & P	(7) ~P v S	(8) S v N	(9) (R & P) & (~P v S)	(10) [(R & P) & (~P v S)] ⊃ (S v N)
T	T	T	T	F	T	T	T	T	T
T	T	T	F	F	T	F	T	F	T
T	T	F	T	F	F	T	T	F	T
T	T	F	F	F	F	F	T	F	T
T	F	T	T	T	F	T	T	F	T
T	F	T	F	T	F	T	T	F	T
T	F	F	T	T	F	T	T	F	T
T	F	F	F	T	F	T	T	F	T
F	T	T	T	F	T	T	T	T	T
F	T	T	F	F	T	F	F	F	T
F	T	F	T	F	F	T	T	F	T
F	T	F	F	F	F	F	F	F	T
F	F	T	T	T	F	T	T	F	T
F	F	T	F	T	F	T	F	F	T
F	F	F	T	T	F	T	T	F	T
F	F	F	F	T	F	T	F	F	T

TABLE 3-18.

(1) L	(2) M	(3) N	(4) L ⊃ M	(5) M v N	(6) N ⊃ L	(7) [(L ⊃ M) & (M v N) & (N ⊃ L)] ⊃ L
T	T	T	T	T	T	T
T	T	F	T	T	T	T
T	F	T	F	T	T	T
T	F	F	F	F	T	T
F	T	T	T	T	F	T
F	T	F	T	T	T	F
F	F	T	T	T	F	T
F	F	F	T	F	T	T

The reader should note that some effort can be saved in the construction of truth tables by realizing that the definition of validity requires that in no case can the premises of a valid argument be jointly true and the conclusion false. This requirement is what allows us to use the test for tautology as a test for validity. However, we could test for validity by simply identifying the rows of the truth table that show the premises jointly true and then checking the truth value of the conclusion in each case. If the conclusion is false in *any* row where the premises are jointly true, the argument is invalid (and the argument proposition is false in that row). This way is shorter in that the construction of the truth table need only proceed up to the point of including each premise and the conclusion. In D columns 4, 5, and 6 describe the premises and column 1, the conclusion. 4, 5, and 6 show joint truth in the first, second and sixth rows and in the sixth row L (the conclusion) is false. Thus, the argument is invalid and the truth table for its argument proposition has **T** in all rows except the sixth as the reader can see in Table 3-18.

The truth table method of evaluation we have described is analogous to the diagram and rule methods of the syllogistic in that it is both effective and mechanical. This can be easily seen since the truth table method for deciding whether a proposition is or is not a tautology is mechanical and effective (i.e., it always gives a definite answer after a finite number of applications of a uniform set of instructions) and validity depends solely on the tautologous structure of the argument proposition. Further, the construction of a truth table is much like the drawing of Venn diagrams. If the reader recalls, we spoke of the Venn diagram method as *model-theoretic* because, in essence, it consists in the construction of abstract models for the premises and conclusion of an argument as means to evaluate it. In constructing a truth table we are figuratively drawing diagrams of all the possible truth situations in which the premises stand to the conclusion. The model, however, is considerably more abstract in this case than it was in the case of the Venn diagram because we have much less information about the structure and meaning of each of the propositions. In general any evaluation procedure that depends on a consideration of the truth or meaning of the premises and conclusion of an argument will be model-theoretic. (For further discussion of this see Chapter 5.)

3.7.1   The ⊃, "implies," and consistency

At this point it will be necessary to caution the reader about a mistake that often arises in connection with the truth table method of evaluation. It is sometimes incorrectly assumed that the ⊃ is the translation of "therefore" or "implies." That is, the material conditional is mistakenly used to express the relationship that obtains between the premises of an argument and the conclusion. This is a natural error in view of the fact that the conditional symbol is used in the evaluation procedure as the main connective of the argument proposition. Also, the usual definition of validity contains an "If . . . then" assertion. Still, the reader should remember that the material conditional is only one of the proposition connectives that occur within a proposition. The "therefore" or "implies" relation is, on the other hand, the name of a relation that obtains between the premises of an argument and the conclusion. We have used the ∴ symbol to stand in place of this relation. It should be noted that the "therefore" or ∴ is used for both valid and invalid arguments and merely serves to set off the conclusion from the premises. If, however, we know that a certain argument is valid and thus that the premises imply the conclusion, then we may note this fact by using the ⊢ or "turnstile" symbol. Thus for A (see p. 96) above we may write

$$P \supset Q, \sim Q \vdash \sim P$$

When using the turnstile we set off the premises with commas. Now we are in a position to clear up all confusion about the ∴ and the ⊢ and ⊃. The ∴ is simply a notational device which means that "what follows is the conclusion." This symbol may be used irrespective of the validity of the argument. The use of the ⊢ symbol indicates that the proposition on the right side of this symbol is a *valid consequence* of the propositions on the left side of the symbol. However, any such sequence such as

$$P \supset Q, \sim Q \vdash \sim P$$

can be rewritten as

"$[(P \supset Q) \mathbin{\&} (\sim Q)] \supset \sim P$" is a tautology.

That is, the ⊢ symbol is justified in just the cases where the argument proposition is a tautology. In no case does the ⊃ symbol itself mean ⊢ or ∴.

The last point in this section concerns a somewhat surprising consequence of the truth table method of evaluation. The astute reader may have already noticed that our procedure is such that, if there were always an **F** in the conjunction of the premises, then the argument proposition would always be **T** (a consequence of the definition of material implication). This means that a contradictory set of premises (which would always be jointly false) validly implies any other statement. To see this in its simplest form consider the following argument:

$$\frac{\begin{array}{c} P \\ \sim P \end{array}}{\therefore S}$$

where S is any statement whatever. The argument proposition would be:

$$(P \& \sim P) \supset S$$

and since $(P \& \sim P)$ would always have an **F** in its table the argument proposition above would be tautologous and the argument would be valid. Surprising as this may seem we should have expected that a contradiction would lead to peculiar problems for evaluating arguments. The best way to avoid this empty sort of validity for our arguments is to require that the premises of an argument be nonself-contradictory or *consistent*. This requirement can be fulfilled if we merely required that at least one row of the truth table made the premises jointly true. Section 3.8 will discuss this requirement in somewhat more detail.

EXERCISES

1 Decide the validity of each of the following argument forms using truth tables:

a. $\dfrac{\begin{array}{l} C \supset (A \& B) \\ \sim A \end{array}}{\therefore \sim C}$

b. $\dfrac{P \supset Q}{\therefore P \supset P}$

c. $\dfrac{\begin{array}{l} N \supset M \\ N \vee M \end{array}}{\therefore M}$

d. $\dfrac{\begin{array}{l} A \vee \sim B \\ A \supset C \end{array}}{\therefore B \supset C}$

e. $\dfrac{\begin{array}{l} P \supset (Q \& R) \\ \sim(\sim Q \vee \sim R) \\ P \supset S \end{array}}{\therefore S}$

f. $\dfrac{\begin{array}{l} P \supset Q \\ \sim(\sim P \& \sim Q) \end{array}}{\therefore P \vee Q}$

g. $(P \lor Q) \supset P$
     $P \supset Q$

     $\therefore \sim(P \& Q)$

h. $(P \& Q) \lor P$
     $\therefore P$

2 Use truth tables to evaluate each of the following arguments:

a. The serum must arrive in 24 hours or Peter will die. If the expert on jungle diseases is available and the serum arrives then Peter will live. The expert will be available. However, if the expert on jungle diseases is available then the serum will arrive. Therefore, Peter will live.

b. If the temperature does not rise tonight, we can go skating tomorrow. If either the temperature rises or the ice is not smooth then we cannot go skating tomorrow. The ice, though, will be smooth. Therefore, we can go skating tomorrow.

c. Joan mailed the letter which was sitting on my desk. Therefore, either Joan mailed the letter or she burned it.

d. Either the capacitor leaked or the resistor burned out. If the capacitor leaked then the resistor burned out. It could not be both that the capacitor leaked and the resistor burned out. Therefore, the resistor burned out.

e. Only if I have a book on Plato and a book on Aristotle can I do my paper. To pass I must do the paper. I will not pass. Therefore, I do not have a book on Aristotle.

f. If Notre Dame beats Army then if Army beats Navy then Navy will not play in a bowl game. Thus, if Navy does not beat Army then Navy does not play in a bowl game.

g. Unless Deitra gets a toy poodle for her birthday, she will be unhappy. Therefore, if Deitra gets a Siamese kitten for her birthday, she will be unhappy.

h. Either Helen will get home before seven or Dora will worry. If Dora does not worry then Helen will get home before seven. Dora worries. Therefore, Helen does not get home before seven.

3.8 SHORTER TRUTH TABLE TECHNIQUE

By carefully considering the working of the truth table test for validity we can devise a method that works as well as the truth table test but that will be considerably shorter. In constructing the full table we began with a listing of all possible combinations of truth and falsity of the various proposition symbols. Next we used these to determine the true-false possibilities of the premises and conclusion. Finally, by suitable construction of the argument proposition we determined validity by evaluating this proposition. Any line of the truth table that made the conclusion false and the premises true, and thus failed to show the argument proposition a tautology resulted in an invalid argument prior to constructing the full table. Now, if we could decide whether an argument would have a row in its table that made the premises true and the conclusion false without constructing the full table then we could shorten our task considerably. In fact, we can do this quite simply by assigning the conclusion the value **F** and attempting to work out an assignment of values to the premise letters that will make them jointly true. When we do this, we are actually constructing the row of the full truth table that invalidates the argument (there may be more than one invalidating row, of course, but one is certainly enough). However, if after sufficient attempts (i.e., all possible ways to make the conclusion false and premises true) we cannot construct an invalidating assignment of truth values, we will have proven the original argument valid. To see how this works consider the following argument:

$$
\begin{array}{c}
\mathbf{F}\quad\mathbf{T} \\
\text{A. 1.}\quad P \supset Q \qquad \mathbf{T} \\
\mathbf{F} \\
\underline{\text{2.}\quad \sim P \qquad \mathbf{T}} \\
\mathbf{T} \\
\therefore \sim Q \qquad \mathbf{F}
\end{array}
$$

First we must assign **F** to $\sim Q$, which would make Q, **T**. The second step requires us to assign values to the remaining proposition letters in such a way that all the premises will be true. Beginning with premise 2 we realize that if $\sim P$ is to be true then P itself will be false, however, making P false results in premise 1 being true and thus we have both premises true and the conclusion false.

This result constitutes a counterexample to the argument A, since we define a counterexample to a propositional argument as an assignment of values that assigns **T** to each premise and **F** to the conclusion. The existence of a counterexample, of course, demonstrates the invalidity of the original argument. Nothing about this procedure requires that we perform any one step before another. Still, the reader can appreciate that the most efficient way of discerning a counterexample will, in general, follow these rules of thumb:

1. Determine which assignments of values will falsify the conclusion and

choose one of these assignments (of course, in the example above there was only one).

2. Using the assignment in step 1 continue by assigning values that will make the premises true. It is always a good idea to begin this assignment with any premises that are single letters or negations of single letters and progress by working on any other premises that can be made true in only one or two ways.

3. If step 2 does not result in a counterexample go back to 1 and use another assignment of values which render the conclusion false and proceed again through 2. There will be two possible outcomes: (a) There will be at least one assignment in 1 that results in a counterexample. (b) No assignment in 1 results in a counterexample. Outcome (a) demonstrates the invalidity of the argument while (b) demonstrates its validity. Do not forget, however, that (b) requires an examination of all the different ways in which the conclusion could be false.

B. 1. $P \supset (Q \supset R)$
   2. $Q \supset (\sim R \supset M)$
   3. $(R \lor M) \supset S$
   $\overline{\quad \therefore P \supset S \quad}$

First, we assign the value **T** to P and the value **F** to S. This results in the falsehood of $P \supset S$ and if given these two assignments, we can make each of the premises true we will have succeeded in invalidating the argument. Note, however, that this assignment is the only one that makes the conclusion $(P \supset Q)$ false and if we cannot assign values to the other letters that will make the premises true then this argument will be valid. We continue our work by noting that since S is **F**, $(R \lor M) \supset S$ will have to contain **F** for $R \lor M$ as this is the only way to make $(R \lor M) \supset S$ true when S is false. This, of course, necessitates the assignment of **F** to both R and M. We can summarize our work so far by the following:

$$
\begin{array}{lll}
 & \text{T} \qquad \text{F} & \\
1. & P \supset (Q \supset R) & \\
 & \qquad\quad \text{F} \quad \text{F} & \\
2. & Q \supset (\sim R \supset M) & \\
 & \quad \text{F} \quad \text{F} \quad \text{F} & \\
3. & (R \lor M) \supset S \qquad & \text{T} \\
 & \overline{\text{T} \quad \text{F}} & \\
 & \therefore P \supset S \qquad\quad & \text{F} \\
\end{array}
$$

Next we must assign **T** to the second premise; since R and M are **F** the formula ($\sim R \supset M$) will be false (R is false, so $\sim R$ is true) and Q must be false if premise 2 is to be true. However, this determines our assignment of values to the atomic propositions in 1 and $P \supset (Q \supset R)$ is true since P is true and Q and R are both false. The final form of the example will be

$$
\begin{array}{lll}
& \mathbf{T} \quad \mathbf{F} \quad \mathbf{F} & \\
1. & P \supset (Q \supset R) & \mathbf{T} \\
& \mathbf{F} \qquad \mathbf{F} \quad \mathbf{F} & \\
2. & Q \supset (\sim R \supset M) & \mathbf{T} \\
& \mathbf{F} \quad \mathbf{F} \quad \mathbf{F} & \\
3. & (R \vee M) \supset S & \mathbf{T} \\
\hline
& \mathbf{T} \quad \mathbf{F} & \\
\therefore & P \supset S & \mathbf{F}
\end{array}
$$

Since, each of the premises is assigned a **T** while the conclusion is **F** the argument is invalid.

C. 1. $N \supset (M \supset \sim N)$
   2. $N \equiv M$
$$\overline{\therefore \sim N \vee \sim M}$$

In case C the only way to make the conclusion false is to make each of the disjuncts false, and this necessitates the assignment of **T** to both M and N. However, since N and M are the only letters in the premises we can determine validity or invalidity without further assignment of values. This gives us

$$
\begin{array}{lll}
& \mathbf{T} \quad \mathbf{T} \quad \mathbf{T} & \\
1. & N \supset (M \supset \sim N) & \mathbf{F} \\
& \mathbf{T} \quad \mathbf{T} & \\
2. & N \equiv M & \mathbf{T} \\
\hline
& \mathbf{T} \quad \mathbf{T} & \\
\therefore & \sim N \vee \sim M & \mathbf{F}
\end{array}
$$

The first premise is false because $M \supset \sim N$ is false when M and N are true and then $\mathbf{T} \supset \mathbf{F}$ is, of course, **F**. As the original assignment was the only one that made the conclusion false we can say that there is no assignment of values that makes the premises true and the conclusion false. In short, the argument is valid.

3.8.1 Consistency

As was seen above, a set of premises such that their conjunction results in a self-contradictory formula validly implies any statement whatever. Since we would usually want to avoid such a set of premises we will now describe a way to test for such a situation without constructing the full truth table. When the conjunction of premises is self-contradictory we will say the premises are *inconsistent* and our method will be a test of the consistency of any list of formulas. Now, the conjunction of an inconsistent set of formulas results in a truth table that has all F's. If we can show that there is at least one assignment of values that makes all of the formulas true then we will have shown the set consistent. Consider the following three propositions:

1. $X \supset (Y \supset Z)$
2. $X \supset (P \supset Q)$
3. $(Y \lor P) \& X$

Beginning with proposition 3 we must make $Y \lor P$ and X true in order to make the whole formula true. We will do this with the following assignment:

    T F   T
3. $(Y \lor P) \& X$

Notice that we could have chosen two other ways to make $Y \lor P$ true, but this one will suffice. The other propositions then look like this:

    T   T
1. $X \supset (Y \supset Z)$
    T   F
2. $X \supset (P \supset Q)$

Since P is F the formula $P \supset Q$ will always be true regardless of the value of Q, and proposition 2 is true. Finally, we can make proposition 1 true by assigning T to Z and we will have found a way to assign values that result in all three formulas being true. This shows that they are consistent, and it requires considerably less effort than the full table.

EXERCISES

1 Use the shorter truth table technique to evaluate the arguments in the exercises at the end of section 3.7.1.

2 Use the shorter truth table method to evaluate each of the following argument forms:

    a. $\sim(A \,\&\, \sim B)$
         $\sim C \lor D$
         $C \lor B$
         $\overline{\therefore A \lor D}$

    b. $(P \,\&\, Q) \supset R$
         $R \supset \sim R$
         $(V \supset P) \,\&\, (W \supset Q)$
         $\overline{\therefore V \supset \sim W}$

    c. $P \supset (F \lor G)$
         $G \supset (N \,\&\, O)$
         $\sim N$
         $\overline{\therefore P \supset O}$

    d. $E \,\&\, (F \,\&\, G)$
         $(F \equiv G) \supset \sim(\sim P \,\&\, \sim Q)$
         $\overline{\therefore Q \lor P}$

3 Which of the sets of formulas below are consistent:

    a. $E \,\&\, (F \lor G)$
      $(E \,\&\, G) \supset \sim(H \lor I)$
      $(\sim H \lor \sim I) \supset \sim(E \,\&\, F)$
      $H \supset I$

    b. $(H \,\&\, I) \lor J$
      $H \supset \sim I$
      $K \,\&\, I$
      $J \supset \sim J$

    c. $P \,\&\, (P \lor Q)$
      $\sim Q \supset \sim P$
      $\sim L \,\&\, \sim Q$
      $\sim(L \lor P)$

3.9 NATURAL DEDUCTION

At this point we have developed and refined a decision procedure for the propositional logic. Further, this procedure has fulfilled all of the requirements we demanded of it, i.e., it is mechanical and effective. However, both because of the cumbersomeness of this method and for more fundamental logical reasons we will present two alternative decision procedures—one in this section and one in the next. The cumbersomeness of the truth table method is obvious when we consider the size of tables for arguments with five or six different propositional letters (not really that large a number); these would have 32 and 64 rows respectively and, though they present no theoretical difficulties, they are unwieldy. Moreover, even the shorter method discussed in section 3.8 becomes laborious when we have a large number of options for assigning an **F** to the conclusion. That is, if the conclusion of an argument were

$(P \& Q) \& R$

we would have seven different assignments of letters that would make the conclusion false and if there were a number of moderately intricate premises then the shorter method would begin to require as much effort as the full table. In spite of these important considerations, however, it would be misleading to insist that the sole basis for our developing alternative decision procedures was this matter of cumbersomeness. The method of natural deduction in this section and the truth tree method in the next are both the result of theoretical investigation of simple propositional and more advanced logics. The necessity of these procedures for further work in logic (see Chapters 4 and 5) and their intrinsic interest are certainly the underlying reason for their inclusion here even though we have already worked out a perfectly complete and acceptable method.

As was discussed in section 3.7 the truth table method is a model-theoretic procedure similar to the Venn diagrams for the syllogism. In this section we will present a *proof-theoretic* method which is in many ways analogous to the use of the syllogistic rules of section 2.7. Before presenting the details of this method, however, let us briefly discuss this notion of proof-theory and its importance for logic. In Chapter 2 we described the syllogistic rule method as proof-theoretic because it could be used to evaluate an argument by reference only to the form of the argument. Of course any evaluation procedure will refer to the form of arguments since validity is a property of argument froms, but a model-theoretic method such as truth tables or Venn diagrams uses extraformal notions such as the truth or meaning of a premise or conclusion. The successful use of the rules of the syllogism did not require any inquiry beyond the purely formal one of inspecting the premises and conclusion for certain properties. There is a certain analogy here with a game such as chess. In chess all the possible moves and the nature of the final outcome are completely described by a list of rules. Further, each of these rules refers only to an arrangement or possible arrangement of pieces on a game board; no rule of chess refers to any notion that involves nonformal properties (i.e., properties that go beyond the schematic description of pieces on a checkered board). Such a set of rules is generally known as *syntactic* because it is restricted to the mention of form or order of elements as opposed to rules of meaning or truth, which are *semantic*. (For more on this distinction see section 6.1). Any proof-theoretic test of validity will be syntactic and much like chess, since it will have a list of form rules or moves that are applied to the structure of premises or an argument and a further general rule that informs us when we have finished the "game" or the evaluation. In Chapter 2 our ending rule was "A syllogism that violates no rule in the list is valid." It should be obvious that the model theory tests that ask questions about truth and meaning are *semantic* procedures. Of course, we want our proof theory test to validate all and only those arguments that are validated by the model-theory test and the demonstration that this is so is not always obvious. In the syllogism this was no problem because there were only a finite number of valid argument forms and we could merely match up the Venn diagram-valid arguments with the rule-valid argument types; in the propositional logic this is not so easily settled and will be considered later (see section 5.3).

The proof-theoretic method, which we will develop in this section, is known as *deduction*. Our list of rules will consist of a number of argument forms that will be used to sanction steps in a sequence that begins with the premises; we will be finished when (1) the last step is the conclusion and (2) every previous step is either a premise or is sanctioned by one of our previously accepted argument forms. When both (1) and (2) are true of a certain sequence then we will describe the sequence as a *deduction* of the conclusion from the premises and the existence of such a sequence will validate the argument. As the reader will see shortly each step and its sanction can be decided by inspection of the form of the step, and so this method will fulfill the syntactic requirements of proof-theoretic decision procedures discussed above. However, before we can properly continue the discussion we must present our rules and demonstrate how they are used. We will do this in two stages because, of the 19 rules we will present, nine are somewhat different from the remaining ten. The first nine rules and their names are:

I.   *Modus Ponens* (M.P.)

$P \supset Q$

P

$\therefore Q$

II. *Modus Tollens* (M.T.)
$P \supset Q$
$\sim Q$
∴ $\sim P$

III. Hypothetical Syllogism (H.S.)
$P \supset Q$
$Q \supset R$
∴ $P \supset R$

IV. Disjunctive Syllogism (D.S.)
$P \vee Q$
$\sim P$
∴ Q

V. Conjunction (Conj.)
P
Q
∴ $P \& Q$

VI. Simplification (Simp.)
$P \& Q$
∴ P

VII. Addition (Add.)
P
∴ $P \vee Q$

VIII. Constructive Dilemma (C.D.)
$(P \supset Q) \& (R \supset S)$
$P \vee R$
∴ $Q \vee S$

IX. Absorption (Abs.)
$P \supset Q$
∴ $P \supset (P \& Q)$

Notice that each of these is a valid argument form (by truth table method) and each is a rather simple or elementary argument form. The proper method of using these elementary valid argument forms as sanctions in a deductive sequence is best illustrated by the following example. We are given three premises:

1. $P \supset (Q \& R)$
2. $Q \supset S$
3. P

and we are required to derive the conclusion $S \vee T$ from them by constructing a deduction. It will be helpful to adopt a uniform method of writing deductions and this will consist in (1) writing the premises in a numbered list with the conclusion set off to the right side of the final premise and (2) continuing the steps (or "moves") by consecutively numbering each one. As will be apparent shortly, the number of each step can be used as a means of referring to it at some later step in the deduction. The above example would appear as follows:

1. $P \supset (Q \& R)$
2. $Q \supset S$
3. $P \quad / \therefore S \vee T$
4. $Q \& R$
5. Q
6. S
7. $S \vee T$

Notice that the last step is the conclusion and so the above proves the validity of the original argument. However, it is not obvious where steps 4-7 come from and it is certainly not obvious that they are justified. As a matter of fact each of them is justified by reference to one of our nine elementary valid argument forms and this can be indicated by reference to the appropriate rule on the right-hand side of each line of the deduction. Thus, our example should be written as follows:

1. $P \supset (Q \& R)$
2. $Q \supset S$
3. $P \quad / \therefore S \vee T$
4. $Q \& R$ 1, 3 M.P.
5. Q 4 Simp.
6. S 2, 5 M.P.
7. $S \vee T$ 6 Add.

The numbers refer to the lines of the proof that result in the line under consideration and, of course, the name (abbreviation is all that is necessary) refers to the justification or sanction of the present step. However, we are still left with the question of where each of the steps comes from. This can be best answered by again considering the chess analogy. The moves in chess are all according to the finite list of rules. Still, one can be familiar with all the rules and yet not be either a good player or even able to play. This is because the rules tell you only what you may or may not do and include no information on what you ought to do in order to win. The same situation obtains in the construction of deductions. The nine rules we have so far presented are not helpful in determining which steps one ought to write in order to most efficiently reach the conclusion. The ability to do this is gotten by practice and trial and error and cannot be taught in the way the truth table method was. The reader should, however, be able to recognize the appropriateness of each of the steps in the above example and their justifications.

The next example to be considered involves certain additional points. The deduction can be written as follows:

1. $N \supset (C \vee B)$
2. $(C \vee B) \supset \sim T$
3. $\sim S \supset T$
4. $N \quad / \therefore \sim\sim S$
5. $N \supset \sim T$ 1,2 H.S.
6. $\sim T$ 4,5 M.P.
7. $\sim\sim S$ 3,6 M.T.

First, one notices that the conclusion is gotten by the following argument:

3. $\sim S \supset T$
6. $\underline{\sim T}$
     $\therefore \sim\sim S$

Now, *modus tollens* is exemplified by

$$P \supset Q$$
$$\underline{\sim Q}$$
$$\therefore \sim P$$

The apparent discrepancy between our use of *modus tollens* and its presentation (rule II) can be explained by the fact that the presentation of the various elementary argument forms does not restrict their application to exact duplication of this form. Thus, *modus ponens*, which is written as

$$P \supset Q$$
$$\underline{P}$$
$$\therefore Q$$

113

has, as allowable instances, the following sorts of arguments:

A. $P \supset \sim Q$
   P
   $\overline{\therefore \sim Q}$

B. $(P \& Q) \supset [(Q \lor T) \supset S]$
   $(P \& Q)$
   $\overline{\therefore (Q \lor T) \supset S}$

These are correct substitution instances of *modus ponens* because they all have the general form of *modus ponens*. In the same way line 7 of the deduction above is a use of *modus tollens* even though it involves additional tilde signs. A second point to note about this deduction is that it is by no means unique. That is, we might have reached the conclusion by using *modus ponens* twice with N and $C \lor B$ instead of using a hypothetical syllogism. In general, there will be alternate ways to construct a deduction and any way is correct if and only if it results in the conclusion as the final step and each step is justified by a rule.

Suppose, though, we had to construct a deduction of S from the premises of the last example? We have proven $\sim\sim S$ and a moment's reflection on the truth table for $\sim\sim S$ shows it to be the same as S so the deduction should be possible. However, our nine rules are not sufficient to get even this simple result and they have to be supplemented by ten additional rules which are known as *replacement rules*. Each of them is a statement of logical equivalence and one may replace all or part of a line in a deduction by its equivalent form as given in the following:

X.   De Morgan's Theorems (De M.)
   $\sim(P \& Q) \equiv (\sim P \lor \sim Q)$
   $\sim(P \lor Q) \equiv (\sim P \& \sim Q)$

XI.   Commutation (Com.)
   $(P \lor Q) \equiv (Q \lor P)$
   $(P \& Q) \equiv (Q \& P)$

XII.   Association (Assoc.)
   $[P \lor (Q \lor R)] \equiv [(P \lor Q) \lor R]$
   $[P \& (Q \& R)] \equiv [(P \& Q) \& R]$

XIII.   Distribution (Dist.)
   $[P \& (Q \lor R)] \equiv [(P \& Q) \lor (P \& R)]$
   $[P \lor (Q \& R)] \equiv [(P \lor Q) \& (P \lor R)]$

XIV.   Double Negation (D.N.)
       $P \equiv \sim\sim P$

XV.   Transposition (Trans.)
       $(P \supset Q) \equiv (\sim Q \supset \sim P)$

XVI.   Material Implication (Impl.)
       $(P \supset Q) \equiv (\sim P \lor Q)$

XVII. Material Equivalence (Equiv.)
       $(P \equiv Q) \equiv [(P \supset Q) \& (Q \supset P)]$

XVIII. Exportation (Exp.)
       $[(P \& Q) \supset R] \equiv [P \supset (Q \supset R)]$

XIX.   Tautology (Taut.)
       $P \equiv (P \lor P)$
       $P \equiv (P \& P)$

Thus, to prove S from $\sim\sim S$ we merely write "D.N." It is important that the reader realize that these replacement rules may operate within a line while the nine elementary valid argument forms refer to whole lines of a proof. This notion of operation "within" a line can be illustrated by the following example:

1. $\sim(P \supset Q) \lor S$
2. $\sim(\sim P \lor Q) \lor S$ 1 Impl.
3. $(\sim\sim P \& \sim Q) \lor S$ 2 De M.
4. $(P \& \sim Q) \lor S$ 3 D.N.

The 19 rules presented are sufficient to allow the construction of a deduction to prove the validity of any argument that can be shown valid with truth table techniques. At this point in the propositional logic it is impossible to prove this sort of completeness but the reader is referred to Chapter 5 for a fuller discussion and must merely assume this completeness here. However, it is clear that this method of evaluation is fundamentally different from the truth table method (the completeness of that method was informally proven as a result of the fact that any proposition was decidedly either tautologous or nontautologous). First, the deduction method of evaluation is not effective. If you will remember an effective decision procedure was one that provided a determinate answer to the question "Is this a valid argument?" As is obvious, the successful construction of a deduction is proof of the validity of a given argument, but suppose someone were to attempt such a construction for an invalid argument? Clearly he would fail, but his failure could not be considered a proof of the invalidity of the argument. This is so because it is impossible to distinguish this situation from one in which the argument is valid, but is so difficult that one cannot see how to proceed; not to know how to construct a deduction is not sufficient grounds for saying the construction is impossible. Thus, this method is only able to definitely validate an argument and cannot conclusively invalidate one; it is, in short, *noneffective.* Also, the deduction procedure is for all practical purposes nonmechanical since there is no reasonably brief sequence of instructions that will show a logician how to construct a deduction.[5] In fact, as the reader can appreciate, the actual construction is a matter of considerable ingenuity and is often described as trial and error. That this decision procedure is most often known as "natural" deduction is a result of the fact that the 19 rules presented are both complete and yet compact enough to allow the construction of proofs without undue repetition. It is possible to get around the use of certain of the rules by using others (i.e., to obtain a complete set with fewer than 19 rules) but these are generally felt to lead to the most "natural" sort of deductions.

EXERCISES

1 Below are five deductions. In each case fill in the correct justification for the lines of the deduction:

a. 1. $P \supset (Q \supset R)$
   2. $\sim R$ $/ \therefore \sim P \vee \sim Q$
   3. $(P \& Q) \supset R$
   4. $\sim (P \& Q)$
   5. $\sim P \vee \sim Q$

b. 1. $A \supset B$
   2. $(A \& B) \supset C$
   3. $\sim C$ $/ \therefore \sim A$
   4. $\sim (A \& B)$
   5. $A \supset (A \& B)$
   6. $\sim A$

c. 1. $A \supset (B \supset C)$
   2. $(D \supset B) \supset A$
   3. B $/ \therefore C$
   4. $B \vee \sim D$
   5. $\sim D \vee B$

[5] As a matter of fact the method of deduction is *mechanical* and this can be proven (see Chapter 5) but the procedure is so complicated that one would be better off with the trial-and-error attempt.

     6. $D \supset B$
     7. A
     8. $B \supset C$
     9. C

d. 1. $(P \& Q) \supset R$
     2. $\sim(N \lor R)$
     3. P $/ \therefore \sim Q$
     4. $\sim N \,\& \sim R$
     5. $\sim R \,\& \sim N$
     6. $\sim R$
     7. $\sim(P \& Q)$
     8. $\sim P \lor \sim Q$
     9. $P \supset \sim Q$
   10. $\sim Q$

e. 1. $E \lor G$
     2. $\sim [F \lor (N \& P)]$
     3. $\sim P \supset \sim G$
     4. $E \supset F$ $/ \therefore \sim N$
     5. $\sim F \,\& \sim(N \& P)$
     6. $\sim F$
     7. $\sim E$
     8. G
     9. $\sim \sim G$
   10. $\sim \sim P$
   11. $\sim(N \& P) \,\& \sim F$
   12. $\sim(N \& P)$
   13. $\sim N \lor \sim P$
   14. $\sim P \lor \sim N$
   15. $\sim N$

2 Use the method of natural deduction to prove the validity of those arguments after sections 3.7 and 3.8 that were shown valid by the truth table methods.

3 Construct a deduction to prove the validity of each of the following:

a. $P \equiv Q$
  $\sim(P \& Q)$ $/ \therefore \sim Q$

b. $A \lor B$
  $C \supset D$
  $A \supset E$
  $\sim(E \lor D)$ $/ \therefore C \lor B$

c. $P \& (Q \lor R)$
  $P \supset \sim Q$ $/ \therefore R$

d. $(N \& O) \supset T$
  $\sim N \supset S$

$\sim(\sim N \;\&\; S)$
$\sim T \quad | \; \therefore \sim O$

e. $(A \supset B) \;\&\; (S \supset R)$
$\sim B \;v\; \sim R$
$S \quad | \; \therefore \sim A$

f. $A \equiv B$
$B \equiv C \quad | \; \therefore A \equiv C$

g. $P \supset S$
$E \;v\; \sim S$
$\sim(\sim P \;v\; N) \quad | \; \therefore E$

h. $L \;v\; (\sim M \;v\; L)$
$M \;v\; (\sim L \;v\; M) \quad | \; \therefore (L \;\&\; M) \;v\; (\sim L \;\&\; \sim M)$

4 Translate each of the following valid arguments into symbolic form and construct a deduction to prove their validity:

   a. If the horse I bet on comes in first, I will win more than \$100 and if he comes in second then I will win \$50. I won neither more than \$100 nor \$50. Therefore, the horse did not come in first and he did not come in second.

   b. If the car fails to start then either the battery is dead or the solenoid is worn out but not both. If the car starts with a push then the battery is dead, but if the car cannot be started with a push then the solenoid is worn out. The car fails to start and a push does not help it start. Therefore, the solenoid is worn out.

   c. If Mrs. Sorel was asleep and her son was in France then the Rolls could not have been driven that night. However, if the Rolls was not driven that night then it would not have gotten that dent on the rear fender. But as any fool can see it does have a dent on the rear fender. Thus, if Mrs. Sorel was asleep her son was not in France.

   d. The murder of Sir Robert was motivated by the hatred he inspired or by the calculated desire to gain his fortune. If it was a calculated crime then it must have been perpetrated by both Lord Ashford and his mistress Sarah, but if it was done out of hatred then either the butler James or Lord Ashford's brother Jonathan did it. Now Sarah was too frightened a woman to have done it and Jonathan has the unassailable alibi of being in Brighton on the evening of the murder. Therefore, the butler did it.

   e. Either the fullback or the halfback will get the ball and if the fullback does not get the ball, the right guard will pull out and block for the halfback. Also, if the right guard will pull out and block for the halfback, the fullback will run out and fake a screen pass. However, if the fullback gets the ball then the halfback will fake a run into the line and the right guard will not pull out and block for the halfback. The fullback does not go out to fake a screen pass so the right guard does not pull out and block unless the halfback gets the ball.

f. Mr. Johnson is in a hurry to get the new building's floor poured. In fact, unless he can get the floor poured before the winter freeze, it cannot be done until spring. Moreover, if Mr. Johnson has very little capital left and the floor will not be poured until spring, the bank will withdraw its loan. If Mr. Johnson is in a hurry, then the bank will not withdraw its loan. Therefore, if Mr. Johnson has very little capital left, he will get the floor poured before spring.

g. Either the country is headed for a recession or the rate of unemployment will go up. If the rate of unemployment goes up then the unions will be unhappy. If the unions are unhappy then even if the war ends, the President will not be reelected. If the war does not end then the protests will continue and if the protests continue, the level of social tension will rise. Therefore, if there is no recession and if the level of social tension does not rise then the President will not get reelected.

h. If I move my king one square to the right I will be checkmated, but if I move it one square to the left, I will be safe. However, if I move the king either one square to the left or right I will not be able to move my castle. If I cannot move my castle then I cannot win in five moves and if I cannot win in five moves then my opponent must be aware of my plan. Also, if I can neither move my king one square right nor left then if my opponent can beat me, he must have a plan of his own. Therefore, if my opponent can beat me and he does not have a plan then I will not win in five moves.

3.9.1 Conditional proofs

In spite of the completeness of the 19 rules, it is desirable to introduce a procedure that can shorten a deduction considerably and that can remove much of the "error" from the trial and error. To understand how the rule of conditional proof operates and is justified, let us return to some of the basic notions surrounding validity. Suppose, we are told that the following premises lead to the conclusion $A \supset B$:

A. $P_1, P_2, P_3 \vdash A \supset B$

What this means, of course, is that $A \supset B$ could not be false while P_1, P_2, and P_3 were jointly true. However, the only way for $A \supset B$ to be false would be for A to be true and B false. This suggests that the validity of argument A could be shown merely by showing that

B. $P_1, P_2, P_3, A \vdash B$

This is so because it just so happens that the invalidity of argument B would result in the invalidity of A and the validity of A would result in the validity of B. In fact, a moment's thought should suffice to show that the two arguments coincide exactly with respect to the question of validity. But, this situation suggests a way in which we can shorten our deductions considerably. Whenever the conclusion is in conditional form we may assume the antecedent of the conclusion and by deducing the consequent we will be validating the original argument. This can best be seen in the following argument:

1. $(N \& O) \supset T$
2. $S \supset N$
3. $S \supset (M \& O)$ $/ \therefore S \supset T$
4. S Assumption
5. N 2,4 M.P.
6. $M \& O$ 3,4 M.P.
7. $O \& M$ 6 Com.
8. O 7 Simp.
9. $N \& O$ 5, 8 Conj.
10. T 1, 9 M.P.
11. $S \supset T$ 4, 10 (C.P.)

What we have done is briefly described as follows: (1) We have proven the validity of 1, 2, 3, $S/ \therefore T$. (2) On the basis of 1 we validated the argument (which is the original argument): 1, 2, 3/ $\therefore S \supset T$. This procedure of conditional proof can be justified by a much more rigorous argument but not with the tools which we have so far presented. Still, the short argument given above will suffice as a sanction to use this conditional proof rule in any deduction. However, we must establish a convention of writing our conditional proofs as problems would arise if more than one assumption was introduced, and if one were to be careless with the steps of the deduction based upon the assumption step. Lines 4-10 are based on the assumption of line 4. Line 11 is not so dependent because we are discharging the assumption in that line and 11 is dependent only on lines 1, 2, and 3. To indicate this we will preface the assumption line 4 by the designation "C1," meaning it is the first conditional assumption. Then each line which is dependent on 4 or on any line which is prefaced by C1 will itself be a C1 line. Finally, we will use a diagonal line (C1̸) on a C prefix number only when the assumption is discharged. These simple but useful conventions would be entered as follows in our above conditional proof:

$$
\begin{array}{lll}
& 1.\ (N \& O) \supset T & \\
& 2.\ S \supset N & \\
& 3.\ S \supset (M \& O) & /\therefore S \supset T \\
\text{C1} & 4.\ S & \\
\text{C1} & 5.\ N & \text{2,4 M.P.} \\
\text{C1} & 6.\ M \& O & \text{3,4 M.P.} \\
\text{C1} & 7.\ O \& M & \text{6 Com.} \\
\text{C1} & 8.\ O & \text{7 Simp.} \\
\text{C1} & 9.\ N \& O & \text{5,8 Conj.} \\
\text{C1} & 10.\ T & \text{1,9 M.P.} \\
\text{C1̸} & 11.\ S \supset T & \text{4,10}
\end{array}
$$

Notice that the first occurrence of the prefix C1 indicates the introduction of an assumption and is self-explanatory, and C1̸ is also self-explanatory of the discharging of the assumption. To see how this procedure would work with a longer proof and two assumptions we will validate the following:

$$
\begin{array}{lll}
& 1.\ P \supset N & \\
& 2.\ N \supset O & \\
& 3.\ (Q \vee R) \supset M & \\
& 4.\ (O \& M) \supset T & /\therefore P \supset [(Q \vee R) \supset T] \\
\text{C1} & 5.\ P & \\
\text{C2} & 6.\ Q \vee R & \\
\text{C1} & 7.\ N & \text{1,5 M.P.} \\
\text{C1} & 8.\ O & \text{2,7 M.P.} \\
\text{C2} & 9.\ M & \text{3,6 M.P.} \\
\text{C1,2} & 10.\ O \& M & \text{8,9 Conj.} \\
\text{C1,2} & 11.\ T & \text{4,10 M.P.} \\
\text{C1̸,2̸} & 12.\ [P \& (Q \vee R)] \supset T & \text{5,6,11} \\
& 13.\ P \supset [(Q \vee R) \supset T] & \text{12 Exp.}
\end{array}
$$

In this example we not only have two assumptions, but we have a line (10) that is dependent on both of them. As can be seen this creates no special problems as long as we write both C numbers for that line. Also, note that we discharged both assumptions at the same time in line 12. This is always valid as long as the antecedent of the discharging conditional is a *conjunction of all the relevant assumptions.* In summary we may give the following rules of thumb for a conditional proof:

1. Prefix all assumption lines with a C number.

2. Any line dependent on a line with a C number must be prefixed with that C number. If there is more than one C number on which the line is dependent then the new prefix must contain all of them.

3. All C number prefixes are removable by conjointly making them the antecedent of a conditional with the consequent being any line of the proof; or any one of the C numbers can be crossed out by making the appropriate assumption the antecedent of the conditional crossing out only the number of that assumption thus:

C1,2 P
C1,$\not{2}$ $R \supset P$
C$\not{1}$ $Q \supset (R \supset P)$

where C1 is Q and C2 is R.

4. If a line is dependent on a line with a crossed out C number it should not be written with that C number (line 13 in the deduction above is dependent on line 12 but has no C number as per this rule).

5. A deduction must not contain a conditional assumption which is not discharged in the proof.

EXERCISE

1 Do problems 4c, f, g, and h of the exercises at the end of section 3.9 by the method of conditional proof.

3.9.2 Indirect proof: an extension of conditional proof

So far in our discussion we have used the rule of conditional proof when the conclusion of the argument was a conditional statement. However, there is nothing in the nature of this rule that entails this restriction. Still, the reader may wonder, what would be the point of using it when the conclusion was not in conditional form? The answer to this can be made apparent in the following deduction:

1. $(N \vee O) \supset B$
2. $\sim B \vee T$
3. $N \quad / \therefore T$

C1	4. ~T	
	5. T v ~B	2 Com.
C1	6. ~B	4,5 D.S.
	7. N v O	3 Add.
	8. B	1,7 M.P.
C1	9. ~B v T	6 Add.
	10. ~ ~B	8 D.N.
C1	11. T	9,10 D.S.
C1	12. ~$T \supset T$	4,11
	13. ~ ~T v T	12 Impl.
	14. T v T	13 D.N.
	15. T	14 Taut.

In this deduction we conditionally assumed the negation of the conclusion and were able to derive the conclusion. This was so because *when an argument is valid, then the negation of the conclusion and the premises must be inconsistent.* This inconsistency appears above in the fact that we are able to deduce both B and ~B (lines 6, 8) from the original premises and the assumption of ~T (the negation of the original conclusion). Once this sort of contradiction is deduced it is easy to derive the original conclusion by lines 9-15. This is so because any statement whatever can be derived from a contradiction. Finally, the reader must recognize that we could not end the deduction at line 11 even though that line is the original conclusion because we are not allowed to end a deduction with a C number that is not crossed out. Now, since the lines which follow the derivation of a contradiction from the original premises and negation of the conclusion will always be of the same form in this sort of proof we may specify a new rule known as *indirect proof* which will be more economical. However, keep in mind that indirect proof is really a type of conditional proof. The rule of indirect proof (I.P.) states:

1. Assume the negation of the conclusion.

2. The original conclusion will be validated when the last line of the deduction is in the form of a contradiction (P & ~P). When using this shortened form of deduction it is not necessary to use C numbers and the justification of the assumption can be given by writing "I.P." to the right of the assumption line.

EXERCISE

Do problems 3a, c, d, and e of the exercises at the end of section 3.9 by the method of indirect proof.

3.9.3 Rules of inference and tautologies

The use of the rules of inference to prove validity is intended to be equivalent to the truth table method in the sense that any argument validated by the rules will be validated by the truth table methods and vice versa. We say "intended" because the presentation of propositional logic in this chapter is not sufficiently advanced to offer any but an intuitive sort of proof for this equivalence. (For more on this issue see the discussions of analyticity and deductive completeness in Chapter 5.) However, our conviction of the correctness of this equivalence can be strengthened by an examination of a way in which the procedures of natural deduction can be used to prove the tautologous character of certain propositions; further the methods of conditional proof will play an important role in this enterprise.

Let us begin by considering a two-premise valid argument:

$$P_1, P_2 \vdash B$$

In saying that this is valid we are in effect saying that $(P_1 \,\&\, P_2) \supset B$ is a tautology. Now if a formula L is a tautology to begin with then it will follow validly from any set of premises whatever. That is, the formula $S \supset L$ (where S is the conjunction of any number of propositional formulas and L is a truth table tautology) will always be tautologous. This, though, means that L could be said to follow from the empty set of premises since $\{\Lambda\} \supset L$ (where $\{\Lambda\}$ means "the empty set of propositional formulas.") is a tautology.[6] Further, if $\{\Lambda\} \supset L$ is a tautology then we may write:

$$\{\Lambda\} \vdash L$$

which may be abbreviated simply as:

$$\vdash L$$

(We may say "abbreviation" but the two statements are perfectly equivalent since $\{\Lambda\}$ means "no premises.") The upshot of this discussion is that any propositional formula which can be proven from no premises will be tautologous. In brief,

[6]The use of the set notation $\{\Lambda\}$ may seem strange in its occurrence as the antecedent of the conditional. However, this simply indicates that the antecedent of the conditional is constructed by conjoining the propositional formulas in the set.

P is tautologous $\equiv \vdash P$.

Again, we will illustrate this by several examples but the above equivalence cannot be demonstrated with any degree of rigor in this chapter.

As our first example we will prove that $P \vee {\sim}P$ is a tautology by showing $\vdash P \vee {\sim}P$. The deduction would look like this:

C1 1. P
C1 2. $P \supset P$ 1,2
    3. ${\sim}P \vee P$ 2 Impl.
    4. $P \vee {\sim}P$ 3 Com.

We simply assume P and since this assumption constitutes a deduction of P we are justified in writing $P \supset P$ as the discharge line for C1. Lines 3 and 4 are quite clear, and since line 4 depends on no premise and no assumption then we may write $\vdash P \vee {\sim}P$, which means that $[P \vee {\sim}P]$ is a tautology. A somewhat more complicated example would be the deductive proof that

$$[(P \supset Q) \supset P] \supset P$$

is a tautology. This proof is given in the following

C1 1. $(P \supset Q) \supset P$
C1 2. ${\sim}(P \supset Q) \vee P$ 1 Impl.
C1 3. ${\sim}({\sim}P \vee Q) \vee P$ 2 Impl.
C1 4. $({\sim}{\sim}P \,\&\, {\sim}Q) \vee P$ 3 De M.
C1 5. $(P \,\&\, {\sim}Q) \vee P$ 4 D.N.
C1 6. $P \vee (P \,\&\, {\sim}Q)$ 5 Com.
C1 7. $(P \vee P) \,\&\, (P \vee {\sim}Q)$ 6 Dist.
C1 8. $P \vee P$ 7 Simp.
C1 9. P 8 Taut.
C1 10. $[(P \supset Q) \supset P] \supset P$ 1,9

EXERCISE

1 Prove the following are tautologies using the method of natural deduction:
   a. ${\sim}{\sim}P \supset P$
   b. $[(R \,\&\, P) \supset Q] \supset (P \supset P)$
   c. $(P \,\&\, Q) \supset P$
   d. $(P \supset Q) \supset [P \supset (P \,\&\, Q)]$
   e. $P \supset (P \,\&\, P)$

3.10 TRUTH TREES

The evaluation procedure presented in this section is, in fact, a blending of the three previous methods—truth table, shorter truth table, and natural deduction. In many situations, however, the tree method will be more efficient and in Chapter 4 (the predicate logic) the use of truth trees will be considerably more convenient. Our treatment of truth trees owes much to the work of R.C. Jeffrey and the method of truth trees can be traced to the work of E.W. Beth and Raymond M. Smullyan.[7]

The basic key to the tree method is the recognition that an argument will be invalid just in the case that the premises can be true when the conclusion is false. In a valid argument this could never occur but consider the following valid argument:

1. $A \supset (N \vee B)$
2. $B \supset T$
3. $A \& \sim N$ $/ \therefore T$

If we were to negate the conclusion then since the argument is valid we would expect the denial of the conclusion to be inconsistent with the premises of the original argument. By "inconsistent" we mean that it could not happen that the premises and the denial of the conclusion were all true at the same time. In essence all the previous decision procedures were also tests of consistency; only the truth tree method will allow us to decide the consistency of any set of premises and the denial of the conclusion with none of the wasted effort of truth tables. Of course, if the denial of the conclusion of an argument is consistent with the premises of the argument this will mean that the original argument is invalid. To see how the tree method works as a decision procedure for both validity and consistency we will work out the tree for the argument form above in five steps. The first step will be the sequential listing of the premises and the denial of the conclusion (we will number each line for ease of reference but this is not a necessary part of the tree). The aim of the rest of our work will be to decide whether this list is consistent.

[7]R.C. Jeffrey, *Formal Logic: Its Scope and Limits* (1967); New York: McGraw-Hill, E.W. Beth, *Foundations of Mathematics* (1959); Amsterdam: North-Holland, and Raymond M. Smullyan, *Theory of Formal Systems* (1961); Princeton: Princeton University Press.

STEP 1

1. $A \supset (N \vee B)$
2. $B \supset T$
3. $A \, \& \sim N$
4. $\sim T$

This is done by writing down the complete list of truth conditions for these formulas in succeeding lines. Line 4 already states its own truth condition so we proceed by writing down the truth conditions for the molecular formula $A \, \& \sim N$. Notice that we place a check to the right of line 3 as a method of recording the fact that the truth conditions for that line have been written. Further, step 2 contains a listing of both A and $\sim N$ as only the truth of both conjuncts makes a conjunction true.

STEP 2

1. $A \supset (N \vee B)$
2. $B \supset T$
3. $A \, \& \sim N \checkmark$
4. $\sim T \checkmark$
5. A
6. $\sim N$

The next step is the writing of the truth conditions for the second line. Since this is a conditional we must decide what would make the conditional true and then write it as line 7 of the tree. From our knowledge of the truth table for the conditional we know that either a false antecedent or a true consequent will make the conditional true. We include this information in the tree by writing line 7 as a branch line. That is, we use branching to show that the conditions in either branch or path would make the original proposition true. In effect this provides two pathways for the tree (either of which contains truth conditions for the original four propositions); the first goes from 1-6 and to the left side of the branch in line 7 and the second from 1-6 and to the right branch of line 7. However, notice that the right-hand path contains both the proposition T and its negation, $\sim T$. Since we are trying to write the truth conditions for the premises and denial of the conclusion, it is clear that this pathway cannot serve as a set of such truth conditions as it contains contradictory requirements. That is, it would require us to assign the value true to both T and $\sim T$ and as this is impossible we "block" this path with an X.

STEP 3

1. $A \supset (N \vee B)$
2. $B \supset T$ ✓
3. A & ~N ✓
4.   ~T ✓
5. A
6.   ~N

7. ~B T
           X

In step 4 we write the truth conditions for $A \supset (N \vee B)$ using the branching that we use for any conditional. Also, our doing so results in one more blocked pathway—the path ending on ~A in line 8. Again, we remind the reader that we are using the tree to test for the consistency of a set of propositions and each pathway is potentially an assignment of values to atomic propositions which make the original set of molecular propositions jointly true. Obviously, then, a path which contains both a proposition and its negation cannot serve as such an assignment of values; we block such paths since they are of no further use in our consistency proof.

STEP 4

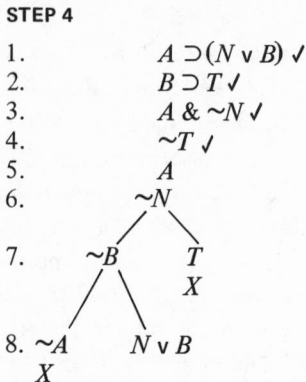

1. $A \supset (N \vee B)$ ✓
2. $B \supset T$ ✓
3. A & ~N ✓
4.   ~T ✓
5. A
6.   ~N

7.   ~B T
              X

8. ~A $N \vee B$
  X

In step 4 we have a path that ends on a molecular proposition. This was the result of writing the truth conditions for $A \supset (N \vee B)$; for one way to make this true was to make $(N \vee B)$ true. However, we cannot allow the construction of the tree to end when it contains unblocked (or "open") paths that end on molecular propositions. This is because we would have to assign the value T to such moleculars and we could not do so without checking for the possibility that the truth conditions for the molecular contradict some other element of that pathway. To avoid this possibility we will write the truth conditions of $N \lor B$ and check it as we did lines 1-4. This results in step 5, which is the completed tree.

STEP 5

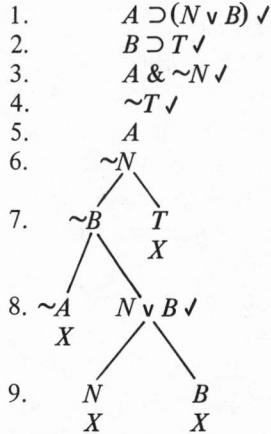

1. $A \supset (N \lor B)$ ✓
2. $B \supset T$ ✓
3. $A \,\&\, {\sim}N$ ✓
4. ${\sim}T$ ✓
5. A
6. ${\sim}N$
7. ${\sim}B$ T
             X
8. ${\sim}A$ $N \lor B$ ✓
    X
9. N B
     X X

All the paths are closed (blocked) and this means that ${\sim}T$ is inconsistent with lines 1-3 (the original premises), which further means that the original argument was valid. The reader should be able to see why the propositions and branching in line 9 represent the truth conditions of $N \lor B$ but this will be discussed shortly. The basic steps in the construction of any truth tree can be summarized as follows:

1. List the premises and the negation of the conclusion.

2. Extend the tree downward by writing the truth conditions for each of the molecular propositions in 1. Check each of these propositions when you have written its truth conditions.

2a. Block or close each path that contains a statement and its negation by writing X below the path.

3. If there are open paths after 2a then determine whether these paths end in atomic or molecular propositions.

3a. If they are atomic and all moleculars in the path are checked then the argument is invalid.

3b. If they are molecular then they must be checked and the tree extended as in 2 and 2a; then the construction continues as in 3-3b.

4. When steps 1-3 have been completed and there are no open paths the argument is valid.

An interesting consequence of the truth tree method is that the open pathway in an invalid argument shows us how to construct a truth table counterexample, i.e., an assignment of values to component propositions such that the premises are true and the conclusion is false. To arrive at this assignment one merely writes **T** for all of the constituents in the open path and this will be the counterexample (one must, however, be careful to recognize that the assignment of **T** to $\sim A$ e.g. means that A is **F**). Finally, the reader may have noticed that our list of instructions did not mention in which order to check the molecular propositions; in fact, the order is immaterial except insofar as it results in a shorter or less complex tree. Clearly, the most efficient method of extending a tree would save all branching until the last (assuming, of course, that the molecular propositions allow this).

The sequence of instructions above is not meant as anything more than a general description of the construction of trees. In step 2 we are asked to "extend the tree downward by writing the truth-conditions for each of the molecular propositions in 1." In our example we did this for molecular propositions such as $A \& \sim N$, $B \supset T$, and $N \lor B$ but we will now list the *extension rules* more formally:

1. $P \& Q$
   P
   Q

2. $P \lor Q$

$$P \qquad Q$$

3. $P \supset Q$

$$\sim P \qquad Q$$

4. $P \equiv Q$

$$\begin{array}{cc} P & \sim P \\ Q & \sim Q \end{array}$$

5. $\sim(P \& Q)$
   ?

6. $\sim(P \lor Q)$
   $\sim P$
   $\sim Q$

7. $\sim(P \supset Q)$
   ?

8. $\sim(P \equiv Q)$
   ?

EXERCISE

1 Using your knowledge of truth tables complete the above list of extension rules.

Notice that the extension rules for truth trees are like the first nine rules of inference for natural deduction in that they only apply to whole lines. Thus, we must choose the extension rule above that corresponds to the main connective of the proposition whose truth conditions we are writing.

EXERCISES

1 Evaluate the arguments given in the exercises after sections 3.7.1 and 3.9 using truth trees.

2 If an argument has a truth tree that is closed does this necessarily mean that the negation of the conclusion is inconsistent with the other premises?

3 Using truth tables the reader should be able to construct the extension rule for any connective and should be able to recognize the relationship between the extension rules and truth tables. If $\emptyset$ is a triadic connective defined by the truth table below, what would the extension rule be for $P\emptyset Q, R$? For $\sim(P\emptyset Q, R)$?

P	Q	R	P∅Q, R
T	T	T	T
T	T	F	F
T	F	T	T
T	F	F	T
F	T	T	T
F	T	F	F
F	F	T	F
F	F	F	T

3.10.1 Tree proofs of tautologies

It is possible to use the truth tree method in contexts other than straightforward evaluation of arguments. We may, for instance, use a little ingenuity to develop a way to examine formulas for being tautological. First, since a tautology is a proposition with all **T**'s in its truth table then by negating it we obtain a self-contradiction. However, in a self-contradiction there is no assignment of values to the atomic propositions that will result in a **T** for the formula. If we construct a tree for the formula then (1) if all paths are closed it is a self-contradiction and (2) if there is an open path it is tautologous or contingent. But if the formula once negated is a self-contradiction then the original formula must have been a tautology. This method can be seen in the following example:

Prove $P \supset (Q \supset P)$ is a tautology. (1) Negate $P \supset (Q \supset P)$ and get

$$\sim[(P \supset (Q \supset P)]$$

(2) Construct a tree

$$
\begin{array}{c}
\sim[P \supset (Q \supset P)]\, \checkmark \\
P \\
\sim(Q \supset P)\, \checkmark \\
Q \\
\sim P \\
X
\end{array}
$$

(3) The only path in (2) is closed so $\sim[P \supset (Q \supset P)]$ is a self-contradiction and $P \supset (Q \supset P)$ is a tautology.

This method has as an obvious corollary the ability to determine whether a formula is a self-contradiction as one merely begins at stage (2). To prove $(A \supset B) \,\&\, (A \,\&\, \sim B)$ is a self-contradiction we can use the following tree:

$$
\begin{array}{c}
(A \supset B) \,\&\, (A \,\&\, \sim B)\, \checkmark \\
A \supset B\, \checkmark \\
A \,\&\, \sim B\, \checkmark \\
\diagdown \\
\begin{array}{cc}
\sim A & B \\
A & A \\
\sim B & \sim B \\
X & X
\end{array}
\end{array}
$$

It might be thought that we could test for a tautology by constructing a tree for the statement without first negating it. This is not correct as a tree with *all* paths open means simply that there is no way to falsify it shown in the tree and not that there is no way at all. Thus consider the following formula:

$$[P \supset (Q \supset P)] \,\&\, N$$

Since we have proven the first part is a tautology the whole proposition will be contingent (N could certainly be false as it is an atomic proposition). However, the tree for this formula given below has all open paths. Thus, all open paths is not a sure sign of being a tautology while all closed paths is a sign of a self-contradiction.

3.11 EXTENSIONS OF THE PROPOSITIONAL LOGIC

Our two-valued, truth functional system of propositional logic is now quite complete. In carrying out this task we began with ordinary language arguments and by use of a formal apparatus and our intuitive understanding of validity, we constructed the logic and its evaluation procedures. However, in doing so we have had to make many stipulations as to the symbolic content of the logic and we have maintained our original propositional restriction throughout (a proposition must be exclusively either true or false). The situation then is this: We have a fairly sophisticated formal system which was created to serve a specific purpose and yet the system itself has many interesting properties which could be explored with only passing concern for ordinary argument evaluation. The type and number of operators that we have introduced is, perhaps, not completely exhaustive and the system as a whole may well be adapted to other contexts. In this section we will consider three different ways in which the propositional logic can be expanded (*generalized* is the appropriate term for this sort of activity in mathematics). Our presentation in each case will be brief as the full development of each of the extensions would require as much space as the present chapter. Still, with this material as a base it is hoped that the reader will be equipped to use the sources that we have grouped in the Selected Reading List under the appropriate headings. The first extension considered will involve the addition of certain operators to the basic list; the second will generalize the truth table notion to matrices (the truth table is sometimes known as a *truth matrix*) of more than two values; and lastly, we will describe certain alternate uses of the entire symbolic machinery of the propositional logic.[8]

3.11.1 Modal logic

Perhaps the most obvious way in which one can enlarge the propositional logic is by the addition of operators to the basic set, $\{\supset \equiv \& \vee \sim\}$. However, in section 3.3 it was pointed out that these operators (indeed even $\sim$ and $\&$ would do) are entirely sufficient for writing all truth functional connectives that might exist between two propositions. Also, in section 3.10 on (truth trees), we raised the possibility of triadic connectives and indicated that they, too, could be handled without adding to the two-value truth table structure. These observations would certainly seem to demand that any addition to our basic set of operators within the two-value framework be *nontruth-functional*. That is, the operator that we would add to the two-value propositional logic will not be completely definable by a truth table (if it were it would be redundant) and will have to be specified in an alternate way. Now, while the notion of an expanded propositional logic has a certain intrinsic interest it would be misleading to suggest that the modal logic of the present section was constructed as a direct result of the desire to add operators to propositional logic. In fact, the interest in modal concepts goes back to Aristotle's *Prior Analytics* and *De Interpretatione* (the original sources of the syllogistic) and has had a fairly continuous history since then. However, the propositional logic of the twentieth century has afforded an appropriate and interesting base on which modal logic can be constructed, and we will briefly discuss the nature of modal concepts and the methods by which they are introduced into propositional logic.

The modal concepts that interested Aristotle are expressed by such words

[8]Many works in logic employ totally different notational conventions than the one in this book. None of these variant notations alters the basic structure of the logic as it has been presented in this chapter but in order to enable the reader to consult these other sources we have included Appendix I, which outlines the conventions of other logic formats.

as "necessarily," "possibly," "contingently," and "impossible." As is evidenced in our ordinary language discussions these modal words are used extensively in our arguments, and we have used them in this book. Thus, we have described an argument as valid when its argument proposition is necessarily true (tautologous), and we have, on occasion, appealed to arguments that might be phrased: "When a proposition is necessarily false then it is false, i.e., when a proposition is self-contradictory then it is always false."

Among logicians, however, there is divided opinion as to the correctness of the use of modalities in logic. They do not see anything wrong with the use of these words to describe validity and the like but there are those who feel that any talk about a proposition being "possible" demands the implicit recognition of the knowledge of the user of the proposition. That is to say, the assertion that "P is possible" seems to require an analysis of the evidence on which P is based and this requirement is felt to be outside the scope of logic.[9] Suffice it to say that modal logic has been developed to a high degree despite this feeling and that the formal machinery that embodies these modal words and operators is still the subject of lively debate especially in such areas as the "proper" interpretation of the formalized concepts. In the remainder of section 3.11.1 we will describe the basis of the formalization of the modal words.

Regardless of the correct interpretation of modal concepts one fact is quite clear: The modal words operate on or "modify" propositions. That is, in the assertion that "P is necessary," the word "necessary" describes a property of the proposition P as a whole. The dispute comes when one tries to understand precisely what sort of property is expressed, but though we will make a few observations on this we will leave it as an open question. To continue, the fact that the modalities operate on whole propositions suggests that we can introduce monadic operators corresponding to the modal words. Thus we can define additional operators as follows:

$$\Box P = \text{df } \text{``}P \text{ is necessary.''}$$
$$\Diamond P = \text{df } \text{``}P \text{ is possible.''}$$

However, it is clear that these modal concepts are not independent and we might have defined both using only one of the operators in the following way:

[9] For example, by G. Frege, *Begriffschrift* (Halle, 1879).

$$\sim \Diamond \sim\!P = \mathrm{df}\ \Box\, P$$

(i.e., "it is not possible that not-P"). This relationship is of great importance, and, in the interest of economy, most systems of modal logic use only the "possibility" operator, introducing the other by the above definition. Now let us see what effect the introduction of these operators has on the propositional logic. (It is important for the reader to recognize that the propositional logic is to be understood as consisting of the ten replacement rule tautologies—see section 3.9, pp. 114-115—and the nine rules of inference—section 3.9, pp. 110-111. We can now use these operators to describe validity without the symbol $\vdash$.[10] Thus,

$$P \vdash Q = \mathrm{df}\ \Box\,(P \supset Q)$$

captures the precise meaning of our assertion that P implies Q if and only if it is impossible that P is true while Q is false. Also we can express the important notions of "consistency" and "logical equivalence" as follows:

P is consistent with Q = df $\Diamond\,(P\,\&\,Q)$
P is logically equivalent to Q = df $\Box\,(P \equiv Q)$

That is, to say that P is consistent with Q is to say that "it is possible for P and Q to be true at the same time," and to say that P is logically equivalent to Q is to say that "it is necessary that $P \equiv Q$." Finally, it is clear that we may define the notions of tautology, contingency, and self-contradiction in the following ways:

P is a tautology = df $\Box\,P$.
P is contradictory = df $\Box \sim\!P$.
P is contingent = df $\Diamond\,P$.

[10] In one of the key works on modal logic in this century, *Survey of Symbolic Logic* (1918), C. I. Lewis uses a symbol that has the same function as our turnstile in place of the material implication sign. This results in the so-called system of "strict implication" (to use $P \vdash Q$ instead of $P \supset Q$ obviously allows one to consider validity as a part of the system itself and not as a consequence of the rules and truths of the system); further, the logic of strict implication is clearly very similar to, and includes modalities as is seen by the modal definition of the "$\vdash$" operator. However, the reader should refer to C. I. Lewis and C. H. Langford, *Symbolic Logic* (New York, 1931) and G.H. von Wright, *An Essay in Modal Logic* (Amsterdam, 1951) for discussions of the differences between systems of modal logic and strict implication.

Having introduced the □ and ◇ operators into the propositional apparatus we must now see what effect they have on deciding the validity of arguments. Earlier we indicated that any genuine extension of the two-valued propositional logic by addition of operators would require (1) the abandoning of truth tables to define the operator and (2) the introduction of alternate (or supplementary) methods of decision. Obviously, the modal operators will not require such drastic steps for two reasons: First, the use of the modal operators does not always result in nontruth-functional propositions, and second, where it results in nontruth-functional propositions, it still retains the propositional nature of the logic. That is, any expression that contains modalities will still be propositional even when it is not truth-functionally decidable. These points can best be illustrated by specific examples. Consider the formula

$$[\Diamond P \,\&\, (\Diamond P \supset \Diamond Q)] \supset \Diamond Q$$

(Note that the modal operators are considered to function like the $\sim$ for purposes of parentheses placement.) This formula is like the argument proposition for *modus ponens* and one could show that it is a tautology by simply writing a truth table for the above based on Table 3-19.

TABLE 3-19.

$\Diamond P$	$\Diamond Q$
T	T
T	F
F	T
F	F

However, if this were the only use of modal operators in the extended propositional logic then it would be a trivial extension. In fact there are formulas that are always true but that cannot be shown true by truth tables; these involve the nontrivial use of modalities. As an example of what might be called an *essentially modal truth* consider:

$$[\Diamond P \,\&\, \Box (P \supset Q)] \supset \Diamond Q$$

This formula captures the argument that (1) If P is possible and (2) If P

logically implies Q then (3) Q is possible. Still, the logical truth of this expression cannot be decided by a truth table (we cannot compare the tables of $\Diamond P$ with $\Box (P \supset Q)$ and $\Diamond Q$ since they would be tables for different symbols and the argument would appear invalid). The presentation of ways in which such formulas are decided is beyond the scope of our discussion of modal logic but in outline it consists in:

1. The introduction of certain fundamental modal truths such as

    a. $P \supset \Diamond P$
    b. $\Diamond (P \vee Q) \equiv \Diamond P \vee \Diamond Q$

2. The introduction of such special rules of inference as

    If P is provable from the propositional logic base (i.e., if $\vdash P$) then $\Box P$.

If a number of these special rules and truths are added to the ten equivalences and nine rules of inference then it is possible to devise a decision procedure much like the procedures of truth tables. This is because these rules and basic truths allow us to put all essentially modal statements into forms that can be handled by truth tables.

As a final note we may observe that the disputes about the correct interpretation and use of modalities is reflected in the choice of truths and rules that are chosen as additions to propositional logic. Obviously, the rule we have used (see 2 above) sanctions the use of "necessary" as a synonym of "tautologous" but there are other rules that give a wider scope to the modal concepts and these can be found in the works cited in footnote 10 and in the works in the Selected Reading List at the end of the book.

3.11.2 Many-valued logics

On more than one occasion in the section 3.11.1 we were careful to point out that the modal logic was constructed within the framework of a two-valued system. The source of our two-valued logic was, of course, the natural observation that a proposition is either true or false. However, in the introductory chapter we indicated that this view of propositions was "oversimplified" to some degree and here we will consider what effect the dropping of the two-value restriction has on the propositional logic as considered in sections 3.1 through 3.10.

First, we repeat that the source of the two-value system was the desire to construct a logic capable of evaluating arguments involving propositions—and propositions lend themselves to the true-false categorization. Now, we could drop this restriction and construct logical systems of any number of values; though the "value" in these logics would certainly not be "truth value" in the true-false sense. Moreover, the logician would be more interested, on the whole, in a system that had an application to some area, i.e., could be interpreted for some subject matter. These considerations have led logicians to construct various many-valued logics and present ways in which these logics could be understood. For example, J. Lukasiewicz in 1930 described a three-valued logic of propositions and used it in an attempt to answer a number of problems that arise with future tensed propositions. Thus, propositions expressed by sentences such as "I am six feet tall" and "I was at home yesterday" can be either true or false while the proposition asserted by "I will be at the office tomorrow" is assigned a third value, which is, perhaps, best rendered as "maybe." As the reader can appreciate this addition requires considerable redefining of the various logical connectives but rather than investigating these changes we will briefly present an *n-valued logic* (a logic with an indefinite number of values) and show how it can be used to formalize an important area of inquiry. Remember, though, the construction of an *n*-valued logic would be possible even if no area of application could be found. Still, the application of *n*-valued logic turns out to be much more interesting and consequential than the three-valued logic.

If we are going to have a logic of *n*-values then we can use any infinite domain as the range of our values. For reasons which will be apparent later we will assign each symbol (at present we will refrain from referring to the symbols as propositions) some value from the set of real numbers between 0 and 1. This can be put as follows:

$$v(P) = n \text{ (where } 0 \leqslant n \leqslant 1).$$

read as "the value of P equals n." Now the logic is not truth-functional since it is not two-valued, but we certainly want it to have the following property: The value of each molecular formula will be computable on the basis of the values of its atomic formulas. Keeping this in mind we may write the following:

$$v(\sim P) = f(v(P))$$
$$v(P \& Q) = f'(v(P), v(Q))$$
$$v(P \lor Q) = f''(v(P), v(Q))$$

Each of these is read as "the value of____is a function of the value of____."
(The other connectives can be defined in terms of these in the usual ways.)

Now these statements do not determine the function for each connective but they do indicate that the value of the molecular formula is a function (f, f', or f'') of the values of the atomic constituent formulas. Before we specify each of these functions we will introduce certain conventions which will be somewhat variant from the propositional format but which will prove very important for our particular application of the n-valued logic. In propositional logic the truth value is assigned to either an atomic or molecular proposition. Instead we will assign our values to pairs of propositions written P/E–the significance of this will be apparent shortly. Keeping this in mind we can write the functions above in the following ways: Assume $v\,(P/E) = j$, $v\,(Q/E) = k$

1. $v\,(\sim P/E) = 1 - j$, $v\,(\sim Q/E) = 1 - k$
2. $v\,[(P\,\&\,Q)/E] = j \times k^{11}$
3. $v\,[(P \vee Q)/E] = j + k - v\,[(P\,\&\,Q)/E]$

It is now possible to compute the value of any molecular formula provided that one knows the value of each formula with respect to the formula on the right side of the solidus. Thus, the formula,

$$[(P \vee Q)\,\&\,R]/E$$

has the value $[(j + k) - (j \times k)] \times l$ when it is known that,

$$v\,(P/E) = j,\ v\,(Q/E) = k,\ v\,(R/E) = l$$

If the numerical value of j was .4, of k was .6, and of l was .1 then the value of the molecular formula would be .076. Also, the functions listed above will always preserve the condition that $0 \leqslant n \leqslant 1$ since even in the case where $v\,(P/E) = 1$ and $v\,(Q/E) = 1$ the disjunction will be $(1 + 1) - 1$ or 1.

Having sketched our n-valued logic and described the ways in which the values of the functions are determined in more complex cases we will now provide an application for this system. That is, we will describe a situation or

---

[11] This is the simplified version of 2 which under certain circumstances will be written in the more general form as $v\,[(P\,\&\,Q)/E] = j \times v\,(Q/E\,\&\,P)$. The significance of this form of 2 and its proper use will be discussed later in the text.

subject matter that will convert the abstract notions of the logic into a fairly familiar relationship. (In doing so we will clear up the ambiguity in function 2—see footnote 11.) The parts of this situation are as follows:

An airplane has crashed and though the cause of the crash is unknown we would like to be able to determine the interrelationship of various probable causes. It will be assumed that a certain amount of knowledge about the aircraft is had and we will call the conjunctive proposition that contains all this knowledge E. That is, E is a conjunction of all the data ascertainable before and up to the crash. Now such data can be said to confer a "probability" on the truth of still other statements. Thus, if P is "the altimeter was inaccurate," Q is "the radio failed," and R is "the right engine had a fire" then the sum of knowledge about this type of aircraft and aircraft in general can serve as evidence for P, Q, and R, and this is indicated by the assignment of a probability value to such expressions as P/E (this is read "the probability of P with respect to evidence E"). Further, when E confers a probability of 1 on some proposition we will say the proposition is certain or true; alternately, when E confers a probability of 0 on a proposition it will be said to be false.

The natural way in which this story fits into the logic can be seen by considering the following issues. Suppose that the data in E make it completely improbable that the altimeter was inaccurate. We would write this as: $P/E = 0$. Now, notice that rule 1 above assigns $\sim P/E$ the value $1 - P/E$, or 1. That is, the truth of the assertion that the altimeter did not fail is certain when there is 0 probability for its having failed. Finally, we can explain the reason for the complication in function 2. Suppose we were trying to compute the probability value of $(P \& Q)/E$. If the value of $P/E = .3$ and the value of Q/E is .6 then the probability of their both being true on the basis of E is .18 (as per function 2). This seems quite reasonable as the probability of two events happening simultaneously should be less than the probabilities of each happening alone. However, suppose Q was $\sim P$; any body of evidence E should confer a probability of 0 on $P \& \sim P$. Still, if $P = .3$ then by function 1 $\sim P = .7$ and $P \& \sim P = .21$. This result cannot stand and we avoid this paradox by putting a condition on function 2, namely, function 2 will be used just in those cases when the probability of P does not have anything to do with the probability of Q. That is, the probabilities of P and Q with respect to E are independent. Now, when Q is $\sim P$ this is most certainly not the case (probability of P is not independent of the probability of $\sim P$) and so we demand that the probability of Q be computed on the basis of $E \& P$—on the basis of

P being part of the evidence. This means that we will assign $\sim P/E \& P$ the value 0 since on the basis of *P* being in the evidence for $\sim P$, then $\sim P$ is certainly false. Now $(P \& \sim P)/E = 0$ and $(P \vee \sim P)/E$ (using function 3) will be 1. This, in brief outline, is a way in which we could use an *n*-valued logic. It is of course limited by the assumption that there is a certain body of evidence *E* that is unchanging and assigns probabilities to other propositions, but the reader can refer to the Selected Readings for more generalized accounts of *n*-valued probability logics. In finishing this section we will present a few very important observations on probability logic that apply to this fragment and to the more complete systems.

First, notice what happens when we demand that the evidence assign only probabilities of zero and one to each proposition. Each computing function reduces to a device for determining whether any molecular proposition has the value zero or one (i.e., we now only have two values); and if zero = **F** and one = **T** then our probability logic becomes the truth-functional logic of sections 3.1-3.10. Thus, the two-valued logic of propositions can be seen as the limiting case of a probability or *n*-valued logic. When we evaluated an argument in two-valued logic, say,

$$P_1, P_2, P_3 \therefore Q$$

we were making the tacit assumption that P_1, P_2, P_3 each had the value one and we called the argument valid when and only when this fact conferred a probability of one on the conclusion. The *E* was not important in this procedure as we simply assumed that the *E* is the same for all propositions.

Second, even in the full *n*-valued probability logic we must use a type of two-valued logic when we speak about the probability which *E* confers on *P*, *Q*, and *R*. When, for instance, we write $P/E = .3$ we are saying that it is true that *E* confers a probability of .3 on *P*. In effect, we used the ordinary propositional logic to order or arrange the *n*-valued logic.

Lastly and most significantly the use of this probability calculus to describe ordinary probability situations requires considerable clarification and interpretation of the notion of probability. Thus, the very well-known question of what is meant by saying the probability of an event happening or a statement's being true is .3. Some philosophers have felt this only makes sense in situations where there is a repetition that allows .3 to be a measure of *relative frequency*—i.e., to say *P* is .3 probable is to say it will be true in 3 out of 10 situations. A second well-known view is that .3 is an estimate of a person's belief that P will be true based on some body of evidence (this is the *subjective probability* view). Disputes about these views and variations of them play a central role in discussions of induction and probability and can be traced through the bibliographical references to this section.

3.11.3 Switching circuits

Each of the two extensions of propositional logic so far considered has involved the alteration of some characteristic of the propositional machinery. Still, both alterations were within the general framework of the logic of propositions. In this section we will present a still further way of expanding the logic of this chapter. Moreover, the technique we use to bring about this extension differs from the previous methods and deserves special consideration. In our exposition of the logic of probability we used a procedure not used up to that point in this chapter. Instead of considering some area of logical inference in an ordinary language context and then formalizing it we did the reverse. That is, we first constructed a purely abstract system of a logic of n values and then we discussed ways in which this abstract system could be applied (the technical term is "interpreted" and the reader is referred to Chapter 5 for a further discussion of this concept). It was clear at the time that this sequence was dictated by the particularly thorny problems which surround the interpretation of the logic of section 3.11.2 as a probability logic. However, the procedure of first considering an abstract system and then applying it is quite valuable and will be used in this section. We will not construct a new formal or abstract system, though, but will use the system of this chapter (sections 3.1-3.10) and attempt to find applications for it that are removed from the propositional. We will do this by providing an alternative use for the table of two-propositional formulas (see Table 3-9). In Table 3-9 we specified a complete description of all possible diadic propositional operators and their interrelationships. Now, we will preserve the formal structure of that table but will provide different meanings to the elements of the table. That is, the letters P and Q and the symbols $\sim$, &, $\supset$, $\equiv$, and v will have new interpretations and the values **T** and **F** will also be reinterpreted. In brief, we could describe the purely abstract system by the following: (1) It will consist of the letters P and Q, each of which may be assigned a value from the set $\{0, 1\}$. We use the numbers so as to sever any relationship with the notions of truth and falsity. (2) It will also contain the symbols $\sim$, v, &, $\equiv$, and $\supset$ which are defined by Table 3-20 (which is identical to Table 3-9 except that 0 is written for **F** and 1 for **T**).[12]

TABLE 3-20.

P	Q	1	2	3	4	5	6	7	8	9	10	11	12	13	14	15	16
1	1	1	1	1	1	1	1	1	1	0	0	0	0	0	0	0	0
1	0	1	1	1	0	0	0	1	0	1	0	1	1	1	0	0	0
0	1	1	1	0	0	1	0	0	1	0	1	1	0	1	1	0	0
0	0	1	0	0	0	0	1	1	1	0	0	0	1	1	1	1	0

The first interpretation we will offer is what might be called the electronic interpretation. The scheme is worked out as follows: (1) Each symbol P, Q is to represent an electronic circuit and since such a circuit is usually said to be "on" or "off" we will assign a circuit the value zero if it has no current flowing and 1 if it has a current flowing. (2) Each symbol $\sim, \vee, \&, \supset, \equiv$ is to be the name of a switching device and is to have the properties as described in Table 3-20. What we mean by "described" above can be illustrated by considering two examples. First the switch $\sim$. This would be an electronic device (a black box for the time being) such that when a circuit P was on and was connected as the input to the switch (Figure 3-1) the output circuit (called $\sim P$) was off; when P was off and connected to the $\sim$ switch the output (again $\sim P$) was on (Figure 3-2).

FIGURE 3-1.   **FIGURE 3-2.**

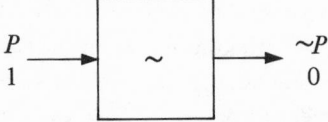

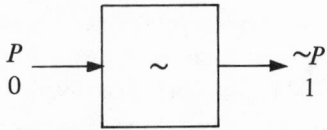

A second example would be the switch $\&$. As a result of Table 3-20 we recognize that this switch requires two input circuits to be properly set up and Table 3-20 demands the conditions shown in Figure 3-3.

These pictorial representations can be given systematically for each of the sixteen columns in Table 3-20.

[12] Strictly speaking our description of the system should include rules about the construction of strings of symbols in 1 and 2. We have not given this here because these issues are handled at length in Chapter 5.

FIGURE 3-3.

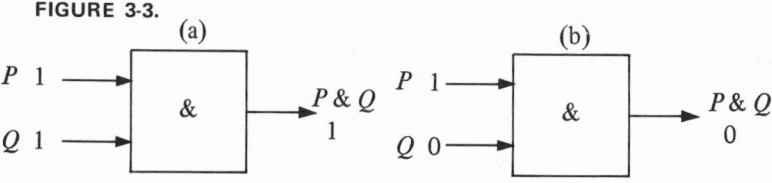

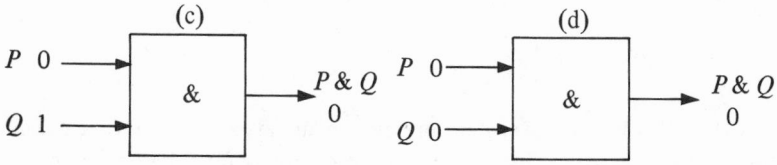

The electronic interpretation can be completed by the recognition that very complex switches for more than two input circuits can be described by systematically reinterpreting the truth tables for molecular formulas as found in section 3.6. Finally, we can find parallels for the notions of contradiction, contingency, and tautology by adopting the following conventions:

1. A circuit will be said to be "tautologous" when it has an output which is *on* regardless of the state of its input circuits.

2. A circuit will be said to be "self-contradictory" when it has an off output regardless of the state of the input circuits.

3. A circuit is "contingent" when it is neither 1 nor 2.

Now to any one with a moderate knowledge of electronic circuitry the physical construction of black boxes such as occurs in Figures 3-1 through 3-3 is simple enough (in the least sophisticated way one could construct switching circuits for all purposes with only relays). This means, though, that one could construct an electronic device that could be used to evaluate an argument. This is so because there is an exact parallel between the structure of propositional logic and the circuit-and-switch interpretation of it which allows us to assert: An argument will be valid just in case the switching circuit constructed on the basis of the associated argument proposition is always on—i.e., is "electronically" tautologous. Further, by constructing a variable device that could be "set" for any finite input switching circuit we would have the logic section of a digital computer. That is, we would have a device that recognizes two discrete inputs—on and off—and that can be used to evaluate any argument set in it by appropriate plugging in of switching elements as per instructions. Let us instruct the computer to devise a switching circuit that will evaluate the argument

$$P \supset Q$$
$$\frac{\sim Q}{\therefore \sim P}$$

It will do so by first arranging itself into the complex switch:

$$[(P \supset Q) \mathbin{\&} \sim Q] \supset \sim P$$

and next it will test this switch for being in an "always on" output condition by putting the four possible input configurations into the points marked P and Q. This switch is given in Figure 3-4 and since it is always on, the original argument is valid.

FIGURE 3-4.

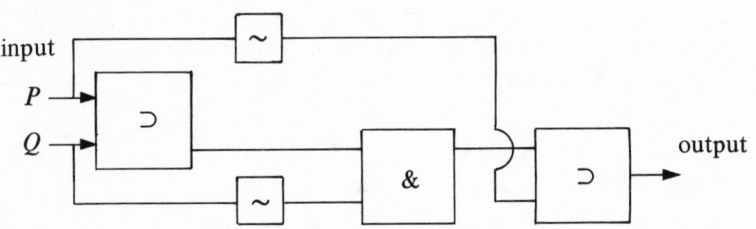

The switches indicated above are constructed according to the conventions shown in Figure 3-5.

FIGURE 3-5.

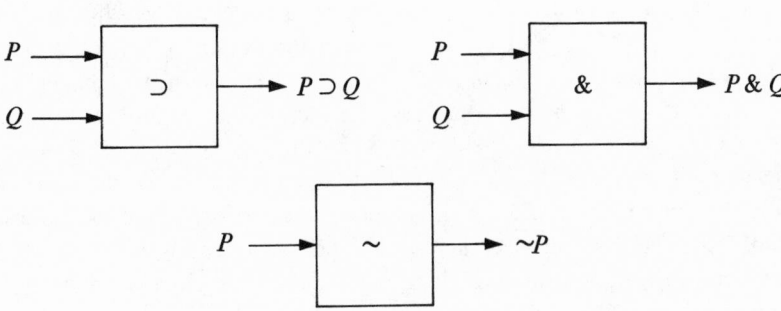

146

The parallel structure of the propositional and switching circuit interpretations is, of course, at the heart of computer construction and many techniques of propositional logic are used to arrange and simplify computer circuits. For more on this subject see the appropriate items in the Selected Readings.

A second interpretation—which the reader can work out for himself—is the water pipe and valve interpretation. The fact that a water flow story can be used in precisely the same way as the electricity story to interpret the abstract structure of propositional logic is behind the fact that most elementary books on electronics use water flow and valves as explanatory devices for electronic circuits.

3.12 AN HISTORICAL NOTE ON THE PROPOSITIONAL LOGIC

Though the reader has probably been under the impression that the propositional logic is, somehow, a more modern replacement for the syllogistic, this is not completely correct. The full development of the propositional logic is, certainly, a nineteenth-and twentieth-century phenomena but the groundwork of the logic can be clearly traced to a period roughly contemporary with Aristotle. Moreover, an examination of the reasons for the long period of general stagnation of the work begun in the fourth century B.C. on the propositional logic would reveal a very intricate and confused chapter in the history of ideas. We will not trace the intricacies but will describe the four main stages of this development.

1. At about the time of Aristotle's formulation of the syllogistic, the Megarian and Stoic schools were studying problems in logic that were independent of the syllogistic. The Megarians (Euclides, Diodorus, Philo) and the Stoics (Zeno of Citium and especially Chrysippus) were primarily concerned with the setting out and understanding of complex propositional arguments.[13] In fact, one great source of confusion for later logicians was the Stoic use of proposition-variable devices (i.e., blanks or numbers that were to be replaced with propositions) in places where the Aristotelian used similar

[13] As is well known, the Stoics were primarily concerned with certain ethical and metaphysical doctrines and their especial concern with logic is most probably owing to their relation to the Megarian philosophers. Typically, Zeno is supposed to have been a pupil of Diodorus. However, this is far from a settled issue in the history of logic.

devices but intended their replacement with predicative expressions. Aside from their overall concern with propositional argument forms, the Megarians, in particular, laid the groundwork for the truth-functional understanding of the conditional. Finally they carried the work on modal logic (within the framework of a propositional logic) much further and were well aware of the notion of "strict implication" discussed in section 3.11.1.

2. Because of confusion and even personal animosity, the Stoic work on logic was seen as a threat to Aristotle's logic and with the rise of importance of the syllogistic during the Middle Ages the Stoic work remained in the background. However, this long period (third to fifteenth centuries A.D.) can be seen as an era in which some reconciliation was brought about between the Stoic and Aristotelian logics and in which many of the problems of logic (e.g., existential import) were raised and considered.

3. The third stage begins with Leibniz, the seventeenth-century German philosopher, and ends with the nineteenth-century English mathematician George Boole. Among Leibniz's many interests was his proposal to construct a universal language of reasoning, *Ars Combinatoria,* in which the processes of reasoning and thought could be reduced to computation procedures of a simple arithmetic nature. This proposal was never worked out in any detail by Leibniz, but Boole, in his small book *The Mathematical Analysis of Logic* (1847), took up the spirit of Leibniz's suggestion and provided an example of a limited logic formulated in a limited algebraic framework. In this work both a logic of classes and a logic of propositions was presented as a special form of algebra and, aside from the mathematical concerns, the work clearly exhibited the basic isomorphism of class and proposition logic. From this point on the early impetus to arithmetize logic became less important than the basic understanding of the role of purely logical inference in mathematical contexts. Such persons as Jevons, Schroeder, Pierce, and Frege are largely responsible for this process, and the reader will be able to appreciate the final result of this work only after reading Chapter 5.

4. The last stage in the history of the propositional logic belongs to the twentieth century and the work of B. Russell, A.N. Whitehead, L. Wittgenstein, and E.L. Post. This is the period in which truth tables (Wittgenstein and more systematically Post) are used as an evaluation procedure and in which the study of propositional logic becomes the study of an abstract, uninterpreted system of axioms. (See Chapter 5.)

4

predicate logic

4.1   THE ELEMENTS OF PREDICATE LOGIC

The methods of the last chapter, though quite powerful, are not adequate for dealing with the kinds of arguments that were considered in Chapter 2, i.e., the syllogism. Consider the argument form

> A.   All A are B.
> $\underline{\text{All } B \text{ are } C.}$
> $\therefore$ All A are C.

How would you symbolize this argument form using the methods of propositional logic? Since each of the constituent propositions here would be atomic propositions by the definitions given in Chapter 2, the correct symbolization would be

> B. P
> $\underline{\quad Q \quad}$
> $\therefore R$

But then we would find argument form A to be invalid since it is possible for P and Q to be true and R to be false. Yet the argument form A that we are dealing with is the paradigm of a valid argument form (see Chapter 1). Perhaps it has occurred to the reader to symbolize our argument form as

C.　$A \supset B$
　　$B \supset C$
　　$\overline{\therefore A \supset C}$

this being a valid argument form that would prove valid under the methods of propositional logic. But this will not do! Whereas the capital letters of propositional logic stand for atomic propositions the capital letters in the symbolization C do not stand for propositions but rather for class names. Since class names are not true or false, formulas like $A \supset B$, where A and B are class names, are not true or false and thus not propositions. Such formulas are then incorrect symbolizations of propositions.

The situation is that whereas the validity of some arguments is dependent on the relationships that exist between the atomic propositions that make them up there are others whose validity is dependent on the relationships that exist between the *internal structures* of the atomic propositions that make them up. The former are adequately dealt with by the methods of propositional logic but the latter require a new logic, or rather an extension of the old. What is needed is a logic that can exhibit the structure of atomic propositions and thus not symbolize an atomic proposition as a capital letter. The logic which is capable of doing this job is called *predicate logic.*

In the predicate logic we have the following initial stock of symbols:

$P, Q, R, S, \ldots$
$\sim, \&, \vee, \supset, \equiv$
$x, y, z, \ldots$
$a, b, c, \ldots$
$(,)$

The capital letters $P, Q, R, S, \ldots$ will not stand in the predicate logic for propositions but rather for predicates. For our purposes a predicate is both the verb and the property said to be possessed by the subject. Thus in the proposition "The book is red," "is red" would be the predicate. Examples of predicates would be "is a color," "is the prince," "is mortal," etc. The monadic operator $\sim$ and the diadic operators $\&, \vee, \supset$, and $\equiv$ will have the same use (definition and meaning) that they have in propositional logic.

The lower case italicized letters from the end of the alphabet are called *individual variables,* i.e., they are variables that range over possible subjects. The lower case italicized letters from the beginning of the alphabet are called *individual constants.* They are used to indicate a particular individual. If we let *a* stand for a particular apple and *R* for the predicate "is red" then the formula

Ra

says that that particular apple is red. Similarly if we allow *c* to stand for "Charley Brown" and *S* for the predicate "is short" then the formula

Sc

says that Charley Brown is short. If we wished to symbolize the proposition "If that particular apple is red then Charley Brown is short" we could do so by writing

$Ra \supset Sc$

Since individual variables do not stand in place of a particular individual the formula

Sx

does not symbolize any proposition at all. It may be taken to symbolize the following, however: "_____ is short." "_____ is short" is not a sentence but might be termed a sentence frame,[1] where the blank indicates the place where the name of an individual might be placed. Such a sentence frame is neither true nor false since it cannot be used to assert anything. If we put a name in the blank, however, our sentence frame becomes a sentence and can then be used to make assertions that are either true or false. Similarly our formula

Sx

is neither true nor false until some individual constant is put in place of the

---

[1] The notion of sentence frame used here is derived from that used by Gilbert Ryle, "Categories," *Proceedings of the Aristotelian Society*, 1938-1939.

individual variable *x*. A formula like *Sx*, which is not a proposition but which becomes one when its individual variables are replaced by individual constants, is called a *propositional function*. Some examples of propositional functions would be

$$Sx \supset Sa$$
$$Sy \supset Py$$
$$Rx \vee \sim Sa$$

There is another way that a propositional function can become a proposition and that is by quantifying it. There are two kinds of quantifiers in our predicate logic. They are the *universal quantifier* written (*x*) and the *existential quantifier* written ($\exists x$). The universal quantifier, (*x*), is to be read "for all *x*." The existential quantifier, ($\exists x$), is to be read "there is an *x* such that" or "for some *x*" where "some" means "at least one."[2] A quantifier is said to be "on" the predicate variable which it contains, thus (*x*) and ($\exists x$) are said to be quantifiers on *x*, while (*y*) and ($\exists y$) are said to be the universal quantifier on *y* and the existential quantifier on *y*, respectively.

The formula (*x*)*Sx* says, given that *S* is the predicate "is short," "For all *x*, *x* is short." Now if we know what things can be *x*, i.e., if we know what the range of *x* is, "For all *x*, *x* is short" becomes a proposition. The range of the individual variables is always to be specified when we have quantified formulas. There are several ways in which this can be done. If all our talk is about numbers we can simply specify that the range of our individual variable is numbers. Or if all our talk is about human beings we could specify that the range of our individual variable is human beings. If we were to specify that the range of *x* is human beings then the formula (*x*)*Sx* would say that for all *x*, where *x* is a human being, *x* is short, or in other words that all human beings are short. If we do not specify the range of our individual variable explicitly it is understood that it ranges over everything, i.e., that it ranges over the members of the universal class. Thus if we did not explicitly specify the range of *x* the formula (*x*)*Sx* would say, for all *x*, where *x* is anything at all, *x* is short, or more simply everything is short.[3] The range specified is usually referred to as the *universe of discourse*.

---

[2] See Chapter 2 for a discussion of this use of "some."

[3] If the range of *x* is numbers then the formula (*x*)*Sx* says that all numbers are short. Is this false or simply nonsense? See p. 314, Chapter 6.

There is, however, another way of symbolizing the proposition "All human beings are short" which does not require us to explicitly specify the range of x, i.e., that allows the range of x to be universal. Consider the formula $(x)(Hx \supset Sx)$ where H is the predicate "is a human being" and S the predicate "is short." This formula then says that for all x, where x is anything at all, if x is a human being then x is short. Which is surely the same as saying that all human beings are short. By the use of such a device we can always allow our individual variable to range over everything.

In the preceding paragraph we made use of the formula $(x)(Hx \supset Sx)$. How, if at all, does this formula differ from $(x)Hx \supset Sx$ or the formula $(x)(Hx) \supset Sx$? Let us define an *occurrence of an individual variable* as an inscription of that variable. Thus in the formula Sx there is one occurrence of the individual variable x. In the formula $Sx \supset Hy$ there is one occurrence of the variable x and one occurrence of the variable y. Since the quantifiers (x) and $(\exists x)$ contain inscriptions of the variable x, they each contain one occurrence of x. Let us now distinguish between free and bound occurrences of an individual variable. This is best done by introducing the notion of the *scope* of a quantifier. First a quantifier is always said to be in its own scope. Second if the quantifier is immediately followed by a left-hand parenthesis (bracket or brace) then everything between that parenthesis and its closing right-hand parenthesis (bracket or brace) is said to be in the scope of the preceding quantifier. For these purposes the parentheses that are parts of quantifiers are to be ignored. Third if the quantifier is not immediately followed by a left-hand parenthesis (bracket or brace) then that predicate and individual variable or constant immediately following the quantifier, and no more, are said to be in the scope of the preceding quantifier. The scope of the quantifier in the formula $(x)(Hx \supset Sx)$ is then the entire formula, which we might indicate as $\underline{(x)(Hx \supset Sx)}$. The scopes of the quantifiers in the following formulas are indicated in the same way:

$$\underline{(x)Hx} \supset Sx$$
$$\underline{(x)(Hx)} \supset Sx$$

An occurrence of an individual variable that lies in the scope of a quantifier on that variable is said to be a *bound occurrence* of that variable. All other occurrences of individual variables are said to be *free occurrences* of individual variables. Thus all occurrences of x in the formula $(x)(Hx \supset Sx)$ are bound occurrences, while only the first two occurrences of x in the formula $(x)Hx \supset Sx$ are bound, the third occurrence being a free occurrence of the variable x. Now consider the formula $(x)(Hx \supset Sy)$. The scope of the universal quantifier on x is the entire formula, and thus all occurrences of the variable x in the formula are bound occurrences. But the occurrence of y is not in the scope of a quantifier on y and is thus a free occurrence of the variable y.

Only those formulas containing no free occurrences of any variables are said to be propositions. All those formulas that contain one or more free occurrences of an individual variable are propositional functions and not propositions. Thus any correct symbolization of a proposition will contain no occurrences of free variables.

The formulas $(x)(Hx \supset Sx)$ and $(x)(Hx) \supset Sx$ have been shown to differ in the scope of the universal quantifier and in that while the former is a proposition the latter is a propositional function. It is to be noted that owing to the difference in scope the first formula, $(x)(Hx \supset Sx)$, is a universally quantified conditional whereas the second formula, $(x)(Hx) \supset Sx$, is a conditional with a universally quantified antecedent. Thus, the antecedent of the propositional function $(x)(Hx) \supset Sx$ is a proposition and its consequent is a propositional function. If we were to use a blank for the free variable the formula could be translated, "If everything is human then _____ is short."

Differences in the scope of a quantifier can be as important as differences in the quantifiers a formula contains. Let us consider the following list:

1. $(x)(Hx \supset Sa)$
2. $(x)(Hx) \supset Sa$
1'. For all x, if x is H then a is S.
2'. If for all x, x is H, then a is S.
1". If anything is H then a is S.
2". If everything is H then a is S.

In the above list 1 and 2 are translated as 1' and 2'. The differences in meaning between 1' and 2' is captured in their restatement as 1" and 2" respectively. Now consider the list:

3. $(\exists x)(Hx) \supset Sa$
3'. If at least one x is H, then a is S.
3". If anything is H then a is S.

Here 3 is translated as 3' and then 3' is restated as 3". Now it can be seen that though 1 and 3 differ in the quantifiers they contain they still say the same thing. Thus it might be said that the scope difference between 1 and 3 amounts to the same thing as a quantifier change, in degree of importance.

In summary we have introduced in this section the following sorts of expressions:

1. Propositions of two types
   a. *Pa, Rb, Ra ⊃ Pb*, etc.
   b.*(x) Px, (∃x) Px, (x)(Hx ⊃ Rx)*, etc.

2. Propositional functions such as
   Px, (x) (Px ⊃ Ry), etc.

And we have seen the importance of the notion of quantifier scope in distinguishing between propositions of the sort in 1b above and propositional functions as in 2 above.

EXERCISE

1 Indicate the scope of quantifiers in each of the following formulas. Locate all free occurrences of variables and indicate which of the following are propositional functions:
   a. *(x)Px ∨ Rx*
   b. *(x)(Pa & ~Sx)*
   c. *(∃y)Sy & ~Ry*
   d. *(y)Px ⊃ (Ry ∨ Sx)*
   e. *(x)(~Px ∨ ~Sx) ⊃ Pb*
   f. *(Py & Ry) ⊃ [(x)Sx ⊃ Px]*
   g. *(∃y) {Px ⊃ [~Ry ∨ (Sx ⊃ Py)]}*
   h. *(x) [(Px & ~Sx) ⊃ (Rx ∨ ~Rx)]*
   i. *(Pa ∨ ~Pa) ⊃ (y)(Sy & ~Sy)*
   j. *(x) {(Px & Ra) ⊃ [(Sx & ~Pa) ∨ Qy]}*

4.2 SINGULARLY GENERAL PROPOSITIONS AND ARGUMENTS

In Chapter 2 we dealt with the four standard form categorical propositions. At the beginning of this chapter we presented a valid argument consisting of those standard form categorical propositions that could not be adequately dealt with by the methods of propositional logic. We can now symbolize this argument so as to exhibit the internal structure of the atomic propositions that make it up. The argument was of the form

    A.   All A are B.
         All B are C.
        $\therefore$ All A are C.

We can now symbolize this argument as

    A. $(x)(Ax \supset Bx)$
         $(x)(Bx \supset Cx)$
       $\therefore (x)(Ax \supset Cx)$

In the next section methods of proof will be introduced that will enable us to show that the argument thus symbolized is, indeed, valid.

All four standard form categorical propositions can now be adequately symbolized. The four propositions and their symbolizations are:

1.	All S are P.	$(x)(Sx \supset Px)$
2.	No S are P.	$(x)(Sx \supset \sim Px)$
3.	Some S are P.	$(\exists x)(Sx \mathbin{\&} Px)$
4.	Some S are not P.	$(\exists x)(Sx \mathbin{\&} \sim Px)$

The adequacy of the symbolization of 1 has already been discussed on page 153, so we will proceed to a discussion of 2. The formula $(x)(Sx \supset \sim Px)$ says that for all x, if x is an S then x is not a P, i.e., if you take anything whatsoever, if it is an S it is not a P, which is to say that no S are P.

Formula 3 says that for at least one x, x is both S and P, i.e., that there is at least one thing that is both an S and a P, or simply some S are P.

The fourth formula can be read, for at least one x, x is S but not P, i.e., that there is at least one thing that is an S but is not a P, or simply, some S are not P.

It is also worthwhile to consider the following two incorrect symbolizations:

    5. All S are P symbolized as $(x)(Sx \mathbin{\&} Px)$.
    6. Some S are P symbolized as $(\exists x)(Sx \supset Px)$.

The first formula, (5), makes the peculiar claim that everything is both an S and a P which is surely very different from saying that everything that is an S is also a P.

The second formula, (6), says that there exists at least one thing such that if that thing is an S then it is also a P. It should be clear then that this formula does not say that there exists at least one thing that is an S, whereas our original proposition, does assert that there exists at least one thing that is an S as does the correct symbolization $(\exists x)(Sx \,\&\, Px)$.

It is to be stressed that one does not symbolize one word at a time, replacing each occurrence of the word "and" with a & and each occurrence of "or" with a v, etc., but rather that one seeks to write an entire formula having the same meaning as the proposition being symbolized. Symbolization is then like translation from one language to another where one does not translate word for word but rather tries to capture the meaning of the whole. Not every occurrence of the word "and" is adequately captured by the &. One must judge by the context and conserve the meaning of the whole. Consider the proposition "All bananas and oranges are delicious." Using "B" for "is a banana," "O" for "is an orange" and "D" for "is delicious," it might be thought that the proposition would be correctly symbolized by $(x)[(Bx \,\&\, Ox) \supset Dx]$. But this formula says that for all x, if x is both a banana and an orange then x is delicious, which is not what our original proposition said at all. Our formula speaks of things that are both bananas and oranges (of which there are none), while our original proposition talks of bananas and of oranges. A correct symbolization would be $(x)[(Bx \vee Ox) \supset Dx]$. This formula says that for all x, if x is a banana or an orange then x is delicious, which is the same as our original proposition. It might also have been symbolized as $(x)(Bx \supset Dx) \,\&\, (x)(Ox \supset Dx)$, i.e., as the conjunction of two formulas, the first saying all bananas are delicious, the second saying all oranges are delicious.

EXERCISE

1 Symbolize each of the following propositions:
   a. The vertebrates are not all warm-blooded.
   b. Every good boy does fine.
   c. Some football players are gigantic but nonetheless intelligent.
   d. Some mushrooms are edible only when cooked.
   e. The whale is dangerous only if attacked.
   f. Some briars are worthwhile smoking if and only if they have been well broken in.
   g. There are people whose moral worth is kept well hidden.
   h. Foreign cars run well only if they are owned by people that are mechanically inclined.
   i. Some unhappy people are pleased only when they are well fed and warm.

j. The truth of some assertions is ascertainable only by diligent investigation.
k. All philosophers and psychologists are patient.
l. No tobacco is worth smoking unless it has been properly cured.
m. Not every philosopher who is an existentialist is an academician.
n. All logicians tell the truth unless they do not tell the truth.
o. All hammer and discus throwers are successful only if they are both strong and graceful.

4.2.1 Testing the validity of singularly general arguments

Can we apply those mechanical means of testing the validity of arguments in propositional logic to the arguments of predicate logic? A partial answer to this question is obtained by considering the applicability of the notion of truth tables to the formulas of predicate logic. As was shown in the previous section predicate logic allows us to display the internal structures of atomic propositions. Thus there is little in common between the formulas $P \supset Q$ of the propositional logic and $(x)(Px \supset Qx)$ of the predicate logic. To write a truth table for the formula $P \supset Q$ is to display its truth values as a function of the truth values of its constituent parts, P and Q. But the truth or falsity of the formula $(x)(Px \supset Qx)$ is not a function of the truth value of its constituent parts, for its constituent parts are not propositions (or more correctly do not stand for propositions) and are not therefore true or false.

Since, however, $(x)(Px \supset Qx)$ does say of each thing in the universe that if it has property P then it has property Q, we may consider $(x)(Px \supset Qx)$ to be equivalent to the conjunction of infinitely many conditionals of the propositional logic. Thus,

$$(x)(Px \supset Qx) \equiv (Pa \supset Qa) \mathbin{\&} (Pb \supset Qb) \mathbin{\&} (Pc \supset Qc) \text{ etc.}$$

in which we would have infinitely many conjuncts and where each individual in the universe is named by our individual constants, $a,b,c, \ldots$ The requisite truth table would then have infinitely many rows and columns, a situation that the reader, no doubt, will wish to avoid. Thus our approach to the testing of validity in the predicate logic will differ in certain specific ways from that of the propositional logic. This section will begin to consider those differences.

We have shown in the preceding section that there are two ways to turn a propositional function into a proposition; first by the replacing of all individual variables with individual constants and second by quantifying all the individual variables. There exists a sense in which both of these methods are the same. Let us consider what the formulas $(x)(Hx \lor Sx)$ and $(\exists x)(Hx \lor Sx)$ are saying in the case where the range of x consists of only one individual. If we designate that individual as a, our first formula will assert the same thing as the formula $Ha \lor Sa$. For to say that for all x, $Hx \lor Sx$ where all the x's consist of nothing but a single individual a is to say nothing more than that that individual is H or S, which is what the formula $Ha \lor Sa$ asserts. But what of the formula $(\exists x)(Hx \lor Sx)$ under these same conditions of a universe of but one individual? To say that at least one x is H or S where x ranges only over a is to say that a is H or S. Therefore the formula $(\exists x)(Hx \lor Sx)$ in a universe of one individual a is the same as the formula $Ha \lor Sa$.

The situation in a universe of two individuals is somewhat different. If we allow x to range over the individuals a and b the formulas $(x)(Hx \lor Sx)$ and $(\exists x)(Hx \lor Sx)$ are not equivalent. When we say that for all x, where x ranges over a and b, x is H or S, we are in fact saying that a is H or S, and b is H or S. The formula $(x)(Hx \lor Sx)$ is therefore equivalent to the formula $(Ha \lor Sa) \& (Hb \lor Sb)$ in a universe consisting of the two individuals a and b. On the other hand the formula $(\exists x)(Hx \lor Sx)$ in the same universe says that at least one member of that universe is H or S, or symbolically $(Ha \lor Sa) \lor (Hb \lor Sb)$.

In a universe of three individuals a, b, and c the formula $(x)(Hx \lor Sx)$ would be the same as the formula

$$(Ha \lor Sa) \& (Hb \lor Sb) \& (Hc \lor Sc)$$

while the formula $(\exists x)(Hx \lor Sx)$ would be the same as the formula

$$(Ha \lor Sa) \lor (Hb \lor Sb) \lor (Hc \lor Sc)$$

In general, where $\emptyset x$ represents some propositional function of x,

$$(x)\emptyset x \equiv [\emptyset a \& \emptyset b \& \emptyset c \& \ldots \& \emptyset n]$$

and

$$(\exists x)\emptyset x \equiv [\emptyset a \lor \emptyset b \lor \emptyset c \lor \ldots \lor \emptyset n]$$

(where n is the number of individuals that x ranges over.)

To say that an argument is valid is to say that there are no conditions under which the premises could be true and the conclusion false. In particular if an argument represented in the predicate logic is valid there will exist no possible range of values for the constituent individual variables that will permit the premises to be true when the conclusion is false. Thus, if for a given argument we can show that a specific universe of individuals makes it possible for the premises to be true and the conclusion false, we have shown the given argument to be invalid.

First let us consider the invalid syllogistic argument form

A.   All A are B.
    All C are B.
    $\therefore$ All A are C.

This argument form would be symbolized in the predicate logic as

B. $(x)(Ax \supset Bx)$
    $(x)(Cx \supset Bx)$
    $\therefore (x)(Ax \supset Cx)$

In a universe of one individual, say a, the above argument form is equivalent to the following argument:

C. $Aa \supset Ba$
    $Ca \supset Ba$
    $\therefore Aa \supset Ca$

This argument is easily shown invalid, since the premises are true and the conclusion false under the following assignment of truth values: Aa true, Ba true, and Ca false. Since we have shown our original argument to be invalid in a universe of one individual we have shown it to be invalid "everywhere."

We will now apply this method of showing invalidity to a more complex argument. Consider the argument:

D.   All princes are quiet fellows.
    Some members of the royal family are quiet fellows.
    Not all members of the royal family are quiet fellows.
    $\therefore$ All princes are members of the royal family.

This argument could be symbolized as follows:

E. $(y)(Py \supset Qy)$
    $(\exists y)(Ry \mathbin{\&} Qy)$
    $(\exists y)(Ry \mathbin{\&} {\sim}Qy)$
    ∴ $(y)(Py \supset Ry)$

In a universe of one individual, say a, this argument becomes:

F. $Pa \supset Qa$
    $Ra \mathbin{\&} Qa$
    $Ra \mathbin{\&} {\sim}Qa$
    ∴ $Pa \supset Ra$

which is valid. This, of course, does not prove the original argument valid for to say that an argument is valid is not to say that there exists some case in which it is impossible to make the premises true and the conclusion false, but is rather to say that there exists no such case. Thus it might be that this argument can be shown to be invalid in a universe of two individuals or, failing that, in a universe of three individuals, etc. In a universe of three individuals, say $a, b,$ and $c,$ our argument becomes

G. $(Pa \supset Qa) \mathbin{\&} (Pb \supset Qb) \mathbin{\&} (Pc \supset Qc)$
    $(Ra \mathbin{\&} Qa) \vee (Rb \mathbin{\&} Qb) \vee (Rc \mathbin{\&} Qc)$
    $(Ra \mathbin{\&} {\sim}Qa) \vee (Rb \mathbin{\&} {\sim}Qb) \vee (Rc \mathbin{\&} {\sim}Qc)$
    ∴ $(Pa \supset Ra) \mathbin{\&} (Pb \supset Rb) \mathbin{\&} (Pc \supset Rc)$

This argument (G) can be shown to be invalid by the method of truth tables or truth trees or the indirect assignment method. One assignment of values that shows its invalidity is as follows: *Pa* **T**, *Pb* **F**, *Pc* **T**, *Qa* **T**, *Qb* **F**, *Qc* **T**, *Ra* **F**, *Rb* **T**, *Rc* **T**.

Though this method suffices to show invalidity it does not suffice to show validity; and it only shows invalidity when one has been fortunate enough to come across a range of the individual variable that exhibits the argument's invalidity. In this way it is much like the method of analogy discussed in connection with syllogistic argument in Chapter 2. There is, however, a happy difference and that is that it can be shown that there exists a crucial case for the method here under discussion. It has been proven that for arguments in the predicate logic of the sort we have been discussing to this point (singularly general arguments) if the number of different predicate symbols is n and the argument is valid for a universe of 2^n individuals then the argument is valid "everywhere."[4] This then represents an effective mechanical test for the validity of the sorts of arguments so far discussed in this chapter. One merely follows the following procedure:

1. Symbolize the argument.

2. Count the number of different predicate symbols the argument contains and raise the number 2 to that power.

3. Designate the number of individual constants indicated in step 2 above and rewrite the argument in its equivalent form for a universe containing that number of individuals.

4. Test the rewritten argument for validity by any of the mechanical means available for determining the validity of arguments in the propositional logic.

Consider the following argument:

> H. No philosophers are unclear thinkers.
> <u>All unclear thinkers are befuddled people.</u>
> ∴ No philosophers are befuddled people.

First we symbolize the argument as:

> I. $(x)(Px \supset \sim Ux)$
> <u>$(x)(Ux \supset Bx)$</u>
> ∴ $(x)(Px \supset \sim Bx)$

Next we note that the number of different predicate symbols is three (P, U, B) and that 2^3 is 8. Now we designate eight individual constants, say, a, b, c, d, e, f, g, and h. And rewrite our symbolized argument for a universe containing just these eight individuals.

> J. $(Pa \supset \sim Ua)$ & $(Pb \supset \sim Ub)$ & $(Pc \supset \sim Uc)$ & $(Pd \supset \sim Ud)$
> & $(Pe \supset \sim Ue)$ & $(Pf \supset \sim Uf)$ & $(Pg \supset \sim Ug)$
> & $(Ph \supset \sim Uh)$
> <u>$(Ua \supset Ba)$ & $(Ub \supset Bb)$ & . . . & $(Uh \supset Bh)$</u>
> ∴ $(Pa \supset \sim Ba)$ & $(Pb \supset \sim Bb)$ & . . . & $(Ph \supset \sim Bh)$

Now we are to test this last argument by means of one of the mechanical methods of Chapter 3, say truth tables. We would find it to be valid and may then conclude that our original argument (H) was valid. The preceding was

---

[4]This was proven by Bernays and Schonfinkel in 1928. In this connection see W. Ackermann, *Solvable Cases of the Decision Problem* (Amsterdam, 1954).

calculated to show that though there is an effective mechanical procedure for determining the validity or invalidity of an argument of the sort so far discussed, the method is extremely cumbersome and time-consuming even for very simple arguments.

We have referred several times to "that class of argument already considered so far in this chapter." These are known as *singularly general arguments.* An argument is said to be singularly general when its premises and conclusion are each adequately symbolized by formulas containing a single quantifier or no quantifier at all. The reader should note that all the arguments discussed so far in this chapter are, in fact, of this sort. There do exist, however, propositions that are not adequately symbolized by a single quantifier. Such propositions are termed *multiply general* and will be discussed in section 4.3. Any argument that contains one or more multiply general propositions either as premises or conclusion is said to be a *multiply general argument.*

Now though we have noted that there exists an effective and mechanical procedure for testing the validity of singlularly general arguments, no such single effective method exists for testing the validity of all multiply general arguments, and more strongly, no set of effective methods exists for testing the validity of all arguments of the predicate logic. This was shown to be true in 1936 by Alonzo Church.[5] Thus, the best that we can expect in our search for methods of determining which arguments are valid and which are invalid in the predicate logic is some set of procedures that, like the method of analogy alluded to above, are one sided. That is, we can develop tests that, if successful, will indicate validity but if unsuccessful will indicate nothing. Methods of this sort will be discussed in the following sections of this chapter.

4.3 MULTIPLY GENERAL PROPOSITIONS AND ARGUMENTS

In section 4.2.1 it was said that there existed propositions that could not be adequately symbolized as singularly general propositions. Our concern in the present section will be to consider the symbolization of such propositions, i.e., multiply general propositions, and arguments that contain at least one such proposition.

[5]"A Note on the Entscheidungsproblem," *Journal of Symbolic Logic*, 1936, 1: 40-41.

Consider the following proposition:

If everyone is here then everyone is happy.

How should such a proposition be symbolized? First it is clear that it is a conditional statement and so our main connective will be a $\supset$. The antecedent of our conditional is the proposition "everyone is here." This is a singularly general proposition which is symbolized using the methods of section 4.1 as:

1. $(x)(Px \supset Hx)$

where P stands for the predicate "is a person" and H for the predicate "is here." Thus our formula 1 says that for all x, if x is a person then x is here, which means the same as everyone is here. The consequent of our original proposition is "everyone here is happy." This could be symbolized once again quite simply, since it is a singularly general proposition as:

2. $(x) [(Px \& Hx) \supset Ax]$

where P stands for "is a person" and H for "is here" and A for "is happy." Our formula 2 can then be read as for all x, if x is a person and x is here, then x is happy, which says the same thing as "everyone here is happy." Now if we take the formulas 1 and 2 and join them by a "$\supset$" we should have a correct symbolization, 3, of our original proposition "If everyone is here then everyone here is happy."

3. $(x)(Px \supset Hx) \supset (x) [(Px \& Hx) \supset Ax]$

Now let us consider the proposition:

If everyone is here then someone here is happy.

Using the same technique as in our previous example we get

4. $(x)(Px \supset Hx) \supset (\exists x) [(Px \& Hx) \& Ax]$

which is a correct symbolization. Is the last occurrence of the individual variable x in formula 4 universally quantified or existentially quantified? This question can be answered by first considering the scopes of the quantifiers that the formula contains. Using our previously established conventions the scopes are

$$(x)(Px \supset Hx) \supset (\exists x) [(Px \& Hx) \& Ax]$$

It is clear from this that the scope of the existential quantifier is the one that the last occurrence of x falls under. But what if our formula was

5. $(x) \{(Px \supset Hx) \supset (\exists x) [(Px \& Hx) \& Ax] \}$

Is the last occurrence of the individual variable x in formula 5 existentially or universally quantified? The answer should be gotten once again by considering the scopes of quantifiers contained in the formula. But in formula 5 the situation is

$$(x) \{(Px \supset Hx) \supset (\exists x) [(Px \& Hx) \& Ax] \}$$

which means that the last occurrence of x is in the scopes of both the existential and universal quantifiers. This ambiguity can be avoided, however, by using a different individual variable in each quantifier and changing each individual variable appropriately, thus 5 is properly written:

5'. $(x) \{(Px \supset Hx) \supset (\exists y) [(Py \& Hy) \& Ay] \}$

In the formula 5' it is clear that the last occurrence of an individual variable, viz., y, is existentially quantified. It is advised that the reader use different individual variables for each quantifier if there is a possible ambiguity of scope. We will follow this practice throughout this book.

In the previous examples of multiply general propositions each proposition consisted of two singularly general propositions joined by some logical connective. Not all multiply general propositions are of this form. Consider the proposition:

If there are any wise men and only philosophers are wise men then they are philosophers.

This proposition cannot be properly symbolized as two singularly general propositions joined by a logical connective. It is properly symbolized as:

6. $(x) \{[Wx \& (y)(Wy \supset Py)] \supset Px\}$

Though we can provide no simple method of symbolizing rather complex multiply general statements, the following is offered as a suggested method of attack. Since all statements of the predicate logic, however complex, are fundamentally propositional we can use this fact to build the predicate devices into the overall propositional nature of each statement. Thus, consider this rather complex statement:

If any woman runs for President, then if all women vote she will win.

If this were symbolized by the methods of Chapter 3 it would be:

$P \supset (Q \supset R)$

where P is "any woman runs for President," Q is "all women vote," and R is "she will win." The next step is the recognition of which propositions are connected by their reference to the same class of individuals. Since the "she" in R refers back to the individual in P we can indicate this by writing an x over both the P and the R:

$$\overset{x}{P} \supset (Q \supset \overset{x}{R})$$

Then, one should consider whether the remaining propositions are general and whether they require variables different from those used previously. Clearly Q is a general statement and requires the use of a different variable, say y, as it will be within the scope of the quantifier we place on x. This is so because the final result will require a quantifier that connects both the x over P and the x over R, and it could not do this, given the propositional structure of the statement, without affecting Q. Also, since the y in Q is not connected with any other variable we can write out Q quite simply as a statement of the form all A are B and get

$$\overset{x}{P} \supset [(y)(Wy \supset Vy) \supset \overset{x}{R}]$$

Next, we convert the

$$x \quad\quad x$$
$$P \text{ and } R$$

into propositional functions that express the properties in the original statement. Thus,

$$x$$
$$P \text{ is } Wx \,\&\, Px$$

(x is a woman and x runs for President)

$$x$$
$$R \text{ is } Ex$$

(x will be elected) so we have

$$(Wx \,\&\, Px) \supset [(y)(Wy \supset Vy) \supset Ex]$$

The final step is the assignment of quantifiers that convert the propositional functions to propositions (in this case we need only assign a quantifier on x). Since our original statement used the word "any" and since the use of an existential quantifier in front of our above formula would not express this we get

$$(x)\{(Wx \,\&\, Px) \supset [(y)(Wy \supset Vy) \supset Ex]\}$$

One advantage of this method is the ease with which both the generality and scopes of quantifiers is determined. Consider the proposition

If any merchandise is missing then all employees will be blamed.

Using the stepwise procedure as above we get

$$P \supset Q$$
$$x \quad y$$
$$P \supset Q$$
$$(Mx \,\&\, Sx) \supset (y)\,(Ey \supset By)$$

167

At this point we are ready to supply the necessary quantification for the variable x. However, if we were to translate the "any" in this example as (x) then our formula would be:

$$(x)(Mx \ \& \ Sx) \supset (y)(Ey \supset By)$$

This, though, would assert

If *all* merchandise is missing then all the employees will be blamed

and this is certainly not what is expressed by our original proposition. What is needed is an existential quantifier to give

$$(\exists x)(Mx \ \& \ Sx) \supset (y)(Ey \supset By)$$

This need could have been recognized in our earlier steps in view of the fact that the P and Q of the original formulation share no variables. It is this that results in our use of $(\exists x)$ for "any" here and (x) for "any" in the former example.

In sum, our recommended procedure for symbolizing statements is:

1. Write the propositional structure of the statement.

2. Provide for cross-referencing by putting appropriate variables on top of propositions.

3. Provide variables for other components where needed and fully symbolize them.

4. Write propositional functions for expressions in step 2.

5. Supply quantifiers in order to change propositional functions to propositions keeping the overall structure of the formula in mind so as to choose correct quantification.

EXERCISE

1 Symbolize each of the following multiply general propositions:
   a. Everyone is here unless someone is there.
   b. Some seek fame and some seek fortune.
   c. If anyone calls someone will take a message.
   d. These are bad times but there will be good times again.
   e. If everybody leaves at five o'clock, then no one gets home on time.
   f. If all the people on Chalfont Road are angry then some people are going to move.

g. Anyone can give advice, but only a wise man accepts advice.
h. If any gas-turbine cars are inexpensive then some gas-turbine cars are successful.
i. If somebody beats Chicago then if no one beats the Mets then the Mets will wind up in first place.
j. If any philosophers are rationalists then, if all rationalist philosophers are idealists, they are idealists.
k. If all propositions are true or false and no commands are true or false then no commands are propositions.
l. If anyone deserves a raise and anyone who deserves a raise gets one then he will get one.
m. All people are sad unless there is something to be happy about.
n. If some doctoral students are not paranoids and some paranoids are not insane, then some doctoral students are not insane.

4.3.1   Testing the validity of multiply general arguments

As was mentioned in the previous section there exists no general effective test of the validity of multiply general arguments. It is, however, sometimes possible to show that a given multiply general argument is invalid. This can be done by showing that in some specific universe the argument has true premises and a false conclusion. The invalidity of the argument:

A. $\dfrac{(x)(\exists y)(Fx \equiv \sim Fy)}{\therefore (x)(Fx \equiv \sim Fa)}$

can be shown by considering A is a universe of two individuals, a and b. The equivalences presented and discussed in section 4.2.1 are to be used here as well. The fact that the premise of A contains two quantifiers requires us to write its equivalent formula in a universe of two individuals in two steps. First we eliminate the universal quantifier by writing

$$(\exists y)(Fa \equiv \sim Fy) \,\&\, (\exists y)(Fb \equiv \sim Fy)$$

We now deal with each conjunct of this formula with the method of section 4.2.1 to get

$$[(Fa \equiv \sim Fa) \lor (Fa \equiv \sim Fb)] \,\&\, [(Fb \equiv \sim Fa) \lor (Fb \equiv \sim Fb)]$$

The conclusion of A in a universe of two individuals a and b, is

$$(Fa \equiv \sim Fa) \ \& \ (Fb \equiv \sim Fa)$$

Thus in a universe of two individuals, a and b, the argument A becomes

$$\frac{[(Fa \equiv \sim Fa) \lor (Fa \equiv \sim Fb)] \ \& \ [(Fb \equiv \sim Fa) \lor (Fb \equiv \sim Fb)]}{\therefore (Fa \equiv \sim Fa) \ \& \ (Fb \equiv \sim Fa)}$$

This argument is easily shown invalid when Fa is true and Fb is false. Thus, since argument A can be shown invalid in a universe of two individuals, it is invalid in any universe.

4.3.2 The relation between universal and existential quantifiers

It is important to note that the existential and universal quantifiers are interdefinable, i.e., they are not independent notions. If we consider the relationship of contradictory categorical propositions, we can see the way in which quantifiers are interdefinable. Consider

All S are P.

and

Some S are not P.

which are contradictory proposition forms.[6]

We have seen that "All S are P" is symbolized as

1. $(x)(Sx \supset Px)$

and "Some S are not P" as

2. $(\exists x)(Sx \ \& \ \sim Px)$

But $Sx \ \& \ \sim Px$ is the same as $\sim(\sim Sx \lor Px)$ by De Morgan's rule (and double negation). This is the same as $\sim(Sx \supset Px)$ by the rule of material implication. Thus we have

[6]See section 2.3

2′. $(\exists x) \sim (Sx \supset Px)$

which is logically equivalent to proposition 2. Now since propositions 1 and 2 are contradictories, so are 1 and 2′. If we negate 2′ it should be then logically equivalent to 1. Thus we have

$$(x)(Sx \supset Px) \equiv \sim(\exists x) \sim (Sx \supset Px)$$

Since $(Sx \supset Px)$ appears on both sides, it would seem that (x) and $\sim(\exists x)\sim$ are truth functionally equivalent or "do the same thing." If we turn to ordinary language, and our reading of the quantifiers, we will find a confirmation of the above. To this end let us compare the propositions,

3. All men are philosophers.

and

4. Some men are not philosophers.

These propositions are of the form of "All S are P" and "Some S are not P" and can thus be symbolized as

3′. $(x)(Mx \supset Px)$

and

4′. $(\exists x)(Mx \,\&\, {\sim}Px)$

As we have seen proposition 4 can be rewritten as

4″. $(\exists x) \sim (Mx \supset Px)$

As propositions 3 and 4 are contradictories, negating one will yield a statement truth functionally equivalent to the other. Thus,

5. $\sim(\exists x) \sim (Mx \supset Px)$

is truth functionally equivalent to proposition 3. Now 3 says that all men are philosophers; what does 5 say? Formula 5 says that it is not the case that there exists an x for which it is false that if x is a man, then x is a philosopher, or in other words, there is no one who is a man and not a philosopher; and finally, as should now be clear, all men are philosophers. Thus we have seen that the universal quantifier (x) functions in the same way as $\sim(\exists x)\sim$. Indeed the universal quantifier (x) is equivalent to $\sim(\exists x)\sim$.

As 3′ and 4″ above are contradictories, by negating one we should get the equivalent of the other. Whereas last time we negated 4″, now let us negate 3′, getting

3″. $\sim(x)(Mx \supset Px)$

which by double negation is the same as

3‴. $\sim(x) \sim\sim(Mx \supset Px)$

But comparing 3‴ with

4″. $(\exists x) \sim (Mx \supset Px)$

we note that they only differ in that 3‴ contains $\sim(x)\sim$ where 4″ contains $(\exists x)$. Since 3‴ and 4″ are equivalent, the expressions $\sim(x)\sim$ and $(\exists x)$ must be functioning in the same way. Or in ordinary language, 4″ says that there exists someone who is a man but not a philosopher; and 3‴ says that it is not the case that everyone is a philosopher. These are clearly equivalent statements. Thus we could have defined the existential quantifier in terms of the universal quantifier as

$(\exists x) =$ df $\sim(x)\sim$

The foregoing discussion is taken to be sufficient justification for the introduction of a new rule called the rule of *quantifier equivalence*, abbreviated **QE**. The rule simply states that (1) We may replace (x) by $\sim(\exists x)\sim$ and (2) We may replace $(\exists x)$ by $\sim(x)\sim$ and vice versa.

Given these facts about quantifier equivalence the reader should attempt to see why the two formulas below are identical:

$\sim(\exists x)(Sx \& Px)$
$\sim[(\exists x)(Sx \& Px)]$

4.4 PREDICATE LOGIC AND RULES OF INFERENCE

In the previous discussions we have been rather careless in our use of the rules of propositional logic and this resulted in a situation which is a possible source of confusion. When we learned the rules of inference and replacement of propositional logic in Chapter 3, it was made quite clear that those rules held between propositions, i.e., between statements that were true or false. But in the preceding discussion, we used these rules to make inferences between things that were not propositions at all. We used De Morgan's rule, for instance, to assert that Sx & $\sim Px$ was logically equivalent to $\sim(\sim Sx \lor Px)$. Now neither Sx & $\sim Px$ nor $\sim(\sim Sx \lor Px)$ are propositions. They are propositional functions and so neither true nor false. How, then, can we speak of inferring one from the other or of their being logically equivalent. Our notion of validity, i.e., that a valid inference is one in which it is impossible for the premises to be true and the conclusion false, cannot apply to propositional functions for they are neither true nor false. We will now expand our notion of validity to accommodate inferences between propositional functions or between propositional functions and propositions.

An inference between propositional functions will be said to be valid if no substitution of individual constants for individual variables (consistently substituting the same constant for the same variable throughout, of course) will lead to a case of true premises and a false conclusion. It should be apparent that under this expanded notion of valid inference all our rules of inference and replacement of Chapter 3, including conditional proof, justify valid inferences amongst both propositional functions and propositions.

We now turn our attention to a whole new set of valid inferences that become demonstrable in a predicate logic though not in a propositional logic. The following are some examples of inferences in the predicate logic which, though obviously valid, are not justified by any of the rules we have so far introduced.

> All men are philosophers.
> John is a man.
> _____
> ∴ John is a philosopher.

> All philosophers are wise men.
> Some philosophers smoke pipes.
> _____
> ∴ Some wise men smoke pipes.

173

Let us consider some even more primitive valid arguments in the predicate logic that are not justified by any of the rules so far presented.

If $(x)Px$ means that everything has the property P, it is surely true that a, some individual thing, has the property P. Thus the argument

$$\frac{(x)Px}{\therefore Pa}$$

is surely valid.

What of the more complicated argument:

$$\frac{(x)(Sx \supset Px)}{\therefore Sb \supset Pb}$$

It is valid also, for if all S are P and b is S, surely b is also P. We might wish to generalize these cases into a rule concerning inferences from universally quantified formulas to those formulas that could have been obtained by dropping the universal quantifier and replacing each occurrence of the individual variable that the dropped quantifier was on by an individual constant. If we were to let the expression $\emptyset x$ represent any propositional function that contained at least one free occurrence of x, our rule might be stated as

$$\frac{(x)\emptyset x}{\therefore \emptyset \alpha}$$

where α stood for some individual constant that had replaced every free occurrence of x in $\emptyset x$.

It should be noted that under our convention for the expression $\emptyset x$, all the following propositional functions could be represented by it.

Px
$Px \supset Sx$
$Pa \supset Sx$
$(\exists y)Py \supset Sx$

and that, therefore, our rule would justify all the following inferences:

$$\frac{(x)Px}{\therefore Pa}$$

$$\frac{(x)(Px \supset Sx)}{\therefore Pb \supset Sb}$$

$$\frac{(x)(Pa \supset Sx)}{\therefore Pa \supset Sa}$$

or $Pa \supset Sb$, etc.

$$\frac{(x)\ ((\exists y)Py \supset Sx)}{\therefore (\exists y)Py \supset Sa}$$

Of course, there is no reason why the universally quantified formula that is our premise must use the individual variable x. In order to be general then, we will use the Greek letter μ to stand for any particular individual variable and rewrite our rule of inference, which we will call *universal instantiation*,

$$\frac{(\mu)\ \emptyset\mu}{\therefore \emptyset\alpha}$$

But our rule is still not as general as it could be. We have previously expanded our notion of valid inference to allow for inferences which involve propositional functions and given our new notion of valid inference the argument

$$\frac{(x)(Px \supset Rx)}{\therefore Px \supset Rx}$$

is valid. Since no substitution of an individual constant for the individual variable, x, in the propositional function, which is the conclusion, will lead to a case of true premises and a false conclusion, the argument is valid. In our last formulation of the rule of universal instantiation, we stated the form of the conclusion as $\emptyset\alpha$, where α stood for some individual constant. But we have now seen that this is too restrictive and so we replace α with the Greek letter ω, where ω will stand for some individual constant or variable. The rule of universal instantiation (abbreviated **UI**) will now be written:

UI $\quad \dfrac{(\mu)\emptyset\mu}{\therefore \emptyset\omega}$

175

where our symbolic conventions indicate:

1. That $\emptyset\mu$ is a propositional function containing at least one free occurrence of the individual variable designated by μ, and

2. That $\emptyset\omega$ is obtainable from $\emptyset\mu$ by replacing each free occurrence of the individual variable designated by μ in $\emptyset\mu$ by the individual variable or constant designated by ω.

The reader should not be perplexed by the reference to the free occurrence of the individual variable designated by μ in $\emptyset\mu$ in statement 2. Of course, there are no free occurrences of the variable designated by μ in $(\mu)\emptyset\mu$, but statement 2 is not referring to $(\mu)\ \emptyset\mu$, but to $\emptyset\mu$, itself, without the universal quantifier (μ). Understanding this, the reader should see that there will always be at least one free occurrence of the individual variable designated by μ.

Let us turn our attention now to some simple examples of valid inference that exhibit our rule of **UI**.

A. $\dfrac{(x)Px}{\therefore Py}$

B. $\dfrac{(x)Px}{\therefore Pc}$

C. $\dfrac{(x)(Sx \lor Rx)}{\therefore Sx \lor Rx}$

D. $\dfrac{(x)\ [(\exists y)(Sx \equiv \sim Sy)]}{\therefore (\exists y)(Sz \equiv \sim Sy)}$

In argument A, μ is x and ω is y; $\emptyset\mu$ is Px and $\emptyset\omega$ is Py. $\emptyset\mu$, being Px, does indeed contain at least one free occurrence of the individual variable designated by μ, namely x. $\emptyset\omega$, here Py, can indeed be gotten from $\emptyset\mu$, here Px, by replacing each free occurrence of the individual variable designated by μ, namely x, by the individual variable or constant designated by ω, here y. Argument A is thus valid by our rule **UI**.

Argument B is precisely like A, except for ω being the individual constant c. It still, however, meets all our conditions, and is thus validated by our rule of **UI**.

In argument C, μ is x, ω is x, $\emptyset\mu$ is $(Sx \lor Rx)$, and $\emptyset\omega$ is $(Sx \lor Rx)$. There is nothing in our symbolic conventions or our statement of the rule that indicates that μ and ω cannot designate the same individual variable, nor is there anything that says that $\emptyset\mu$ and $\emptyset\omega$ may not be the same formula. Argument C is validated by our rule as it stands since $(Sx \vee Rx)$ does contain at least one free occurrence of x and $(Sx \vee Rx)$ can be gotten from $(Sx \vee Rx)$ by replacing each occurrence of x in $(Sx \vee Rx)$ by x.

We have a somewhat more complicated case in argument D, which is a multiply general argument. But our rule applies in precisely the same way. In D: μ is x, ω is z, $\emptyset\mu$ is $(\exists y)(Sx \equiv {\sim}Sy)$, and $\emptyset\omega$ is $(\exists y)(Sz \equiv {\sim}Sy)$. We determined that μ was x by noting that the universal quantifier on x appeared in the premise, but not in the conclusion. We determined that ω was z by noting what letter "took the place of" x in the conclusion. Now let us consider whether the argument in D meets our symbolic conventions and our rule of **UI**. First we note that $\emptyset\mu$, $(\exists y)(Sx \equiv {\sim}Sy)$, does contain at least one free occurrence of x which is the individual variable designated by μ. Second we see that $\emptyset\omega$, $(\exists y)(Sz \equiv {\sim}Sy)$, can be gotten from $\emptyset\mu$, $(\exists y)(Sx \equiv {\sim}Sy)$, by replacing every free occurrence of x in $\emptyset\mu$ by z. Thus D is also validated by our rule of **UI**.

What would have happened if, in argument D, x had been instantiated to y instead of to z? D would have then read:

$$\text{D}'. \quad \frac{(x)\,[(\exists y)(Sx \equiv Sy)]}{\therefore (\exists y)(Sy \equiv {\sim}Sy)}$$

According to our rule and its attendant symbolic conventions, D′ is validated by our rule of **UI**, but it is invalid. For it is clear that the premise is true in a case where there are some things that are S and some things that are not S, e.g., in a universe consisting of a, which has property S, and b, which does not have property S. But the conclusion is false in any universe since it is self-contradictory.

In order to avoid invalid arguments such as D′, we must add a restriction to our rule of **UI**.

3. Where ω is an individual variable, ω must occur free in $\emptyset\omega$ wherever μ occurs free in $\emptyset\mu$.

Argument D′ violates this restriction. For whereas x occurs free in $\emptyset\mu$, $(\exists y)(Sx \equiv {\sim}Sy)$, the occurrence of y that replaces it in $\emptyset\omega$, $(\exists y)(Sy \equiv {\sim}Sy)$, is bound by the existential quantifier on y.

One further point should be considered regarding **UI**. The rule of **UI**, as stated, indicates that the premise of a universal instantiation must have a universal quantifier as its left-most unit. This condition must be met in applications of **UI**, as invalidity may result if it is not. Consider the statement,

"Adam is the sole owner of Spot and it cannot be the case that both Adam is the sole owner of Spot and everyone else is the sole owner of Spot." Let us symbolize this proposition as

Sa & $\sim(Sa$ & $(x)Sx)$[7]

If we were to ignore the implicit restriction on **UI**, that the universal quantifier must come first, we might infer

$$\frac{Sa \ \& \ \sim(Sa \ \& \ (x)Sx)}{\therefore Sa \ \& \sim (Sa \ \& \ Sa)}$$

This is invalid since the premise is obviously true and the conclusion is self-contradictory and thus false. If we take the original proposition and try to move the universal quantifier to the left-most position, we find that

1. Sa & $\sim(Sa$ & $(x)Sx)$		
2. $\sim(Sa$ & $(x)Sx)$ & Sa	1	Com.
3. $\sim((x)Sx$ & $Sa)$ & Sa	2	Com.
4. $\sim((x)Sx$ & $Sa)$	3	Simp.

When we get to step 4, the quantifier is not the left-most symbol, since it is preceded by a $\sim$. If we continue:

5. $\sim(x)Sx$ v $\sim Sa$	4	De M.

the $\sim$ still precedes (x). It is, in fact, impossible to get the universal quantifier to the first position. Indeed the best we can do is use our rule of quantifier equivalence, from section 4.3.2, to get,

6. $(\exists x) \sim Sx$ v $\sim Sa$	5	**QE**

We have managed to get a quantifier to the left-most position, but it is an existential quantifier and thus not of a form suitable for **UI**.

There are, however, valid inferences, of a sort we have not yet considered, that follow from existentially quantified formulas. If it is true that some philosophers are wise, then it must follow that there is an individual, call

---

[7]This example is due to Richard B. Angell.

him a, who is both a philosopher and wise. Symbolically,

$$\frac{(\exists x)(Px \ \& \ Wx)}{\therefore Pa \ \& \ Wa}$$

Who is a? a is the, or one of the, wise philosophers that must exist, if it is true that some philosophers are wise. Some confusion arises here over the role of the individual constant. So long as we have an existential statement, asserting that there is one individual having some particular property, we are free to give that individual some arbitrarily chosen name. The key term here is "arbitrarily chosen." We cannot choose to call the individual by a name that has already appeared in the context of the argument under consideration, for that would be to assume what is not given.

We must now seek to generalize our example into a rule of inference, which we will call *existential instantiation* (**EI**).

$$\textbf{EI} \quad \frac{(\exists \mu)\phi\mu}{\therefore \phi\omega}$$

where ω is an *individual constant* that appears at no prior stage in the proof. Here, as before, our symbolic conventions avoid the "proving" of certain invalid arguments. For example,

1. $(\exists x)(Px \equiv Px)$ $/ \therefore Pa \equiv Pb$
2. $Pa \equiv Pb$ 1 **EI** (erroneous)

This obviously erroneous proof violates our symbolic convention, since $Pa \equiv Pb$ cannot be gotten from $Px \equiv Px$ by replacing the free occurrences of x by an individual constant. Similarly our restriction that in an **EI** ω must be an individual constant that appears in no prior line will avoid such erroneous "proofs" as

1. $(\exists x)Px$
2. $(\exists x) \sim Px$ $/ \therefore Pa \ \& \sim Pa$
3. Pa 1 **EI**
4. $\sim Pa$ 2 **EI** (erroneous)
5. $Pa \ \& \sim Pa$ 3,4 Conj.

This "proof" of our invalid argument is stopped at step 4 by our restriction. Since *a* appears in step 3, we may not existentially instantiate to *a* in line 4.

We have insisted that ω be an individual constant in uses of **EI** because our extended notion of validity, as presented on page 173, would not countenance as valid the inference:

$$\frac{(\exists x)Px}{\therefore Py}$$

since it is clearly possible that for some substitution instances the conclusion is false while the premise is true.

We will soon have to add a complication to our uses of **EI** in the light of certain difficulties that arise in connection with another kind of inference involving quantifiers, viz., universal generalization. But before considering universal generalization and the added complication to existential instantiation, we turn our attention to still another kind of valid inference involving quantifiers.

Consider the clearly valid inference:

$$\frac{\text{Socrates is a wise philosopher.}}{\therefore \text{Some philosophers are wise.}}$$

or symbolically,

$$\frac{Ps \ \& \ Ws}{\therefore (\exists x)(Px \ \& \ Wx)}$$

From the fact that a given individual has a certain property it surely does follow that some individual has that property. We will call this rule of inference, of which the argument above is an application, the *rule of existential generalization* (**EG**). We will write the rule of **EG**

$$\mathbf{EG} \ \frac{\varnothing\omega}{\therefore (\exists\mu)\varnothing\mu}$$

once again using our symbolic conventions to avoid certain erroneous uses of our rule. The invalid argument

$$\frac{(x)(\exists y)(Fx \equiv \sim Fy)}{\therefore (\exists x)(Fx \equiv \sim Fx)}$$

might be thought to be proven by the steps

1. $(x)(\exists y)(Fx \equiv \sim Fy)$ $/\therefore (\exists x)(Fx \equiv \sim Fx)$
2. $(\exists y)(Fx \equiv \sim Fy)$ 1 **UI**
3. $Fx \equiv \sim Fa$ 2 **EI**
4. $(\exists x)(Fx \equiv \sim Fx)$ 3 **EG** (erroneous)

That the argument is invalid can be seen by considering that the conclusion is self-contradictory and thus false in every universe, whereas the premise is true in a universe of more than one individual where some individuals in the universe have the property F and some do not. The "proof" goes wrong at step 4 since you cannot get $Fx \equiv \sim Fa$ by replacing the free occurrences of x in $Fx \equiv \sim Fx$ by a (or x, for that matter).

No further restrictions beyond those contained in the way we have written **EG** are needed. We thus go on to our final new rule of inference, *universal generalization* (**UG**).

If we recall our expanded notion of validity, we will see that the following argument is valid:

$$\frac{Py}{\therefore (x)Px}$$

For if it is true that every individual we choose has the property P, it follows that all individuals have the property P.

We can state the rule of which this is an instance as,

UG $$\frac{\emptyset\omega}{\therefore (\mu)\emptyset\mu}$$

where ω must be a variable. It should be noted that severe restrictions must be placed on our rule since clearly the individual variable that ω designates may not have arisen in just any way.

The method of conditional proof introduced in Chapter 3 is, as has been noted, justifiably used in the predicate logic. The only new factor in the use of conditional proof is that given our expanded notion of valid inference, we may introduce propositional functions as well as propositions as conditional assumptions. We must, however, place certain restrictions on our rule of **UG** insofar as it is used on a $\emptyset\omega$ that lies in the scope of a conditional assumption.

Consider the following invalid argument and its "proof,"

$$\frac{(x)(Fx \supset Fx)}{\therefore (x)(Fx \supset (y)Fy)}$$

	1. $(x)(Fx \supset Fx)$	$/\therefore (x)(Fx \supset (y)Fy)$
C1	2. Fx	
C1	3. $(y)Fy$	2 **UG** (erroneous)
C1	4. $Fx \supset (y)Fy$	2,3
	5. $(x)(Fx \supset (y)Fy)$	4 **UG**

The reader can verify the invalidity of the argument by considering it in a universe of two individuals. In order to "stop" the "proof" we add the follow-restriction to our rule of **UG**.

1. ω must be a variable that does not occur free in any conditional assumption on which $\emptyset\omega$ depends.

In the "proof" we find that the **UG** at line 3 is performed on a $\emptyset\omega$ that depends on a conditional assumption (in this case, itself). And we find that ω does occur free in that conditional assumption on which $\emptyset\omega$ depends; thus the **UG** at line 3 is erroneous by restriction 1.

A further restriction on **UG** is needed to avoid such "proofs" as the following:

1. $(x)(Fx \equiv Fx)$	$/\therefore (x)(y)(Fx \equiv Fy)$
2. $Fx \equiv Fx$	1 **UI**
3. $(y)(Fx \equiv Fy)$	2 **UG** (erroneous)
4. $(x)(y)(Fx \equiv Fy)$	3 **UG**

The argument "proved" is invalid, as can once again be shown in a universe of two individuals. The "proof," however, violates none of our rules or restrictions so far given. We thus introduce the further restriction,

2. ω must not occur free in $(\mu) \emptyset\mu$.

There remains one further difficulty with our rule of **UG** as it now stands. This difficulty arises in proofs involving universal generalization where previous existential instantiations have taken place. Consider the following "proof" of an invalid argument.

1. $(x)(\exists y)(Fx \equiv \sim Fy)$ $/\therefore (x)(Fx \equiv \sim Fa)$
2. $(\exists y)(Fx \equiv \sim Fy)$ 1 **UI**
3. $Fx \equiv \sim Fa$ 2 **EI**
4. $(x)(Fx \equiv \sim Fa)$ 3 **UG**

The reader can easily show that the argument "proved" is invalid, yet it violates none of our rules or restrictions as given to this point. In order to avoid such erroneous "proofs" we will insist that all occurrences of ω introduced by **EI** must be subscripted with all free variables occurring in $(\exists \mu) \emptyset \mu$ and that when using **UG**, μ must not be a variable that occurs as a subscript in $\emptyset \omega$.

Thus our "proof" becomes

1. $(x)(\exists y)(Fx \equiv \sim Fy)$ $/\therefore (x)(Fx \equiv \sim Fa)$
2. $(\exists y)(Fx \equiv \sim Fy)$ 1 **UI**
3. $Fx \equiv \sim Fa_x$ 2 **EI**
4. $(x)(Fx \equiv \sim Fa_x)$ 4 **UG** (erroneous)

The individual variable a introduced by **EI** in step 3 is subscripted with an x since x occurs free in step 2, which is $(\exists \mu) \emptyset \mu$. The use of **UG** at step 4 is in violation of our new restriction on **UG**, since x occurs as a subscript in step 3 which is $\emptyset \omega$. It is important that all subscripts introduced through **EI** be treated as occurrences of individual variables as regards our quantification rules and their restrictions. Thus if we have

1. $(\exists x)(Pa_y \,\&\, Rx)$

as some line in a proof, we would not get

2. $(Pa_y \,\&\, Rb)$

by **EI** on 1; we would get instead

3. $(Pa_y \,\&\, Pb_y)$

where the b is subscripted with a y because the occurrence of y in 1 is a free occurrence of y and our rule of **EI** states that all occurrences of ω introduced by **EI** must be subscripted with all the free variables occurring in $(\exists \mu) \emptyset \mu$.

183

This treatment of subscripting will also keep us from trying to get around the erroneous step 4 in the above "proof" by writing the erroneous "proof"

1. $(x)(\exists y)(Fx \equiv \sim Fy)$ $/\therefore (y)(Fy \equiv \sim Fa)$
2. $(\exists y)(Fx \equiv \sim Fy)$ 1   **UI**
3. $Fx \equiv \sim Fa_x$ 2   **EI**
4. $(y)(Fy \equiv \sim Fa_x)$ 3   **UG**   (erroneous)

since step 4 is erroneous for it contains a free occurrence of ω, i.e., x, as the subscript of a.

4.4.1   Summary of rules of quantification

UI $\dfrac{(\mu)\emptyset\mu}{\therefore \emptyset\omega}$

UG $\dfrac{\emptyset\omega}{\therefore (\mu)\emptyset\mu}$

where ω is a variable.

Restriction 1. ω must not occur free in any conditional assumption on which $\emptyset\omega$ depends.

Restriction 2. ω must not occur occur free in $(\mu)\emptyset\mu$.

Restriction 3. μ must not be a variable that occurs as a subscript in $\emptyset\omega$.

EI $\dfrac{(\exists\mu)\emptyset\mu}{\therefore \emptyset\omega}$

where ω is a constant and all occurrences of ω introduced by **EI** must be subscripted with all the free variables occurring in $(\exists\mu)\emptyset\mu$.

Restriction 1. ω must not appear in a prior line.

EG $\dfrac{\emptyset\omega}{\therefore (\exists\mu)\emptyset\mu}$

It is to be noted that we have not placed any restrictions on our quantification rules that would keep us from validating the inference from $(x)\emptyset x$ to $(\exists x)\emptyset x$. We may simply write

1. $(x)\phi x$ $/\therefore (\exists x)\phi x$
2. ϕa 1 **UI**
3. $(\exists x)\phi x$ 2 **EG**

without violating our rules of **UI** or **EG**. It is clear, then, that our predicate logic makes an existential presupposition but that that presupposition is very limited. All that we assume is that the universe of discourse is nonempty, and so long as we take the universal class to be our universe of discourse, as we have suggested, our existential presupposition is the even more limited claim that there is at least one member of the universal class, i.e., the universal class is nonempty. It is to be noted that under this presupposition there may be many empty classes, but not all classes may be empty. Thus the inference from "All A are B" to "Some A are B" is still blocked, since A may be empty.

The reader should convince himself that our rules will not allow a validation of the inference from $(x)(Ax \supset Bx)$ to $(\exists x)(Ax \mathbin{\&} Bx)$.

Having completed the introduction of our new rules for the predicate logic we now include several examples of arguments and their proofs using the rules now at our disposal.

    A.   All philosophers are wise.
          All intellectuals are snobs.
       $\therefore$ If all who are wise are intellectuals all philosophers are snobs.

which we symbolize as

$(x)(Px \supset Wx)$
$(x)(Ix \supset Sx)$
$\therefore (x)(Wx \supset Ix) \supset (y)(Py \supset Sy)$

and prove

       1. $(x)(Px \supset Wx)$
       2. $(x)(Ix \supset Sx)$ $/\therefore (x)(Wx \supset Ix) \supset (y)(Py \supset Sy)$
C1   3. $(x)(Wx \supset Ix)$
       4. $Px \supset Wx$ 1 **UI**
       5. $Ix \supset Sx$ 2 **UI**
C1   6. $Wx \supset Ix$ 3 **UI**
C1   7. $Px \supset Ix$ 4,6 H.S.

185

C1   8. $Px \supset Sx$ 7,5 H.S.
C1   9. $(y)(Py \supset Sy)$ 8 **UG**
C1 10. $(x)(Wx \supset Ix) \supset (y)(Py \supset Sy)$ 3,9

    B.   If all unicorns are red then all unicorn tapestries are incorrect
           representations.
        There are no unicorns.
        There are unicorn tapestries.

        ∴ There are incorrect representations.

which we symbolize as

      $(x)(Ux \supset Rx) \supset (y)(Ty \supset Iy)$
      $\sim(\exists x)Ux$
      $(\exists x)Tx$
      $\therefore (\exists x)Ix$

and prove

     1. $(x)(Ux \supset Rx) \supset (y)(Ty \supset Iy)$
     2. $\sim(\exists x)Ux$
     3. $(\exists x)Tx$ /∴ $(\exists x) Ix$
     4. $\sim\sim(x) \sim Ux$ 2 **QE**
     5. $(x) \sim Ux$ 4 D.N.
     6. $\sim Ux$ 5 **UI**
     7. $\sim Ux \lor Rx$ 6 Add.
     8. $Ux \supset Rx$ 7 Impl.
     9. $(x)(Ux \supset Rx)$ 8 **UG**
   10. $(y)(Ty \supset Iy)$ 1, 9 M.P.
   11. Ta 3 **EI**
   12. $Ta \supset Ia$ 10 **UI**
   13. Ia 11,12 M.P.
   14. $(\exists x)Ix$ 13 **EG**

    C.   If anyone is tall then someone is short.
       No one is short.
      ∴ No one is tall.

which we symbolize

      $(x)(\exists y)(Tx \supset Sy)$
      $\sim(\exists x)Sx$
      $\therefore \sim(\exists x)Tx$

and prove

1. $(x)(\exists y)(Tx \supset Sy)$
2. $\sim(\exists x)Sx$ /∴ $\sim(\exists x)Tx$
3. $(\exists y)(Tx \supset Sy)$ 1 **UI**
4. $Tx \supset Sa_x$ 3 **EI**
5. $\sim\sim(x)\sim Sx$ 2 **QE**
6. $(x)\sim Sx$ 5 D.N.
7. $\sim Sa$ 6 **UI**
8. $\sim Tx$ 4,7 M.T.
9. $(x)\sim Tx$ 8 **UG**
10. $\sim(\exists x)\sim\sim Tx$ 9 **QE**
11. $\sim(\exists x)Tx$ 10 D.N.

It is again to be noted that Sa and Sa_x are to be treated as identical for all purposes except **UG** and **EI**. Thus step 8 in the last proof is quite legitimate.

EXERCISES

1 Locate all the errors in each of the following erroneous "proofs."

  a. 1. $(x)(Px \supset Rx)$ /∴ $(\exists x)Px \supset Ra$
      2. $Px \supset Ra$ 1 **UI**
      3. $(\exists x)Px \supset Ra$ 2 **EG**

  b. 1. $(x)(\exists y)(Px \supset Ry)$ /∴ $(\exists x)(Px \supset Rx)$
      2. $(\exists y)(Py \supset Ry)$ 1 **UI**
      3. $Pa \supset Ra$ 2 **EI**
      4. $(\exists x)(Px \supset Rx)$ 3 **EG**

  c. 1. $(x)(\exists y)[(Sx \& \sim Ry) \supset Px]$ /∴ $(y)[(Sy \& \sim Ra) \supset Py]$
      2. $(\exists y)[(Sx \& \sim Ry) \supset Px]$ 1 **UI**
      3. $(Sx \& \sim Ra_x) \supset Px$ 2 **EI**
      4. $(y)[(Sy \& \sim Ra_x) \supset Py]$ 3 **UG**

  d. 1. $(\exists y)(\exists x)[(Py \lor Sx) \& Rx]$ /∴ $(y)(x)(Px \lor Sy)$
      2. $(\exists x)[(Pa \lor Sx) \& Rx]$ 1 **EI**
      3. $(Pa \lor Sa) \& Ra$ 2 **EI**
      4. $Pa \lor Sa$ 3 Simp.
      5. $(x)(Px \lor Sa)$ 4 **UG**
      6. $(y)(x)(Px \lor Sy)$ 5 **UG**

  e. 1. $(x)(\exists y)[Px \equiv (Ry \& Sy)]$ /∴ $(x)[Px \supset (Ra \& Sa)]$
      2. $(\exists y)[Px \equiv (Ry \& Sy)]$ 1 **UI**
      3. $Px \equiv (Ra_x \& Sa_x)$ 2 **EI**
      4. $[Px \supset (Ra_x \& Sa_x)] \& [(Ra_x \& Sa_x) \supset Px]$ 3 Equiv.
      5. $Px \supset (Ra_x \& Sa_x)$ 4. Simp.
      6. $(x)[Px \supset (Ra_x \& Sa_x)]$ 5 **UG**

f. 1. $(x)(\exists z)(\exists y) [(Rz \supset Sy) \& Px]$
    2. $(y)Sy \supset Ra$ $/\therefore (\exists y)(Sy \supset Sy)$
C1 3. Sy
    4. $(\exists z)(\exists y) [(Rz \supset Sy) \& Px]$ 1 **UI**
    5. $(\exists y) [(Ra_x \supset Sy) \& Px]$ 4 **EI**
    6. $(Ra_x \supset Sb) \& Px$ 5 **EI**
    7. $Ra_x \supset Sb$ 6 Simp.
C1 8. $(y)Sy$ 3 **UG**
C1 9. Ra 2,8 M.P.
C1 10. Sb 7,9 M.P.
C1 11. $Sy \supset Sb$ 3,10
    12. $(\exists y)(Sy \supset Sy)$ 11 **EG**

g. 1. $(\exists x)(y)(Fx \supset \sim Fy)$
    2. $(x)(y)(\sim Fy \supset Sx)$ $/\therefore (y) \{Fy \supset [(Fa \supset Sy) \& (x)Fx] \}$
C1 3. Fy
    4. $(y)(Fa \supset \sim Fy)$ 1 **EI**
    5. $Fa \supset \sim Fy$ 4 **UI**
    6. $(y)(\sim Fy \supset Sx)$ 2 **UI**
    7. $\sim Fy \supset Sx$ 6 **UI**
    8. $Fa \supset Sx$ 5,7 H.S.
C1 9. $(x)Fx$ 3 **UG**
C1 10. $(Fa \supset Sx) \& (x)Fx$ 8,9 Conj.
C1 11. $Fy \supset [(Fa \supset Sx) \& (x)Fx]$ 3,10
    12. $(y) \{Fy \supset [(Fa \supset Sy) \& (x)Fx] \}$ 11 **UG**

h. 1. $(\exists z) \sim Pz \supset (x)Rx$ $/\therefore (z)(y) [(\sim Py \vee Sy) \& \sim Sz] \supset (x)Rx$
C1 2. $(y) [(\sim Py \vee Sy) \& \sim Sx]$
C1 3. $(\sim Pz \vee Sz) \& \sim Sx$ 2 **UI**
C1 4. $(y) [(\sim Py \vee Sy) \& \sim Sy]$ 3 **UG**
C1 5. $(\sim Pa \vee Sa) \& \sim Sa$ 4 **UI**
C1 6. $\sim Pa \vee Sa$ 5 Simp.
C1 7. $\sim Sa \& (\sim Pa \vee Sa)$ 5 Com.
C1 8. $\sim Sa$ 7 Simp.
C1 9. $Sa \vee \sim Pa$ 6 Com.
C1 10. $\sim Pa$ 8,9 D.S.
C1 11. $(\exists z) \sim Pz$ 10 **EG**
C1 12. $(x)Rx$ 1,11 M.P.
C1 13. $(y) [(\sim Py \vee Sy) \& \sim Sx] \supset (x)Rx$ 2,12
    14. $(z)(y) [(\sim Py \vee Sy) \& \sim Sz] \supset (x)Rx$ 13 **UG**

2 Construct proofs of the following valid arguments:
    a. $(\exists x)(Px \& Qx) \supset (y)(Wy \supset Ly)$
          $(\exists y)(Wy \& \sim Ly)$
         $\overline{\therefore (x)(Px \supset \sim Qx)}$

    b. $(x)(Qx \supset Vx)$
          $(x) [(Vx \& Qx) \supset Px]$
         $\overline{\therefore (x) [\sim Qx \vee (Vx \& Px)]}$

c. $(x) [(Px \lor Rx) \supset Sx]$
$(\exists x)(Px \& Ex)$
$(\exists x)(Px \& Fx)$
$(\exists x)(Rx \& \sim Sx)$
$\overline{\therefore (\exists x)(Ex \& Fx)}$

d. $(x)(\exists y) [Px \supset (Rx \lor Sy)]$
$\sim(\exists x)(Rx \lor \sim Qx)$
$(x)Px$
$\overline{\therefore (\exists x)Sx}$

e. $(x)(\exists y)(Fx \equiv \sim Fy)$
$(x) [(Px \& \sim Rx) \supset Fx]$
$\overline{\therefore (y) [(Py \& \sim Ry) \supset (\exists x) \sim Fx]}$

3 Symbolize and prove the following valid arguments:

a. Anyone who wants to lose weight must work hard at it. You cannot work hard at something if you have little spare time. You will succeed in losing weight if you have spare time. Therefore, if someone who wants to lose weight has spare time then if he works hard at it he will succeed.

b. Anytime when some politician is dishonest the country suffers. The time is now and Senator Q is dishonest. Therefore, the country is suffering.

c. If anyone is worthy of praise then all Nobel Prize winners are to be congratulated. All great physicists are worthy of praise. Some Nobel Prize winners are great physicists. Therefore, some of those worthy of praise are to be congratulated.

d. Any existentialist who is a positivist is both confused and derided. Therefore, if any existentialist is a scientist and all scientists are positivists then he is confused.

e. All mothers are either worried about their children or are asleep. No mothers who are insomniacs are asleep. Therefore, if all insomniacs are mothers then all insomniacs are worried about their children.

f. If there are any pessimists then all existentialists are pessimists. If there are any unhappy people then all pessimists are unhappy people. Therefore, if there are unhappy pessimists then all existentialists are unhappy.

g. All beef and chicken is to be eaten immediately or frozen. Anything is a chicken if and only if it is an irrational feathered biped. No irrational feathered biped is to be frozen. Therefore, all chicken is to be eaten immediately.

h. Pragmatists and rationalists are philosophers. Philosophers and psychologists are erudite. Erudite people are entertaining but perplexing. Some pragmatists are neither entertaining nor kind. Therefore, some rationalists are kind but not entertaining.

    i. There is nothing which is not either feathered or not a bird. All things that are feathered or winged are oviparous. Therefore, all birds are oviparous.

    j. There is nothing that is valuable and not rare, and there is nothing that is rare and not coveted. Anything is valueless if and only if it is unwanted. All unwanted things are discarded and all discarded things are rubbish. Therefore, there is nothing that is not coveted and not rubbish.

4.4.2 Proving logical truths

In Chapter 3 the reader was shown how certain formulas could be proven to be tautologies by means of the method of conditional proof and our 19 rules. Tautologies were defined as those formulas that never had the value false in the defining column of their truth tables. Thus, only those formulas which have truth tables can be tautologies. We have seen that there are formulas of the predicate logic that cannot be adequately captured by truth tables[8] and, therefore, cannot be tautologies. On the other hand, it is quite clear that there are formulas of the predicate logic that are never false, e.g.,

$$(x)(Fx \equiv Fx)$$

yet we do not want to call them tautologies as you cannot write the truth table for $(x)(Fx \equiv Fx)$. Any formula that is always true will be called a *logical truth*. By our definition all tautologies are logical truths but not all logical truths are tautologies.

Several logical truths have played important roles in the preceding sections. In section 4.1 we argued that the formula

$$(x)(Hx \supset Sa)$$

was equivalent to the formula

$$(\exists x)Hx \supset Sa.$$

which was to say that the formula

[8] See section 4.2.1.

1. $[(x)(Hx \supset Sa)] \equiv [(\exists x)Hx \supset Sa]$

is a logical truth. We can now prove a more general logical truth of which this formula is a special case. The logical truth in question is

2. $[(x)(\emptyset x \supset Q)] \equiv [(\exists x)\emptyset x \supset Q]$

where $\emptyset x$ is any propositional function containing at least one free occurrence of x and Q contains no free occurrences of x.[9] We will proceed by first proving

3. $[(x)(\emptyset x \supset Q)] \supset [(\exists x)\emptyset x \supset Q]$

and then,

4. $[(\exists x)\emptyset x \supset Q] \supset [(x)(\emptyset x \supset Q)]$

From 3 and 4 we get 2 by the rules of conjunction and material equivalence.

The proof of 3 is:

C1	1. $(x)(\emptyset x \supset Q)$	
C2	2. $(\exists x)\emptyset x$	
C2	3. $\emptyset a$	2 **EI**
C1	4. $\emptyset a \supset Q$	1 **UI**
C1,2	5. Q	3,4 M.P.
C1,2	6. $(\exists x)\emptyset x \supset Q$	2,5
C1	7. $[(x)(\emptyset x \supset Q)] \supset [(\exists x)\emptyset x \supset Q]$	1,6

The proof of 4 is:

C1	1. $(\exists x)\emptyset x \supset Q$	
C2	2. $\emptyset x$	
C2	3. $(\exists x)\emptyset x$	2 **EG**

[9]We specify that $\emptyset x$ contains at least one free occurrence of x in order to prevent 2 from degenerating into the trivially true

$(P \supset Q) \equiv (P \supset Q)$

since when there are no free occurrences of x in $\emptyset x$ the quantifiers (x) and $(\exists x)$ are non-operative.

C1,2	4. Q	1,3 M.P.
C1,2	5. $\emptyset x \supset Q$	2,4
C1	6. $(x)(\emptyset x \supset Q)$	5 **UG**
C1	7. $[(\exists x)\emptyset x \supset Q] \supset [\emptyset x \supset Q]$	1,6

In section 4.3.2 we introduced the rule of quantifier equivalence, which we can now justify more fully by proving that the following two formulas

5. $(x)\emptyset x \equiv \sim(\exists x)\sim\emptyset x$
6. $\sim(x)\sim\emptyset x \equiv (\exists x)\emptyset x$

are logical truths.

We prove 5 to be a logical truth by proving that 5'

$5'. (x)\emptyset x \supset \sim(\exists x)\sim\emptyset x$

and

$5''. \sim(\exists x)\sim\emptyset x \supset (x)\emptyset x$

are logical truths from which the logical truth of 5 follows by the rules of conjunction and material equivalence.

The proof of $(x)\emptyset x \supset \sim(\exists x)\sim\emptyset x$ runs

C1	1. $(x)\emptyset x$	
C2	2. $(\exists x)\sim\emptyset x$	
C2	3. $\sim\emptyset a$	2 **EI**
C1	4. $\emptyset a$	1 **UI**
C1	5. $\emptyset a \vee \sim(\exists x)\sim\emptyset x$	4 Add.
C1,2	6. $\sim(\exists x)\sim\emptyset x$	5,3 D.S.
C1,2	7. $(\exists x)\sim\emptyset x \supset \sim(\exists x)\sim\emptyset x$	2,6
C1	8. $\sim(\exists x)\sim\emptyset x \vee \sim(\exists x)\sim\emptyset x$	7 Impl.
C1	9. $\sim(\exists x)\sim\emptyset x$	8 Taut.
C1	10. $(x)\emptyset x \supset \sim(\exists x)\sim\emptyset x$	1,9

The proof of $\sim(\exists x)\sim\emptyset x \supset (x)\emptyset x$ is as follows:

C1	1. $\sim(\exists x)\sim\emptyset x$	
C2	2. $\sim\emptyset x$	
C2	3. $(\exists x)\sim\emptyset x$	2 **EG**

C2	4. $\sim\emptyset x \supset (\exists x) \sim\emptyset x$	2,3
C1	5. $\sim\sim\sim\emptyset x$	4,1 M.T.
C1	6. $\emptyset x$	5 D.N.
C1	7. $(x)\emptyset x$	6 **UG**
C1	8. $\sim(\exists x) \sim\emptyset x \supset (x)\emptyset x$	1,7

The proof of the logical truth $\sim(x) \sim\emptyset x \equiv (\exists x)\emptyset x$ is left to the reader.

EXERCISE

1 Prove that the following formulas are logical truths, where $\emptyset x$ and ψx are propositional functions containing at least one free occurrence of x, and A contains no free occurrence of x.

a. $\sim(x)\emptyset x \equiv (\exists x) \sim\emptyset x$

b. $\sim(\exists x)\emptyset x \equiv (x) \sim\emptyset x$

c. $(\exists x) [\emptyset x \vee \psi x] \equiv [(\exists x)\emptyset x \vee (\exists x) \psi x]$

d. $[(x)\emptyset x \vee (x)\psi x] \supset (x) [\emptyset x \vee \psi x]$

e. $\sim\{(x) [\emptyset x \vee \psi x] \supset [(x)\emptyset x \vee (x)\psi x] \}$

f. $(\exists x) [\emptyset x \& A] \equiv [(\exists x)\emptyset x \& A]$

g. $(\exists x) [\emptyset x \supset A] \equiv [(x)\emptyset x \supset A]$

h. $(\exists x) [A \supset \emptyset x] \equiv [A \supset (\exists x)\emptyset x]$

i. $(x) [A \supset \emptyset x] \equiv [A \supset (x)\emptyset x]$

j. $[(\exists x)\emptyset x \supset (\exists x)\psi x] \supset (\exists x) [\emptyset x \supset \psi x]$

4.5 RELATIONAL PREDICATES

The predicate logic, as so far presented, is still not adequate for the job of evaluating all arguments given in natural language. In particular it cannot deal with the valid argument:

A. Some Vice Presidents hate all intellectuals.
_____

∴ If Mr. C is an intellectual some Vice Presidents will hate him.

The reader will note, on trying, that this argument is more than a little difficult to symbolize using the predicate logic as so far presented. The difficulty lies specifically with the predicates we have so far allowed.

All the predicates we have dealt with to this point have been properties, or qualities, etc. that were properly predicated of an individual. But not all predicates are of this sort. Consider the propositions

1. John is the father of George.
2. The number four is larger than the number two.
3. Spiro hates Mr. C.

If we allow F to be the predicate "is the father of George" we could symbolize 1 as

Fj

But we could better display the structure of 1 if we allowed F to be the predicate "is the father of." Now the phrase "is the father of" cannot be sensibly completed by the name of a single individual. Thus "is the father of George" is not a proposition, nor is "John is the father of" a proposition. But "is the father of" is sensibly completed by the names of two individuals, e.g., by "John" and "George." We will then write 1 using F for "is the father of," j for "John," and g for "George" as

Fj, g

Any predicate that is naturally completed by two individuals is termed a *diadic predicate* or diadic relation. Some examples of diadic predicates would be,

is greater than
is to the right of
is taller than

The propositions 2 and 3 above both contain diadic predicates. Using L for "is larger than," proposition 2 can be symbolized

$L\ 4,2$

While using H for "hates," s for Spiro, and c for Mr. C, proposition 3 can be symbolized

Hs, c

In general, using R for a diadic predicate and x and y for individual variables, all propositions of the form 1, 2, and 3 can be written

Rx, y

It should be recognized that Rx, y is a propositional function and therefore can be turned into a proposition not only by replacing x and y with individual variables, but also by quantifying them.

Consider the proposition

4. Everyone is taller than John.

Using Tx, y for "x is taller than y," Px for "x is a person," and j for "John," we may symbolize it as

$(x)(Px \supset Tx, j)$

The formula says that for all x, if x is a person then x is taller than John, or everyone is taller than John.

Now consider the proposition

5. Everyone is taller than someone or other.

Using Tx, y for "x is a taller person than y," we can symbolize it as

$(x)(\exists y)(Tx, y)$

which says that for all x there exists a y such that x is a taller person than y, which says the same thing as proposition 5.

We can now symbolize the argument in A above using Vx for "x is a Vice President," Hx,y for "x hates y," Ix for "x is an intellectual," and c for "Mr. C," getting

A'. $\underline{(\exists x)\ [Vx\ \&\ (y)(Iy \supset Hx, y)]}$
$\therefore Ic \supset (\exists x)(Vx\ \&\ Hx, c)$

Nothing new needs to be said regarding our rules of inference in our expanded predicate logic. We have all that we need to prove A' and the proof follows:

1. $(\exists x)\ [Vx\ \&\ (y)(Iy \supset Hx, y)]$ $/\therefore Ic \supset (\exists x)(Vx\ \&\ Hx, c)$
2. $Va\ \&\ (y)(Iy \supset Ha, y)$ 1 **EI**

	3. $(y)(Iy \supset Ha,y)$ & Va	2 Com.
	4. $(Ic \supset Ha,c)$ & Va	3 **UI**
	5. $Ic \supset Ha,c$	4 Simp.
C1	6. Ic	
C1	7. Ha,c	5,6 M.P.
	8. Va	2 Simp.
C1	9. Va & Ha,c	8,7 Conj.
C1	10. $(\exists x)(Vx$ & $Hx,c)$	9 **EG**
C1	11. $Ic \supset (\exists x)(Vx$ & $Hx,c)$	6,10

The reader should carefully scrutinize this proof and note that every step does conform to the indicated rule despite the presence of our diadic predicate. One thing that does change regarding our quantifiers when we allow diadic predicates is that their order becomes much more significant. Consider the diadic predicate Lx, y meaning "x loves y" in all the following quantificational possibilities:

6. $(x)(y)Lx,y$
7. $(y)(x)Lx,y$
8. $(\exists x)(\exists y)Lx,y$
9. $(\exists y)(\exists x)Lx,y$
10. $(x)(\exists y)Lx,y$
11. $(\exists y)(x)Lx,y$
12. $(\exists x)(y)Lx,y$
13. $(y)(\exists x)Lx,y$

Let us try to see what each of these formulas say assuming that our universe of discourse is persons, i.e., that x and y range only over persons. Formula 6 says that for all x and all y, x loves y, or

Everyone loves everyone.

Formula 7 says that for all y and all x, x loves y, which says,

Everyone is loved by everyone.

Thus formulas 6 and 7 seem to say the same thing. Proposition 8 says that there exists at least one x and at least one y, such that x loves y, or more naturally,

Somebody loves somebody.

It should be obvious that 9 says the same thing,

Somebody is loved by somebody.

Thus it would seem that when both quantifiers are universal or when both quantifiers are existential, the quantifier order does not matter, at least in the case of the predicate "loves."

In each of the propositions 10-13, we have both existential and universal quantifiers. Proposition 10 says that for all x, there exists a y, such that x loves y. But what does this mean? Does proposition 10 say that there is some particular individual such that everybody loves him or does it say rather that for every person there exists someone or other that he loves? It can be shown that the latter is the meaning of 10. If we consider what 10 says in a universe of three individuals, e.g., we can see that this is the case. In such a universe containing the individuals a, b, and c, proposition 10 becomes

10'. $[(La, a) \vee (La, b) \vee (La, c)]$ & $[(Lb, a) \vee (Lb, b) \vee (Lb, c)]$ &
$[(Lc, a) \vee (Lc, b) \vee (Lc, c)]$

Now 10' is clearly saying of a that he loves himself, or he loves b, or he loves c, i.e., that he loves someone or other in his universe. And 10' also says the same thing about b and c, each of them loves someone or other in their universe. Thus we may conclude that proposition 10 says

Everyone, individually, loves somebody or other.

Now let us consider

11. $(\exists y)(x)Lx, y$

Does proposition 11 say the same thing as 10 or does it rather say that there is someone or other who is loved by everyone collectively? By using the same techniques we used in our investigation of 10 we can see that 11 means the latter. In a universe of the three individuals a, b, and c proposition 11 becomes

$[(La, a)$ & (Lb, a) & $(Lc, a)]$ $\vee$ $[(La, b)$ & (Lb, b) & $(Lc, b)]$
$\vee$ $[(La, c)$ & (Lb, c) & $(Lc, c)]$

which clearly says that either every member of the universe loves a, or every member loves b, or every member loves c. Thus proposition 11 does say that

Someone or other is loved by everyone, collectively.

It should be noted then that whereas "Someone or other is loved by everyone, collectively" implies "Everyone, individually loves somebody or other," the converse is not the case, and therefore propositions 10 and 11 are not equivalent. We can prove that proposition 11 implies 10 thus:

1. $(\exists y)(x)Lx, y$ $/\therefore (x)(\exists y)Lx, y$
2. $(x)Lx, a$ 1 **EI**
3. Lx, a 2 **UI**
4. $(\exists y)Lx, y$ 3 **EG**
5. $(x)(\exists y)Lx, y$ 4 **UG**

It is left to the reader to prove that proposition 10 does not imply 11; a universe of two individuals is suggested.

In a similar fashion the reader should convince himself that

12. $(\exists x)(y)Lx, y$

means

There exists someone or other that loves everyone, collectively.

and that

13. $(y)(\exists x)Lx, y$

means

Everyone, individually, is loved by someone or other.

The importance of quantifier order in cases of relational predicates can also be seen by considering the following two formulas:

14. $(x)(\exists y)Sx, y$
15. $(\exists y)(x)Sx, y$

where x and y range over numbers and Sx, y means "x is less than y." On the basis of our foregoing discussion it should be clear that $(x)(\exists y)Sx, y$ says

Every number, individually, is less than some number or other.

whereas $(\exists y)(x)Sx, y$ says

Some number or other is less than every number, collectively.

More simply proposition 14 says that there is no largest number, whereas 15 says that there is a number smaller than any number. Thus propositions 14 and 15 are quite different, indeed one is true and the other false.

All the relational predicates we have considered, so far, have been diadic, i.e., relations that hold between two individuals. There are, however, triadic relational predicates with which we are all familiar. An example of such a predicate is "between" as in "a is between b and c." We will symbolize "a is between b and c" by

Ba, b, c

The simple proposition

16. Not everything is between two other things.

may be symbolized using Bx, y, z as "x is between y and z" thus

$\sim(x)(\exists y)(\exists z)Bx, y, z$

which the reader should prove is equivalent to

$(\exists x)(y)(z) \sim Bx, y, z$

Some other triadic predicates are

x is the only child of y and z.
x is the arithmetic mean of y and z.
x and y are the extremities of z.

199

In English there exist quadratic predicates as well, e.g., "w and x are the twin daughters of y and z," which might be symbolized, Tw, x, y, z. There is no reason why there might not be a relational predicate standing between any given number of individuals, though there may not in fact exist such a predicate in natural language.

EXERCISES

1 Symbolize the following propositions:
  a. If anyone can beat Irving at chess Ralph can.
  b. If everyone is taller than Tara then Mark is taller than Tara.
  c. There are philosophers who do not understand any existentialists.
  d. Every existentialist understands every philosopher.
  e. There is a gymnosophist who is disliked by all gymnosophists.
  f. At least one gymnosophist does not like all gymnosophists.
  g. Anyone who knows everything should be on the faculty.
  h. Everyone hates someone at some time or other.
  i. If Simon loves Sandy, then someone loves someone.
  j. Causes always precede their effects.
  k. Anyone shorter than someone is not the tallest person.
  l. It is a wise father who knows his own child.
  m. If Sidney is to the left of Sophie and Sophie is to the left of Myrna and Sidney is to the right of Myrna, they must all be standing in a circle.
  n. If someone is taller than everyone, and someone is smarter than everyone then someone is both taller and smarter than everyone.
  o. Anyone who is worse at arithmetic than Bert and who tires more easily than Frieda had better have someone do their arithmetic for them.

2 Prove each of the following arguments valid:
  a. $(x)(Qx \supset (\exists y)Sx, y)$
     $(x)(Sx, a \supset Lx, a)$
     _____
     $\therefore \sim Qa$
  b. $(\exists x)\,[Vx \,\&\, (y)(Vy \supset Ry, x)]$
     _____
     $\therefore (\exists x)(Vx \,\&\, Rx, x)$
  c. $(x)(y)(Px \supset Rx, y)$
     $(x)(y)\,[(Rx, y \lor Ly) \supset Tx]$
     $(x)Px$
     $(\exists x) \sim Tx$
     _____
     $\therefore (\exists y)Ly$

d. $(x)(Sx \supset (y)(Py \supset Rx, y))$
$(\exists x)Sx$

$\overline{\therefore (\exists y)Py \supset (\exists x)(\exists z)Rz, x}$

e. $(x)(y)(Px \supset (Sy \supset \sim Lx, y))$
$(\exists x)(\exists y)((\sim Px \vee \sim Sy) \supset Hx, y)$
$(x)(y)(\sim Rx \supset \sim Hx, y)$
$(x)(y)Lx, y$

$\overline{\therefore (\exists x)Rx}$

3 Symbolize and prove each of the following arguments:
   a. Charles loves Mary. Charles does not love anyone who hates him. Therefore, Mary does not hate Charles.
   b. Everyone who disagrees with Plato likes Russell. Anyone who reads Locke is not read by Russell. Hume likes everyone who reads Berkeley. Thus, Berkeley reads Locke only if Hume agrees with Plato.
   c. Some philosophers are revered by every philosopher. Therefore, some philosophers revere themselves.
   d. Carol can solve every exercise in this book. The average beginning student of logic cannot solve the more difficult exercises in this book. Anyone who can solve exercises that an average beginning student of logic cannot solve is more logical than the average beginning student of logic. Therefore, Carol is more logical than the average beginning student of logic.
   e. No number is larger than itself. Therefore, any number which was larger than every number would not be a number.

4.5.1 Some Properties of Diadic Relations

Diadic relational predicates are by far the most common relational predicates in natural languages. Such predicates have therefore been investigated in a general way and various properties belonging to them have been defined and their interrelations traced. In the current section we will discuss some of these properties and their interrelationships.

Consider the three relational predicates in the propositions:

1. *a* has the same color hair as *b*.
2. *a* is a smaller positive integer than *b*.
3. *a* loves *b*.

and how they are related to those propositions formed by simply interchanging the individuals that stand in each of the relations, i.e.,

    1'. *b* has the same color hair as *a*.
    2'. *b* is a smaller positive integer than *a*.
    3'. *b* loves *a*.

If 1 is true, then surely 1' is true no matter who *a* and *b* are. This is to say, where Cx, y means "*x* has the same color hair as *y*."

$$(x)(y)(Cx, y \supset Cy, x)$$

In general, any relation that, like "*x* has the same color hair as *y*," satisfies, i.e., makes true, the formula

    4. $(x)(y)(Rx, y \supset Ry, x)$

is said to be a *symmetrical relation*.

On the other hand, it is to be noted that no matter what numbers *a* and *b* stand for in 2 and 2', it is never the case that if 2 is true, 2' is true. Indeed, no matter what numbers *a* and *b* are, if 2 is true then 2' is false. Which is to say, where Sx, y means "*x* is a smaller positive integer than *y*,"

$$(x)(y)(Sx, y \supset {\sim}Sy, x)$$

In general, any relation that, like "*x* is a smaller positive integer than *y*," satisfies, i.e., makes true, the formula

    5. $(x)(y)(Rx, y \supset {\sim}Ry, x)$

is said to be an *asymmetrical relation*.

Finally, if proposition 3 is true, i.e., if it is true that *a* loves *b*, it may or may not be the case that 3', *b* loves *a*. This is to say that the relation *x* loves *y* satisfies neither formula 4 nor 5. Any relation, such as *x* loves *y*, that is neither a symmetrical nor an asymmetrical relation, is said to be a *non-symmetrical relation*.

The reader should convince himself that each of the relations in the following three lists belongs where it is.

SOME SYMMETRICAL RELATIONS

x is married to *y*.
x is adjacent to *y*.
x has the same number of members as *y*.

SOME ASYMMETRICAL RELATIONS

x is the father of y.
x is a larger positive integer than y.
x is older than y.

SOME NONSYMMETRICAL RELATIONS

x likes y.
x is the sister of y.
x is no taller than y.

Any diadic relation such that every individual stands in that relation to itself is said to be a *reflexive relation.* This is to say that every reflexive relation satisfies the formula

$$(x)Rx, x$$

Some examples of reflexive relations are

x has the same number of members as y.
x has the same color hair as y.
x is identical to y.

There are relations such that no individual stands in that relation to itself. For instance, no number is greater than itself, no one is his own father, no one is older than himself. All such relations, for which it is the case that:

$$(x) \sim Rx, x$$

are said to be *irreflexive relations.*

There are other diadic relations such that some individuals stand in that relation to themselves and others do not. For instance, x loves y. Some people love themselves and some people do not love themselves. Such relations that are neither reflexive nor irreflexive are said to be *nonreflexive relations.*

The final set of properties of diadic relations that we will consider are *transitivity, intransitivity,* and *nontransitivity.* Any relation for which it is true that

$$(x)(y)(z) \ [(Rx, y \ \& \ Ry, z) \supset Rx, z]$$

203

is said to be a *transitive relation.* An example of a transitive relation would be "is a greater positive integer than," since, for any x, y, and z, if x is a greater positive integer than y and y is a greater positive integer than z, then x is a greater positive integer than z. Those relations that, like "is the father of," satisfy the formula

$$(x)(y)(z) \; [(Rx,y \; \& \; Ry,z) \supset {\sim}Rx,z]$$

are said to be *intransitive relations.* And finally those relations that fail to satisfy both

$$(x)(y)(z) \; [(Rx,y \; \& \; Ry,z) \supset Rx,z]$$

and

$$(x)(y)(z) \; [(Rx,y \; \& \; Ry,z) \supset {\sim}Rx,z]$$

are said to be *nontransitive relations.* Some examples of each follow.

SOME TRANSITIVE RELATIONS

x is a smaller positive integer than y.
x is older than y.
x is harder than y.

SOME INTRANSITIVE RELATIONS

x is the son of y.
x is twice as tall as y.
x is the mother of y.

SOME NONTRANSITIVE RELATIONS

x likes y.
x is adjacent to y.
x loves y.

Given any diadic relation we can now determine its properties in accordance with the above definitions. The relation "x loves y," e.g., is nonreflexive, nonsymmetrical, and nontransitive. The relation "x is the father of y" is irreflexive, asymmetrical, and intransitive. Not all these properties of relation are independent, however. Every relation that is transitive and irreflexive, e.g., is also asymmetrical. This can be proved as follows:

1. $(x)(y)(z) [(Rx,y \& Ry,z) \supset Rx,z]$
2. $(x) \sim Rx,x$ $/\therefore (x)(y)(Rx,y \supset \sim Ry,x)$

C1	3. Rx,y		
	4. $(y)(z) [(Rx,y \& Ry,z) \supset Rx,z]$	1	UI
	5. $(z) [(Rx,y \& Ry,z) \supset Rx,z]$	4	UI
	6. $(Rx,y \& Ry,x) \supset Rx,x$	5	UI
	7. $\sim Rx,x$	2	UI
	8. $\sim(Rx,y \& Ry,x)$	6,7	M.T.
	9. $\sim Rx,y \vee \sim Ry,x$	8	De M.
C1	10. $\sim\sim Rx,y$	3	D.N.
C1	11. $\sim Ry,x$	9, 10	D.S.
C1	12. $Rx,y \supset \sim Ry,x$	3,11	
	13. $(y)(Rx,y \supset \sim Ry,x)$	12	UG
	14. $(x)(y)(Rx,y \supset \sim Ry,x)$	13	UG

EXERCISE

There are theoretically 27 different ways of describing relations using the three sets of three properties of diadic relations we have introduced. However, not all of these 27 are possible since the properties are not fully independent. We have seen, for instance, that there are no relations that are irreflexive, symmetrical, and transitive.
a. Which of the 27 are possible sets of properties of diadic relations?
b. Find a diadic relation for each of the possible sets of properties.
c. Given that the relation "smaller than" is irreflexive, prove that $(\exists y)(x)Sx, y$ is not only false, but self-contradictory.

4.5.2 The relation of identity

All those relations that are reflexive, symmetrical, and transitive are called *equivalence relations*. The most important such relation is the relation of *identity*. We will write "x is identical to y" as

$$x = y$$

The identity sign = corresponds to one of the senses of the word "is" in natural language. Consider the two propositions

1. The book is red.
2. Lewis Carroll is Charles L. Dodgson

Proposition 1 asserts that the book has the property red, i.e., that the word "is" functions to indicate that red is predicated of the book. This use of "is" is known as the *is of predication*. The "is" in proposition 2 is not being used to assert that Lewis Carroll has the property Charles L. Dodgson; it is not predicating Charles L. Dodgson of Lewis Carroll. Thus it is not the "is" of predication. What proposition 2 is asserting, is that the names "Lewis Carroll" and "Charles L. Dodgson" both refer to the same individual. The sense of "is" that allows us to make such an assertion is called the *is of identity*.

The symbol = can be used to symbolize propositions that specify a given number of entities. If, for instance, we have the proposition

Exactly one thing is both green and large.

we may symbolize it as

$$(\exists x) \{(Gx \ \& \ Lx) \ \& \ (y) \ [(Gy \ \& \ Ly) \supset (x = y)] \}$$

which says that there is something that is green and large and if anything is green and large it is that thing. In other words, our formula says that there is at least one thing that is green and large and there is at most one thing that is green and large. In a similar fashion we can symbolize the proposition

Exactly two things are both green and large.

by first writing a formula that says that at least two things are green and large and then conjoining it with a formula that says that at most two things are green and large. In this way we get,

$$(\exists x)(\exists y) \{[(Gx \ \& \ Lx) \ \& \ (Gy \ \& \ Ly) \ \& \ {\sim}(x = y)] \ \& \ (z) \ [(Gz \ \& \ Lz) \supset ((z = x) \lor (z = y))] \}$$

The identity symbol can also help us symbolize such statements as

There is a number that is smaller than any other number.

We can handle the notion "other number" by the use of identity. We get

$$(x)(\exists y)(Sy, x \ \& \ {\sim}(y = x))$$

which says that there is a number smaller than any number but not smaller than itself.

Consider now the propositions:

    3. Lewis Carroll wrote *Through the Looking Glass.*
    4. Charles L. Dodgson wrote *Through the Looking Glass.*

Given propositions 3 and 2, that Lewis Carroll is Charles L. Dodgson, the truth of proposition 4 immediately follows. For what 2 tells us indicates that 3 and 4 are predicating the same property of the same individual, in which case, 3 and 4 are truth functionally equivalent. In general it would seem that

A. $x = y$
$$\overline{\therefore \emptyset x \equiv \emptyset y}$$

which is to say that if $x = y$, then given any assertion involving x, if we replace any number of occurrences of x in it by y, the resulting assertion will have the same truth value as the original assertion. As an immediate consequence of argument A we have the following rule:

If $x = y$, then from $\emptyset x$ we may infer $\emptyset y$.[10]

We will incorporate this as a rule of predicate logic and call it the *rule of identity* (**ID**). We will make use of our new rule of identity in the proof of the valid argument

[10] This is a form of Leibniz's principle of the identity of indiscernibles, which can also be expressed as a rule of substitution as follows: "Things are the same (or identical) when one of them can be substituted in place of the other with preservation of truth." It can be found in this form in C. I. Gerhardt, ed., *Die philosophischen Schriften von G. W. Leibniz* (Berlin: Weidmann, 1875-1890), vol. 4, p. 219. It should be noted, however, that there are contexts in which the principle seems to fail. Consider the proposition, "The reader believes that Lewis Carroll wrote *Through the Looking Glass.*" Given proposition 2 above and our principle it should follow that, "The reader believes that Charles L. Dodgson wrote *Through the Looking Glass.*" It is clear, no doubt, that the former can be true and the latter false. Such examples, however, are not taken to be violations of our rule, but rather to point to the general difficulty of dealing with belief statements in truth-functional logic.

B. Lewis Carroll wrote *Through the Looking Glass*.
Lewis Carroll was Charles L. Dodgson.
Charles L. Dodgson was a logician.

∴ A logician wrote *Through the Looking Glass.*

which we symbolize:

B′.   *Wc, t*
c = d
Ld

∴ $(\exists x)(Lx$ & $Wx, t)$

using *Wx, y* for "*x* wrote *y*," *Lx* for "*x* is a logician," *c* for "Lewis Carroll," *d* for "Charles L. Dodgson," and *t* for "*Through the Looking Glass.*" We prove B′ by

1. *Wc, t*
2. *c = d*
3. *Ld*   /∴ $(\exists x)(Lx$ & $Wx, t)$
4. *Wd, t*   1,2 **Id**
5. *Ld & Wd, t*   3,4 Conj.
6. $(\exists x)(Lx$ & $Wx, t)$ 5 **EG**

We also introduce at this point the *rule of identity introduction*, abbreviated **II**, which allows us to write an identity of the form

$$\omega = \omega$$

at any point in a proof. That such a rule is justified should be clear from the fact that any identity of the form $\omega = \omega$ is a logical truth, and a logical truth would follow validly from any premise, and indeed from no premise at all.

By means of our new rules of **Id** and **II**, we can now prove that identity is both symmetric and transitive. First we prove that identity is symmetric, i.e.

$$(x)(y) \, [(x = y) \supset (y = x)]$$

The proof follows.

C1 1. *x = y*
2. *y = y*   **II**

208

C1 3. $y = x$ 1,2 **Id**
C1 4. $(x = y) \supset (y = x)$ 1,3
    5. $(y) [(x = y) \supset (y = x)]$ 4 **UG**
    6. $(x)(y) [(x = y) \supset (y = x)]$ 5 **UG**

Next we prove that identity is transitive, i.e.

$$(x)(y)(z) [((x = y) \& (y = z)) \supset (x = z)]$$

The proof follows:

C1 1. $(x = y) \& (y = z)$
C1 2. $x = y$ 1 Simp.
C1 3. $(y = z) \& (x = y)$ 1 Com.
C1 4. $y = z$ 3 Simp.
C1 5. $x = z$ 2,4 **Id**
C1 6. $((x = y) \& (y = z)) \supset (x = z)$ 1,5
    7. $(z) [((x = y) \& (y = z)) \supset (x = z)]$ 6 **UG**
    8. $(y)(z) [((x = y) \& (y = z)) \supset (x = z)]$ 7 **UG**
    9. $(x)(y)(z) [((x = y) \& (y = z)) \supset (x = z)]$ 8 **UG**

EXERCISES

1 Symbolize the following propositions:
   a. Susan is Terry's only sister.
   b. John's father is Helen's only brother.
   c. There is only one positive integer greater than three and less than five.
   d. If Harry is taller than John and John is taller than George, then if Harry is George, John is sometimes taller than himself.
   e. If the Morning Star is Venus and the Evening Star is Venus, then since the Evening Star appears before the Morning Star, Venus appears before itself.

2 Prove the following arguments valid.
   a. $(\exists x) [(Rx, h \& Lx) \& (y) (Ry, h \supset (y = x))]$
       $\sim Ls$
       _____
       $\therefore \sim Rs, h$

   b. Ra, b
       $(x)(Ra, x \supset (b = x))$
       $\sim (b = c)$
       _____
       $\therefore \sim Ra, c$

c. $\dfrac{(\exists x)(\sim(x = a)\ \&\ Px)}{\therefore (\exists x)Px\ \&\ \{Pa \supset (\exists y)(\exists z)\ [\sim(y = z)\ \&\ (Py\ \&\ Pz)]\ \}}$

d. $\dfrac{(\exists y)(x)\ [Px \equiv (x = y)]}{\therefore (x)Fx \supset (\exists y)(Py\ \&\ Fy)}$

e. $\dfrac{(\exists y)(x)\ [(\sim Px \vee (x = y))\ \&\ ((x = y) \supset Px)]}{\therefore (\exists x)(Px\ \&\ Lx) \equiv (y)(Py \supset Ly)}$

3. Prove

$$\phi x$$
$$\sim\!\phi y$$
$$\overline{\therefore \sim(x = y)}$$

4.6   TRUTH TREES AND PREDICATE LOGIC

The rules and methods of Chapter 3, combined with the new rules and methods of the present chapter, give us a method of proof for valid arguments in the predicate logic. However, this method of proof is not effective, i.e., though it will prove a valid argument valid, it cannot indicate the invalidity of an invalid argument. As has previously been mentioned, no effective method for testing validity in the predicate logic is possible.

Within Chapter 3 several effective and mechanical methods for the testing of validity of arguments in the propositional logic were introduced. The two major such methods were those of truth tables and truth trees. In section 4.2.1 it was explained that truth tables are not useful as a means of testing validity in the predicate logic, but nothing was said of the possibility of generalizing truth trees for use in the predicate logic.[11]

Though truth trees cannot provide us with an effective test for the validity of arguments in the predicate logic, they can be used in such a way as to indicate a valid argument's validity. Thus, whereas truth tables cannot be generalized from the propositional logic to the predicate logic, truth trees can be, though they do not remain an effective test in the predicate logic. In this section we will extend the method of truth trees to the predicate logic.

In section 3.10 it was seen that truth trees enable us to enumerate the conditions under which each of the original formulas in a tree can be true,

[11] It is not true that truth tables are of *no* use in predicate logic, since they are used when we consider an argument of the predicate logic in a universe containing a finite number of individuals. Such applications are discussed in sections 4.2.1 and 4.3.1.

individually, and then decide whether any set of these conditions will allow all the formulas to be true, together. The advantages of the tree method over other methods, say truth tables, is its efficiency in limiting the number of cases that have to be considered. The extension rules of Chapter 3 for the trees served to state the conditions for the truth of the formula checked. If there was only one way in which the formula could be true, the extension rule involved a listing of that one set of conditions. If there was more than one way in which the formula could be true, the extension rule involved a branching with one set of conditions at the bottom of each branch.

The first task to be considered in extending the method of truth trees to the predicate logic is the presence of such formulas as:

$(x)\emptyset x$

and

$(\exists x)\emptyset x$

There is an immediate and obvious difficulty in writing the extension rules for $(x)\emptyset x$ and $(\exists x)\emptyset x$. The complete truth conditions for the formula $(x)\emptyset x$ would be exceedingly difficult to write, for though there is only one such set of conditions, the set has infinitely many members. The extension rule for $(x)\emptyset x$, then, will be a listing rule, since there is only one set of conditions for its truth and it would look like this:

$(x)\emptyset x$
$\emptyset a$
$\emptyset b$
$\emptyset c$
.
.
.

The situation is somewhat different in the case of $(\exists x)\emptyset x$. A formula of this form can be true under infinitely many different sets of conditions, though now each set is quite simple. The extension rule for $(\exists x)\emptyset x$ is a branching rule, since there is more than one set of conditions for its truth, and it would look like this:

$(\exists x)\emptyset x$
$\emptyset a \quad \emptyset b \quad \emptyset c \quad \ldots$

there being infinitely many branches.

In a universe of a finite number of individuals, say the three a, b, and c, the extension rules for $(x)\emptyset x$ and $(\exists x)\emptyset x$ can be written out quite easily as

$(x)\emptyset x$
$\emptyset a$
$\emptyset b$
$\emptyset c$

and

$(\exists x)\emptyset x$

$\emptyset a$ $\emptyset b$ $\emptyset c$

As was explained in Chapter 3, extension rules always come in pairs, e.g.,

$A \supset B$

$\sim A$ B

$\sim(A \supset B)$
A
$\sim B$

Thus we should have an extension rule for

$\sim(x)\emptyset x$

as well as the one for $(x)\emptyset x$ and one for,

$\sim(\exists x)\emptyset x$

as well as one for $(\exists x)\emptyset x$. Utilizing our rules of **QE** and D.N., however, $\sim(x)\emptyset x$ and $\sim(\exists x)\emptyset x$, respectively, become

$(\exists x) \sim\emptyset x$

and

$(x) \sim\emptyset x$

Since $(\exists x) \sim\emptyset x$ is a formula of the form

$$(\exists x)\emptyset x$$

and $(x)\sim\emptyset x$ is a formula of the form

$$(x)\emptyset x$$

we find that we do not need four different extension rules. All quantified formulas and their negations are reducible to the forms $(x)\emptyset x$ and $(\exists x)\emptyset x$. Thus in utilizing the tree method in predicate logic, we will change all formulas beginning with negated quantifiers into formulas beginning with unnegated quantifiers through the use of **QE** (and D.N. where necessary).

But we turn again, now, to the question of how one can use an extension rule such as that for $(x)\emptyset x$, that seems to involve, in an unrestricted universe, the writing of infinitely many formulas. The solution is not to write the entire set of conditions for the truth of $(x)\emptyset x$ at once, in the hope that there will be no need to write all of them. Consider, for instance, the valid argument:

> Everything is green.
> ――――――――――
> ∴ Albert is green.

which we symbolize:

$$\frac{(x)Gx}{\therefore Ga}$$

In utilizing the tree method we begin as usual by listing the premise and the negation of the conclusion getting

$$(x)Gx$$
$$\sim Ga$$

Next we write at the bottom of every open path that contains $(x)Gx$ one of the members of the set of truth conditions for $(x)Gx$, namely Ga, thus we get

$(x)Gx$
$\sim Ga$
Ga

Notice that here we have not checked $(x)Gx$. The reason we have not checked it is that we have not written all of the conditions for its truth when we have written Ga. Indeed, since you will never write all the conditions for the truth of a universally quantified formula, you will never check one. In the above case we are fortunate since all that we need write is one of the conditions for the truth of $(x)Gx$; having written Ga the tree closes since the one and only path contains both a formula and its negation. Since we now have

$(x)Gx$
$\sim Ga$
Ga
X

the argument is valid and we are done.

Why write Ga instead of Gb or Gc since they are all part of the truth conditions for $(x)Gx$? Since an a already appears in the tree when we list the premise and negation of the conclusion, we increase the possibility of closing the tree quickly by introducing a part of the truth condition for $(x)Gx$ that contains an a.

In general if we have an open path that contains a formula of the form $(x)\emptyset x$, we will write a $\emptyset \omega$ at the bottom of the path for each individual constant ω that appears in that path. This is precisely what we did in the previous tree, where there was only one ω in the single path, viz., the individual constant a.

Consider the more complicated valid argument

> If anyone can climb a rope, Adam and Bill can.
> Adam cannot climb a rope.
> _____
> ∴ Bill cannot climb a rope.

which we symbolize as

$(x)\,[Cx \supset (Ca\ \&\ Cb)]$
$\sim Ca$
_____
$\therefore \sim Cb$

Step 1. List premises and negation of conclusion

$(x) [Cx \supset (Ca \& Cb)]$
$\sim Ca$
$\cancel{\sim\sim}Cb$ (erase double tildes)

Step 2. Write $\emptyset\omega$'s at bottom of open path that contains $(x)\emptyset x$. Note that there are two ω's, a and b, and thus there will be two $\emptyset\omega$'s

$(x) [Cx \supset (Ca \& Cb)]$
$\sim Ca$
Cb
$Ca \supset (Ca \& Cb)$
$Cb \supset (Ca \& Cb)$

Step 3. Use all extension rules on nonquantified formulas in tree

Since all paths are closed the argument is valid.

If a given argument containing a formula of the form $(x)\emptyset x$, does not contain any individual constants, we simply choose any individual constant whatsoever for our ω. If, for instance, we have the valid argument:

Everything is green.
_____
∴ Something is green.

which we symbolize as:

$(x)Gx$
_____
$\therefore (\exists x)Gx$

Step 1. We list the premises and the negation of the conclusion.

$(x)Gx$
$\sim(\exists x)Gx$

Step 2. We check the formula beginning with a negated quantifier and write the equivalent unnegated formula at the bottom of every open path containing the formula checked.

$(x)Gx$
$\sim(\exists x)Gx$ ✓
$(x)\sim Gx$

Step 3. Choose an individual constant, say a, as our ω and write $\emptyset\omega$ at the bottom of every open path containing $(x)\emptyset x$. But in our case there are two formulas of the form $(x)\emptyset x$, so we treat each one individually, writing first

$(x)Gx$
$\sim(\exists x)Gx$ ✓
$(x)\sim Gx$
Ga

having chosen to write one of the truth conditions for $(x)Gx$.

Step 4. We could go on and write another truth condition for $(x)Gx$, say Gb, if we wished, but clearly that would not lead to a rapid closure of the path. In light of this we will write a truth condition for $(x)\sim Gx$ instead. Since at this point an individual constant appears in the tree, our ω for $(x)\sim Gx$ will be that individual constant, i.e., a. Thus we get

$(x)Gx$
$\sim(\exists x)Gx$ ✓
$(x)\sim Gx$
Ga
$\sim Ga$
X

We have always checked formulas only when we were able to write the necessary and sufficient conditions for the formula's truth by means of the extension rules. It is for this reason, as we have noted, that universally quantified formulas are never checked, since we never can write more than part of the necessary conditions for their truth. The situation is different in the case of an existentially quantified formula in that we can write a sufficient condition for its truth but never the necessary conditions for its truth. However, a sufficient condition will do, so long as we are careful not to state as a sufficient condition a $\emptyset\omega$ containing as ω an individual constant, already appearing in the path. Thus when we encounter a formula of the form $\emptyset\omega$ in that path we check $(\exists x)\emptyset x$ and choose as an ω, an individual constant not appearing in the path, and write a formula of the form $\emptyset\omega$ at the bottom of every open path containing the formula checked. Consider the valid argument

> All philosophers are wise men.
> All wise men are pipe smokers.
> _____
> ∴ All philosophers are pipe smokers.

which we symbolize as

$$(x)(Px \supset Wx)$$
$$(x)(Wx \supset Sx)$$
$$\overline{\therefore (x)(Px \supset Sx)}$$

Step 1. We list the premises and the negation of the conclusion

$$(x)(Px \supset Wx)$$
$$(x)(Wx \supset Sx)$$
$$\sim(x)(Px \supset Sx)$$

Step 2. We check the last formula and write the appropriate formula at the bottom getting

$$(x)(Px \supset Wx)$$
$$(x)(Wx \supset Sx)$$
$$\sim(x)(Px \supset Sx) \checkmark$$
$$(\exists x) \sim(Px \supset Sx)$$

Step 3. We now check our existentially quantified formula first, choosing some individual constant, say a, for our ω, we get

$(x)(Px \supset Wx)$
$(x)(Wx \supset Sx)$
$\sim(x)(Px \supset Sx)$ ✓
$(\exists x) \sim(Px \supset Sx)$ ✓
$\sim(Pa \supset Sa)$

Step 4. Now we turn to one of our two universally quantified formulas, say the first, and write one of its truth conditions. Since the individual constant, a, already appears in the tree, it will be our ω.

$(x)(Px \supset Wx)$
$(x)(Wx \supset Sx)$
$\sim(x)(Px \supset Sx)$ ✓
$(\exists x) \sim(Px \supset Sx)$ ✓
$\sim(Pa \supset Sa)$
$Pa \supset Wa$

Now we must do the same thing for our second universally generalized formula, getting

$(x)(Px \supset Wx)$
$(x)(Wx \supset Sx)$
$\sim(x)(Px \supset Sx)$ ✓
$(\exists x) \sim(Px \supset Sx)$ ✓
$\sim(Pa \supset Sa)$
$Pa \supset Wa$
$Wa \supset Sa$

Step 5. Now we deal with all unquantified formulas in accordance with our extension rules for connectives, getting:

$(x)(Px \supset Wx)$
$(x)(Wx \supset Sx)$
$\sim(x)(Px \supset Sx)$ ✓
$(\exists x) \sim(Px \supset Sx)$ ✓
$\sim(Pa \supset Sa)$ ✓
$Pa \supset Wa$ ✓
$Wa \supset Sa$ ✓
Pa
$\sim Sa$

$\sim Pa$ Wa
X

        $\sim Wa$ Sa
        X X

at which point all the paths are closed indicating that we are finished and that the argument is valid.

Our discussion so far will suffice to cover both multiply general arguments (though there are some special consequences regarding multiply general arguments which we will discuss later) and arguments containing relational predicates excluding identity. Consider the logical truth

$(x)(x = x)$

In Chapter 3 we saw that one could prove a formula to be a tautology by writing its negation and applying the method of the trees. The same method will prove a given formula to be a logical truth. Thus we negate $(x)(x = x)$ and write its tree, getting

$\sim(x)(x = x)$ ✓
$(\exists x) \sim(x = x)$ ✓
$\sim(a = a)$

from which point there is no way to proceed using our previous rules. We thus introduce a new reason for closing a path. *A path is to be closed if it contains a formula and its negation or if it contains a formula of the form* $\sim(\omega = \omega)$. Our tree for $(x)(x = x)$ would then close, proving it to be a logical truth.

Just as we were able to prove for $(x)(x = x)$ that identity is reflexive, we ought to be able to prove that identity is symmetrical, which is to prove

$(x)(y) ((x = y) \supset (y = x))$

a logical truth. We proceed as before by negating the formula and writing its tree. In this way we get

$\sim(x)(y) [(x = y) \supset (y = x)]$ ✓
$(\exists x) \sim(y) [(x = y) \supset (y = x)]$ ✓
$\sim(y) [(a = y) \supset (y = a)]$ ✓
$(\exists y) \sim [(a = y) \supset (y = a)]$ ✓
$\sim [(a = b) \supset (b = a)]$ ✓
$a = b$
$\sim(b = a)$

We have exhausted our available rules, yet we cannot close the tree, though it is obvious that we should be able to do so. What is needed is some analogue to our rule of **Id**. The following procedure will suffice: *If there are formulas of the form* $\omega = \alpha$ *and* $\emptyset\omega$ *in an open path, write the formula* $\emptyset\alpha$, *obtained by replacing one of the occurrences of* ω *in* $\emptyset\omega$ *by* α, *at the bottom of the open path.* Applying this rule to our tree above allows us to write

$$\sim(b = b)$$

closing the tree. The formula $(a = b)$ is of the form $(\omega = \alpha)$, where ω is a and α is b. The formula $\sim(b = a)$ is a $\emptyset\omega$, where ω is a, we obtained $\sim(b = b)$ in accordance with our rule by replacing one (in this case the only) occurrence of ω in $\emptyset\omega$ with α. (In our case replacing a in $\sim(b = a)$ by b.)

We now summarize our new procedures for the tree method.

SUMMARY OF THE TREE METHOD FOR THE PREDICATE LOGIC

1 List the premises and the negation of the conclusion.

2 a. Erase all double tildes.

2 b. Check all formulas of the forms $\sim(x)\emptyset x$ and $\sim(\exists x)\emptyset x$ and write the equivalent formula of the forms $(\exists x)\sim\emptyset x$ and $(x)\sim\emptyset x$, respectively, at the bottom of every open path that contains the formula checked.

2 c. Close all paths that contain a formula and its negation, or a formula of the form $\sim(\omega = \omega)$. If all the paths are closed you are finished and the argument is valid; if not go on to step 3.

3 a. If there are any unchecked formulas in an open path to which the extension rules for connectives (Chapter 3) can be applied, apply them and return to step 2 above; if not, continue to step 3b.

3 b. If there are formulas of the form $\omega = \alpha$ and $\emptyset\omega$ in an open path, write the formula $\emptyset\alpha$, obtained by replacing one of the occurrences of ω in $\emptyset\omega$ by α, at the bottom of the open path; if not go on to step 4.

4 If an open path contains a formula of the form $(\exists x)\emptyset x$ and no formula of the form $\emptyset\omega$, check the formula of the form $(\exists x)\emptyset x$ and choose as ω an individual constant not appearing in the path, and write a formula of the form $\emptyset\omega$ at the bottom of every open path containing the formula checked; if not go on to step 5.

5 If a formula of the form $(x)\emptyset x$ occurs in an open path, write one formula of the form $\emptyset\omega$ for each individual constant, ω being that

constant, that appears in any formula in the path, at the bottom of the path. If there are no occurrences of individual constants in the path, choose any individual constants as your ω and write a formula of the form $\emptyset\omega$ at the bottom of the path. If no formula of the form $(x)\emptyset x$ occurs in an open path go on to step 6.

6 If you have made no changes in the tree since last beginning at step 2, you are through and the argument is invalid; if you have made a change return to step 2.

It should be obvious from the above that the tree method is mechanical. When the tree method is used on singularly general arguments, it is also effective; i.e., given any singularly general argument, we will finish the tree either having an open path (invalid) or all paths closed (valid). In the case of multiply general arguments, the tree method is not effective. If a multiply general argument is valid, its tree will eventually close; but if an argument is invalid, there are two ways in which the tree may fail to close. It may fail to close at a point where we are told that we are finished, i.e., a case where we have considered all the possibilities and the argument is then known to be invalid, but it may also fail to close while having an infinite path. In the latter case, though the tree does not close, we are never told by the tree method procedure that we are finished. If we can show that the tree will never close, then we know the argument is invalid. But it can happen that though there is an infinite path, we cannot tell that there is one. We may go on expecting that at any moment we will be able to close the tree. It is in this sense, that the tree method is not effective in the predicate logic.

The following truth tree (or more properly, incomplete truth tree) is generated in an attempt to prove the formula

$(\exists x)(y)(Fx \equiv \sim Fy)$

to be a logical truth

$\sim(\exists x)(y)(Fx \equiv \sim Fy)$ ✓
$(x) \sim(y)(Fx \equiv \sim Fy)$
$\sim(y)(Fa \equiv \sim Fy)$ ✓
$(\exists y) \sim(Fa \equiv \sim Fy)$ ✓
$\sim(Fa \equiv \sim Fb)$
$\sim(y)(Fb \equiv \sim Fy)$ ✓
$(\exists y) \sim(Fb \equiv \sim Fy)$ ✓
$\sim(Fb \equiv \sim Fc)$

221

$\sim(y)(Fc \equiv \sim Fy)$ ✓
$(\exists y) \sim(Fc \equiv \sim Fy)$ ✓
$\sim(Fc \equiv \sim Fd)$
.
.
.

It should be obvious that this is a tree with an infinite path. We can tell that there will be an infinite path, because our tree has taken on a definite pattern. The third, sixth, ninth, and twelfth formulas occurring in our tree after the point at which we have stopped will be $\sim(Fd \equiv \sim Fe)$, $\sim(Fe \equiv \sim Ff)$, and $\sim(Ff \equiv \sim Fg)$. From the pattern found it is clear that our tree will never close. In this way we can tell that $(\exists x)(y)(Fx \equiv \sim Fy)$ is not a logical truth.

EXERCISES

1 Use the method of truth trees to test the following arguments for validity.

a. $(x)Sx \supset Hb$
$\sim Hb$
_____
$\therefore \sim(\exists x)Sx$

b. $(\exists y)(Ty \lor Qy)$
_____
$\therefore Ty \lor (\exists x)Qx$

c. $(\exists x)Lx$
$(x)(Lx \supset Sx)$
_____
$\therefore (\exists x)Sx$

d. $(x)Lx \& (y)Vy$
_____
$\therefore (z)(Lz \& Vz)$

e. $(x) [Lx, a \supset La, x]$
$(\exists x) \sim La, x$
_____
$\therefore (\exists x) \sim Lx, a$

f. $Qa \equiv Qb$
_____
$\therefore a = b$

g. $(x)(\exists y)Rx, y$
_____
$\therefore (\exists y)Rb, y$

h. $(x)(Tx \supset Cx)$

$\therefore (y)\,[(\exists x)(Tx\,\&\,Ry,\,x) \supset (\exists z)(Cz\,\&\,Ry,\,z)]$

i. $(\exists x)Sx$
$(x)(y)\,[(Sx\,\&\,Sy) \supset (x = y)]$

$\therefore (\exists x)\,[Sx\,\&\,(y)(Sy \supset (x = y))]$

j. $(x)(\exists y)Ly,\,x$
$(x)(y)(Lx,\,y \supset Rx,\,y)$

$\therefore (x)(\exists y)Ry,\,x$

2   Construct an argument whose tree contains an infinite path.

4.7.   AN HISTORICAL NOTE ON THE PREDICATE LOGIC

The use of algebraic formulas to represent logical relations is due to George Boole (1815-1864). But the introduction of quantifiers to bind variables is due to the American philosopher Charles Sanders Peirce (1839-1914) and the German mathematician Gottlob Frege (1848-1925). The introduction of quantifiers was probably the most important single advance in the history of symbolic logic. Frege, in his publication of *Begriffschrift*, in 1879 predated Peirce by four years in the introduction of quantification. Frege's symbolism was extremely complex and cumbersome as compared with that of Peirce. In 1883 Peirce, pursuing various suggestions made in an article of 1859[12] by Augustus De Morgan (1806-1871) concerning relations, introduced the method of symbolizing relations we have used. In the same article[13] Peirce also introduced the symbols Π and Σ as the universal and existential quantifiers respectively. These quantifier symbols function in the same way as our symbols (x) and $(\exists x)$.

The work of Frege was pursued by the English philosopher Bertrand Russell and Alfred North Whitehead in their *Principia Mathematica* (1913), from which most modern logic derives. Most early systems of logic based on the work of Russell and Whitehead used a single rule of quantification, usually **UG**. Our system of *natural deduction* originates from the work of Gerhard Gentzen and Stanislaw Jaskowski (1934), though the use of **EI** as a rule

[12] "On the Syllogism IV and on the Logic of Relations," *Cambridge Philosophical Transactions*, (1864), 10: 331-358.
[13] Printed as an appendix to *John Hopkins Studies in Logic*.

was introduced by Willard Van Orman Quine and J. Barkley Rosser in 1946. The symbolic conventions and subscripting device used in our formulation of the quantification rules are due to Irving M. Copi and P. Suppes, respectively.

formal systems

5.1 GEOMETRY AND ITS HISTORY

Geometry no doubt had its beginning in the development of rules of measurement. It seems very likely that with the advent of agriculture and the associated importance of land it became essential to be able to determine the boundaries of one's land. Owing, most likely, to the special importance of redetermining boundaries every year after the flooding of the Nile, Egypt became the center of geometry as a "science of measurement." When Euclid came on the scene in the third century B.C. a great many "geometrical truths" had already been compiled. Euclid was not the first to see that these geometrical truths were not independent of one another, for various of these truths had been shown to follow from other geometrical truths by the Pythagoreans and such geometers as Eudoxus, Theaetetus, Archytas, Hippocrates of Chios, Democritus, Theodoros of Cyrene, and Antiphon the Sophist. What seems so unique about Euclid's work was that it showed that a very great number, indeed a whole system, of such geometrical truths could be shown to follow from a small number of other such truths.

There is, however, a further difference between the truths of Egyptian geometry and those of the Greeks besides the degree and way that they were able to organize those truths. The two sets of truths seem to be about different things, or even further, about different kinds of worlds. For, whereas the Egyptian geometry spoke of land, Euclid's geometry spoke of one and two dimensional objects nowhere to be found in this world. This is something we often lose sight of, for we come to think that Euclidean geometry is about the diagrams we find in the textbook or that are drawn on the blackboard by our teachers; but one cannot draw a "breadthless length," which is Euclid's definition of a line. And if one cannot draw a line one cannot draw a triangle or a square or any other figure of Euclidean plane geometry. This difference in the development of geometry was due to a mathematical mysticism, which became the metaphysics of the Pythagorean philosophy and led eventually to Plato's theory of forms. The geometry that flourished in Plato's academy and culminated in the work of Euclid was of this tradition. We do not know whether or not Euclid himself was a Platonist, but we can be fairly certain that the men he studied with were students of Plato and it was from them that he received the notions of point, line, and plane.

Owing to the character of otherworldliness that is found in Euclidean geometry a question arises as to what sort of truths it deals with. There is little difficulty in knowing how one would go about establishing the findings of Egyptian geometry, one merely checks them against what one finds in the world, i.e., one makes observations. Such methods are not available, however, for checking the statements of Euclidean geometry for there is nothing we can observe; the geometry is not about observable things. How then does one establish their truth? Euclid's geometry is divided into four kinds of statements, viz., definitions, postulates, axioms, and theorems. The truth or falsity of the definitions is not a problem since the definitions are stipulations.[1] The axioms and postulates are of exactly the same nature so far as their truth or falsity is concerned and so we will follow the common practice of calling them all axioms. Before we discuss the way in which the truth or falsity of the axioms is determined let us consider the truth or falsity of the theorems. The theorems are propositions that validly follow from the axioms, or that, at least, is what is claimed of them. Their truth follows then from the truth of the axioms, for the theorems are, in effect, the conclusions of valid arguments having the axioms as their premises; from which it follows that if the axioms are true the theorems must be true. The question of the nature of the truths of Euclidean geometry then can be reduced to the question of the truth of the axioms. For the Greeks the

[1] See section 6.3 on stipulative definitions.

answer was simple. The method to be used was intuition and the result was that the axioms were *self-evident truths.* All that one had to do was consider the axioms and one would "see" their truth. It was, however, argued from the very beginning that one of the axioms of Euclid was not self-evident or at least not so self-evident as the others. It was the fifth postulate (axiom) whose self-evidence was questioned. It states: "That, if a straight line falling on two straight lines makes the interior angles on the same side less than two right angles, the two straight lines, if produced indefinitely, meet on that side on which are the angles less than the two right angles."[2] For some it was the word "indefinitely" that removed self-evidence. For others it was the already noted existence of asymptotes, those lines that approach each other but never meet, that made it seem that the fifth postulate (axiom) required proof. In any case, many attempts were made to prove the fifth postulate (axiom) from the remaining nine axioms. All these proofs were failures, though many are of great interest.[3] It has since been shown that all such attempts were doomed to failure since the fifth postulate is independent of the remaining axioms. To say that an axiom A is independent of the set of axioms $\{B\}$ is to say that no use of the rules of inference will allow you to derive axiom A from the set of axioms $\{B\}$. To say of a set of axioms that they are independent is to say that each axiom which is a member of the set is independent of the rest of the axioms in the set. In section 5.2 we will consider a proof of the independence of a specific set of axioms.

Since little progress had been made in the attempt to directly prove the fifth postulate from the remaining axioms, the method of indirect proof was tried. By denying the fifth postulate, it was hoped a contradiction could be derived thus showing that the denial of the postulate was impossible and thereby proving the postulate itself. Since there are at least two ways of denying the fifth postulate there are at least two different sets of theorems that can emerge from the new axiom sets. We could deny the fifth postulate by saying that our two lines never meet no matter how far extended on the side "on which the angles are less than the two right angles." When denied in this way the postulate (when added to the remaining unchanged postulates) gives rise to such "strange" theorems as "the sum of the interior angles of a triangle is less than 180 degrees."[4] When we deny the fifth postulate by saying that the two lines when extended meet more than once we get the

[2] Euclid, "Elements," *The Thirteen Books of Euclid's Elements,* 2d ed., ed. Sir T. L. Heath (New York, 1956), vol. 1, p. 202.

[3] See Roberto Bonola's *Non-Euclidean Geometry* (New York: Dover, 1955).

[4] This actually requires a change in another of the axioms of Euclid as well as the fifth.

theorem that the sum of the interior angles of a triangle is greater than 180 degrees. Now, though these denials of the fifth postulate give rise to some rather peculiar theorems no one such denial gives rise to a contradiction. Thus, this method of proof also failed to give a demonstration of the fifth postulate.

Attempts were also made to replace the fifth postulate by more self-evident statements and then to derive the fifth postulate itself as a theorem. Though it is quite easy to replace the fifth postulate with "other" statements from which the fifth can be derived all such statements must be equivalent to the fifth postulate, due we know now, to the independence of the postulate. Since the new postulate and the old are then equivalent[5] it is hard to see in what sense the new could be any more self-evident than the old. The most famous such axiom is Playfair's "Through a given point outside a given straight line only one parallel can be drawn to that line."

The outcome of these disputes about Euclid's geometry was the recognition that other geometries were possible, which is to say that a geometry was a system of statements some of which had been designated *axioms* and from which other statements were deduced called *theorems.* The question of truth or falsity of the geometry arose out of a misconception of what geometry was. One could ask if a geometry was consistent or if its axioms were independent but not if it was true or false. But it must be noted that we do use geometry of the world; we survey land, we use the Pythagorean theorem to compute the diagonal of a field, etc. and all this despite the fact that geometry is about breadthless lengths and points that have no parts. What we are using is not geometry but rather an interpretation of geometry. We have replaced "straight line" with "the path of a ray of light" and Euclid's "points" with "locations." Thus, the statement that the shortest distance between two points is a straight line becomes the statement that the shortest path between two locations is the path that a ray of light would take between those locations. Now whereas the first statement is neither true nor false of this observable world, the second statement is true of this world. Thus, though geometries are neither true nor false their interpretations are either true or false. Once this was understood the development of uninterpreted geometry could head off in new directions and one realized that the previous attempts to prove the fifth postulate of Euclid by means of indirect proof had resulted in the construction of the beginnings

---

[5]Strictly speaking the new axiom must say at least what the old says but may say more. Charles Dodgson argues this of Playfair's axiom.

of new geometries no less respectable as uninterpreted geometries than Euclid's. The first non-Euclidean geometry presented in this light was that of Nicolas Lobachevski (1793-1856) in 1826, though the great mathematician Gauss claimed to have realized the independence of the fifth postulate as early as 1792 but was hesitant to put such a notion in print, maintaining that he wished to avoid "the shrieks of the dullards."

5.1.1 Some features of formal deductive systems

Let us now consider some of the features of a formal uninterpreted deductive system. First it should be noted that not all the terms of such a system can be defined within the system without circularity. So that if a deductive system contained terms A, B, and C, and A was defined by B and C it would no longer be possible to define B and C by means of A without our definitions being circular. Thus any formal deductive system must contain certain undefined terms which we will call the *primitives* of the system. All other terms of the system will then be defined as certain combinations of the primitives. Thus in a system containing the terms

$P\ Q \sim v\ \&\ \supset)\ ($

it is possible to designate P, Q, $\sim$, v,), and (as primitives and define $\supset$ and & with them as follows:

$(P \supset Q)$ is the same by definition as $(\sim P \lor Q)$.
$(P\ \&\ Q)$ is the same by definition as $\sim(\sim P \lor \sim Q)$.

Once the terms have been introduced some rule must be given for the identification of "properly constructed" groups of the terms. If our terms were the words of the English language the rule (or in this case rules) that would be called for would be the rules of grammar. These would enable us to determine that the group of terms "A and the but" was an unacceptable group of terms (in this case an ungrammatical sentence) while the group "The ball is red" was an acceptable, i.e., grammatical, group. In general, those groups of terms that satisfy these rules of the system (known as *formation rules*) are to be called *well-formed,* whereas those groups that do not satisfy the formation rules are to be called *ill-formed.*

The axioms of the formal deductive system can now be given. The axioms are some subset of the well-formed groups of terms of the system. The formal deductive system must also contain some rule or rules of inference that allow the drawing of one well-formed group of terms from one or more other well-formed groups of terms.

Some notion of *demonstration* is also needed that will allow for the definition of a theorem as the outcome of the use of the rule or rules of inference on the axioms of the system.

Such uninterpreted formal deductive systems are called *syntactical deductive systems*. If one of the possible interpretations of a given formal deductive system is the sort of natural deduction discussed in Chapters 3 and 4 the system is said to be a *formal logistic system*.

5.2 A FORMAL SYSTEM IN THE PROPOSITIONAL LOGIC

Formal logistic systems have various properties that can be discussed relative to their interpretation as the logic of two-valued truth functions. We will now introduce a formal logistic system in an uninterpreted form and then discuss its interpretations and its properties relative to these interpretations.

We must first establish certain conventions of a notation that will enable us to distinguish between uses of the terms of the system and discussions about those terms. There is an obvious difference between speaking of George Washington, the man, and "George Washington," the name of the man. Whereas the name "George Washington" can be said to contain 16 letters the man George Washington cannot. When I speak of the man George Washington, I use his name in order to do so; when I speak of his name, on the other hand, I do not make use of his name; I instead mention it. There exists a convention in written English for distinguishing cases of use and mention, a device that has been used in the preceding. When a word is being used it is written without quotation marks and when it is being mentioned it is written within quotation marks. Thus we have the following two sentences meaning quite different things.

1. The tallest mountain contains three parts.
2. "The tallest mountain" contains three parts.

Sentence 1 speaks of an object you can climb whereas 2 speaks of something you can utter but cannot climb. This distinction is even more thoroughgoing then the preceding perhaps indicated. If you were studying German in an American classroom you would speak about the German language in English, whereas when you spoke German you would not be speaking about German but rather using it. If we call the language that you are trying to learn the *object language* then we might well call the language that you use to talk about it the *metalanguage* since the prefix "meta" means above or about. Now in our example, German words would appear in the metalanguage but they would be mentioned rather than used as for instance in the sentence, "The German word 'ich' is only capitalized at the beginning of a sentence."

There is, of course, no necessity for the object language and metalanguage to be different languages in the sense that German and English are different languages. When one studies the English language in an American classroom both the object language and the metalanguage are English. When the English language is being used to talk about the English language we are speaking in the metalanguage. The language that we are talking about in an English class is called the object language. Now, obviously, this is a relative distinction, for we can, after all, talk about a metalanguage (as in fact we have been doing). When one does so the metalanguage becomes the object language and the talk about it is taking place in the "new" metalanguage. If we wish, however, we can keep our original distinction between object language and metalanguage and call our new level of discourse the *metametalanguage*. There is no limit we can set to the number of levels that are possible. Consider the sentence

> The sentence "The word 'ball' contains four letters" contains six words.

If we consider the word "ball" as in the object language then the sentence "The word 'ball' contains four letters" would be in the metalanguage in which case "The sentence 'The word "ball" contains four letters' contains six words" would be in the metametalanguage. If on the other hand it better suits our purpose to consider "The word 'ball' contains four letters" as in our object language then the latter is in the metalanguage.

Our object language will be the formal system we are constructing. Our metalanguage will be English supplemented with the names of the various items in the object language. Now if the letter "P" is in our object language we will need to know its name in order to speak about it. The standard convention of placing the letter "P" between quotation marks for its name is too cumbersome for our purposes so we will instead write the name of *P* in italic type and **P** itself in boldface type. This convention will be followed from this point on.

Our formal system[6] contains the following primitives

A, A₁, A₂, A₃, . . .
B, B₁, B₂, B₃, . . .
C, C₁, C₂, C₃, . . .

called *letter symbols*, and

~, v

called *operator symbols*, and

(,)

called *grouping symbols.* Though the use of the word "symbol" ordinarily implies that there is something that is being symbolized that is not meant to be the case here. The letter symbols symbolize nothing; they are meant to be nothing more than marks on paper. The same is true of the operator and grouping symbols. It should be noted that the symbols above appear in boldface type because they are being displayed as part of the object language; they are not being spoken about.

It is convenient to introduce into the metalanguage at this point various devices for naming things in our object language. We have already introduced the names of our primitive symbols or at least the device for giving those names, but it is useful to also have a way of naming groups of those symbols. A horizontal listing of a finite number of the symbols of our object language will be called a formula. Thus

ABvv))
C
(AvC)
~A₁

are all formulas of our system. Their names can be written by writing the

[6]Our formal system is a form of the Hilbert-Ackermann system and so will be referred to as H.A.

name of each constituent symbol in the same order in a horizontal listing. Thus the names of the four formulas above may be written as

$ABvv))$
C
(AvC)
$\sim A_1$

We will now, however, introduce into the metalanguage a set of names P, Q, R, S, etc. that will stand for any formula whatsoever in the object language. Thus whereas the name $ABvv))$ names only one formula in the object language (the formula **ABvv))**) the name P may name any formula in the object language. If we wished to talk about some specific formula in the object language but could not, or wished not, to name a specific formula we would make use of the name P.

We can now formulate a rule that will allow us to pick out that subset of formulas of the object language that are to be termed well-formed. To that end we give the following recursive definition of well-formed formula:[7]

    1. A letter symbol alone, i.e., $A, A_1, \ldots$ is well-formed.
    2. If P is well-formed then $\sim P$ is well-formed.
    3. If P and Q are well-formed then $(P \vee Q)$ is well-formed.
    4. No formula is well-formed unless its being so follows from 1-3 above.

The following is a list of a few well-formed formulas (wff):

A
$\sim B$
$(Av\sim B)$
$(\sim (AvB_2) \vee C)$

We now can use the recursive definition of well-formed formula to decide whether the formula $\sim ((AvB) \vee \sim (CvA))$ is well-formed. We use the following form of proof:

    1. A, B, and C are all wff's by part 1 of the recursive definition.
    2. (AvB) is a wff by step 1 and part 3 of the recursive definition.

---

[7] A property, P, is said to be *recursively* defined if there exists a definition that (1) identifies the most basic entities that have the property P and (2) specifies the rules by which if anything has P, something else, having P, can be constructed and (3) states that nothing else has P.

233

3. $(C \lor A)$ is a wff by step 1 and part 3 of the recursive definition.
4. $\sim(C \lor A)$ is a wff by step 3 above and part 2 of the recursive definition.
5. $((A \lor B) \lor \sim(C \lor A))$ is a wff by steps 2 and 4 and part 3 of the recursive definition.
6. $\sim((A \lor B) \lor \sim(C \lor A))$ is a wff by step 5 and part 2 of the recursive definition.

It should be noted that the failure to construct such a proof for a given formula does not necessarily mean that the formula is not well-formed, since your failure may be due to your abilities rather than to the form of the formula. That such a proof can be constructed does, however, guarantee that the given formula is well-formed.

From this point on it will be convenient to restrict the use of the names P, Q, R, S, etc. to well-formed formulas in our object language rather than to any formula well-formed or not.

Since our interest will be in the properties of our formal system and since for this reason we will almost exclusively be using the metalanguage it is valuable to introduce still further devices for simplifying the metalanguage. Consider the following group of formulas

(A∨B)
(~A∨B)
((C∨D) ∨ (C∨ ~A))

These formulas have something in common, viz., they can all be named by the name $(P \lor Q)$. As we have indicated the names P and Q can name any wff in our object language. If P names the same letter symbol as A (viz., **A**) and Q names the same letter symbol as B (viz., **B**) then $(P \lor Q)$ names the same thing $(A \lor B)$ names (viz. (**A ∨ B**)). And if P names the same thing $\sim A$ names and Q names the same thing B names then $(P \lor Q)$ names the same thing that $(\sim A \lor B)$ names. This is what we mean when we say that these formulas all have the form $(P \lor Q)$, viz., that they can all be named by $(P \lor Q)$.

We can now introduce the symbols &, $\supset$, and $\equiv$ into our metalanguage to simplify the naming of certain formulas in our object language. Consider the formulas

(~A ∨ B)
(~~A ∨ B)
(~(~C ∨ D) ∨ (~C ∨ ~A)

They are all nameable by the name $(\sim P \vee Q)$. We now introduce the following definition

$$(P \supset Q) = \mathrm{df}\,(\sim P \vee Q)$$

which is to say that whenever we encounter a formula of the form $(\sim P \vee Q)$ we can write its name by eliminating the $\sim$ and replacing the $\vee$ by $\supset$. Thus we can write the names of the formulas above as

$(A \supset B)$
$(\sim A \supset B)$
$((C \supset D) \supset (C \supset \sim A))$

It should be noted before we continue that whereas the name P can name any formula in the object language this is not true of the name $\sim P$. It is useful to think of $\sim P$ as a compound name made up of two parts; first the name of the $\sim$ and second the name of any formula in the object language. Since the name $\sim$ names only the $\sim$, the compound name $\sim P$ will name only those formulas that are preceded by a $\sim$ and no others. The name P can, however, name both those formulas preceded by $\sim$ and those that are not preceded by $\sim$. Thus P can name the formula A, while $\sim P$ cannot; but, on the other hand, $\sim P$ can name the formula $\sim A$ and so can P. Thus the name $\sim P$ names a subset of the formulas named by the name P.

Just as the definition $P \supset Q = \mathrm{df}(\sim P \vee Q)$ helps us to simplify the naming of those formulas named by $(\sim P \vee Q)$ we can introduce other definitions that will provide us with shorthand names of other formulas. To that end we give the following definitions

$(P \,\&\, Q) = \mathrm{df} \sim (\sim P \vee \sim Q)$
$(P \equiv Q) = \mathrm{df}((P \supset Q) \,\&\, (Q \supset P))$

Some idea of the usefulness of such shorthand ways of writing names can be gotten by considering the definition that would be given for $(P \equiv Q)$ if we had not first defined $(P \,\&\, Q)$ and $(P \supset Q)$. The definition of $(P \equiv Q)$ just using the primitive operators of our system would be

$(P \equiv Q) = \mathrm{df} \sim (\sim (\sim P \vee Q) \vee \sim (\sim Q \vee P))$

and a name of such formidable size as

$$\sim(\sim(\sim(\sim A \lor B) \lor C) \lor \sim(\sim C \lor (\sim A \lor B)))$$

can now be shortened to $((A \supset B) \equiv C)$.

It is important to realize that the symbols $\&, \supset$, and $\equiv$ do not exist in the object language and that we have not defined them in the object language. They are devices introduced into the metalanguage in order to allow us to shorten the names of formulas of the object language.

Our system will contain infinitely many axioms, which we will be able to designate by the naming procedures we have introduced.[8] There are four classes of these axioms, those named by the following four names

Ax. I $\quad ((P \lor P) \supset P)$
Ax. II $\quad (P \supset (P \lor Q))$
Ax. III $\quad ((P \lor Q) \supset (Q \lor P))$
Ax. IV $\quad ((P \supset Q) \supset ((R \lor P) \supset (R \lor Q)))$

Due to the fact that P, Q, and R each name any formula in H.A. each of the axiom names above name infinitely many axioms in the object language. Since these axiom names contain the symbol $\supset$ they do not resemble the formulas that they name even in form. If we were to replace the symbols defined into the metalanguage by their definitions the resulting names would resemble the formulas named in form. The following list is composed of two formulas in the object language named by each of the axiom names above.

I. $\quad (\sim(A \lor A) \lor A)$
$\quad (\sim((B \lor C) \lor (B \lor C)) \lor (B \lor C))$

II. $\quad (\sim A \lor (A \lor B))$
$\quad (\sim(C \lor D) \lor ((C \lor D) \lor D_2))$

III. $\quad (\sim(A \lor B) \lor (B \lor A))$
$\quad (\sim((C \lor D) \lor B) \lor (B \lor (C \lor D)))$

IV. $\quad (\sim(\sim A \lor B) \lor (\sim(C \lor A) \lor (C \lor B)))$
$\quad (\sim(\sim B \lor (C \lor D)) \lor (\sim(A_2 \lor B) \lor (A_2 \lor (C \lor D))))$.

[8]This method of giving axiom schemata rather than axioms was first introduced by J. von Neumann, "Zur Hilbertschen Beweistheorie," *Mathematische Zeitschrift,* 1927, 26: 1-46. The original Hilbert-Ackermann system contains a finite number of axioms and two rules. Our form of it, making use of von Neumann's device, has infinitely many axioms and one rule.

We will follow the practice of referring to our four axiom names simply as "axioms," but it must be borne in mind that they are actually names and not the axioms themselves.

Our system will contain a single rule which, like the rules of inference with which the reader is familiar, will serve to justify infinitely many inferences of a single form. The rule (R1) is

$$P, P \supset Q \vdash Q$$

where the symbol $\vdash$ can be read "yields." This says that if we have two formulas, one named by P and the other named by $P \supset Q$, we are entitled to write the formula named by Q. Thus if we have

$$(A \supset B)$$

and

$$(A \supset B) \supset C$$

we may write C according to our rule of inference. But since our formulas $(A \supset B), (A \supset B) \supset C$ are shorthand names, the actual inference that is being justified between formulas of the object language is

(~A v B)
~((~A v B) v C)
C

The reader should satisfy himself that the third formula in each of the sets of three formulas below follows from the others by our stated rule:

1. $(\sim \sim A \vee \sim A_2)$
   $\sim A$
   $\sim A_2$
2. $(\sim\sim(\sim A \vee \sim\sim B) \vee \sim(\sim C_1 \vee \sim B))$
   $\sim(\sim A \vee \sim\sim B)$
   $\sim(\sim C_1 \vee \sim B)$

It would also be useful if the reader were to specify the inference in the object language that was being named by each of the following:

1. a. $((\sim A \vee B) \supset D)$
   b. $(\sim A \vee B)$
   c. D by R1 on a, b
2. a. $(C_2 \supset (A \& \sim C))$
   b. C_2
   c. $(A \& \sim C)$ by R1 on a, b
3. a. $((A_1 \equiv (B \vee C)) \supset R)$
   b. $(A_1 \equiv (B \vee C))$
   c. R by R1 on a, b

To simplify the writing of names still further, we now introduce into the metalanguage the symbols [,], {, and } to be used from time to time to clarify the grouping of symbols. They will thus be used to replace some of the left-hand and right-hand parentheses in the names of formulas of the object language. In this way we will write

$$(((A \& \sim A) \& B) \vee C)$$

as

$$\{[(A \& \sim A) \& B] \vee C\}$$

We will also allow the dropping of grouping symbols altogether where the grouping is clear without them. Thus in the metalanguage we can write $A \supset \sim B$ for $(A \supset \sim B)$.

Further devices are available for simplifying the grouping of symbols in the metalanguage. Though no further such devices will be used here the reader should try to supply such devices as an exercise.

The formal system we are considering, H.A., was so constructed as to have propositional logic as one of its interpretations. Given this "intended" interpretation, there are various questions that we can ask about our system. However, before we ask and answer these questions, we must spell out the intended interpretation of our system.

The letter symbols of our system stand, on intended interpretation, for propositions. The operator symbols $\sim$ and $\vee$ stand, on intended interpretation, for "not" and "or" as discussed in Chapter 3, and the grouping symbols are of course the parentheses. Since on this interpretation our letter symbols (now propositional symbols) take on the values of truth or falsity we will incorporate into our metalanguage the entire device of truth tables in order to facilitate our talk of the properties of the system on intended interpretation. We can, for instance, now indicate that on the intended interpretation our operator symbols are defined by Tables 5-1 and 5-2.

TABLE 5-1.

P	$\sim P$
T	F
F	T

TABLE 5-2.

P	Q	$(P \vee Q)$
T	T	T
T	F	T
F	T	T
F	F	F

The first property of our formal system that we will discuss is *functional completeness*. A formal system is said to be functionally complete if on intended interpretation every possible truth-functional formula is expressible in the system, where "expressible in the system" means a logically equivalent formula containing only the connectives $\sim$ and $\vee$ can be written. It is easy to show that for every truth functional formula that is a function of the truth value of a single proposition, a logically equivalent formula can be written in our system. There are, of course, only four such unique formulas. General truth tables can be written for them as in Table 5-3,

TABLE 5-3.

P	$f(P)$
T	
F	

where the "$f(P)$" column can either be **T, T; T, F; F, T;** or **F, F.** The formulas in our system having these same values, i.e., which are the same function of their constituent propositions, are $P \vee \sim P, P, \sim P$ and $\sim (P \vee \sim P)$ respectively

It can also be easily shown that all 16 possible truth functions of two different propositional symbols can be written in our system. The general truth table for these 16 is shown as Table 5-4,

TABLE 5-4.

P	Q	$f(P, Q)$
T	T	
T	F	
F	T	
F	F	

where there are but 16 possible different ways of filling the "$f(P, Q)$" column.[9] Where $f(P, Q)$ is **T,T,F,T**, e.g., we can write in our system the formula $P \vee \sim Q$, which expresses the same function. It is left to the reader to show that all remaining 15 functions are expressible in our system, given the intended interpretation. But what of those truth-functional formulas that are functions of three propositional symbols, or four, or five, etc.? We introduce the truth table, Table 5-5, to express any possible truth-functional formula as a function of its constituent propositional symbols,

TABLE 5-5.

Row	P_1	P_2	P_3	...	P_{n-1}	P_n	$f(P_1, P_2, P_3, \ldots P_{n-1}, P_n)$
1	T	T	T	...	T	T	
2	T	T	T	...	T	F	
.	.	.	.	...	.	.	
.	.	.	.	...	.	.	
.	.	.	.	...	.	.	
2^{n-1}	F	F	F	...	F	T	
2^n	F	F	F	...	F	F	

Given a formula that contains, say, n different propositional symbols, to say that it is truth-functional is to say that the given formula's truth value is entirely determined by the truth value of its n constituent propositional symbols. The table that exhibits the function will contain 2^n rows, since that is the possible number of different combinations of truth values that the constituent propositional symbols can have, and each one of these possi-

[9] See discussion of this point in section 3.3.

bilities will assign a truth value to the given formula. Given the method, indicated in section 3.6, of writing all the possible truth values of the constituent propositional symbols, for a given n, we can specify the values assigned to each propositional symbol in any particular row. If there are three constituent propositions, $n = 3$, then the number of rows, being 2^n, is 8. Now given our method of constructing truth tables, we can construct the required table, Table 5-6.

TABLE 5-6.

Row	P_1	P_2	P_3	$f(P_1, P_2, P_3)$
1	T	T	T	
2	T	T	F	
3	T	F	T	
4	T	F	F	
5	F	T	T	
6	F	T	F	
$2^{n-1} = 7$	F	F	T	
$2^n = 8$	F	F	F	

Thus we have a method for constructing the truth table of any truth-functional formula consisting of any number of constituent propositional symbols.

5.2.1 Metatheorem I: H.A. is functionally complete

Proof: It is true of all truth-functional formulas that either:

1. they have the value true in just one of their defining rows and false in all the others, or

2. they have the value true in more than one of their defining rows, or

3. they have the value true in none of their defining rows, i.e., they have the value false in all their defining rows. Now since all truth-functional formulas fall into one or another of these three classes, it will suffice to prove the functional completeness of our system, if we show that we can construct in our system every formula of each class.

CASE 1 There is a **T** in just one of the defining rows, **F** is in all the others.

241

Let us assume for the moment that the **T** is in the first row. In that case we construct the following formula in our system:

1. $\sim(\sim P_1 \vee \sim P_2 \vee \sim P_3 \vee \ldots \vee \sim P_{n-1} \vee \sim P_n)$

which will have a **T** in its first row, since all the P_i's of which it consists will have the value **T** in the first row, and their negations, $\sim P_i$'s, will thus have the value **F**. The disjunction of the n false disjuncts will have the value false, and since the entire disjunction is negated, the formula will have the value **T**. But in any other row, one or more of the P_i's will have the value **F**, since only in the first row do all the P_i's have the value true. But then the negation of those false P_i's will be true and the disjunction as a whole will be true, since a disjunction is true if one or more disjuncts are true. But then formula 1 will be false, since it is the negation of the disjunction. Thus formula 1 is true in the first and false in all other rows.

Now what if the **T** were in the second row and all other rows were false? Then the requisite formula in our system would be

2. $\sim(\sim P_1 \vee \sim P_2 \vee \sim P_3 \vee \ldots \vee \sim P_{n-1} \vee P_n)$

This formula is true in the second row and nowhere else, for only in the second row are all its disjuncts false. In a similar way all formulas having just one **T** in any one of their defining rows can be written in our system. Simply take the row in which the **T** appears and construct a disjunction, writing $\sim P_i$ for each P_i that has the value **T** in that row and P_i for each P_i that has the value **F** in that row. Then place a tilde in front of the entire disjunction and you will have the requisite formula in our system.

CASE 2 There are two or more **T**'s in the defining rows.

Let us consider first the case where there are just two **T**'s and these in the first and second rows. In this case we simply take formulas 1 and 2 above and write

3. $\sim(\sim P_1 \vee \sim P_2 \vee \sim P_3 \vee \ldots \vee \sim P_{n-1} \vee \sim P_n) \vee$
    $\sim(\sim P_1 \vee \sim P_2 \vee \sim P_3 \vee \ldots \vee \sim P_{n-1} \vee P_n)$

and this is the requisite formula in our system. Consider Table 5-7.

TABLE 5-7.

	(3)	
(1)	(1) v (2)	(2)
T	T	F
F	T	T
F	F	F
.	.	.
.	.	.
.	.	.
F	F	F
F	F	F

Since formula 1 is true in the first row and false in all others and formula 2 is true in the second row and false in all others, the disjunction of the two formulas, 3, will be true in the first two rows and false in all others. In a similar fashion we can construct formulas in our system that have two or more T's in their defining tables. Say the T's are in rows j, k, and l. We first construct formulas as in case 1, i.e., a formula that is true in the jth row and false in all others, and a formula that is true in the kth row and false in all others, and finally a formula that is true in the lth row and false in all others. Now we write the disjunction of these three formulas and we have the requisite formula in our system.

CASE 3   There are no T's in any row.

In this case the requisite formula is:

4. $\sim(P_1 \vee \sim P_1 \vee P_2 \vee P_3 \vee \ldots \vee P_{n-1} \vee P_n)$

Thus we have shown that given any truth-functional formula whatsoever, we can write an equivalent formula in our system. Our system is thus functionally complete. Since the only factor in our system that figured in the above proof was that it contained the $\sim$ and $\vee$, it follows that any formal system containing the $\sim$ and $\vee$ is, on intended interpretation, functionally complete.

The reader should now prove that the formal system containing the following connectives are, on intended interpretation, functionally complete: $\sim$, &; $\sim$, $\supset$; and the symbol /, defined on intended interpretation as in Table 5-8.

TABLE 5-8.

P	Q	P/Q
T	T	F
T	F	T
F	T	T
F	F	T

We turn now to the concept of *demonstration.* A formal notion of demonstration will not only allow us to define "proof" and "theorem," it will enable us to prove many things about our formal system. A demonstration will be a vertical listing of formulas such that each formula (called a step) is either an axiom or follows from two previous steps by R1, or is a premise. Any formula that is the last step of a demonstration, in which every step is either an axiom or follows from two previous steps by R1 is called a *theorem* of our system.

Any demonstration that contains premises as steps will be called a demonstration of a *derived rule,* the derived rule being that the last formula in the demonstration follows from the premises contained as steps in the demonstration. Thus,

$(P \lor Q)$ Premise
$(P \lor Q) \supset (Q \lor P)$ Ax. III
$Q \lor P$ By R1

is a demonstration of the derived rule (DR1)

$P \lor Q \vdash Q \lor P$

It should be noted that every axiom is a theorem according to our definition. When the symbol $\vdash$ appears alone before a formula, it is to be read "is a theorem." Thus, $\vdash (P \lor P) \supset P$ says that the formula $(P \lor P) \supset P$ is a theorem of our system.

Before we demonstrate any theorems of our system a few words must be said about the notion of *replacement.* Any original name may be replaced by another name that names a subset of the things named by the original name. Thus, remembering that the symbols P, Q, R, S, etc. are names, the name P may be replaced by the name $\sim P$, since everything named by $\sim P$ is already named by P. Similarly the name P may be replaced by the name $Q \& R$, since everything named by $Q \& R$ is already named by P. P may, of course, be replaced by R since P and R are equally general names, i.e., they both can name the same thing.

Since our four axioms are actually names of the infinitely many axioms of the object language, they too can be replaced by other names that name some subset of the axioms of the object language. Any name that replaces an axiom name is then, itself, an axiom name. We will call any name that replaces an original name a form of the original name. For simplicity's sake each name and its forms will receive the same designation. Thus we will call both

$$(P \vee P) \supset P$$

and

$$((P \& Q) \vee (P \& Q)) \supset (P \& Q)$$

Axiom I, though the latter is a *form* of $(P \vee P) \supset P$. Similarly, we will call both

$$P, P \supset Q \vdash Q$$

and

$$R \supset Q, (R \supset Q) \supset P \vdash P$$

R1, though the latter is a form of $P, P \supset Q \vdash Q$.

It must be borne in mind that replacement is an operation that exists between names and hence takes place in the metalanguage.

We will now proceed to develop our system by demonstrating several theorems and derived rules.

Theorem 1: $\vdash (Q \supset R) \supset [(P \supset Q) \supset (P \supset R)]$
Demonstration: $(Q \supset R) \supset [(\sim P \vee Q) \supset (\sim P \vee R)]$ Ax. IV
       $(Q \supset R) \supset [(P \supset Q) \supset (P \supset R)]$ By def.

It should be noted that what we call "by definition" is a case of replacement since our defined symbols are shorthand names.

We now introduce the notion of *proof*. A proof is a vertical listing of formulas, called steps, each of which is an axiom, *or* a step derived from two previous steps by a use of R1, *or* a premise, *or* a theorem, *or* a step derived from one or more previous steps by a derived rule. Every proof can be turned into a demonstration by replacing each theorem in it with a form of its own demonstration and each derived rule in it with a form of its own demonstration. We will use proofs rather than demonstrations when space demands.

DR2:	$(P \supset Q), (Q \supset R) \vdash (P \supset R)$	
Proof:	$(Q \supset R) \supset [(P \supset Q) \supset (P \supset R)]$	Th. 1
	$Q \supset R$	Premise
	$(P \supset Q) \supset (P \supset R)$	By R1
	$P \supset Q$	Premise
	$P \supset R$	By R1
Theorem 2:	$\vdash P \supset P$	
Proof:	$P \supset (P \vee P)$	Ax. II
	$(P \vee P) \supset P$	Ax. I
	$P \supset P$	By DR2

For purposes of illustration, we will now write the demonstration of Theorem 2.

Theorem 2:	$\vdash P \supset P$	
Demonstration:	$[(P \vee P) \supset P] \supset \{[\sim P \vee (P \vee P)] \supset (\sim P \vee P)\}$	Ax. IV
	$[(P \vee P) \supset P] \supset \{[P \supset (P \vee P)] \supset (P \supset P)\}$	By def.
	$(P \vee P) \supset P$	Ax. I
	$[P \supset (P \vee P)] \supset (P \supset P)$	By R1
	$P \supset (P \vee P)$	Ax. II
	$P \supset P$	By R1
Theorem 3:	$\vdash P \supset (Q \supset P)$	
Proof:	$P \supset (P \vee \sim Q)$	Ax. II
	$(P \vee \sim Q) \supset (\sim Q \vee P)$	Ax. III
	$P \supset (\sim Q \vee P)$	By DR2
	$P \supset (Q \supset P)$	By def.

It should be noted that the inferences allowed by a rule are independent of the interpretation of the rule because the rule is purely syntactic. Thus, if we introduce the primitive connective $*$ and state the following rule

$P * Q, \sim Q \vdash \sim P$

it is perfectly clear that

$$(\sim P \vee R) * (S \& R)$$
$$\sim(S \& R)$$
$$\sim(\sim P \vee R)$$

is allowed by the rule without one's knowing what $*$ is. In the same way R1 of our system allows exactly the same inferences, no matter what interpretation we give the symbols $\sim$ and $\vee$. On intended interpretation R1 of our system is hereditary with respect to truth, i.e., if the premises are true, then what our R1 allows us to write will be true. That this is the case can be seen from Table 5-9.

TABLE 5-9.

P	Q	P ⊃ Q
T	T	T
T	F	F
F	T	T
F	F	T

If, instead of our intended interpretation, we had allowed our letter symbols to take on the values 1 or 0, and interpreted our operator symbols as in Tables 5-10 and 5-11,

TABLE 5-10.

P	~P
1	0
0	1

TABLE 5-11.

P	Q	(P ∨ Q)
1	1	1
1	0	1
0	1	1
0	0	0

our R1 would have been hereditary with respect to "1-ness" since Table 5-12 would follow by our definition of the ⊃. But it would remain the same rule for it would still allow exactly the same inferences. Indeed, it would not matter

TABLE 5-12.

P	Q	P ⊃ Q
1	1	1
1	0	0
0	1	1
0	0	1

if our interpretation was such that our letter symbols took on one of three values 0, 1, 2 and ~ and v were defined as in Tables 5-13 and 5-14.

TABLE 5-13.

P	~P
0	1
1	0
2	2

TABLE 5-14.

P	Q	P v Q
0	0	0
0	1	0
0	2	0
1	0	0
1	1	1
1	2	2
2	0	0
2	1	2
2	2	0

Though our R1 is, under this interpretation, hereditary with respect to "0-ness" (see Table 5-15) it *still* allows the same inferences.

TABLE 5-15.

P	Q	P ⊃ Q
0	0	0
0	1	1
0	2	2
1	0	0
1	1	0
1	2	0
2	0	0
2	1	2
2	2	0

5.2.2 Metatheorem II: the axioms of H.A. are independent

Let us turn now to the question of the independence of our axioms. To say that our axioms are independent is to say that no one of them is deducible from the others by means of the rule of our system. We have now seen that the property of independence can be discussed irrespective of any particular interpretation of our system, for our rule allows precisely the same deductions no matter what the interpretation. But we can use just this fact to show that our axioms are independent. If we could find an interpretation of H.A. such that R1 was hereditary with respect to some value, say δ, and we could show that under that interpretation, axioms I-III had the value δ when axiom IV did not, we would show axiom IV to be independent of the others. For since R1 is hereditary with respect to δ, it would not enable us to get from a set of formulas with the value of δ to a formula that does not have the value δ. Further, since a rule allows the same inferences under any interpretation and we have shown the rule does not allow the inference from axioms I-III to axiom IV under this interpretation, we have shown that it does not allow it under any interpretation. Which is simply to say, you cannot use axioms I-III to validly deduce axiom IV by means of R1 and thus axiom IV is independent.

CASE 1   Axiom I is independent

TABLE 5-16.

P	$\sim P$
0	1
1	0
2	2

TABLE 5-17.

P	Q	$P \vee Q$
0	0	0
0	1	0
0	2	0
1	0	0
1	1	1
1	2	2
2	0	0
2	1	2
2	2	0

On the interpretation afforded by Tables 5-16 and 5-17 R1 is hereditary with respect to 0-ness. When P has the value 2, Q has the value 0, and R has the value 0, axioms II, III, and IV all have the value 0, but axiom I has the value 2. Thus R1 allows no inferences from axioms II, III, and IV to axiom I. Axiom 1 is thus independent.

CASE 2 Axiom III is independent.

Let the values of P, $\sim P$, Q, and $P \lor Q$ be as shown in Tables 5-18 and 5-19.

TABLE 5-18.

P	$\sim P$
0	1
1	0
2	0
3	2

TABLE 5-19.

P	Q	$P \lor Q$
0	0	0
0	1	0
0	2	0
0	3	0
1	0	0
1	1	1
1	2	2
1	3	3
2	0	0
2	1	2
2	2	2
2	3	0
3	0	0
3	1	3
3	2	3
3	3	3

On this interpretation R1 is hereditary with respect to 0-ness. When P has the value 2, Q has the value 3, and R has the value 0, axioms I, II, and IV all have the value 0 while axiom III has the value 3. Thus R1 allows no inferences from axioms I, II, and IV to axiom III. Axiom III is thus proven independent.

CASE 3 Axiom IV is independent.

Let the values of P, $\sim P$, Q, and $P \vee Q$ be as shown in Tables 5-20 and 5-21.

TABLE 5-20.

P	$\sim P$
0	1
1	0
2	3
3	0

TABLE 5-21.

P	Q	$P \vee Q$
0	0	0
0	1	0
0	2	0
0	3	0
1	0	0
1	1	1
1	2	2
1	3	3
2	0	0
2	1	2
2	2	2
2	3	0
3	0	0
3	1	3
3	2	0
3	3	3

On this interpretation R1 is hereditary with respect to 0-ness. When P has the value 3, Q has the value 1, and R has the value 2, axioms I, II, and III all have the value 0, while axiom IV has the value 2. Thus R1 will not allow the deduction axiom IV from axioms I, II, and III. Thus axiom IV is independent.

CASE 4 Axiom II is independent.

251

Let the values of P, $\sim P$, Q, and P v Q be as shown in Tables 5-22 and 5-23.

TABLE 5-22.

P	$\sim P$
0	1
1	0
2	3
3	2

TABLE 5-23.

P	Q	P v Q
0	0	0
0	1	0
0	2	0
0	3	0
1	0	0
1	1	1
1	2	1
1	3	1
2	0	0
2	1	1
2	2	2
2	3	2
3	0	0
3	1	1
3	2	2
3	3	3

On this interpretation R1 is hereditary with respect to 0-ness or 2-ness as can be seen from Table 5-24. Axioms I, III, and IV on this interpretation take on only the values 0 and 2 and R1 is hereditary with respect to this property, i.e., any formula deducible from axioms I, III, and IV by R1 will take on only the values 0 and 2. That this so follows not just from the fact that on this interpretation 0 and 2 are hereditary, but also from the fact that if R1 is used on two formulas, one of which has the value 0 and the other of which has the value 2, the resultant formula will have the value 0. Axiom II, on the other hand, has the value 1 when P is 2 and Q is 1, from which it follows that axiom II cannot be deduced by the use of R1 from axioms I, III, and IV. Axiom II is thus independent. We now have proven each of the axioms of H.A. independent of the others.

TABLE 5-24.

P	Q	$P \supset Q$
0	0	0
0	1	1
0	2	1
0	3	1
1	0	0
1	1	0
1	2	0
1	3	0
2	0	0
2	1	1
2	2	2
2	3	3
3	0	0
3	1	1
3	2	2
3	3	2

In order to facilitate the proving of further metatheorems of H.A. we now introduce into our metalanguage the method of *mathematical induction.* "Mathematical induction" is actually a misnomer, as the method is purely deductive. The principle of mathematical induction follows immediately from Peano's fifth axiom,[10] "Any property which belongs to 1 and also to the successor of any number which has it belongs to all numbers." If we are able to order some group of things by means of the natural numbers so that there is a first, a second, a third, etc., and we are able to show that the first of these things has the property *f,* and that if we assume any one of these things to have the property *f,* it follows that the next one will also have the property *f,* then it follows by mathematical induction that all things have the property *f.*

One does not ordinarily try to prove mathematical induction due to its place as one of Peano's axioms; but if we replace Peano's fifth axiom with what is sometimes called the *axiom of well ordering*, mathematical induction (or its equivalent) can be proven. We will proceed by first giving a definition that will allow us to restate the principle of mathematical induction in set theoretic

[10] Giuseppe Peano (1858-1932) presented his five axioms in an attempt to formalize a part of the theory of natural numbers. The first four of his axioms may be expressed as follows: (1) Zero is a natural number. (2) The immediate successor of any natural number is a natural number. (3) Distinct natural numbers never have the same immediate successor. (4) Zero is not the immediate successor of any natural number.

terms. We will then prove this restatement of mathematical induction.

A set G of positive integers is called *inductive* if, whenever we take any member of the set and add 1 to it, the result is a member of the set.

The principle of mathematical induction can now be stated as follows:

> If we have any set G and we find that
> α. 1 is in G, and
> β. G is inductive,
> then all integers will be in G.

Suppose that we have a set G of positive integers with properties α and β, then we will show that *all* positive integers are in G.

In order to prove the foregoing, let us assume that there are positive integers not in G. Pick the smallest such number, call it Q.

Q is not 1, since 1 is in G, so $Q = P + 1$ for some positive integer P. However, $P < Q$ and therefore P is in G. But if P is in G and G is inductive, $P + 1$ must be in G also. But $P + 1$ is Q, so Q is in G. Thus our assumption that there are positive integers not in G leads to a contradiction, viz., that Q is and is not in G. Therefore, all positive integers are in G.

The form of mathematical induction we have so far discussed is called *weak induction.* There is, however, another form called *strong induction,* which differs only in the way the conditions are stated for the induction.

If we are able to order some group of things by means of the natural numbers so that there is a first, a second, a third, etc., and we are able to show that the first of these things has the property f and that if we assume that some arbitrarily chosen thing and all those things that precede it in the ordering each have the property f, it follows that the next one will also have the property f, then it follows by mathematical induction that all the things have the property f.

We can state weak induction as

> If $f(1)$
> and for any arbitrary n,
> if $f(n)$ then $f(n + 1)$,
> then for all m, $f(m)$

where n is any arbitrarily chosen integer and m ranges over all the positive integers and $f(a)$ is read, a has the property f. The numbers should be read as ordinals rather than cardinals for our purposes.

Strong induction could then be written

If $f(1)$
and for any arbitrary n,
if $f(k)$ for every $k < n$, then $f(n)$
then for all $m, f(m)$.

We now turn our attention to the question of the consistency of our system. A formal deductive system is said to be consistent if no contradiction is deducible by means of the rules of the system from the axioms of the system. We will proceed by first proving that every theorem of our system is a tautology. Any system in which every theorem is a tautology is said to be analytic.

5.2.3 Metatheorem III: H.A. is analytic

Every theorem of our system is a tautology, i.e., if $\vdash P$ then P is a tautology. We will prove this by mathematical induction on the number of uses of R1 in the demonstration of $\vdash P$. It should be noted before we proceed with the mathematical induction that if there are no uses of R1 in the demonstration of $\vdash P$, P must be an axiom and all our axioms are tautologies as Tables 5-25 through 5-28 show.

TABLE 5-25. Axiom I.

P	$P \vee P$	$(P \vee P) \supset P$
T	T	T
F	F	T

TABLE 5-26. Axiom II.

P	Q	$P \vee Q$	$P \supset (P \vee Q)$
T	T	T	T
T	F	T	T
F	T	T	T
F	F	F	T

TABLE 5-27. Axiom III.

P	Q	$P \vee Q$	$Q \vee P$	$(P \vee Q) \supset (Q \vee P)$
T	T	T	T	T
T	F	T	T	T
F	T	T	T	T
F	F	F	F	T

TABLE 5-28. Axiom IV.

P	Q	R	$P \supset Q$	$R \vee P$	$R \vee Q$	$(P \supset Q) \supset$ $((R \vee P) \supset (R \vee Q))$
T	T	T	T	T	T	T
T	T	F	T	T	T	T
T	F	T	F	T	T	T
T	F	F	F	T	F	T
F	T	T	T	T	T	T
F	T	F	T	F	T	T
F	F	T	T	T	T	T
F	F	F	T	F	F	T

We will now proceed with our proof by strong induction on the number of uses of R1, in the demonstration of ⊢ P.

> α **CASE**   There is one use of R1 in the demonstration of ⊢ P. In this case R1 is used on two previous steps each of which must be an axiom.

These two steps must have the form

$$S_j \supset S_k$$
$$S_j$$

where S_k is P. We will show that P must be a tautology in this case by assuming that P is not a tautology and deriving a contradiction. Let us also assume that we have constructed a truth table containing the formulas $S_j \supset S_k$, S_j and S_k which, of course, we can do for any given case. Now, if P, i.e., S_k, is not a tautology it must have the value **F** in some row of the truth table, say the mth. Since the formula S_j is an axiom and thus a tautology it is true in every row including the mth. Since in the mth row the formula S_j has the value **T** and the formula S_k has the value **F**, the formula $S_j \supset S_k$ must have the value **F** in its mth row. But the formula $S_j \supset S_k$ is an axiom and thus a tautology so it must have the value **T** in its mth row. From our assumption that P is not a tautology we have arrived at the contradiction that $S_j \supset S_k$ is both **T** and **F** in its mth row; thus P must be a tautology.

β **CASE**   Our assumption here is that in each of the $k < n$ uses of R1 in the demonstration $\vdash P$, the result was a tautology. We will prove then that the nth use of R1 will result in a tautology. The nth use of R1 will take place on two previous steps that must be of the form

$S_j \supset S_k$

and

S_k

Each of these formulas, being steps in the demonstration of a theorem, is either an axiom or derived from two previous steps by a use of R1. If one or the other is an axiom, then they are tautologies. If one or the other resulted from a use of R1, it must have been one of the $k < n$ uses of R1, and by our β case assumption, if they resulted from any of the $k < n$ uses of R1 they are tautologies. Thus our formulas $S_j \supset S_k$ and S_k are both tautologies. Now by the same reasoning found in the α case above the result of the nth use of R1 on $S_j \supset S_k$ and S_j, i.e., S_k, will be a tautology.

Having proven both the α and β case, it follows that for any number of uses of R1 in the demonstration of $\vdash P$, P is a tautology. Thus, all the theorems of H.A. are tautologies and so H.A. is said to be *analytic*.

5.2.4   Metatheorem IV: our system, H.A., is consistent

If a formal deductive system is inconsistent, i.e., if its axioms are inconsistent, contradictories are demonstrable from its axioms. That is to say two theorems of the system will be contradictory. Given contradictory theorems in our system it is possible to prove any other formula a theorem by the following technique: Let us prove that Z is a theorem, where Z is any formula, given that we already have as theorems $\vdash P$ and $\vdash \sim P$.

$\sim P \supset (\sim P \vee Z)$	Ax. II
$\sim P$	Theorem
$\sim P \vee Z$	By R1
$P \supset Z$	By def.
P	Theorem
Z	By R1

Thus every formula will be a theorem of our system, if our system is inconsistent. If we can show that there is a formula that is not a theorem of our system it will follow then that our system is consistent.[11]

We have already shown that our system is analytic, i.e., that every theorem is a tautology. From this it immediately follows that any formula not a tautology is not a theorem. The formula $\sim(P \vee \sim P)$ is a formula of our system that is not a tautology and therefore, not a theorem. We have thus shown that there is a formula of our system that is not a theorem and thus our system must be consistent.

We will now continue with the development of H.A.

Theorem 4:	$\vdash P \vee \sim P$	
Proof:	$P \supset P$	Th. 2
	$\sim P \vee P$	By def.
	$(\sim P \vee P) \supset (P \vee \sim P)$	Ax. III
	$P \vee \sim P$	By R1
Theorem 5:	$\vdash P \supset \sim\sim P$	
Proof:	$\sim P \vee \sim\sim P$	Th. 4
	$P \supset \sim\sim P$	By def.
DR 3:	$P \supset Q \vdash \sim Q \supset \sim P$	
Proof:	$P \supset Q$	Premise
	$Q \supset \sim\sim Q$	Th. 5
	$P \supset \sim\sim Q$	By DR2
	$\sim P \vee \sim\sim Q$	By def.
	$(\sim P \vee \sim\sim Q) \supset (\sim\sim Q \vee \sim P)$	Ax. III
	$\sim\sim Q \vee \sim P$	By R1
	$\sim Q \supset \sim P$	By def.
Theorem 6:	$\vdash P \supset (P \& P)$	
Proof:	$(\sim P \vee \sim P) \supset \sim P$	Ax. I
	$\sim\sim P \supset \sim(\sim P \vee \sim P)$	By DR 3
	$P \supset \sim\sim P$	Th. 5
	$P \supset \sim(\sim P \vee \sim P)$	By DR 2
	$P \supset (P \& P)$	By def.

[11] This is known as the *Post criterion of consistency*; it is due to C. L. Post.

DR4: $P, Q \vdash P \& Q$
Proof: $Q \supset (P \supset Q)$ Th. 3
           Q Premise
           $P \supset Q$ By R1
           $\sim Q \supset \sim P$ By DR3
           $(\sim Q \supset \sim P) \supset [(\sim P \vee \sim Q) \supset (\sim P \vee \sim P)]$ Ax. IV
           $(\sim P \vee \sim Q) \supset (\sim P \vee \sim P)$ By R1
           $\sim(\sim P \vee \sim P) \supset \sim(\sim P \vee \sim Q)$ By DR3
           $(P \& P) \supset (P \& Q)$ By def.
           $P \supset (P \& P)$ Th. 6
           $P \supset (P \& Q)$ By DR2
           P Premise
           $P \& Q$ By R1

Theorem 7: $\vdash \sim\sim P \supset P$
Proof: $\sim P \supset \sim\sim\sim P$ Th. 5
             $(\sim P \supset \sim\sim\sim P) \supset [(P \vee \sim P) \supset (P \vee \sim\sim\sim P)]$ Ax. IV
             $(P \vee \sim P) \supset (P \vee \sim\sim\sim P)$ By R1
             $P \vee \sim P$ Th. 4
             $P \vee \sim\sim\sim P$ By R1
             $(P \vee \sim\sim\sim P) \supset (\sim\sim\sim P \vee P)$ Ax. III
             $\sim\sim\sim P \vee P$ By R1
             $\sim\sim P \supset P$ By def.

Theorem 8: $\vdash (P \& Q) \supset P$
Proof: $\sim P \supset (\sim P \vee \sim Q)$ Ax. II
             $\sim(\sim P \vee \sim Q) \supset \sim\sim P$ By DR3
             $(P \& Q) \supset \sim\sim P$ By def.
             $\sim\sim P \supset P$ Th. 7
             $(P \& Q) \supset P$ By DR2

Theorem 9: $\vdash (P \& Q) \supset Q$
Proof: $\sim Q \supset (\sim Q \vee \sim P)$ Ax. II
             $(\sim Q \vee \sim P) \supset (\sim P \vee \sim Q)$ Ax. III
             $\sim Q \supset (\sim P \vee \sim Q)$ By DR2
             $\sim(\sim P \vee \sim Q) \supset \sim\sim Q$ By DR3
             $(P \& Q) \supset \sim\sim Q$ By def.
             $\sim\sim Q \supset Q$ Th. 7
             $(P \& Q) \supset Q$ By DR2

Theorem 10: $\vdash P \equiv P$
Proof: $P \supset P$ Th. 2
             $P \supset P$ Th. 2
             $(P \supset P) \& (P \supset P)$ By DR4
             $P \equiv P$ By def.

DR5:	$P \equiv Q \vdash \sim P \equiv \sim Q$	
Proof:	$P \equiv Q$	Premise
	$(P \supset Q) \& (Q \supset P)$	By def.
	$((P \supset Q) \& (Q \supset P)) \supset (P \supset Q)$	Th. 8
	$P \supset Q$	By R1
	$\sim Q \supset \sim P$	By DR3
	$((P \supset Q) \& (Q \supset P)) \supset (Q \supset P)$	Th. 9
	$Q \supset P$	By R1
	$\sim P \supset \sim Q$	By DR3
	$(\sim P \supset \sim Q) \& (\sim Q \supset \sim P)$	By DR4
	$\sim P \equiv \sim Q$	By def.

DR6:	$P \supset Q, R \supset S \vdash (P \vee R) \supset (Q \vee S)$	
Proof:	$(P \supset Q) \supset [(S \vee P) \supset (S \vee Q)]$	Ax. IV
	$P \supset Q$	Premise
	$(S \vee P) \supset (S \vee Q)$	By R1
	$(R \supset S) \supset [(P \vee R) \supset (P \vee S)]$	Ax. IV
	$R \supset S$	Premise
	$(P \vee R) \supset (P \vee S)$	By R1
	$(P \vee S) \supset (S \vee P)$	Ax. III
	$(P \vee S) \supset (S \vee Q)$	By DR2
	$(S \vee Q) \supset (Q \vee S)$	Ax. III
	$(P \vee S) \supset (Q \vee S)$	By DR2
	$(P \vee R) \supset (Q \vee S)$	By DR2

DR7:	$P \equiv Q, R \equiv S \vdash (P \vee R) \equiv (Q \vee S)$	
Proof:	$P \equiv Q$	Premise
	$(P \supset Q) \& (Q \supset P)$	By def.
	$((P \supset Q) \& (Q \supset P)) \supset (P \supset Q)$	Th. 8
	$P \supset Q$	By R1
	$R \equiv S$	Premise
	$(R \supset S) \& (S \supset R)$	By def.
	$((R \supset S) \& (S \supset R)) \supset (R \supset S)$	Th. 8
	$R \supset S$	By R1
	$(P \vee R) \supset (Q \vee S)$	By DR6
	$((P \supset Q) \& (Q \supset P)) \supset (Q \supset P)$	Th. 9
	$Q \supset P$	By R1
	$((R \supset S) \& (S \supset R)) \supset (S \supset R)$	Th. 9
	$S \supset R$	By R1
	$(Q \vee S) \supset (P \vee R)$	By DR6
	$[(P \vee R) \supset (Q \vee S)] \& [(Q \vee S) \supset (P \vee R)]$	By DR4
	$(P \vee R) \equiv (Q \vee S)$	By def.

EXERCISE

1 Prove the following theorems and derived rules of H.A.
   a. Theorem 11: $\vdash P \equiv \sim\sim P$
   b. Theorem 12: $\vdash (P \& Q) \supset (Q \& P)$
   c. DR8: $P \supset Q, R \supset S \vdash (P \& R) \supset (Q \& S)$
   d. Theorem 13: $\vdash [P \lor (Q \lor R)] \supset [(P \lor Q) \lor R]$
   e. Theorem 14: $\vdash [(P \lor Q) \lor R] \supset [P \lor (Q \lor R)]$
   f. DR9: $P \supset (Q \supset R) \vdash (P \& Q) \supset R$
   g. DR10: $(P \& Q) \supset R \vdash P \supset (Q \supset R)$

5.2.5   Metatheorem V: the substitution metatheorem

We are now ready to prove the substitution metatheorem, metatheorem V. We have previously spoken of replacement as an operation that one can carry out with names, i.e., we can replace one name with any other name that names a subset of the things named by the original name. Thus we have seen that the name P can be replaced by the name $\sim P$. Substitution is quite different from replacement. A rule of substitution would say that we could write P for Q if $P \equiv Q$, i.e., if P and Q had the same truth values. Now though the name $\sim P$ can replace the name P, it is never the case that $\sim P$ can be substituted for P, since it is never the case that $\sim P \equiv P$. Though there is no explicit rule of substitution in our system, the only explicit rule being R1, we can now prove that substitution is implicit in our system. It is implicit in the sense that given H.A.'s infinite number of axioms and the system of naming and replacement inherent in it, we can do all the things we could do if we had a rule of substitution and only a finite number of axioms.

We must first formulate the substitution metatheorem: If we let P_1, P_2, P_3, ..., P_n be any formulas of our system and let Q be any formula that does not occur as, or as a part of any P_i; and let S be any formula made up of only Q and P_i $(1 \leqslant i \leqslant n)$, then if S' is a formula obtainable by putting R in place of any number of occurrences of Q in S, then $Q = R$, $S \vdash S'$. That this formulation adequately captures the notion of substitution can be seen by first considering some examples of S and S' (Table 5-29) and then considering what the metatheorem says about them.

In row 1 of Table 5-29 our S formula is P_1 and since P_1 can be gotten from P_1 by putting R in place of any number of occurrences of Q in P_1, since there are none, P_1 is also an S' formula. In row 2 we find that for the S formula $P_2 \supset Q$ there are two possible S' formulas. One is gotten by replacing none of the occurrences of Q by R (a possibility left open by our use of the phrase

TABLE 5-29.

Row	S	S'
1	P_1	P_1
2	$P_2 \supset Q$	$P_2 \supset Q, P_2 \supset R$
3	$(P_1 \vee Q) \supset Q$	$(P_1 \vee Q) \supset Q, (P_1 \vee R) \supset Q, (P_1 \vee Q) \supset R, (P_1 \vee R) \supset R$

"any number" in our formulation); and the other is gotten by replacing all occurrences of Q by R. Row 3 should now be clear to the reader. Our metatheorem says that if $Q \equiv R$ and you also have $P_2 \supset Q$, you will be able to derive, for instance, $P_2 \supset R$ in our system.

We will proceed by first proving that $Q \equiv R \vdash S \equiv S'$ and then proving $Q \equiv R, S \vdash S'$ as a corollary.

Let $P_1, P_2, P_3, \ldots, P_n$ be any formulas of our system; let Q be any formula that does not occur as, or as a part of any P_i, and let S be any formula which is made up of only Q and P_i $(1 \leqslant i \leqslant n)$. If S' is a formula obtainable by putting R in place of any number of occurrences of Q in S, then $Q \equiv R \vdash S \equiv S'$.

Proof is by strong induction on the number of symbols in S counting each occurrence of $\sim$, $\vee$, Q, and P_i $(1 \leqslant i \leqslant n)$ as a single symbol.

α**CASE**: There is only one symbol in S and that symbol must be either a Q or a single P_i.

    CASE 1 S is Q and S' is Q.

Since $\vdash Q \equiv Q$ is Theorem 10, and since in this case S, S', and Q are merely different names for the same thing, we have by replacement (not substitution)

    $\vdash S \equiv S'$

Given that $S \equiv S'$ is a theorem and that to say that it is is to say that $S \equiv S'$ is demonstrable from the axioms alone, it is also true to say that $S \equiv S'$ is demonstrable from the axioms plus some (any) additional premise, thus

    $Q \equiv R \vdash S \equiv S'$

    CASE 2 S is Q and S' is R.

Given the premise $Q \equiv R$ and that in this case S and Q name the same thing and S' and R name the same thing, we have by replacement (not substitution) that

$$S \equiv S'$$

Thus,

$$Q \equiv R \vdash S \equiv S'$$

CASE 3 S is P_i and so S' is P_i also.

$\vdash P_i \equiv P_i$ Th. 10
$\vdash S \equiv S'$ By replacement
$Q \equiv R \vdash S \equiv S'$

β **CASE:** Assume our metatheorem true for any S formula containing less than m symbols. Given this assumption we will show the metatheorem true for any S formula containing exactly m symbols. Consider an S formula containing m symbols $(m > 1)$. S has either the form $\sim S_1$ or $S_2 \vee S_3$.

CASE 1 S is of the form $\sim S_1$.

Since S contains exactly m symbols and the $\sim$ counts as a symbol, S_1 contains less than m symbols ($m - 1$ to be exact) and thus by our β case assumption

$$Q \equiv R \vdash S_1 \equiv S_1'$$

Since by DR5

$$S_1 \equiv S_1' \vdash \sim S_1 \equiv \sim S_1'$$

we have

$$Q \equiv R \vdash \sim S_1 \equiv \sim S_1'$$

and since

$$S \text{ is } \sim S, S' \text{ is } \sim S_1'$$

(since the $\sim$ in $\sim S_1$ will not be affected by replacing any number of occurrences of Q in S_1 by R). We have then, by replacement

$$Q \equiv R \vdash S \equiv S'$$

CASE 2 S is of the form $S_2 \vee S_3$.

Since S contains m symbols and the $\vee$ counts as a symbol, S_2 and S_3 each contain fewer than m symbols and so by our β case assumption we have

$$Q \equiv R \vdash S_2 \equiv S_2'$$

and

$$Q \equiv R \vdash S_3 \equiv S_3'$$

by DR7 we then get

$$Q \equiv R, Q \equiv R \vdash (S_2 \vee S_3) \equiv (S_2' \vee S_3')$$

which clearly is the same as

$$Q \equiv R \vdash (S_2 \vee S_3) \equiv (S_2' \vee S_3')$$

and since S is $(S_2 \vee S_3)$, S' is $(S_2' \vee S_3')$ (since the $\vee$ in $(S_2 \vee S_3)$ will not be affected by replacing any number of occurrences of Q in S_2 and S_3 by R). We then have by replacement

$$Q \equiv R \vdash S \equiv S'$$

Thus for any S formula containing any number of symbols

$$Q \equiv R \vdash S \equiv S'$$

Now as a corollary to Metatheorem V, we will prove

$$Q \equiv R, S \vdash S'$$

If we have $Q \equiv R$ as a premise, then by our previous metatheorem we have

$$S \equiv S' \qquad \text{By M.T. V}$$
$$(S \supset S') \,\&\, (S' \supset S) \qquad \text{By def.}$$
$$((S \supset S') \,\&\, (S' \supset S)) \supset (S \supset S') \qquad \text{Th. 8}$$
$$S \supset S' \qquad \text{By R1}$$
$$S \qquad \text{Premise}$$
$$S' \qquad \text{By R1}$$

Thus

$$Q \equiv R, S \vdash S'$$

We could go on developing our system and proving further metatheorems about it. We could, for instance, show that on intended interpretation every tautology will be a theorem of our system, i.e., our system is *deductively complete*; which, given our proof of the analyticity of our system, leads to the conclusion that the set of theorems of H.A. is identical to the set of tautologies. We could indeed show that if any nontautology is added to our set of axioms, our resulting system would be inconsistent, i.e., our system is *strictly complete*. We turn now, however, to a discussion of why one should bother to formalize at all.

5.3 WHY FORMALIZE?

Two aspects of formalization should be discussed. First, why do we present an uninterpreted syntactical system only to end up talking about its properties on what we have called the intended interpretation? Second, why do we axiomatize instead of working with a group of rules as in natural deduction?

In dealing with uninterpreted syntactical systems, we are, in a sense, abstracting certain features of logic from others. In this way we end up with something considerably more general than the logic of Chapters 3 and 4. The syntactical features of truth-functional logic are shared by other systems. We have seen in Chapter 3, e.g., that electronic switching circuits share the syntactical features of propositional logic. It was also mentioned that something so seemingly distant from logic as plumbing shares many of these same syntactical features. The similarity of syntactical features in plumbing and electronic circuitry has often served as a pedagogic device, that of making the unfamiliar features of electronic circuitry familiar. When propositional logic is presented as an uninterpreted syntactical system, the possibility of multiple interpretations becomes manifest. Perhaps the enormous power of this treatment of logic is best seen when it is realized that the recognition of the syntactical similarities between logic and switching circuits has made the electronic digital computer possible. C. E. Shannon, in an article published in 1938, laid the groundwork for this advance.[12]

Once the syntactical similarities are seen, or, what is the same thing, once the various possible interpretations are noted, we can go on to prove various things about our system on one of those interpretations. Since our major concern has been the evaluation of arguments, it is natural for us to be concerned with what we have called the intended interpretation. However, since these properties (consistency, analyticity, functional completeness, etc.) arise in large part from the syntactical features of our system, proving them of our system on a given interpretation, has definite consequences on any possible interpretation.

When we proved our system consistent on intended interpretation, we in fact proved that no formula of the form (P & $\sim P$) is a theorem of our system. This is a syntactical feature of our system and no matter what interpretation is given to the notion of "theorem" and "formula" (P & $\sim P$) is excluded. Thus, though consistency is a property of the system only on intended interpretation (consistency dealing with truth and falsity) having proved our system consistent has proved something about the system on every interpretation. The significance of what has been proved will, of course, vary from interpretation to interpretation.

With respect to truth-functional logic, itself, the advantage of considering it as one possible interpretation of an uninterpreted syntactical system allows us to see quite clearly the dependence of the semantic properties of logic on its syntactical properties.[13]

Another significant consequence of dealing with logic through uninterpreted syntactical systems is that it allows us the sort of freedom pure mathematics affords the mathematician. Just as advances in pure mathematics can prove quite surprising and indeed counterintuitive when interpreted, the same is true of the formal approach to logic. Indeed pure mathematics treats mathematics as an uninterpreted syntactical system. In this way our

[12] C. E. Shannon, "A Symbolic Analysis of Relay and Switching Circuits," *Transactions of the American Institute of Electrical Engineers*, 1938, 7: 713-723.

[13] For further discussion of the relation between syntactical and semantic aspects of a language see section 6.1.

intuitions do not interfere with our development of the syntactical features of our system. The significance of these developments can then be judged on interpretation. Later in this chapter we will see, at least in part, the development of a very surprising consequence concerning formal systems of a certain degree of syntactical complexity that would probably not have been reached except through the high level of abstraction afforded by uninterpreted syntactical systems.

We now turn to our second question: Why axiomatize? One possible reason is that we desire simplicity. When we axiomatize, we reduce our system to as few elements as possible. This quest for simplicity is reflected in our interest in the independence of the axioms. If our axioms are not independent all that follows is that we could have done with fewer of them. There is an obvious aesthetic element in this quest for simplicity, an element that is manifested in the application of such terms as "sloppy" and "inelegant" to systems that do not have independent axioms. Still, the quest for simplicity in itself is not the sole reason for axiomatization. Through formal axiomatization one makes explicit all the syntactical relations that exist in the material being formalized. This can lead to the exposure and avoidance of error as well as the exposure of as yet, unexpected aspects of the material under consideration.

Consider, e.g., the question of whether the 19 rules of Chapter 3 are complete in the sense that every valid argument can, in principle, be proven so by means of those rules. How would one go about proving that they are, in fact, complete? Certainly not by enumeration. It is, actually not too difficult to prove that they are complete once we have constructed an axiomatized system in which all 19 rules of inference are contained as rules or derived rules and in which substitution is possible. In fact, H.A. is such a system, and if we had proven H.A. deductively complete, it would follow almost as a corollary that the 19 rules of Chapter 3 are complete.

To prove H.A. deductively complete is to prove that every tautology is demonstrable in the system; but we have already seen in Chapter 3 that an argument is valid if and only if its associated argument proposition is a tautology. So if every tautology is demonstrable in H.A. then every valid argument is proven valid.

Formalization thus affords us a means to answer the question raised in Chapter 3 of whether the proof-theoretic method of natural deduction will suffice to show all the arguments valid that can be shown valid by model-theoretic methods such as truth tables.

Historically, axiomatized systems such as H.A. predate systems of natural deduction. Systems of natural deduction like that of Chapter 3 came into use only after they had been proven deductively complete as axiomatized systems.

With respect to the evaluation of arguments, our main concern in this book, natural deduction has obvious advantages over axiomatized systems. Natural deduction is far less cumbersome than axiomatization, and it is indeed more natural in that it corresponds more nearly to our ordinary notions of evaluation. But this naturalness would count for nothing if we could not prove the system of natural deduction adequate to its task, and this we do through axiomatization.

5.4   THE FORMALIZATION OF THE PREDICATE LOGIC

In section 5.2 we introduced the formal system H.A. of the propositional logic and developed it to the point of proving some of its major metatheorems. We will not do the same thing for the predicate logic. Instead, we will consider some of the unique problems posed by the axiomatization of the predicate logic. But, in order to facilitate our discussion, a system of the predicate logic will be introduced and its development discussed, though not carried out.

Our system will be an extension of the system in section 5.2 and so we will call it H.A.'. The primitives of H.A.' are

1. Infinitely many capital letters from the beginning of the alphabet, with and without subscripts—to be called *propositional constants*

$A, A_1, A_2, \ldots$
$B, B_1, B_2, \ldots$
$C, C_1, C_2, \ldots$

2. Infinitely many capital letters from the middle of the alphabet, with and without subscripts. These are to be called *propositional variables*

$P, P_1, P_2, \ldots$
$Q, Q_1, Q_2, \ldots$
$R, R_1, R_2, \ldots$

3. Infinitely many capital letters from the beginning of the alphabet, all with superscripts and with and without subscripts. These are to be called *predicate constants*,

$$A^1, A^2, A^3, \ldots$$
$$B^1, B^2, B^3, \ldots$$
$$C^1, C^2, C^3, \ldots$$
$$A_1^1, A_1^2, A_1^3, \ldots$$
$$B_1^1, B_1^2, B_1^3, \ldots$$
$$C_1^1, C_1^2, C_1^3, \ldots$$
$$A_2^1, A_2^2, A_2^3, \ldots$$

. . . . . .
. . . . . .
. . . . . .

4. Infinitely many capital letters from the middle of the alphabet, all with superscripts and with or without subscripts. These are to be called *predicate variables*

$$P^1, P^2, P^3, \ldots$$
$$Q^1, Q^2, Q^3, \ldots$$
$$R^1, R^2, R^3, \ldots$$
$$P_1^1, P_1^2, P_1^3, \ldots$$
$$Q_1^1, Q_1^2, Q_1^3, \ldots$$
$$R_1^1, R_1^2, R_1^3, \ldots$$
$$P_2^1, P_2^2, P_2^3, \ldots$$

. . . . . .
. . . . . .
. . . . . .

5. Infinitely many lower case letters from the beginning of the alphabet with or without subscripts. These are to be called *individual constants*,

$$a, a_1, a_2, \ldots$$
$$b, b_1, b_2, \ldots$$
$$c, c_1, c_2, \ldots$$

6. Infinitely many lower case letters from the end of the alphabet with or without subscripts. These are to be called *individual variables*.

$$x, x_1, x_2, \ldots$$
$$y, y_1, y_2, \ldots$$
$$z, z_1, z_2, \ldots$$
•

7. Two *operator symbols*

$\sim$, $\vee$

8. Two *grouping symbols*

$(,)$

We institute the same sorts of naming procedures for our metalanguage that we established in section 5.2 for H.A. Thus we introduce $\supset$, &, and $\equiv$ into our metalanguage as before. We require one new shorthand name in our metalanguage, which we introduce by the following definition,

$$(\exists x) P = \mathrm{df} \sim (x) \sim P$$

It is also to be noted that the superscripts of our predicate constants and variables represent the order of the predicate, i.e., whether it is monadic, dyadic, triadic, . . . , n-adic.

Now we give a recursive definition of what will constitute a well-formed formula (wff) in H.A.$'$.

1. If F is a propositional symbol, then F is a wff.

2. If F is an n-adic predicate symbol, then $F(\omega_1, \omega_2, \ldots, \omega_n)$ is a wff where $\omega_1, \omega_2, \ldots, \omega_n$ are individual constants or variables.

3. If F is a wff, then $\sim F$ is a wff.

4. If F and G are both wff's, then $(F \vee G)$ is a wff.

5. If F is a wff and x is an individual variable, then $(x)(F)$ is a wff.

6. No formula is a wff unless its being so follows from 1-5 above.

Now, finally, we introduce the six axiom names and two rules of our system.

Axiom I. $(P \vee P) \supset P$.
Axiom II. $P \supset (P \vee Q)$.
Axiom III. $(P \vee Q) \supset (Q \vee P)$.
Axiom IV. $(P \supset Q) \supset [(R \vee P) \supset (R \vee Q)]$.
Axiom V. $(x)(P \vee Q) \supset [P \supset (x)Q]$, where x is any individual variable,

P is any wff containing no free occurrences of x; and Q is any wff.

Axiom VI. $(x)P \supset Q$, where x is any individual variable, ω is any individual variable or constant, P is any wff, Q is obtainable from P by replacing every free occurrence of x in P by ω; and where if ω is a variable, ω is free in Q wherever x is free in P.

R1. $P, P \supset Q \vdash Q$

R2. $P \vdash (x)P$

The reader should formulate the definitions of demonstration, theorem and derived rule for H.A.' on analogy with those of H.A.

It can be seen immediately that every theorem and derived rule of H.A. is a theorem and derived rule of H.A.', since the first four axioms and R1 of H.A. and H.A.' are the same. Thus H.A. is contained in H.A.'.

The consistency of H.A.' is easily established by first associating with every wff of H.A.' a propositional formula, i.e., a formula of the propositional logic. The rules for finding the associated propositional formula are simply (1) If F is a propositional formula, then its associated propositional formula is F, itself. (2) If F is a quantified formula, its associated propositional formula is obtained by (a) dropping all quantifiers and their associated parentheses, and (b) replacing every well-formed part of the formula (resulting from step a) which is of the form $P^n(x_1, x_2, \ldots, x_n)$ by a propositional symbol, using different propositional symbols for each different part beginning with different P^n's but using the same symbol for each occurrence of the same P^n regardless of differences in the individual symbols $x_1, x_2, \ldots, x_n$.

It is then easy to prove that

1. If F is a theorem of H.A.', then its associated propositional formula is a tautology.

This is not the same as analyticity since analyticity in a predicate logic would amount to every theorem being a logical truth and we have noted in Chapter 4 that the class of logical truths is larger than that of tautologies.[14]

The reader should prove that if 1 is true of H.A.', then H.A.' is consistent by the Post criterion. On development of H.A.', various metatheorems can be proved, such as the substitution metatheorem and functional completeness.

[14] Or more correctly, the set of tautologies is a proper subset of the set of logical truths.

We will not concern ourselves with these metatheorems, but rather turn our attention to the special problems of proving the deductive completeness of systems like H.A.$'$. Deductive completeness here, as in H.A., is the converse of analyticity. As we have noted analyticity for H.A.$'$ consists in every theorem being a logical truth. Thus to say that H.A.$'$ is deductively complete is to say that every logical truth is a theorem of H.A.$'$. We have defined "logical truth" by saying that any formula that is a logical truth is always true, but we did not elaborate on what "always" means other than to say that it did not mean "true for every condition in its truth table." A logical truth is always true in the sense that it is *true in every possible nonempty universe.*[15]

Though we did not prove H.A. to be deductively complete it is relatively clear, we hope, that such a proof would have involved the truth table definition of tautology. Deductive completeness was formulated in H.A. as the statement that every tautology was a theorem of H.A., which was to say that any formula that had the value true in every row of its truth table was a theorem of H.A. Since the notion of truth table is a precise notion, in the sense that it can be rigorously defined, it is used to facilitate the proof.

In the same way a proof of the deductive completeness of H.A.$'$ requires some formalized notion of logical truth. Having identified the notion of logical truth with that of being true in every possible nonempty universe, it is the latter concept that usually is formalized. One method of formalizing this notion of "true in every possible nonempty universe" that might present itself to the reader is that implicit in sections 4.2.1 and 4.3.1. There we introduced the logical truths

$$(x) \emptyset x \equiv [\emptyset a \; \& \; \emptyset b \; \& \; \emptyset c \ldots]$$
$$(\exists x) \emptyset x \equiv [\emptyset a \lor \emptyset b \lor \emptyset c \ldots]$$

which we utilized in showing the invalidity of certain arguments in the predicate logic by considering those arguments in universes of small numbers of individuals. We said there that to say that our argument is valid is to say that there is no nonempty universe in which the premises are true and the conclusion false. We have also developed the notion of argument proposition, that being the proposition obtainable by conjoining the premises and having them materially imply the conclusion. Since any given argument is valid if and only if its associated argument proposition is a logical truth, we have

[15] The reason we specify "nonempty universe" is so that the proposition $(x) Px \supset (\exists x) Px$ will be a logical truth under our definition.

what seems to be a possible way to formalize the notion of logical truth. It would follow that if a given argument is valid its associated propositional formula would be a *tautology* when rewritten in any universe containing a finite number of individuals, and, further it would seem that by the method of mathematical induction we should be able to show it a tautology in a universe of any number of individuals. Unfortunately, this will not work for it can be proven that though a quantified formula is a tautology in every universe up to size n, you cannot show, in general, that it will be a tautology in a universe of size $n + 1$. This is one of the consequences of Church's theorem mentioned in section 4.2.1.

In order to develop a more adequately precise formulation of the notion of "true in every nonempty universe" one must first develop the notions of *model, interpretation with respect to a model, satisfiable with respect to a given model,* etc. The consideration of these notions, however, lies beyond the scope of this book.[16]

5.5 GÖDEL'S INCOMPLETENESS THEOREM

Gottlob Frege, whose name has appeared several times in our discussions of the history of logic, was the first to conceive *and* formulate the program of reducing mathematics to logic. Frege was convinced that arithmetic was a part of logic. He developed a symbolism that made possible the formulation of arithmetical statements within the formalism of logic. As a part of this development, Frege introduced the use of quantifiers to bind variables. Frege's work and his program produced little interest in the world of mathematics with the exception of Bertrand Russell, whose interest in the foundations of mathematics led him to study Frege's *Die Grundgestze der Arithmetik* (1893 and 1903). Russell was convinced that Frege's program was essentially correct, but he discovered a contradiction in Frege's premises. Using the development in axiomatic method theory due to David Hilbert (particularly in *Grundlagen der Geometrie,* 1899), Bertrand Russell and Alfred North Whitehead sought to carry out Frege's program in their *Principia Mathematica.*

The program of Hilbert differed from that of Frege and Russell in that he conceived of arithmetical statements as being about nothing, i.e., as just being marks on paper, whereas Frege and Russell conceived of arithmetical

[16] The reader may pursue this matter further in section V of the Selected Readings.

statements as being truths in the calculus of classes (a branch of logic). Clearly, then, for Frege and Russell arithmetical statements could be tested for truth by reference to their subject matter. On the other hand the notion of arithmetic truth for Hilbert was not testable in this way as he did not conceive of arithmetical statements as referring to any subject matter.

The Gödel theorem of 1931, which constitutes the subject matter of this section, had important consequences for the program of Frege, Russell, and Hilbert. Gödel proved that any axiomatized deductive system in which the truths of arithmetic can be written will be fundamentally incomplete if it is consistent. This is to say that there are infinitely many truths of arithmetic that are not demonstrable from any set of consistent axioms in any system that has the symbolic richness to symbolize the truths of arithmetic.[17]

One of the consequences of Hilbert's program would be the reduction of the notion of truth in pure mathematics to that of demonstrability or theoremhood, thus dissolving an enormously puzzling problem of the philosophy of mathematics. According to this view, to say that a given proposition of pure mathematics is true, say the Goldbach conjecture that every even number greater than or equal to six is the sum of two odd primes, is merely to say that it is deducible by means of the rules of the system from the axioms of the system. It is evident from the Gödel theorem, as stated above,[18] that the problem of the nature of mathematical truth remains.

Our concern in the remainder of this section will be to discuss in more detail the Gödel result. Since Gödel's proof makes special use of self-reference,[19] we will turn now to a consideration of a very simple set of languages in which self-reference is possible and very explicit.[20]

Our language will consist of primitives:

$P, n, *$

[17] The Gödel theorem applies only to those systems in which the notion of demonstration is recursively defined (as it is in H.A. on page 244).

[18] The statement we have called the Gödel theorem is not the Gödel theorem, but an important corollary of it. For the original proof see Kurt Gödel, *On Formally Undecidable Propositions of Principia Mathematica and Related Systems* (Oliver & Boyd: London, 1962).

[19] The reader might well profit by reading section 6.2.4 regarding self-reference before proceeding.

[20] This treatment of self-reference and the Gödel theorem is drawn largely from an article by Raymond M. Smullyan, "Languages in Which Self-Reference Is Possible," *Journal of Symbolic Logic*, 22: 55-67. Many of the refinements and simplifications are due to Richard C. Jeffrey of the University of Pennsylvania.

We will use the term *expression* to refer to any finite string of the primitives. Our language will be so constructed that we may say things about names and about things named. To this end we will need rules of name formation and interpretation, as well as rules of sentence formation and interpretation. The rules of name formation are

1. The result of writing an expression between asterisks is a name.
2. The result of writing *n* before a name is a name.
3. Nothing is a name unless its being so follows from 1 and 2 above.

By these rules there are two ways of writing a name. Consider the following:

P
****
n*P*

The above list consists of two names of the first type and one of the second Both *P* and **** are examples of names that are expressions between asterisks, whereas n*P* is an example of a name formed by placing an *n* before a name. It should be realized that placing an *n* before any of the names above will result in another name.

For completeness we include the following list of expressions that are not names:

**
n**
Pn

The rules of name interpretation are:

1. A name that begins and ends with asterisks denotes the expression obtained by deleting the first and last asterisks.
2. A name that begins with an *n* denotes the norm of the expression denoted by the expression obtained by deleting the initial *n*.

The first rule is simple enough. We take any name of the first type and remove the first and last asterisks and what remains is what the name named. Taking the names *P* and **** above and applying our first rule of name interpretation, we find that they name:

P and
**

In order to understand the second rule of name interpretation, we must first define *norm*. The *norm of an expression* is the expression prefixed to its own type 1 name. Consider the following list of norms of expressions:

n∗n∗
P∗∗P∗∗
∗∗∗∗

The type 1 name of *n* is ∗*n*∗. If we prefix *n* to its type 1 name, we get *n∗n∗*, which is thus the norm of *n*. Similarly *P∗∗P∗∗* is the norm of *P*∗ and ∗∗∗∗ is the norm of ∗.

Our second rule of name interpretation tells us that type 2 names, i.e., names beginning with an *n*, name the norm of some expression. We can determine which expression by simply finding out what is named by that part of the type 2 name following the initial *n*. Consider the type 2 name,

n∗P∗

According to our second rule of name interpretation it names the norm of an expression, the expression named by ∗*P*∗. Now the expression named by ∗*P*∗ is *P* and so *n∗P∗* is the name of the norm of *P*. The norm of *P* is

P∗P∗

Thus, *n∗P∗* names *P∗P∗*. But *n∗P∗* is not the only name of *P∗P∗* since the latter is also named by

∗*P∗P∗∗*

Let us again consider the expression,

n∗n∗

which is a type 2 name, since it is a type 1 name preceded by an *n*. What does it name? Being a type 2 name, it designates the norm of the expression named by ∗*n*∗. Since ∗*n*∗ names *n*, *n∗n∗* names the norm of *n*. The norm of *n* is *n* prefixed to its type 1 name, but that is *n∗n∗*. Thus *n∗n∗* names the norm of *n* and the norm of *n* is *n∗n∗*; *n∗n∗* names *n∗n∗*.

We now proceed to our rules of sentence formation and interpretation. The rule of sentence formation is

1. An expression is a sentence if and only if it is obtainable by writing *P* before a name.

By our rule of sentence formation the following are all sentences:

*P*n**
*P****
*Pn*n**

since each consists of a name, either of type 1 or type 2, preceded by a *P*.

The rule of sentence interpretation is

1. The result of writing *P* before the name of an expression is true if the expression named has the property *P* and false otherwise.

Under this rule of sentence interpretation, the sentence *P*n** says that *n* has the property *P*; *P**** says that * has the property *P*; and *Pn*n** says that the norm of *n* has the property *P*.

Now finally consider the very interesting expression

*Pn*Pn**

which is a sentence, since it consists of a *P* preceding a name. The sentence says that the norm of *Pn* has the property *P*. Well the norm of *Pn* is *Pn* prefixed to its type 1 name, i.e., *Pn*Pn**. Thus *Pn*Pn** says of itself that it has the property *P*. We have thus constructed a self-referring expression. Now depending on what the property *P* is the sentence *Pn*Pn** is true, false, or paradoxical. If *P* means "contains asterisks," e.g., the sentence *Pn*Pn** says that *Pn*Pn** contains asterisks, which is true. If, on the other hand, *P* means "contains no asterisks," then obviously what *Pn*Pn** says of itself is false. Finally if *P* means "is false," then what *Pn*Pn** says of itself is paradoxical; for if what it says is true then it is false; and if what it says is false then it is true.

The foregoing indicates that it is not self-reference, itself, that leads to paradox, but rather self-referring statements that predicate their own truth or falsity.

Let us now consider what would occur if our sentence *Pn*Pn** was a well-formed formula in a formal deductive system in which the predicate *P* meant on intended interpretation, "is a nontheorem." The sentence *Pn*Pn** would then say of itself that it is a nontheorem. If this sentence is true then what it says of itself is true; and it is therefore a nontheorem. But then our system will be incomplete for there will be a truth, $Pn*Pn*$, that is not a theorem of the system. If, on the other hand, our sentence is false, then what it says of itself is false, and it is therefore a theorem. But then our system will be non-analytic, for there will be a theorem, $Pn*n*$, that is false.

The foregoing paragraph represents the format of the Gödel proof. Gödel showed that a formula like $Pn*Pn*$ with a predicate meaning "is a nontheorem" is constructable in (is a well-formed formula in) any system with sufficient complexity to symbolize the truths of arithmetic.[21]

[21] It should be noted that the Gödel result can also be proven for certain fragments of arithmetic that do not contain all the usual arithmetic operations. For more on this see R. Robinson, "An Essentially Undecidable Axiom System," *Proceedings of the International Congress of Mathematicians*, 1952, 1: 729-730.

6

logic and language

6.1   LOGIC AND LANGUAGE

One pervasive feature of Chapters 2-5 (the chapters on formal deductive logic) was the interconnection of the symbolic apparatus with the casual knowledge of ordinary language. Most often it turned out that ordinary English needed to be made more precise before it could serve as a basis for formal devices, but, nonetheless, there is an unquestionable dependence of formal logic on language and we propose to discuss that dependence in this chapter. After a brief preliminary outlining of some of the general aspects of logic's relationship to ordinary language, we will discuss (1) the sort of errors in reasoning that occur most often in ordinary language and that cannot be handled properly by the evaluation methods of Chapters 2-4 and (2) various aspects of the concept of *definition,* which itself plays a crucial role in the logic-language relationship.

The close relationship between logic and language is not surprising. The ability to speak a language (or, if not speak, then simply use in some way) is often taken as one of the intellectual features that separates men from other animals. Also, the ability to "reason," one of Aristotle's defining characteristics of man, has been generally—if vaguely—held to mark off human from animal intelligence. It does not require much effort to recognize that linguistic and reasoning ability are not independent features of human intelligence but are connected and overlapping. The ability to formulate arguments and make inferences is certainly a type of linguistic ability. However, we have devoted considerable space to the precise specification of the notion of *logical inference* and we ought to be more exact about the nature of the linguistic aspects of logic. In section 1.5 a brief attempt was made to describe the various aspects of language. This sort of analysis is necessary here, because however sophisticated a notion of logic one might have, it cannot be compared to ordinary language unless this latter idea is refined. This, of course, does not mean that we must include a textbook on linguistics within one on logic but simply that our casual references to such entities as "ordinary language" or "natural language" must be sharpened. In Chapter 1 we indicated that the study of language can be divided into three categories: the syntactic, semantic, and pragmatic. We had occasion to use the first two of these concepts in application to logic rather extensively in Chapters 2 and 3, but a brief review will be presented. Any example of the use of language (written or spoken) will consist of an orderly arrangement of some physical objects, whether these be sound waves or ink marks on a printed page. We say "orderly" not because language is highly ordered, but merely to indicate that certain arrangements of sounds or ink marks are not part of the language, in that they are improper or unacceptable arrangements. Typically, in English, the letter combination "bc" whether uttered or written, is not part of the ordinary variety of English sounds or letter patterns. On a larger scale we can all recognize the inappropriateness of the following sort of word string:

The the house hot than ran.

The rules in a language that determine which order of elements are part of the language and which are not are *syntax* rules. Of course, a complex natural language may not have these rules completely and explicitly formulated. One of the tasks of a linguist will be just such formulation, but here it is only necessary for the reader to understand what is meant by the syntactical aspect of language. Most, if not all, languages (and certainly all natural languages) can be used to describe, refer to, and express various events or states of affairs in the nonlinguistic world (the world of chairs, tables, ideas, events, etc.). In order for this to be possible there must be rules or conventions that connect the linguistic elements to nonlinguistic items. The study of the ways in which this connection is made is known as *semantics*. When it is determined that the word "dog" can be used to refer to a certain class of creatures, we have made a semantic discovery. Also, when someone says of a certain sentence that it is true he is expressing a very general semantic property of sentences, for in order for some string of linguistic elements to have the property of truth there must be a state of affairs corresponding to that string. Typically, when someone utters the sentence

John is here.

his utterance is true only when appropriate observations would determine that John is, in fact, present.[1] In Chapter 3 we described the truth table methods as *semantic* because any question about the truth of a proposition is a semantic question, as is any question about meaning, reference, etc.

The final aspect of language we will distinguish is known as *pragmatics,* or the concern with the uses of linguistic expressions. That there is a pragmatic aspect to ordinary language is quite certain, but there can be difficulty in differentiating pragmatics from semantics. One can most easily distinguish the semantic from the pragmatic aspects by considering the situation in which a person uses less than parliamentary language, i.e., when he swears. Any particular oath may have some semantic content, i.e., it may mean something. However, it is immediately apparent that an oath is usually not meant literally. It is employed for certain psychological reasons and in certain situations quite irrespective of the precise meaning of its words (and many oaths and exclamations have no semantic content). The study of the context and use of linguistic expressions is pragmatics, and our example is meant to show that it is possible to distinguish the pragmatic aspect from the semantic even though the use of an expression is often taken to define its semantic content. As a matter of fact no one of these aspects is completely independent of the others; think what havoc one wreaks with the meaning of a sentence by altering its word order.

Having distinguished these aspects of any natural language we must now determine how logic fits into the pattern. In the most straightforward sense the logics of Chapters 2-5 were attempts to construct artificial languages, and as such resembled the natural languages on which they were based. They differed mostly in that the syntactic rules of formation and semantic rules

[1] For more on this see A. Tarski, "The Semantic Conception of Truth", *Philosophy and Phenomenological Research:* (1944) 4: 341-376

were explicit and allowed no ambiguity or vagueness. Still, the relationship between logic and language is more than this rather trivial one of artificial vs. natural language. The significant central concept of logic is the notion of logical consequence, its importance arising, of course, from the many additional concepts it ties together, viz., validity, truth, decision procedure, etc. In a very general sense we may say that logical consequence is a relation of certain sentences in a language (natural or artificial) to other sentences in the language. The question of the relationship between logic and language can then be put into the following form: "What sort of linguistic concept is the concept of logical consequence?"

To repeat, it is possible to see this notion of logical consequence as a linguistic one because it is, at bottom, a relation between linguistic entities—albeit a very special one. Before presenting a tentative answer to the above question we must make sure that certain points are well understood. In Chapter 1 and throughout our development of formal logic in Chapters 2, 3, and 4 we were careful to point out that the items that served as premises and conclusions of arguments were *propositions.* We used this term to express the subtle but vital point that sentences (the actual physical ink marks or sounds, i.e., tokens) were different from propositions and that (1) a proposition might be expressed by many different sentences and (2) logic was concerned with propositions. Now by speaking of the notion of logical consequence as a relation between sentences we do not mean to undermine the distinction we have made all along. It is, however, true that sentences can be used to express propositions, and since logical consequence relates propositions we can still make sense of the notion that sentences can be related by a property of logical consequence. To summarize this digression we may say that logical consequence can only be viewed as a linguistic property or relation when suitable allowance has been made for the issues surrounding the distinction between sentence and proposition. Still we are left with the interesting question of the nature of this relation.

In developing an answer to this it might be helpful to give examples of some other sorts of linguistic relations, e.g., when we come across the procedure of adding the suffix "ed" to a regular verb such as "walk." This procedure might be described as the *past tense relation* and, given examples of regular verbs, we would have no difficulty in both determining which verbs were present and which were past, and we would also have no difficulty in describing the semantic significance of the addition of "ed" to regular verbs. The point of this example is to show that a syntactic alteration (adding "ed") can result in a semantic change (expression of past action instead of present). Additionally, we might point out that often syntactic changes result in no semantic change, e.g., the substitution of "the_____of John" for "John's_____." However, these latter cases are far less frequent than the former and usually require much qualification.

Now, when one examines the premises of a valid argument one can sense the fact that they are related to the conclusion in some way, even though we do not speak of the conclusion as constructed from the premises in the way we speak of the past tense as constructed from the present. Our primary concern up to this point in the book has been to determine whether this relation held in a specific case. Well, which linguistic aspect did we use to determine this? That is, a good clue to the nature of logical consequence is given by the method we use to determine whether that relation holds between a particular set of premises and a conclusion. As a matter of fact we had two sorts of tests for this relation—one semantic and one syntactic. We saw that the idea of consequence attached to *argument form* and was a syntactic property. It was in a very important sense, like the *past tense relation,* in that we recognized it by a sort of formal inspection (allowing for the obvious differences in difficulty between determining the "past tense-ness" of a verb and the validity of an argument). Still, we were able to devise semantic tests for this relation (truth tables, Venn diagrams), and it cannot be denied that *logical consequence* is a relation with semantic ramifications. In the face of the dual methods of evaluating arguments we will tentatively say that logical consequence is a syntactic property of arguments (or a syntactic *relation* between premises and conclusions) but that the presence or absence of this property has important effects on the semantic content of the premises and conclusions of the argument. The reader is probably not surprised by this since we have just considered a rather trivial case of this type of relation. "Walk" and "walked" are related syntactically, and their syntactic relation has semantic consequences. Surely, there must be differences between the linguistic status of logical consequence and that of the past tense relation. The most apparent difference is generality; the past tense relation is a narrow one, which does, or does not hold when a specific suffix is, or is not present. On the other hand, the syntactic basis of logical consequence is much broader and is by no means determined by simple inspection. Still, there are more significant differences. The semantic effect of the presence or absence of the consequence relation is entirely different from the one that obtains between present and past tense verbs. When a set of premises and a conclusion are logically connected (i.e., the argument they embody is valid) then we know that the truth of the premises results in the truth of the conclusion. Truth, itself, is rather different as a semantic concept from the past or present tense relation and the consequence relation is thus much more general in its semantic consequences. In addition, there seems to be something considerably more binding about logical consequence. We all recognize that the addition of "ed" to regular verbs is only one way to bring about the tense change and further, that a language could get along without the simple present-past dichotomy that most modern languages have. However, it seems hard to imagine a language with either no consequence relation or with a different kind of consequence relation. This is not to say that the words used in one language to express validity and its many instances could not be different, but what would a language that, e.g., rejected the validity of *modus ponens* look like?[2] It does not seem that *modus ponens* is merely a syntactic relation that has a semantic function and that might be accepted or rejected as a matter of linguistic convention (even though the words used to express *modus ponens* can vary considerably from one language to another). The problems associated with this seeming "necessity" of the forms of logical consequence will be briefly discussed in section 6.1.1. For the present we may summarize our discussion by the following:

1. Logic is contained (or embedded) in language and this is perhaps the source of our considering linguistic ability and intelligence (reasoning ability) as two forms of expression of the same ability—the ability most cited as a distinguishing feature of human intelligence.

2. When the logic, which is implicitly contained in language, is made explicit in order to devise evaluation procedures, we clearly recognize the parallels between logic and language.

3. These parallels, which are best brought out by consideration of the sorts of evaluation procedures employed, lead to the idea of logic as concerned with certain syntactic properties. Moreover, these syntactic properties have very special semantic consequences.

4. In spite of the parallels between logical consequence and other linguistic devices there are important differences—one of which is the apparent "bindingness" of particular forms of logical consequence.

---

[2] Clearly, the language does not literally reject *modus ponens*; what is meant is that the grammatical rules that govern the construction of elements of the language do not allow the construction of the argument proposition that embodies *modus ponens*.

6.1.1 The basis of logic

So far in this book we have had a lot to say about the nature of logic and its relation to language. In Chapter 1 we described logic as *normative* or *prescriptive* in that it, in part, described the standard to which we appeal in justifying our inferences. This view has the merit of allowing for the fact that (1) many persons fail to use logic as a standard and it is thus not a description of human reasoning and (2) even when we construct valid arguments (or evaluate them correctly) we do not usually do so by the procedures found in Chapters 2-4. In other words, logic sets a certain norm or standard that may or may not be met by our everyday inferential devices but that ought to be met (though not necessarily with the same inference devices). This description of logic as normative together with our recent observations on the syntactical and semantical aspects of logic go a long way to clarifying the position that logic occupies in the area of human knowledge. However, neither of these views explains the special necessity that seems to surround the rules of logic. That is, we saw in section 6.1 that our logic (whether syllogistic, propositional, or predicate) consisted of certain syntactic relations (not unlike grammatical relations) but they differed from ordinary grammatical relations in that we did not seem at liberty to alter them. We might change the words or the symbols we use to describe *modus ponens,* but we cannot devise our rules in such a way that *modus ponens* is no longer a valid argument form. We will outline here the various ways in which philosophers have attempted to provide the basis for this "cannot," and the reader is referred to the selected readings for more complete discussions of this area known most often as the *philosophy of logic.* Note that when we described logic in Chapter 1 as normative we were allowing for this necessity in our description. However, consider two cases where we have to deal with normative rules:

1. One ought to be kind to animals.
2. One ought to accept *modus ponens* as valid.

Now, though we may not approve of a world in which people mistreated animals we can certainly conceive of the possibility of a world in which 1 was not so. However, what would happen if 2 was denied, i.e., if *modus ponens* were not classified as a valid argument? To find out we will write the argument in a special way:

$$P \supset P$$
$$\underline{P}$$
$$\therefore P$$

This argument is a special case of *modus ponens*, and if it is not valid then *modus ponens* will not be valid. To say it is not valid is to say that its argument proposition, $[(P \supset P) \& P] \supset P$, is not a tautology. Before considering how this proposition could be false let us use our other rules to simplify it.[3]

1. $[(P \supset P) \& P] \supset P$
2. $[(\sim P \vee P) \& P] \supset P$ 1 Impl.
3. $[P \& (\sim P \vee P)] \supset P$ 2 Com.
4. $[(P \& \sim P) \vee (P \& P)] \supset P$ 3 Dist.
5. $[(P \& \sim P) \vee P] \supset P$ 4 Taut.
6. $\sim[(P \& \sim P) \vee P] \vee P$ 5 Impl.
7. $[\sim(P \& \sim P) \& \sim P] \vee P$ 6 De M.
8. $[(\sim P \vee \sim\sim P) \& \sim P] \vee P$ 7 De M.
9. $[(\sim P \vee P) \& \sim P] \vee P$ 8 D.N.
10. $[(P \vee \sim P) \& \sim P] \vee P$ 9 Com.
11. $P \vee [(P \vee \sim P) \& \sim P]$ 10 Com.
12. $[P \vee (P \vee \sim P)] \& (P \vee \sim P)$ 11 Dist.
13. $[(P \vee P) \vee \sim P] \& (P \vee \sim P)$ 12 Assoc.
14. $(P \vee \sim P) \& (P \vee \sim P)$ 13 Taut.
15. $P \vee \sim P$ 14 Taut.

Now step 15 is equivalent to $[(P \supset P) \& P] \supset P$, and if this latter proposition is nontautologous (i.e., if we deny validity to *modus ponens*) so is $P \vee \sim P$. Yet, how could an assertion of this form be false?[4] It would seem that we

[3]Though we have not spoken about the use of the rules of inference to simplify or change formulas, it should be apparent that this is possible. In the case at hand we are using the replacement rules to rearrange and simplify the initial expression. This procedure will always be possible since the initial expression has two propositional symbols and will, therefore, be equivalent to some shorter expression that has the same two propositional symbols and less repetition. In fact, though we are only using this procedure to explicitly exhibit certain features of our initial formula, it can be used as an important tool for studying the propositional logic. By putting formulas into suitable forms (known as *normal forms*) one can determine the various properties of the formula at a glance. Also, the use of simplification procedures allow one to construct simpler switching circuits which have the same result as the more complex ones.

[4]It should be noted that there is a branch of logic that is, in part, based on the notion that statements of the form $P \vee \sim P$ are not necessarily true. However, this logic (known as *intuitionistic logic*) is based on assumptions about the nature of logic that transcend our present discussion of *modus ponens,* and a full consideration of these assumptions and the restructuring they entail is beyond the scope of this book. In this connection the reader is referred to Y. Bar-Hillel and A. Fraenkel, *Foundations of Set Theory* (Amsterdam, North Holland 1958), Chap. 4.

cannot alter *modus ponens* without allowing our logic to contain a contradiction (the denial of $P \vee \sim P$ is $P \,\&\, \sim P$) and, of course, we can validly infer everything from a contradiction. Further, the denial of any of the rules of inference and equivalences of the syllogistic, propositional and predicate logics result in the assertion of self-contradictory propositions. Thus, there does seem to be a more than ordinary "normativeness" to the rules of logic, and it is this property of logic that seems to require some explanation. In what follows we will call this the problem of the *basis of logic*.

In general there seem to be two ways of providing this basis and both have been appealed to by philosophers—albeit with varying emphasis and details. We can either say that logic derives its necessity from certain properties of our world or we can explain its necessity by appeal to properties of the human intellect. In short, either the laws of logic are laws of nature or laws of thought.[5] We will explain these two positions by considering briefly two older works on logic (mid-nineteenth century). In *System of Logic* (1858), J.S. Mill makes the following observation about geometry, though his remarks are meant to apply equally to any deductive disciplines supposed to have the special sort of necessity we are investigating:

> Since then neither in nature nor in the human mind, do there exist any objects exactly corresponding to the definitions of geometry, while yet that science cannot be supposed to be conversant about non-entities; nothing remains but to consider geometry as conversant with such lines, angles, and figures as really exist; and the definitions as they are called must be regarded as some of our first and most obvious generalizations concerning those natural objects. The correctness of those generalizations *as* generalizations is without a flaw . . . the peculiar accuracy, supposed to be characteristic of the first principles of geometry, thus appears to be fictitious.[6]

It is clear from the above that Mill sees geometric, arithmetic, and logical truths as a special form of laws of nature. They are "our first and most obvious generalizations concerning natural objects."[7] Now, this view suffers

---

[5] This dichotomy may appear naïvely simple, but viewing the issue this way does allow one to make interesting observations on the many different works in this area.

[6] J. S. Mill, *System of Logic* (1858), p. 149.

[7] Mill had a special view on the structure of syllogistic arguments that does not conflict with the view presented here but should be mentioned in this context. He felt that the syllogism was not itself a generalization from empirical situations but a device for recording such generalizations. This, though, does not affect the notions discussed here.

from two basic problems: The first of which is its failure to account for the special necessity which logical laws seem to demand, and the second that it is not at all obvious that the various geometric, algebraic, and logical truths are or could be generalizations from empirical observations of "natural objects." This second possible objection cannot be properly handled here (the reader is advised to study Chapter 7 as a means of understanding what sort of thing a law of nature is and then comparing logical laws to these), but we will briefly discuss the first. Mill realized that his view seems to conflict with the feeling that logical laws are of extraordinary necessity. He accepted the fact (a "fact" to most empiricist philosophers) that laws of nature—however well established—can be denied without self-contradiction and that any of them could, conceivably, be false in some other world. Further, he is consistent in his position, in that he is perfectly willing to consider logical laws as no more necessary or binding than other natural laws. The problem, though, is that logical laws do not seem to be deniable without self-contradiction. Mill could, of course, argue that the special necessity we are trying to explain is simply a result of the great degree of evidential support that logical laws can claim and that is lacking in all other instances of physical, chemical, and biological laws. However, it is by no means obvious that such a difference in degree could ever account for the difference in kind that obtains between laws of logic and mathematics, on one hand, and the physical sciences, on the other. Finally, we would expect that if the laws of logic and mathematics were simply very abstract but nonetheless empirical generalizations then there would be at least conceivable counterexamples. So far from this being so, we usually consider any apparent violation of logical and mathematical truths no violation at all. If we found two entities that when placed together formed one object we would not consider this a case where $1 + 1 = 1$ (and thus a counterexample to $1 + 1 = 2$) but a case where the objects or entities chosen were not genuine instances of the law $1 + 1 = 2$. If $1 + 1 = 2$ or $P \vee \sim P$ were empirical truths then our rejection of such a counterexample would be very odd indeed.[8]

A second way of construing the truths of logic and mathematics is as "laws of thought." The philosopher Immanuel Kant felt that the truths of geometry were necessary truths because they were the rules or laws by which our perceptions were organized. This, he felt, explained both why these truths seemed inescapably true and why they applied, if only approximately, to the empirical world. More to the issue of logical laws, George Boole in *An*

[8]The reader is referred to Chapter 7 for a more complete discussion of the issue of "confirmation of empirical laws."

Investigation of the Laws of Thought (1854) tries to explain both the necessity of logical truths and the fact that we often fail to properly employ them; i.e., we often reason invalidly. This latter fact is a problem for anyone with Boole's philosophy of logic for if *modus ponens* and the others were laws of thought why would we ever reason improperly?

> there exist among the intellectual laws a number marked out from the rest by this special character, viz., that every movement of the intellectual system which is accomplished solely under their direction is *right*, that every interference therewith by other laws is not interference only, but *violation*. It cannot but be felt that this circumstance would give to the laws in question a character of distinction and pre-dominance. They would but the more evidently seem to indicate a final purpose which is not always fulfilled, to possess an authority inherent and just, but not always commanding obedience.[9]

The problems that one has in justifying a psychological view of the necessity of logical truths are clearly brought out in this passage. Boole would have us agree that the laws of logic are seen as necessary by human reasoners because they are embedded in the psychological structure of human reasoners. This is certainly a plausible explanation for the bindingness of logic on our mental workings, but it is hard to see why, if this were true, we could ever go wrong in our inferences. Why, that is, are the laws of logic—which are taken to be psychological laws—both inviolable and still often violated in everyday inferences? Any law of psychology (if there are any as yet) would be true of the majority of humans, but if it appeared false in some instance we would not recommend that the individual in that instance change his behavior to fit the law. If there is a psychological law that can be put roughly as "All persons in such-and-such a situation become morose," then if an individual in that situation behaves with great ebullience and gives no indication of being morose, would we say that the law was violated or that the individual had better begin acting morosely so as to support the law? In effect, Boole is asking us to consider the laws of logic as both psychological and different from other psychological laws in that we change our behavior to conform to these laws when we have violated them. Also, and this leads into rather far-flung regions of philosophy, a "laws of thought" view might have some difficulty in explaining the fact that the empirical world does fit logical and mathematical laws as well as it does. It is not prima facie obvious that the

[9]George Boole, *An Investigation of the Laws of Thought* (1854), p. 459.

physical world ought to conform to laws of the human mind, and this consideration is central to a philosopher such as Kant who considers the mind the basis of all order.

It is quite clear that in the forms presented above neither the Mill nor the Boole view of logic is ultimately satisfying, though both seem to have the ingredients of an acceptable position.[10] Suffice it to say that there is vast literature in the philosophy of logic and that answers to the question "What is the basis of logic?" are far less satisfactory than answers to the question "What is logic?"

6.2   INFORMAL FALLACIES

It is clear that the most basic logical error that anyone can make is to present an argument that on evaluation, turns out to be invalid. However, there are many argument forms that, though invalid, are not considered fallacies because the notion of *fallacy* entails the belief that the argument form involved is one that often or repeatedly misleads. Many syllogistic, propositional, and quantificational arguments are so obviously invalid that they would mislead no one or, at least, very few. Thus anyone who argues, e.g.,

> If John eats his dinner he will get dessert.
> ∴ John got dessert.

i.e.,

> A. $\dfrac{P \supset Q}{\therefore Q}$

is arguing invalidly, but the argument form A is so obviously invalid (i.e., Q obviously does not follow from $P \supset Q$) that it would not seriously tempt anyone to give it his assent. Because of this we do not speak of argument A as a fallacy. However, consider

[10] For more subtle views on this subject the reader is referred to C. I. Lewis, *Mind and the World Order* (New York: Dover, 1956) and W. V. O. Quine "Two Dogmas of Empiricism," in *From a Logical Point of View* (Cambridge: Harvard University Press, 1961), and "Truth by Convention" in Benacerraf and Putnam's collection, *Philosophy of Mathematics* (Englewood Cliffs, N.J.: Prentice Hall, 1964).

If John eats his dinner he will get dessert.
He will get dessert.

∴ He will eat his dinner.

B. $P \supset Q$
     Q
     ∴ P

Now this argument seems, at first glance, all right. In fact many people would not hesitate to declare argument form B valid; yet we know (or should know) that this argument—though it resembles both *modus ponens* and *modus tollens*—is invalid. Since arguments such as B closely resemble ordinary valid argument forms and for that reason can mislead people; we will call B an example of a fallacy, specifically the *fallacy of affirming the consequent*. We will present others shortly.

The next point that we must consider is that not all fallacies are so easily shown to be cases of formally invalid arguments. Many fallacious arguments arise from considerations that could never be captured in a purely symbolic system, and yet these arguments are both invalid and persuasive. One of the most typical of these is the argument known as *appeal to authority*. Suppose you are disputing the issue of who has the responsibility for the use of scientific discoveries in military areas. Your opponent maintains that scientists should not be responsible for uses governments find for their inventions and he cites the testimony of some eminent biologist for his position:

Dr. A, a well-known biologist, believes a scientist is not responsible for uses others find for his discoveries.

∴ We should not hold him responsible.

We surely feel that there is something wrong with this argument as it involves an unjustified appeal to authority. That is, an argument that depended on Dr. A's testimony on a biological matter might be a valid argument since Dr. A is well informed about biology; but in a social/political argument as given above Dr. A is not really more of an authority than a nonscientist and appeal to his testimony is unjustified.

In this section we will describe and exemplify the more common fallacies. This undertaking will be made considerably more systematic if we divide these fallacies into categories by some definite type distinction. Perhaps the best way of doing this is in terms of the sources of their fallaciousness. To this end, we will divide these logical errors into three classes based on the tripartite division of the aspects of language as discussed in Chapter 1 and the first section of this chapter. If the source of the fallacy is formal it will be included in the section on *syntactic* fallacies (the above example of affirming the consequent is obviously syntactic). If, on the other hand, there is some sort of confusion about the meaning of terms in the argument and this results in its fallaciousness, then the argument will fall under the heading of *semantic* fallacies. Finally, we will consider the sorts of fallacies that arise from improper use of certain premises (such as the above-discussed appeal to authority), and these will be classed together as *pragmatic* fallacies. We turn first to the syntactic fallacies.

6.2.1 Syntactic fallacies

As has been discussed above it is possible to regard all of the errors and invalid arguments that might be revealed by the symbolic machinery of Chapters 2-4 as, in some sense, fallacies. However, we saw fit to detail only those formal errors likely to occur fairly often and rather systematically mislead. The fallacy of affirming the consequent was just such an error. Closely related to this is the *fallacy of denying the antecedent* as exemplified in the following:

> If you are intelligent you will succeed.
> You are not intelligent.
> _____
> ∴ You will not succeed.

In symbolic form this argument would be written as

$$P \supset Q$$
$$\sim P$$
$$\overline{\qquad\qquad}$$
$$\therefore \sim Q$$

It is clear that however closely this argument resembles *modus tollens* it is invalid and can be proven so by the methods of Chapter 3. However, it does have a certain persuasiveness when presented in ordinary language and can be used to mislead.

The reader should realize that each violation of the rules of the syllogism was, in effect, a fallacy. However, because the exhaustive exemplification of every possibly misleading invalid argument form would duplicate material already covered, we will leave this to the reader and move on to sources of fallacies that have not yet been discussed in the book.

6.2.2   The semantic fallacies

We will now consider those arguments that contain confusions in meaning that result in their being invalid. Of course, the phrase "confusions in meaning" is itself rather unclear and in the ensuing discussion we will more precisely identify the areas of confusion. The first sort of confusion arises from the ambiguity of a word or phrase. It is a familiar fact of everyday language that the same word can often have different meanings. Thus, the word "bank" can be a place where business is transacted or the shore of a river. Moreover, there are considerably more subtle shades of meaning ambiguity of a word or phrase, and these are often the source of puns, *double entendre,* and other witticisms. However, when such ambiguity is found in an argument it can often mislead one into evaluating the argument as valid, even though closer inspection would have revealed some error. When word ambiguity brings about such a situation we will identify it as the *fallacy of equivocation.* Our first example of equivocation is contained in the following syllogism:

> All things that are spoiled are inedible.
> Timmy is spoiled.
> ─────────────────────────────
> ∴ Timmy is inedible.

In this case we can identify two different senses of the word "spoiled," one meaning "chemically ruined" and the other meaning "overindulged." Since there are two clearly different senses to this word we do not really have a proper syllogism, i.e., there are really four terms in the above argument. The proper form of this argument would be

> All things chemically spoiled are inedible.
> Timmy is psychologically spoiled.
> ─────────────────────────────
> ∴ Timmy is inedible.

Now in this case even though the conclusion may be true the argument is invalid because the middle term is not the same in each case. In short it is not a syllogism at all. We describe this as *equivocation* on the word "spoiled."

The reader may have noted that this semantic fallacy is, underneath, one of improper form and it could have been classified as a syntactical fallacy. However, since any invalid argument must violate a syntactic rule of some sort we could have classified all fallacies as syntactic. This, though, would defeat the purpose of our original plan of classifying the fallacies by source of error and so we will continue to call the fallacy of equivocation a *semantic fallacy* even though it can be translated into a formal or syntactic fallacy. To continue, the particular equivocation in the above example is, of course, very obvious (if not humorous) and certainly would not mislead the average reader. This is not to say that equivocation is always so direct. Quite often the meaning of a term will "shift" very subtly in an argument, and this will slip by all but the most careful listener. The following example is somewhat more subtle than the above.

> It is certainly true that men are of the animal kingdom, and it is natural for an animal to exhibit characteristic patterns of behavior. However, human society restricts man's animalistic behavior and so human society is, to that extent, unnatural.

The equivocation in this case is on the word "animal." It is first introduced as a morally neutral term meaning "member of a certain biological class." However, it takes an additional, but not completely different, meaning in the phrase "animalistic behavior." The point of this second term is that animals often behave in ways we would consider unfit for human imitation and we describe this behavior with the strongly pejorative term "animalistic." Thus, while it is true that society restricts this latter type of behavior it is not true that it restricts our ordinary natural behavior as Homo sapiens—members of the animal kingdom. To sum up, equivocation is the semantic fallacy that arises from ambiguity in a term of an argument.

It is sometimes the case that each term of a proposition is clear enough but that the entire proposition has alternative interpretations. When the entire premise (or conclusion) of an argument is ambiguous and this results in the invalidity of the argument, we call this the fallacy of *amphiboly*. Suppose, you were to come across the following sentence in an argument:

> Toscanini's son did not know how to conduct himself.

It could be taken to mean that the famous conductor's son was not a conductor himself, or that on some particular occasion, he did not know how to conduct himself socially. All the words are fairly unambiguous when taken separately but the statement, as printed—is amphibolous. If it were to occur in an argument then one would be hard put to determine which meaning was intended, and this could result in an invalid argument's appearing valid. There is a rather famous case where just such a circumstance occurred. Croessus, king of Lydia, is supposed to have consulted the Delphic oracle before embarking on a campaign against Persia and is supposed to have been told, "If you make war on Persia you will destroy a great kingdom." Croessus assumed that this meant that he would defeat Persia but learned the amphibolous nature of this statement when, after suffering defeat, he realized that the kingdom was his own.

Another ambiguity that can create problems in evaluating an argument is the *fallacy of accent.* In many situations a speaker can convey different shades of meaning with the same words by suitably accenting certain parts of the utterance. Thus, the following statement can be given two different "readings," and the choice of interpretations would have significant effect on any argument that contained the statement:

John ought not to overtly belittle his associates.

The two senses of the above can be brought out most clearly by the following rewritten versions.

John *ought not to* overtly belittle his associates.
John ought not to *overtly* belittle his associates.

The italics in each sentence above indicate the stress that a speaker could use in delivering each version and the drastic difference between the two should be apparent. The fallacy of accent is not, however, necessarily tied to spoken arguments or utterances. In fact, it is often more effectively employed as a means of misleading readers of various advertising signs and even some newspapers. Thus, imagine picking up the morning newspaper and seeing the headline:

CAMPUS VIOLENCE AT
STATE UNIVERSITY
averted

The visual impression of the above is such that you might very well be led to believe that there was unrest at State University when, in fact, the opposite was true. The newspaper would, of course, have achieved this deception by printing certain parts of the headline in larger type and thus, accenting them disproportionately—hence the fallacy of accent.

The final two semantic fallacies are closely related and somewhat intricate. They are related in that one concerns arguments relating parts to the whole while the other considers the relation of the whole to the part. This will become clearer if we consider the following situation. It is a familiar fact that sportswriters, in deciding who will win a certain game, will examine and compare each man of one team with his opposite number on the other. Thus, the argument runs, when a certain team has a man-to-man advantage it will win the game. If the purpose of this argument is merely to establish the fact that one team seems more likely to win than another this procedure is perfectly sound. However, it is quite often the case that this analysis of the "parts" (individual players) of one team is used as the premise for the certain prediction that one team will beat some other team. This latter argument is described as the *fallacy of composition* because conclusions reached on the basis of the parts of an entity do not necessarily relate to the whole. In the extreme case this is seen by the absurdity of arguing that the United States is not a member of the United Nations because each of the states that make up the United States are not members of the United Nations. Also classified as a fallacy of composition is the following semantically confused argument:

> A pin makes hardly any sound when it falls, so if you spill the contents of that box no one will notice as it is a box of pins.

Clearly, the lack of sound that a pin makes when it falls is a property of it as an individual pin and does not apply to a large number of pins. To argue that it does is to commit the fallacy of composition.

For an even clearer example consider the following two sentences:

> Dogs are numerous.
> Dogs are friendly.

Even though both sentences have a similar structure it can be seen that the class term "dogs" in the first is modified by a composite property word (i.e., "numerous") while in the second the modifier is a distributive property word. The first sentence says of the entire class "dogs" that it is a large class while the second says of each dog that it is friendly. Since the errors in the above examples arise from confusing the distributive or individual use of a class with the composite use this type of mistake comes under the heading of the fallacy of composition.

As the reader can imagine there is a fallacy that is the converse of the fallacy of composition, in that it is based on the invalid argument from the whole to the part. This will be known as the *fallacy of division* and is exemplified in the following argument:

> The army is notoriously inefficient.
> Captain Smith is a soldier.
> _____
> ∴ Captain Smith must be inefficient.

The fallacy of division, like the fallacy of composition, can show up in predicates as well as in arguments such as the above. Thus, the following two sentences contain the shift from the collective use of a predicate to the distributed use, and an argument based on this shift would commit the fallacy of division:

> Television sets are common in America.
> Television sets are intricate electronic devices.

6.2.3   The pragmatic fallacies

There are a number of often used lines of argument that are neither clearly fallacious nor valid and that usually demand considerable contextual clarification before they can be evaluated. Typical of these was the previously discussed argument known as the *appeal to authority* (or *argumentum ad vericundiam*). In the example cited it was pointed out that it is perfectly reasonable to argue by appealing to an authority on some matter, as long as the matter is within the area of competence of the authority. Thus Dr. A was recognized as an authority on biological matters but not necessarily on moral issues (if there is ever such a thing as an "authority" in this field). Indeed, it is because of the importance of the circumstances of the argument that this section is entitled "pragmatic fallacies." There is nothing intrinsically fallacious about appeal to an authority in an argument, but all too often the appeal is to an improper authority and this is the source of error which we have labeled *ad vericundiam*. In all the following cases the reader will be given descriptions of circumstances in which the particular argument considered is invalid. However, it is generally possible to describe special contexts in which the same pattern of argument is valid. This, of course, means that the use of labels for evaluating arguments such as *ad vericundiam* is not by any means mechanical. However, our intention in this section is merely a description of some of the more common pragmatic fallacies and not an exhaustive analysis of their possible contexts.

The name *ad baculum* is translated as "to the stick," and this argument is usually one that involves the threat of violence. When someone is told:

> It is only reasonable that you should not testify against our employer because if you do we will get you.

We characterize this as *ad baculum* or appeal to force and in a logical context it is fallacious. The source of the fallacy here is that the "because" in the above is not a logical or inferential "because" but the result of a threat. Of course, as with other pragmatic fallacies, it is possible to imagine circumstances in which it is valid. Thus, if the argument were rewritten with the following premises and altered conclusion, it would be valid.

> Either you do not testify or you are killed.
> No one wants to be killed.
> ∴ You do not testify.

The fallacy of *ad baculum* need not involve the use of overt threat; any use of penalty or retribution which serves as a premise for an argument and involves a nonlogical "because" as above is classed as an appeal to force.

Of all the pragmatic fallacies *ad hominem* is perhaps the most important and the most misunderstood. It is a rather obvious fact that any particular argument you come across in speeches, newspapers, or ordinary conversation is authored by some individual or group. In earlier chapters we evaluated any number of arguments without any special concern for who used them but, in our everyday existence, arguments are used by people in specific situations. On occasion an argument may be used by someone in circumstances which seem to undermine the argument's conclusion, and it is in such circumstances that the fallacy of *ad hominem* is often committed. For example, suppose that someone presents an argument against the poor quality of certain mass-produced goods:

> We often hear that poor quality merchandise is a natural outcome of the market demand. That is, people are not willing to pay the higher price for better workmanship. However, this line of argument is mistaken. Quite

often the manufacture of a better product is not much more costly than the poorer designed item and no one really tries to test public acceptance by putting a really well-made item out.

This argument, whatever its intrinsic merit, would seem invalid if it were put forward by a manufacturer who was himself guilty of the sort of misrepresentation the argument condemns. However, the validity of an argument is always independent of the circumstances of its presentation and is certainly independent of the utterer of the argument. To include a consideration of the source of an argument in its evaluation is to commit the fallacy of *ad hominem circumstantial.* That is, arguing "toward the circumstances of the man" instead of to the argument itself.

Another fairly common form of the *ad hominem* fallacy is known as *abusive* and is illustrated in the following:

John says that there will always be a tension between inflation and the unemployment rate in a capitalist economy but he is not to be trusted as he was once a Communist party member.

It is obvious that John's statement about the capitalist economy is based on some sort of evidence and can be examined only by reference to this information. The attempt to discredit his statement by attacking him directly is *ad hominem abusive* and is not logically valid.

Another one of the most common forms of pragmatic ad hominem fallacy is *tu quoque* ("you, yourself"), the attempt to discredit an argument by pointing out something in the background or situation of the speaker. Suppose you are trying to convince someone of the dishonesty of keeping the incorrectly computed change that one may get from a grocery store clerk. During the discussion he turns to you and says: "It is not dishonest. Why, if you were to get too much change you would probably keep it yourself." This argument is invalid when it is meant to establish the honesty of the action because it is clear that the honesty of the action is not proven or disproven by the fact that you would or would not keep the money. If it is true that you would keep the change then he would be right in claiming that your words and your actions were inconsistent, but that would not validate the honesty of keeping undeserved change. The fallacy is called *tu quoque* because a conclusion is purported to be proven by reference to the beliefs or actions of the speaker and is clearly fallacious. Another context in which it arises can be outlined as follows: An elected official is questioned about the impropriety

299

of some of his dealings with the local business community and he argues that his actions were not improper since such dealings are a common and apparently accepted part of political life. He is, in effect, claiming that it is all right because everybody does it and this is a general form of the *tu quoque* fallacy.

On occasion you will hear an argument, such as

> Cigarettes do not cause cancer because there is no conclusive evidence that they do.

Of course, as we realized in our attempts to construct deductions, the failure to prove a statement does not mean that its negation is provable. That is, it is invalid to insist that cigarettes are safe because all attempts to prove them unsafe have failed. The Latin name of this pattern of fallacious reasoning *ad ignorantium,* is aptly translated as arguing "toward ignorance" referring to the fact that one's ignorance or inability to prove some proposition is used as a premise to allegedly imply the opposite of this proposition.

Let us now consider the fallacy of *ad misericordiam* ("appeal to pity"). Suppose an instructor is presented with the following argument by a student in his class:

> You have to pass me because I need the credit for this course to graduate and I need the degree to get a better job to support my family.

There is no doubt that we all feel the emotional force of such an argument, but it is not a good argument. The "because" in the above is not deductively valid as the proper reason for a passing grade is usually based on the class work and not the circumstances of the student. In this case the appeal to pity is clearly not logically compelling as presented. The source of the persuasiveness of the above argument, however, is that the wider context of the student's situation may warrant extra consideration and leniency in the assignment of the grade may be the result of such consideration. Still, the *ad misericordiam* argument is always invalid.

Rendered into English *ignoratio elenchi* denotes the fallacy of arguing when "ignorant of the purpose (goal)" of some argument. Of all the pragmatic fallacies this is perhaps the most blatant, and the reader will shortly appreciate that it only appears valid under specially constructed conditions. In essence, a person who is guilty of *ignoratio elenchi* is using some argument to support a conclusion that is not the proper conclusion of the original argument. Most often the argument used is a valid one, but valid only for the conclusion that is not the one explicitly argued for. If this sounds somewhat intricate let us simplify it by reference to an example. A classic case of *ignoratio elenchi* is contained in the following:

> The Indian Valley conservation bill deserves the support of each and every citizen of our state. Conservation, though it is often "too little, too late," is the only means we have for ensuring a continued natural environment for our society. Without considered conservation legislation this worthy purpose would be frustrated and we will surely ruin our planet.

Now the speaker is allegedly presenting an argument to support the Indian Valley conservation bill but, in fact, his argument is one for the merit of conservation. One may assent to this latter argument and be a whole-hearted supporter of "considered" conservation legislation and still not support the Indian Valley bill. Perhaps the bill, though called a "conservation bill," has the ultimate effect of giving large areas of the valley to private industrial contractors. In any case the *ignoratio elenchi* is apparent because an argument for conservation is presented as an argument for the Indian Valley bill and though the former may be valid the latter is not.

Of all the pragmatic fallacies, *accident and converse accident* are most often cited as fallacious by persons who have had no formal training in logic, and the reader will probably recognize them under different names (*hasty generalization, glittering generalities,* etc.). In the fallacy of accident a person argues that some specific case is to be subsumed under a general rule or principle when, in fact, that subsumption is questionable. A typical example is contained in the following:

> The constitution allows every citizen the right to bear arms and thus my right to own this gun is in accordance with the constitution and should not be challenged.

Now, the general rule mentioned in the constitution is not necessarily a premise from which we can validly deduce a conclusion relating to an individual case. It may very well be that aspects of the specific case would rule it out as a subcase of the general rule. For instance, suppose a person were to claim that the constitutional rule allowed criminals to "bear arms." It would seem that this case is not one which was meant to fall under the Bill of Rights and to claim that it did would be a clear case of the fallacy of

301

accident. The name arises from the fact that the individual instance has accidental or special characteristics that disqualify its inclusion under the general rule. Similarly, there are often cases where a person argues invalidly from some specific case or cases to a general rule, and this is known as the *fallacy of converse accident* or *hasty generalization.*[11] A particularly blatant example of this fallacy is found in the following:

> Persons on welfare are extorting our tax money under false pretenses since I know of several cases where welfare recipients earn money without declaring it. In fact, they earn more than many people who are not on welfare.

However persuasive such an argument may appear to many people it is thoroughly invalid as it may very well be true that there are abuses of the welfare structure without our rejecting the entire structure.

We are all familiar with the rather humorous situations in which one is asked a question such as: Have you stopped your heavy drinking lately? Clearly, either a yes or a no answer is incriminating and yet questions, in general, seem to be settled by either a yes or a no. The source of the peculiarity of this particular sort of question is that it is complex. That is, it is composed both of a straightforward question and a hidden supposition; in this case the supposition that you are or have been a heavy drinker. When this complex question construction is incorporated into an argument then it is known as the *fallacy of complex question.* The following would be an example:

> You ought to leave school since most of the stuff you learn there is from books and is of no practical value. And a person should do something worthwhile with his life.

If you attempted to argue that you ought not to leave school then, unless you attacked the complex assumptions in the premises, you would appear to be saying that you did not want to do anything worthwhile with your life.

The *fallacy of petitio principii* (or "begging the question") is most interesting in that the arguments given as examples are, on evaluation, valid. However, the fallaciousness of this type arises more from the context of

---

[11] A person may argue from specific cases to a general rule in ways which we accept (sound *inductive* arguments), but no converse accident will be a *deductively* valid argument. For more on inductive reasoning see Chapter 7.

presentation than the form of the argument. In the play *Le Medicin Volant* by Molière, a character who is impersonating a doctor tells a rather gullible client, "Hippocrates has said—and Galen confirmed it with many persuasive arguments—that when a girl is not in good health she is sick." In this case, it is clear that the doctor and his distinguished sources as represented in this passage have begged the question in that the premises of this facetious argument are nothing more than the assertion of the conclusion in different words. The Latin *petitio principii* means literally "petitioning the premises" and points up the fact that the premises are insufficient to establish the conclusion, as they are equivalent to the conclusion. The example cited is, of course, rather humorous and hardly convincing, but when the premises are expanded and it is difficult to trace their equivalence to the conclusion then *petitio principii* can be misleading.

EXERCISE

1 Identify the fallacy in each of the following arguments:
   a. Giant turtles are almost extinct. This animal is a giant turtle so this animal must be almost extinct.
   b. The FBI has solved many criminal cases by using wire-tapping so it should be allowed to use it whenever it wants.
   c. We ought to see the movie that I want to see since I am the only one with a car that can get us to the movies.
   d. Man has the power to be immortal but he loses it when he sins and since every man, to date, has committed some sin, no one has yet lived forever.
   e. No one has really shown that our environment will be irreversibly damaged by pollution so, until this is shown, manufacturers should continue with their present waste disposal methods.
   f. Our team's losing is no news so since no news is good news, the news of our team's loss must be good news.
   g. The sign of a good-hearted man is his concern for others. So to be good-hearted one ought to do things that will show concern for others.
   h. If a person does not like the way this country is run he should leave it.
   i. A: I will give no more money to the alumni association as I do not approve of its policies.
      B: That's all right. We will put you down for the same amount as last year.
   j. Since practically every heroin addict has tried marijuana first, we ought to outlaw marijuana as it is a major cause of heroin addiction.

    k. Was greed or incompetence the reason for Senator A's backing of the new tax bill? In either case there is no reason to continue to support him.

    l. There is something wrong with a medical association which licenses its members to practice medicine. Should not the physicians have finished practicing before they get their licenses?

    m. Professor Johnson did not like the parts of the *Republic* in which Plato advocates communal cohabitation. Did not the good professor ever wish for such a pleasant situation and if so how can he, in all fairness, criticize Plato?

    n. Nothing tastes better than lobster. But even gruel is better than nothing so gruel must taste better than lobster.

    o. We have been engaged in the Cold War with the communists since World War II and in that time the crime rate in America has gone way up and the level of decency has plummeted. Thus, one can only assume that we have been losing the Cold War.

6.2.4   A note on two paradoxes

Before beginning our discussion of definition it would be useful to outline a number of problematic or paradoxical aspects of language that have direct bearing on logic. These paradoxes have far-reaching consequences for logic and they can be best introduced in this context—a linguistic context in which we have been careful to distinguish the aspects of natural language and logic. The first of these is usually classified as a pragmatic paradox—and this is for reasons which fit very well with our use of the term *pragmatic.* Consider the sentence:

> John cannot assert even one complete and grammatically correct English sentence.

It is quite clear what this sentence asserts and there would seem to be no paradox in its assertion. However, suppose this perfectly clear sentence were asserted by John (the person mentioned in the sentence) on some occasion. Well, its meaning is still unambiguous, but its very utterance by John seems to falsify it. This is so, of course, because the above sentence is a "complete and grammatically correct sentence" and on our supposition it is asserted by John. The paradox is clearly *pragmatic* in that the problem arises as a result of the conflict between what the sentence asserts and the context in which it is asserted; in most contexts there is no problem but when the context includes a mention of the speaker there is a conflict.

A second paradox is one that depends on somewhat different linguistic properties but with a similar result. Suppose we were to assert the following:

The only sentence in this book on page 305 line 3 is false.

Careful checking would reveal that the sentence referred to in the above was itself! But this would mean that it was false if it were true and true if it were false—surely a paradoxical result. The most common presentation of this paradox is the puzzle:

If you were in Crete and met a Cretan who said, "All Cretans are inveterate liars" would you believe him?

Because of this way of phrasing the paradox it is most often known as the *paradox of the liar,* though it is sometimes referred to as the *vicious circle paradox.* Logicians have had a special interest in this puzzle, and though we cannot present their observations on and uses of this paradox, we can give the reader an idea of how the paradoxical result is achieved and how it differs from the pragmatic paradox we gave as an example above.[12] First, let us note that we have been rather casual about this term *paradox.* A paradox is not just any statement or belief that is peculiar—though the word is sometimes used that way. In the context of our discussion, a paradox will be a situation in which our analysis leads to two conclusions or options that are either logically incompatible or whose joint truth seems unacceptable. The logical paradox of the liar consists of two possible positions—either the proposition on page 305, line 3 is true or it is false and yet by simple argument each of these seems to lead to contradictions (if the proposition is true, then it is false and if it is false, then it is true). The only alternative to this would seem to be a rejection of the true-false interpretation of the original proposition. That is, we can reject the idea that this proposition is exclusively either true or false. This option, though, seems unacceptable since we have described all propositions as either true or false (and have built a system of logic on this notion) and, on the face of it, the proposition in question is not different from many others. In sum, the liar paradox is built from the following:

1. Construct a proposition as in page 305, line 3.
2. If we accept it as a proposition it will either be **T** or **F**.

[12] Those interested in a fuller discussion of this and still other, more formal, paradoxes should refer to C. I. Lewis and C. H. Langford, *Symbolic Logic* (1932).

3. If it is **T** then it is **F** but if it is **F** then it is **T** so option 2 is problematic.

4. If we reject 2 then we have a meaningful and otherwise acceptable sentence which is not propositional (not exclusively **T** or **F**).

When summarized in this way the source of the paradox and avenues of reduction become obvious. The proposition in question must be shown to be significantly different from other propositions and then we will be able to reconstruct step 4 so as to disqualify the proposition in question from the ranks of the more ordinary propositions. Two points become obvious: First, the proposition refers to itself, and second, it makes an assertion about its own truth. Self-reference is not, in itself, a cause of paradox. Many sentences can be constructed with harmless self-reference, e.g.,

This sentence has five words.

However, the self-reference of this sentence is syntactical, i.e., it refers to a syntactical property of the sentence (number of words) whereas truth is a semantical property. Still the paradox is not generated by self-reference to other semantical properties e.g.,

The meaning of this sentence is not vague.

The liar paradox, then, gets its peculiarities by its containing reference to its own truth, and recognizing this can be grounds for disarming the paradox. Note, though, the great difference between the pragmatic and liar paradoxes. The former is peculiar because the context of utterance of a sentence falsifies the proposition. The liar paradox does not have to depend on the context of assertion (in the case of the Cretan it does but this is only incidental) as the problems arise from the assertion itself. For more on self-reference the reader should see section 5.5.

6.3 DEFINITION

When one recognizes the significance of the language-logic relationship it is not difficult to further recognize the central role the process of defining plays in this area. In a general way it may be said that all of language becomes useful and meaningful only through some sort of definition. Also, in setting up the symbolic machinery of Chapters 2-5 we constantly made use of certain methods of defining our terms. Finally, it was noted that the avoidance of the traditional semantic fallacies depended on being careful with respect to the assumed definitions of our terms. Though this section will present only a basic approach to this topic it is not overstating the case to say that much of philosophy consists in extended study of this concept.[13]

Since we have spent considerable effort in delineating the syntactic, semantic, and pragmatic aspects of language it will be useful to determine in which of these aspects the process of definition belongs. As a first approximation it may be said that *definition* is the general name of the ways in which linguistic forms become associated with objects and situations in the world; it is, in short, primarily concerned with the semantical aspect of language. We have described this as a "first approximation" because there is considerable controversy about the ultimate roles that pragmatics and syntactics play in the various processes of definition and we do not want to appear misleadingly dogmatic on this point. Perhaps the most basic way in which a linguistic term derives its semantic content is by the procedure known as *ostensive definition*. The familiar example of the parent pointing to the household pet and uttering the word "dog" as the child looks on is an example of ostensive definition. The role of this misleadingly simple method of definition can be seen quite clearly when one refers to the dictionary, the traditional source of the definitions of most words in a language. Consider the structure of the typical dictionary: To the right of each entry (and each entry is a linguistic item, i.e., a string of symbols) is a sequence of symbols. Now, by "looking up" any one of these items we are able to associate it with some string of further items (i.e., each word will be followed by another word or string of words). In fact, if we were very diligent in this process of looking up dictionary entries we would discover that the construction of a dictionary is a large-scale variation of *petitio principii* in that every "word" is itself defined by other words which, in the end, are defined by the original word. This circularity is, of course, not very problematic for the user of a dictionary because he comes to it with a certain minimum of known or defined words. The dictionary is used to enlarge his stock of defined words by depending on those that are defined without any dictionary. In general, one gets this basic, nondictionary stock of words from ostensive definition. Most larger dictionaries are themselves capable of giving ostensive definitions by the use of those pictures that are often encountered to the right of the printed definition.

[13] See Aristotle, *Categories* and L. Wittgenstein, *Philosophical Investigations* (New York: Macmillan, 1953) for an instructive comparison of differing analyses of definition.

However, it is significant that ostensive definitions lie behind the attempt to construct dictionaries.[14]

The second sort of definition to consider has already been discussed. This is the *verbal* definition typically found in a dictionary or in any attempt to define one word (or phrase) with others. However, one can make a significant distinction between two main types of verbal definition—the *explicit* and the *implicit*. A dictionary entry is an explicit verbal definition inasmuch as it presents a string of words as defining a particular word. This, though, is not the only way we can use words to define a word. Quite often we can gather the meaning of words from some linguistic context that uses but does not explicitly define the unknown. It is not uncommon to read a newspaper article that contains an unfamiliar word (it could be a seldom-used English word, a technical term you have never heard of before, or even a foreign word used in an English language context). However, in most cases it is not necessary to "look it up" in the dictionary (and it may not be there anyway if the word is newly coined). Still, the meaning of the term is gleaned from the context, from the subtle dependencies which this word has on other, more familiar words in the selection. This method of defining a word is known as *implicit verbal* definition.

In a sense all definitions are either ostensive or verbal, but there are so many additional nuances to the concept of definition that merely distinguishing ostensive and verbal is unhelpful. That is , there are many additional ways to view definitions and even though each of them will be either ostensive or verbal our inquiry should consider them. The first new distinction is that between a *lexical* (or reporting) definition and a *stipulative* definition. Consider the actual construction of most English dictionaries (the standard French dictionary is constructed somewhat differently); many sources are gathered together and words are looked up in each of them. Each word is then excerpted from the source (novels, plays, poetry, essays, etc.), but it is excerpted with its immediate context. After suitable allowance for repetition the word is entered in the dictionary with its one or more meanings, on the basis of the implicit definition present in each context of the word. In short, a dictionary entry is an explicit report of how a word is used in current situations. No attempt is made to legislate or alter the reported widespread usage, and hence the name *reportive* or *lexical* definition. There are times, however, when one is not interested in a lexical

[14] Ostensive definition is easily described but in any particular case this method can lead to confusion and ambiguity, see L. Wittgenstein, *Philosophical Investigations.*

definition of a term. It may be that the word is newly coined or that you want to use an older word in a new way, but in either case the idea of stipulating the definition of a term is the appropriate description of this type of activity. In Chapter 2 we stipulated that the word "some" was to mean "at least one" and in Chapters 2-5 we often stipulated the meaning of our symbolic devices. Any problems that arise in connection with stipulative definitions usually involve the use to which they are put. In a straightforward sense it is fair to say that there can be no quarrel with the stipulated definition itself but only with the justification behind the definition. Thus, if you stipulate that "wrong" is to mean "whatever I disagree with," then your definition could not be described as incorrect so much as, in this case, unjustified. Depending on the context, the justification provided will be the most significant aspect of the stipulative definition, and this was apparent in our attempts to justify the stipulations we placed on our logical devices.

Closely related to the notion of stipulative definition is that of *precising* definition. In certain situations the meaning of some rather vague word might become especially important to discussion and the only way to properly carry on the discussion would be by pinning down the meaning of the word more exactly. This need is most likely to occur in contexts such as the legal or philosophical. Thus, while in ordinary affairs a word such as "airplane" suffices to describe most man-made, flying devices, in the laws relating to air traffic it is necessary to state precisely what is an airplane and what is not. The word "airplane," in being given a precising definition, still retains its basic ordinary usage; it is not the intent of a precising definition to change the meaning so much as eliminate its vagueness.

The final sort of definition we will discuss, which is also a species of stipulative definition, is known as *operational* definition and its most familiar context is natural science. Any student of elementary physics is aware of the definitions of such concepts as time, distance, and mass in terms of some procedure of measurement. Thus, the distance from A to B is defined as the result of putting measuring sticks end to end from A to B and then counting them. Also, these measuring sticks are defined as being of a certain number of units (meters, feet, etc.) by comparing them to some standard unit (until recently, the famous "meter bar" in Paris). This process of definition, which is certainly stipulative, is given the more precise name, *operational,* as the definition describes an operation or procedure by which the concept is to be understood. Clearly, operational definitions of such concepts as time and mass are necessary in physics since these concepts enter into various physical laws and must be both measurable and experimentally identifiable. Physics is not particularly concerned with philosophical definitions of time, though the operational definitions of time, mass, etc. in physics have entered into philosophical discussions.

At this point we have presented various types of definitions, but the reader should recognize that we have not discussed the actual process of defining. That is, we have not considered the ways in which one would use the definitions discussed above to actually define something. We now know, e.g., that "table" can be defined ostensively or verbally, lexically or stipulatively but not how one would frame each definition. The most well-known method for constructing a definition is due to Aristotle and is generally known as the *genus and differentia* method. One first states what general class the entity being defined belongs to (i.e., its genus) and then specifies the ways in which this particular entity differs from other members of the genus (i.e., one gives its differentia). We have, in fact, used the Aristotelian method of definition on the concept of definition itself. That is, we first said that definition was the way in which one associates words with nonlinguistic items (this is its genus) and then we described the different subclasses of definition within this general frame. Further, all this was done as both a verbal and lexical process since we have no choice but to use words in our definition of "definition" and we were concerned to describe the actual way in which people define words. The reader has probably been most aware of the Aristotelian method of constructing definitions in biological contexts and, in fact, the Linnaean system of biological classification is derived from the Aristotelian method. Earlier, we mentioned the fact that definition is related to some of the central problems in philosophy, and it is the failure of the Aristotelian method in many contexts and the underlying presuppositions this method requires us to have that have resulted in views such as that of Wittgenstein.[15] Some of these criticisms will be brought out in our following discussion of "meaning."

6.4 MEANING

The full understanding of the concept of meaning and its related ideas (i.e., truth, reference, etc.) is certainly no simple matter and is beyond the scope of an introductory book on logic. However, on the basis of our previous discussions of logic, language, fallacies, and definitions we can

[15] See note 13, this chapter.

provide the reader with a general background that will allow him to more effectively grasp the thorny problems in this area.

Earlier we described semantics as the study of the ways in which a syntactical system gets connected to, or associated with the nonlinguistic world. Now while this statement is certainly in need of qualification, it was useful in our understanding of the concept of definition. Thus, any definition was considered as a device for connecting a linguistic sign with some aspect of the empirical world; since this is done in many different ways, there are many different sorts of definitions. Now, it would seem that the concept of meaning is a direct product of definition. That is, the meaning of a word would seem to be what one ends up with when one defines the word. Actually, though, there is a very important asymmetry between the concept of meaning and that of definition, and this has made the concept of meaning seem more philosophically significant. The asymmetry is the result of the fact that defining is an activity that can be clearly explained and seems to involve no mysteries, whereas meaning is not an activity but a property that appears to come with a language. It is an uncomplicated but important fact that we (as individuals) are not the authors of our language. When we are young we learn a language that seems to have been created without our consultation. As a result of this it is perfectly natural that we would think of the meanings of the parts of the language as quite independent of individuals and as properties of the language itself. Thus, the process of finding the meaning of a word is ordinarily conceived of as a search for what is in the language and what, after diligent effort, can be discovered. Further, since there are certainly different types of words in any natural language, the search for one sort of meaning that encompasses all of these types becomes a near impossible task. This difficulty, in turn, gives rise to the general notion that "meaning" is an especially complex and enigmatic concept. During the twentieth century the preponderance of linguistic and philosophical research has been concerned with the dissolution of what are considered the illusive problems associated with the word "meaning."[16] This is not to say that there are not many genuine semantic problems that concern the linguist and philosopher, but only that the notion that words come with fixed meanings and that there is one idea behind the concept of meaning has been generally abandoned. Philosophers recognize that there are different bases to the way in which each of the following are meaningful linguistic entities:

[16] The reader who is interested in this would do well to consult C. K. Ogden and I. A. Richard's *The Meaning of Meaning.* (New York: 1938)

1. Names
2. Class terms or universals
3. Predicate expressions—including words that describe mental states
4. Descriptions—definite and indefinite
5. Ethical terms
6. Aesthetic terms
7. Scientific concepts

This list is only partial but if one were to examine the historical and contemporary literature on each of these one would have to touch on most of the major problems in philosophy, and the problems that have arisen in connection with just class terms, would result in a fairly complete examination of traditional metaphysics. Because of the direct connection between the notion of definite description and formal logic, we have included Appendix II, which discusses definite descriptions; but any further inquiry into the types of meaning found in the other categories will require the use of the recommended reading at the end of the book. In what remains of this chapter, we will discuss two issues that are natural outgrowths of our previous discussions and that have a direct bearing on issues surrounding the concept of meaning.

In sections 6.1 and 6.2 we were concerned to differentiate three aspects of language and discuss the role of logic in terms of these. We also indicated that these three aspects were not independent of one another but were, on the contrary, interdependent. We will now consider the more precise nature of the interdependencies by first discussing the relation of the semantic aspect of language to the syntactic and then the semantic to the pragmatic. Since the concept of meaning is a part of this semantic aspect, our discussions in both cases will provide the reader with some very general observations about this concept; these, it is hoped, will serve as a base for any further inquiry.

It is clear that the syntactic aspect of any natural language is closely related to the semantic. Earlier, we pointed out that the violation of the grammatical rules of English could result in an expression such as

The the house hot than ran.

Now, though this expression would be most often described as "meaningless," we can recognize that the source of its absurd character is its ungrammatical construction. That is, the string of words above fails to have any meaning because it violates a considerable number of the syntactical rules of the English language.[17] This does not mean, however, that syntactic abuse always results in semantic defects or that one can determine some syntactic failure for each case of the use of meaningless expressions. In fact, one of the most lively areas for dispute in linguistics and the philosophy of language is precisely this topic, i.e., how far one can correlate the semantic with the syntactic aspects of a language (either a natural or an artificial language). Linguistic and philosophical research on this question has taken two main forms. The first is concerned with the project of constructing a grammar (a body of syntactic rules) that will partially enable one to determine the meaningfulness of expressions in the language. Since this is done by first determining the necessary and sufficient grounds for the grammaticalness of expressions the first requirement would be a complete grammar for the language under consideration. This grammar would have to univocally determine which expressions in the language were well formed and which were not. In Chapter 5 we did this quite simply for the propositional calculus, but the task is much harder when the language is one with the syntactic richness of English. Though such a grammar has yet to be completed there is considerable work going on in this field.[18] The second area of investigation into the relationship of semantics and syntactics has had many ramifications in philosophical discussions and will be discussed at somewhat greater length.

In the above discussion we focused on an ungrammatical and meaningless example. However, as has been indicated, it is perfectly possible for an ungrammatical expression to be quite meaningful, and this without need of special contextual clarification. For example, consider the expression

John attached the picture onto the inside of his wallet.

In general, we try to avoid such awkward expressions, but they are certainly not so devoid of meaning as was the previous example. Further, there is a large class of expressions perfectly correct in the syntactical sense but

[17] There is, of course, a sense in which even such apparently nonsensical expressions have "meaning"; they can be used to evoke emotion or even express a fairly clear statement if set in the proper context. For example, imagine the expression above uttered hastily by someone running away from a fire.

[18] For more on this see Noam Chomsky, *Syntactic Structures* (The Hague: Mouton, 1957) J. Katz and Fodor, "The Structure of a Semantic Theory," in J. Katz and Fodor, *Readings in Philosophy of Language* (Englewood Cliffs, N.J.: Prentice Hall, 1964). Much of the work on transformational grammar described in these works is not concerned with the direct relation of syntactics to semantics but they are useful in this connection.

decidedly peculiar in semantic content. Typically the sentence

Green ideas sleep furiously.

is grammatically well formed but asserts, or attempts to assert, something that would be classed as nonsense. Still, the reader can appreciate why it is inappropriate to assimilate this example to the ones above. Also, the peculiarity of such sentences as this one creates special problems for any attempts to correlate syntactic and semantic elements. In philosophical discussions this sentence (or, rather, the author of this sentence) is generally felt to commit a special sort of semantic fallacy known as a *category mistake*. Precisely what is involved in this fallacy is this: Certain concepts are supposed to be appropriate to others and thus the semantics of a language does not allow the full range of syntactic combination. Thus, the concepts red, blue, orange, etc. are appropriate to physical objects such as paintings, cars, chairs, etc. However, nothing in the syntactical structure of English rules out the attribution of such color words to abstract nouns such as justice, ideas, or health. This is what is meant by our statement that semantic considerations rule out certain correct syntactic expressions. Grammatically both of the following are well formed

1. The dress is blue.
2. The health is orange.

but 2 is clearly nonsense of some sort and it is generally taken to be a category mistake in which predicates of one category are improperly used to modify nouns of another category. In our example above, the predicates red, blue, orange, etc. belong to the physical object category and not to the abstract concept category as is implied in 2; hence, the category mistake in 2. It should be obvious that the assumptions behind the possibility of such a mistake are considerable. There is the implicit recognition that words are "shaped" in such ways that they cannot be joined with one another even when the usual syntactic conventions are observed and that the result of category violation is a form of nonsense or is, in some way, not well formed. Further, the notion of a category mistake seems to undermine the uses of metaphor that abound in most natural languages. Were someone to describe a thought as "impenetrable" we would not genuinely be tempted to reject this utterance as a violation of semantic categories though we do not ordinarily speak of intangibles such as thoughts as either penetrable or impenetrable.[19]

We indicated above that the notion of a category mistake has had philosophical ramifications. These arise when the supposed mistake is made in a conceptual area which has philosophic connections. In *Concept of Mind,*[20] Gilbert Ryle argues that there are systematic category mistakes made in the traditional discussions of the philosophy of mind. It is, thus, his contention that certain well-known philosophic problems can only be resolved when these mistakes are brought to light.

Having given a general outline of the semantic-syntactic relation we turn now to the semantic-pragmatic. It is quite apparent that the meaning of a word and the use to which it is put in some specific context are practically inseparable. In fact, when we were attempting to distinguish these aspects, we were forced to use the rather atypical example of swearing as a linguistic instance in which the semantic and pragmatic elements of an utterance were fairly separate. However, it had been the traditional view that the pragmatic element of an utterance was wholly dependent on the semantic and this view has come under considerable fire in the contemporary philosophy of language. Proponents of the traditional view would maintain that the meanings of terms in a language are logically prior to their use on particular occasions and that semantic investigation necessitates excursions into the thought processes of speakers of a language.[21] Thus, on this view the meaning of a term is a result of some mental process on the part of the speaker, and this process leads to his using a word in a particular way on some specific occasion. When, e.g., I wish to assert something about a cat, I will (on the traditional view) utter the word "cat" and the meaning of this utterance will be explicable only in terms of the mental image of "catness" which I can, presumably, entertain. The objections to this view of the meanings of terms are formidable but our primary interest is merely in showing the reader how this position attempts to account for the semantic-pragmatic relationship.[22]

[19] For more on the attempt to formulate a category structure for a natural language which will be analogous to the syntactical rules of grammaticality consult F. Sommers, "The Ordinary Language Tree," *Mind,* April 1959.

[20] Gilbert Ryle, *Concept of Mind* (New York: Barnes & Noble, 1949)

[21] Exactly what is meant by "logically prior to" is, of course, a difficult but significant issue. In general the recognition that this priority is just wrong when one studies the learning of a language has been a main stimulus to the abandoning of the traditional view.

[22] The objections, briefly, center around the difficulties one would have in explicating this mental image and in showing how it is that we can use language without these images in most situations. In the ordinary cases one uses expressions quite meaningfully without ever conjuring up such images and many words in English ("or," "but," etc.) have no possible image.

Both because of objections to this view and because of its unworkability in linguistics, research since the latter part of the nineteenth century has gradually resulted in a shift. In fact, pragmatic criteria have become the basis for determining the meaning of linguistic entitles both for the empirical linguist and the philosopher. The philosophic basis for this position can be found in L. Wittgenstein and J. L. Austin's works and the linguistic side of this shifted view can be found in the work of Leonard Bloomfield and Zelig Harris among others. As was mentioned earlier in this section, many philosophical problems can arise when one initiates a search for *the* meaning of linguistic expressions as diverse as those in 1-7 in the above list. The Wittgensteinian dictum (which has been an accepted linguistic principle since at least 1930) that the meaning of an expression is its use has served to untangle some of the knotty problems that surround many philosophical issues. Also, the use of purely pragmatic criteria in empirical linguistics has resulted in a more natural and rigorous understanding of languages—understanding that would have been impossible on a view of meaning such as is contained in the mental image view.[23] Still, the reader should recognize that the issues surrounding the semantic-pragmatic relationship are far from settled. Though the more traditional views seem too objectionable there are still a large number of problems in the pragmatic-distributional approach.

[23] In Zelig Harris, *Structural Linguistics,* such criteria are known as *distributional* and the basic aim of Harris's linguistics is the isolation and classification of the "meaningful" elements of a language by purely statistical data. Thus, individual elements of a language are isolated, determined synonymous, etc. by means of distributional analysis of their occurrences in various contexts or "environments."

the logic of science

7.1 SCIENCE AND EXPLANATION

We turn now to that system of justification of claims that we call science. Science is, of course, more than just a system of justification of claims; it is also a method for arriving at claims. These two aspects of science are two sides of the same coin, for the system of justification and the method of inquiry are interwoven in a way that we must try to make explicit.

Scientists make various sorts of claims that differ in the ways they are to be justified. The following list comprises some of these various sorts of claims:

1. The other side of the moon is as heavily cratered as the side that faces the earth.
2. All satellites travel in elliptical orbits.
3. There will be a total eclipse of the sun on January 4, 2015.
4. The existence of carbon dioxide in the earth's atmosphere is due, for the most part, to plant life.

Statement 1 is an example of a reported observation; 2 is an example of a natural law; 3 is an example of a prediction; and 4 is an example of an explanation. Scientists make observations, do experiments, discover laws, invent theories, make predictions, give explanations, uncover causes, etc. In all these activities the scientist is making claims of one sort or another and the interest of the philosopher lies in what sorts of claims these are and what forms of justification exist for them. We are also interested in seeing how these various activities are related one to another. Does, for instance, the fact that a phenomenon x can be predicted imply that it can also be explained? How are laws and theories related?

In Chapter 1, and indeed throughout this book, we have emphasized the relation between the justification of claims and the notion of argument. Since we have just described science as a method of arriving at and justifying claims science can be viewed as making use of arguments toward the ends of explanation, prediction, etc., while placing particular kinds of restrictions on what can play the role of premises in such arguments. We have termed that area of logical inquiry that concerns itself with the use of argument "pragmatics," and we may then consider the philosophy of science to belong primarily to this area.[1]

There will then be two major trends in this chapter. One that investigates the types of justification involved in the scientific enterprise (or, what amounts to the same thing, what in general are the kinds of grounds that scientists use for accepting or rejecting various claims). The other trend will be an examination of the interrelationship of various concepts in the logical structure of the sciences and, to this end, a discussion of each of these various notions such as law, theory, explanation, prediction, etc. In the course of doing this we will in fact be explicating the notion of *induction*. In Chapter 1 we distinguished deductive and inductive arguments by reference to the degree of connection between the premises and conclusions of such arguments. This difference in degree of connection is often accounted for by reference to the fact that deductive arguments proceed from the general to the particular whereas inductive arguments proceed from the particular to the general. It will be a part of the task of this chapter to discuss some of the ways in which science seems to move from particular observations to general assertions about the nature of the world. In this way we hope to clarify the sense in which science is inductive.

It should be noted before we continue that the position that will be expressed in this chapter has not gone undisputed, though it does reflect, in large part, what might be termed the classical view in the philosophy of science.

[1] A discussion of the division of logical inquiry into the areas of syntactics, semantics and pragmatics is to be found in sections 1. 5 and 6. 1.

The primary endeavor of science is the explanation of "the world." Before we consider what is meant in the sciences by "the world," we will concern ourselves with the nature of explanation in general and scientific explanation in particular.

We begin by considering the following request for an explanation,

Why were you late for dinner, Mr. S?

The presence of the word "why" characterizes it as a request for an explanation. One does not as a matter of course ask for an explanation of every event that occurs; we are motivated to ask for explanations only in cases of special interest. Interest can be grounded in many things, but in general we can argue that it is the unusual that we ask to have explained. If everyone was always late for his dinner appointments we would not ask anyone why he was late.

Let us take Mr. S's explanation as

I was caught in a monumental traffic jam.

In what sense does this explain being late for dinner? It explains it in the sense that since everyone knows that if one is caught in a monumental traffic jam on one's way to an appointment one will be late, then they will also know that Mr. S was necessarily late since Mr. S was caught in a monumental traffic jam. The explanation is so constructed that, given a certain set of conditions (e.g., that Mr. S was caught in traffic) a given consequence, the thing we wish to explain, necessarily follows. Thus, the explanation is enthymematic in that there is a suppressed premise. We now make the explanation explicit as follows:

> Anyone who has a dinner appointment and is caught in a monumental traffic jam will be late for his dinner appointment.
> Mr. S had a dinner appointment and was caught in a monumental traffic jam.
> ∴ Mr. S was late for his dinner appointment.

The reader has surely noted that the above has the form of a valid deductive argument; indeed it is an example of a use of *modus ponens* after an application of universal instantiation. Using the methods of Chapter 4, we may symbolize it as,

$$(x) [(Dx \& Tx) \supset Lx]$$
$$(Ds \& Ts)$$
$$\therefore Ls$$

which is proven valid as follows

1. $(x) [(Dx \& Tx) \supset Lx]$
2. $(Ds \& Ts)$
3. $(Ds \& Ts) \supset Ls$ 1 **UI**
4. Ls 2,3 M.P.

The fact that our explanation has this deductive pattern is indicative of the nature of explanation. When one explains A in terms of B, one shows that, given B, one should expect A. Since we initially set out to explain that which is unusual and unexpected we attempt to remove the element of surprise and show that this is just the sort of thing that was to be expected, given the facts of our explanation. The relation that exists between the premises and the conclusion of a valid argument serves the purpose of making the conclusion a consequence to be expected given the premises. Of course, any deductive argument form fulfills this aspect of "expectation," but the form of explanation goes beyond this to make the thing to be explained a particular instance of a general situation.

In order to facilitate our further discussion of explanation we introduce two new terms. We will call the statement of the thing to be explained the *explanandum* and the assertions offered in explanation of the explanandum the *explanans*. The explanans of an explanation consists of two statements, one a general assertion and the other a description of a state of affairs obtaining before the event described by the explanandum. In the above we have the explanans of an explanation. It consists of the general assertion (or law),

> Anyone who has a dinner appointment and is caught in a monumental traffic jam will be late for his dinner appointment.

and the other assertion, which we will call the statement of *initial or antecedent conditions*,

> Mr. S. had a dinner appointment and was caught in a monumental traffic jam.

To this point we have seen that explanations have a deductive form in which the explanandum follows from the explanans by universal instantiation and *modus ponens.*[2] In this way it is seen that the initial conditions and the explanandum are special cases of the antecedent and consequent, respectively, of the general statement of the explanans. Since, as we shall see, the general statement that is a part of the explanans is usually a law, the model of explanation we have so far sketched is called the *covering law model.*[3] According to this model, as we have seen, an event is explained by subsuming it under some general law called the *covering law.*

We turn now to a discussion of some of the general properties that adequate scientific explanations must possess. The most obvious such condition is that the explanans be true (or confirmed, which as we shall see later is not the same thing as true). Since in scientific explanation the truth (or confirmation) of the explanans is determined through observational evidence the explanans must be *testable in principle,* which is to say that observational evidence must be relevant to the truth or falsity of the explanans. A statement is said to be testable in principle when the result of some observation *could* count as evidence for the falsity of that statement. The word "could" is stressed here to indicate that it is not necessary that there be something that counts as evidence against the truth of a statement in order for it to be testable, but rather that we know what would constitute evidence for its falsehood.

Consider the assertion

There exist entities that do not effect any of our senses either directly or indirectly.

which is clearly untestable in principle. Nothing *could* count as observational evidence for its falsehood. Such a statement could never be a part of the explanans of an adequate scientific explanation. For, in order to be adequate, its explanans must be true (or confirmed) and if its explanans is untestable there is no way to establish its truth (or confirm it).

A further condition that a scientific explanation must meet is that of

[2]It has been maintained, e.g., by Carl G. Hempel, that there are nondeductive explanations, sometimes called *probabilistic* or *statistical-inductive* explanations. A short discussion of such explanations is to be found on pages 348-349. For further consideration see Carl G. Hempel, *Philosophy of Natural Science* (1966), pp. 58-69.

[3]The covering law model is due to Carl G. Hempel and Paul Oppenheim, "The Logic of Explanation," *Philosophy of Science,* 1948, 15: 135-178.

noncircularity. Consider the enthymematic explanation below, which has been constructed to answer the question "Why does opium put Mr. S to sleep?"

Opium has soporific powers, therefore, it puts Mr. S to sleep.

Clearly, this would not be an adequate explanation. For all that is meant by "soporific powers" is that it puts one to sleep. Thus the explanans tells us no more than the explanandum. What we have here then is a kind of equivalence between the explanans and explanandum. Since in the covering law model we have seen that the explanans always implies the explanandum and since we know that by the law of material equivalence

[(explanans ⊃ explanandum) & (explanandum ⊃ explanans)] ≡ (explanans ≡ explanandum)

we can see that the condition that guarantees noncircularity is that the explanandum not imply the explanans.

There is another kind of circularity, of a more subtle sort, that is to be avoided. This sort of circularity, which we will call *ad hocity*, exists when the sole evidence for the explanans is the explanandum. In such a case the explanans is said to be ad hoc. Consider the following explanation:

> Fish can breathe underwater whereas men drown underwater because there exists a great water spirit that hates men but loves fish. It is this spirit who kills all men who enter his domain and allows the fish to survive.

If the sole evidence for the existence of the water spirit is that men drown underwater and fish do not then we have a case of an ad hoc explanans. In such a situation it is clear that one ad hoc explanation has nothing to recommend it over another ad hoc explanation since the evidence for every explanans for a given explanandum will be the same, viz., the explanandum itself. Thus a necessary condition for the adequacy of a scientific explanation is that there be evidence for the explanans other than the state of affairs described in the explanandum.

7.1.1 The explanandum

We turn now to an investigation of the explanandum. It is sometimes asserted simply that the explanandum is a phenomenon or event, i.e., a state of affairs we wish to explain. This is, however, a gross oversimplification. First, it is to be noted that it is not the phenomenon itself that we seek to explain but rather some description of it. Consider the occurrence of some event, say a man throwing a piece of chalk and its subsequent shattering on the floor. Unfortunately, we have had to give a description of the event in question but we ask the reader to imagine that he has witnessed such an event and that it has, therefore, actually taken place. If such an event were witnessed by a group of people would all their descriptions of the event be the same? It is very unlikely indeed that their descriptions would all be the same. Now we are not concerned here with the possibility of their having given contrary descriptions but rather the more likely situation that some observers will mention elements, say A, B, and C in their descriptions of the event while others mention factors D, E, and F in their descriptions while not mentioning the elements A, B, and C. That this is more than likely to occur can easily be seen when one considers the impossibility of any observer giving a complete description of the event. A complete description of the event would have to include such things as the color of the man's clothes, the size of the room in which he threw the chalk, the relation of the room to the star Alpha Centauri, and an infinite list of other such items. As this is the case, the best that any observer can do is to describe some relatively small number of elements of the event. Given this factor of choice over such a large number of elements there is little reason to believe that our observers will all decide to include the same elements in their descriptions. Indeed it would be strange if any two of them were to give exactly the same description. Could we give reasons why Mr. A gave the description that he gave rather than the description that Mr. B gave? It is supposed that such explanations are possible in relation to certain sociopsychological factors, such as Mr. A's interests and concerns. But it would be more profitable to consider whether the situation would change if all the members of our group of observers were, say, physicists. Would this not increase the possibility of our observers giving the same descriptions? Surely it would for what we have at least done is narrowed the probable range of interests and concerns of our observers. But there would seem to be an even more important factor at work, for there is a notion of a "proper" way of describing an event in physics. Our physicists are required by their science to state such things as the mass of the chalk, its initial velocity, its position, and the forces acting on it. The physicist would consider such things as the chalk's color and texture as irrelevant and thus omit them from his description. More will be said about this notion of relevancy later, but it should be noted that when we seek to explain something the something we wish to explain consists not of the "entire" event but rather of those aspects of it that are of interest to us and that are reflected in our description of the event. It is for this reason that we have used the term *explanandum* to refer to a description of the event to be explained rather than to the event itself.

7.1.2   The explanans

The antecedent conditions, i.e., the set of events that took place before the event to be explained, are always enormous in number. In the explanans above we have given two things as the antecedent conditions

Mr. S had a dinner appointment.

and

Mr. S was caught in a monumental traffic jam.

But, these clearly are not the only conditions that obtained before Mr. S was late. There was, e.g., the fact that Mr. S was clothed, that he was in a given country, that he was on a given planet, that the Andromeda galaxy had a given angular momentum in relation to him, etc. All these, and infinitely more, were conditions that existed before the event described in our explanandum. In any given explanation only a small number of the initial conditions are stated. The reader has no doubt recognized that the decision as to which conditions to include and which to exclude is based on the notion of *relevance.* "After all the angular momentum of the Andromeda galaxy had nothing to do with my being late and it would be quite insane to include it as a part of my explanation" would be a proper response to being criticized for incompleteness in this matter. But what if the question of relevance is not so easily settled? In the case we have been considering the explanans are readily at hand, i.e., the individual knows why he was late, but what of a request for an explanation where the explanans are not so easily determined. In the sciences this is surely the more typical case. We usually pick an explanandum that requires some inquiry in order to discover the appropriate explanans.

Let us consider a situation in which a man, on entering a room places a heavy parcel of books on a chair. After 20 minutes the chair suddenly collapses. The man asks why did the chair break? Our explanandum is then

The chair broke.

Assuming we cannot state the appropriate law, we should be able to at least state the initial conditions. But here we once again face the problem of relevance. There are infinitely many conditions (events) that obtained before the chair broke. How do we know which ones to pick out? If we were able to state the law involved it would determine which of the initial conditions were relevant. This is so because, as we have noted, the initial conditions are an instance of the antecedent class of our general statement or law.

Our problem can be restated in the following way. Before the occurrence of the event described in our explanandum, there occurred infinitely many states of affairs described by the infinitely many statements

$$C_1, C_2, C_3, C_4, C_5, \ldots$$

Some subset (hopefully proper subset) of these descriptions constitutes the description of the relevant initial conditions. Since there are infinitely many subsets of an infinite set our problem is a formidable one. In the case of most explanations our problem amounts to determining which of the infinitely many subsets, i.e., states of affairs, constitutes the cause of the event described by the explanandum.

We have seen that the determination of the applicable law would result in the determination of the relevant initial conditions. It is evident, however, that the converse is also true, i.e., if we have determined the relevant initial conditions we have also determined the relevant law. The relevant law is simply the result of generalizing (universally) the assertion

If these particular initial conditions . . . then the particular event as described in the explanandum occurs.

We will proceed by considering the nature of the general statement or law and the method of its establishment, thereby also showing the way the relevant initial or antecedent conditions are determined.

7.2 LAWS

In our previous examples of explanations one of the statements of our explanans has been of the form

All *A* are *B*.

We have called the statement in the explanans of this form the *general statement* or *covering law*. It should be evident, however, that not every proposition of the form "All *A* are *B*" is a covering law (nor what we have meant by general statement in this context). Consider the two statements

      1. All of Mr. S's books are tattered.

and

      2. All satellites travel in elliptical orbits.

We are certain that the reader would agree that whereas the second is a law, the first is not. What we would now like to consider is the difference between them that leads us to say that one is not a law and the other is a law.

The difference between statements 1 and 2 does not lie in their truth or falsity. Though the reader did not know whether 1 was true or false, it was not this fact that led him to deny that it was a law. Even if 1 is true it is still not a law. Of course this is not to say that truth or falsity has nothing to do with a statement's being a law. A statement can only be a law[4] if it is true, but the converse, and this was our point above, does not follow. Thus it is not the truth of a statement of the form "All *A* are *B*" that characterizes it as a law.

Let us consider how statements 1 and 2 function or fail to function within an explanation in hope of shedding some light on our question. To this end consider the explanation

    A.   All Mr. S's books are tattered.
         The book Mr. S just bought is Mr. S's book.
         ──
        ∴ The book Mr. S just bought is tattered.

---

[4] The word "law" is ambiguous. We can distinguish at least two senses of it; first, the sense of "law" used in talking of a "natural law" and second, the sense of "law" as used in talking of the "law of the land." The first sense is relevant to science, while the second is relevant to the study of legal systems. Whereas it makes sense to speak of the truth or falsity of natural laws it does not seem to make sense to speak of the truth or falsity of the laws of the land. Our discussion of laws in this chapter is restricted to that of natural laws.

and

B. All satellites travel in elliptical orbits.
The ball of gas that erupted from the sun's surface is a satellite.

∴ The ball of gas that erupted from the sun's surface travels in an elliptical orbit.

It is obvious that whereas B constitutes a possibly adequate explanation, A certainly does not. Let us try and specify the reasons for the failure of A. When Mr. S says that all of his books are tattered he of necessity has to say it at a given time. Moreover when Mr. S says at a given time that all his books are tattered the truth of his statement is relative to the time that he made it. In other words, whereas it is true that all of Mr. S's books are tattered at time t_1, it may be false that all Mr. S's books are tattered at some later time t_2 since Mr. S may have acquired a new untattered book in the intervening time. It is just this that leads to the failure of A.

The statement that all satellites travel in elliptical orbits may also be made at a specific time, say t_1, but this fact seems to have nothing to do with its truth. It would seem that at least a part of what is meant in calling the statement "All satellites travel in elliptical orbits" a law is that it is always true. The generality of laws seems, however, to be even broader than mere temporal generality. There is a sense in which the statement that all satellites travel in elliptical orbits is about everything, while the statement that all Mr. S's books are tattered is about nothing but Mr. S's books.

When we say that

All satellites travel in elliptical orbits.

we are not only speaking of all those things that are now satellites. Indeed we are not only speaking of all those things that were, are now, or will be satellites. We seem to be speaking of anything that could have been a satellite, and that would include this book, Mount Everest, the battleship Missouri, the reader, etc.

To put this another way, when we say that a statement of the form "All A are B" is a law we assent not only to the statement that "All A are B," but also to the statement that if something were an A it would also be a B. A conditional statement in the subjunctive mood is called a counterfactual

327

conditional,[5] and thus we can summarize by saying that a law is said to support its counterfactual conditional.[6] We have seen that statement 2 supports its counterfactual conditional

If something were a satellite it would travel in an elliptical orbit.

meaning thereby that if we take statement 2 to be a law we take its counterfactual conditional to be true.

The fact that we do not take statement 1 to be a law is reflected in the fact that though we may assent to its truth we would deny the truth of its conterfactual conditional

If something were Mr. S's book it would be tattered.

In summary then we have seen that by a law we mean a true, universal affirmative statement whose subject class is open in the sense that it refers to everything that could possibly be a member of that class. And we have seen that this criterion of openness of the subject class is reflected in our acceptance of the counterfactual conditional of a statement that we have accepted as a law.

7.2.1   The establishment of laws

We turn now to the question of how we determine if a given statement is in fact a law. This is, as we have seen, the question of how we establish the truth of a universal affirmative statement with an open subject class. There is little difficulty in establishing the truth of a universal affirmative with a closed subject class, such as All Mr. S's books are tattered. This can be done by the method of enumeration, i.e., all we need do is look at each member of the subject class and see if it is a member of the predicate class. The truth of Mr. S's claim about all his books is established by looking at each book and seeing if it is tattered. This method is not available for the establishment of a law, however, since the subject class is open and thus of unlimited

---

[5]The term *counterfactual* arises from the fact such statements have antecedents that express their own falseness, i.e., that indicates that they are contrary to fact.

[6]A discussion of some of the difficulties with this account of the relation between laws and counterfactual conditionals is to be found in Nelson Goodman, *Fact, Fiction, and Forecast* (New York: Bobbs-Merrill, 1965).

membership. How then do we establish that a given assertion is a law?

Though there is a prima facie difficulty with establishing the truth of a hypothesis (law candidate), there seems to be no such difficulty with seeing how we establish the falsehood of such hypotheses. If, e.g., we find a satellite that does not travel in an elliptical orbit we have shown that the hypothesis that all satellites travel in elliptical orbits is false. We will call a phenomenon of this sort, i.e., one that shows a given hypothesis to be false, a *disconfirmation* of the hypothesis. Now though we have seen that no number of observations of satellites traveling in elliptical orbits establishes the truth of the hypothesis that all satellites travel in elliptical orbits in the way that a given number of observations of each of Mr. S's books being tattered establishes the truth of the claim that all Mr. S's books are tattered, these observations do at least seem to eventually convince us of the truth of the hypothesis. The matter seems to be something like the following: Though no number of cases absolutely establishes the truth of the hypothesis, each case seems to lend some support for the hypothesis. We will call a phenomenon that lends such support to the hypothesis a *confirmation* of the hypothesis. To say of any phenomenon that it is a confirming instance of the hypothesis is, in part, to say that it is not a disconfirming instance. But we must be careful here to make clear what we mean by saying that a given phenomenon is not a disconfirming instance of a hypothesis. Consider the hypothesis

All marsupials are herbivorous.

It is clear that any case of a marsupial that is not herbivorous constitutes a disconfirmation of this hypothesis. It is also clear that a case of a specific marsupial that is herbivorous is not a disconfirmation but a confirmation of it. But surely the fact that a specific book is red also fails to disconfirm our hypothesis, yet we do not want to call this fact a confirmation of "All marsupials are herbivorous."[7] Every marsupial constitutes a possible confirmation or disconfirmation of our hypothesis. A marsupial confirms the hypothesis if it is herbivorous and disconfirms it if it is not herbivorous.

Despite the need for all of the foregoing qualifications it is still useful to think of a confirmation as being a case of a nondisconfirmation. To say that a given event is a confirmation of our hypothesis is to say that the event was a

[7] Many philosophers of science would want to consider this a confirmation, but one that lends very little support to the hypothesis. This is generally a part of what is called the Bayesian approach to confirmation.

possible disconfirmation which did not disconfirm the hypothesis.

In the cases of the hypotheses we have so far considered it has been quite clear what would count as a confirming or disconfirming instance and thus one would know what observation to make in order to "test" the hypothesis. The matter, however, is not always so simple. Often the hypothesis in question is such as to preclude confirmation or disconfirmation by direct observation. Consider, e.g., the hypothesis:

All electrons have a negative charge of 4.8×10^{-10} abs. e.s.u.

Since there is no way to directly observe an electron nor for that matter the amount of charge of an electron, the question of what we are to observe in order to confirm or disconfirm our hypothesis is a good deal more complex than in our previous examples. These cases can be dealt with by considering the fact that no hypothesis is presented completely without context. And one part of the context of any given hypothesis is the body of scientific knowledge that existed prior to the consideration of the hypothesis. This we will call the *preexisting body of scientific knowledge.* In general, it is possible to deduce some observable consequence from our hypothesis and some part of the preexisting body of scientific knowledge. Let us assume that from our hypothesis and two propositions of the preexisting body of scientific knowledge, call them P_1 and P_2, we have validly deduced a proposition R that describes a directly observable event. (See Figure 7-1.)

FIGURE 7-1.

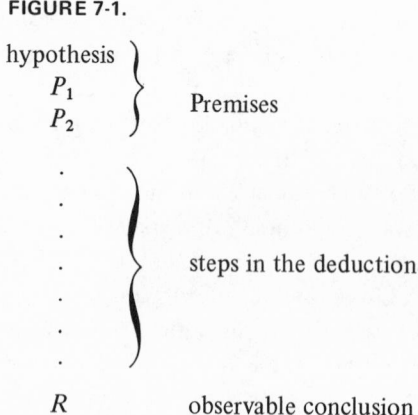

We can now see that our hypothesis is testable by means of the event described in R. If, for instance, the state of affairs described in R does not prevail, i.e., if R is false, at least one of our premises must also be false, since a valid argument with a false conclusion must have false premises. Since P_1 and P_2 are parts of the preexisting body of scientific knowledge and thus considered to be established truths the foregoing situation constitutes the disconfirmation of our hypothesis, the hypothesis being the premise whose truth is under consideration.

If, on the other hand, we find R to be true, we have a confirming instance of the hypothesis since R was a possible disconfirming instance. In this case the usefulness of treating confirmation as nondisconfirmation becomes evident. If our deduction of R from our premises is valid and R is true, nothing whatsoever deductively follows about the truth or falsity of our premises. Thus our feeling that the truth of R constitutes some support for our hypothesis derives from the fact that R could have disconfirmed our hypothesis, but it did not. We will call this process of deriving some directly observable consequence from a hypothesis and some part of the preexisting body of scientific knowledge *elaboration of the hypothesis.*

The distinction drawn here between hypotheses that are confirmable by direct observation and those that are confirmable by indirect observation is often termed that between *experimental* and *theoretical hypotheses.* The model of science that recognizes this distinction and the associated distinction of the two kinds of confirmation is called the *hypothetico-deductive model.*

It is important to note that the hypothetico-deductive model can be taken to distinguish between two sorts of induction. In the case of experimental hypotheses we have an induction that is little more than an extension of what we have called the method of enumeration beyond the observed cases to all cases of the same sort, i.e., from instances of the hypothesis to the hypothesis itself. The situation is quite different with regard to theoretical hypotheses. In their case the induction is not direct for we are making our induction from a case that is an observable consequence drawn deductively from the hypothesis and some part of the preexisting body of scientific knowledge and that, therefore, could not be called an *instance* of the hypothesis. This sort of induction then cannot be viewed as a kind of extension of the method of enumeration.

Though, our hypothesis or, more usually, its elaborations, indicate what things ought to be looked at as possible disconfirming or confirming instances, the "looking" itself may be quite complicated. The elaboration of a hypothesis might lead, e.g., to the statement that all the readings of a meter hooked into a complicated device will be divisable by 4.8×10^{-10}. In order to "look" and "see" that this is the case one must first construct the indicated device and make sure that no extraneous factors are present. The carrying out of such a procedure is one of the things that is generally called doing an *experiment*.

To recapitulate then, a law candidate or hypothesis is established as a law through repeated confirmation. Given the nature of confirmation there seems to be no way of determining how many confirmations are required before a law candidate is to be considered a law.

We are now able to return to the problem posed in section 7.1.2 of how we determine what the relevant initial conditions are for the explanation of an event, say x. We have seen that all the subsets of the initial conditions are true, i.e., they consist of states of affairs that did in fact obtain before the occurrence of the phenomenon described by the explanandum. The determination of the correct explanans cannot then proceed by asking which subset of initial conditions is true. The question that should be asked, viz., "Which subset constitutes the relevant initial conditions?" turns out to be answerable, as we have in part seen, by determining which of many possible hypotheses is true (or well confirmed). The list of possible hypotheses is easily determined. Let us call our explanandum x and identify the complete set of initial conditions as

$$C_1, C_2, C_3, \ldots, C_n$$

and the 2^n subsets of these conditions as

$$I_1, I_2, I_3, \ldots, I_{2^n}.$$

Each of these 2^n subsets, as we have seen, describes an actual state of affairs and is, therefore, true. Under these conditions the form that an explanation of x would take is

$$\frac{\text{If } I_? \text{ then } x}{\therefore x}$$

where the question mark indicates that at this point we do not know which subset of initial conditions is the relevant one. Now for each possible relevant subset of initial conditions we have a corresponding possible law or hypothesis. Thus we have the following list of hypotheses:

1. If I_1 then x
2. If I_2 then x
3. If I_3 then x

$\qquad \cdot$

$\qquad \cdot$

2^n. If I_2n then x

If we tested these hypotheses in turn by the methods outlined in this section and we found one of them to be well confirmed and thus took it to be a law, we would have discovered the explanation of x. The establishment of one of our hypotheses as a law would determine the relevant initial conditions and our explanation would be complete. Thus if the first hypothesis became well confirmed our explanation of x would be,

$$\frac{\text{If } I_1 \text{ then } x \qquad I_1}{\therefore x}$$

"I_1" is true being a subset of the initial conditions, "If I_1 then x" is taken to be true being a well confirmed hypothesis and so the truth of x must follow.

If the second hypothesis had been the one confirmed then our explanation of x would have been

$$\frac{\text{If } I_2 \text{ then } x \qquad I_2}{\therefore x}$$

Since the number of possible relevant initial conditions is always enormously large one does not, in fact, simply list all the possible hypotheses. The scientist, being familiar with the preexisting body of scientific knowledge, begins by feeling that some subsets of initial conditions are more likely to be relevant than others and that, therefore, some hypotheses are more likely to be laws than others. He then, on this basis, considers only a small number of hypotheses, a number that may increase if none of the beginning group becomes well confirmed.

We have so far considered how law candidates are established as laws; we turn now to a consideration of the issue of rejection of previously established laws. Consider the case of an elaboration from a law, say L_1, and two other propositions from the preexisting body of scientific knowledge, say P_1 and P_2, and let us call the deduced proposition E. Schematically then we have Figure 7-2.

FIGURE 7-2.

$$
\left.
\begin{array}{l}
L_1 \\
P_1 \\
P_2
\end{array}
\right\}
\quad \text{three statements from the preexisting body of scientific knowledge.}
$$

$$
\left.
\begin{array}{c}
\cdot \\
\cdot \\
\cdot \\
\cdot \\
\cdot
\end{array}
\right\}
\quad \text{steps in the deduction}
$$

$$E \qquad \text{observable conclusion}$$

Let us now consider the significance of finding E to be false. As we have seen if L_1 were a law candidate rather than a part of the preexisting body of scientific knowledge, the falsity of E would be taken as indicative of the falsity of L_1. But in the case now under consideration L_1 is a previously established law, and this considerably complicates matters. Since, as before, our elaboration consists of validly deducing E from the premises L_1, P_1 and P_2, the falsehood of E does indeed imply the falsehood of our premises. The difference, however, lies in the fact that in the case where one of our premises is a hypothesis and the other premises are preestablished "truths," clearly we say that it is the hypothesis that is false, whereas in our new case all our premises are preestablished "truths," and it is not clear at all which of them we have shown to be false. Such matters are usually decidable, however, through a consideration of a property of laws which we will call *entrenchment*.[8] A law is said to be entrenched to a greater or lesser degree as its rejection would cause a greater or lesser degree of disturbance to the rest of the preexisting body of scientific knowledge. It is clear that the rejection of certain portions of the preexisting body of scientific knowledge would have little effect on what remains. Such portions would have a very low degree of entrenchment. There are, however, other portions, or more specifically laws,

[8]For a discussion of a related notion of entrenchment see Nelson Goodman, *Fact, Fiction, and Forecast* (New York: Bobbs-Merrill, 1955).

that are very greatly entrenched and whose rejection would necessitate a complete overhaul of the science in question. It would seem that the degree of entrenchment of a given law is a product of the frequency of use of that law in the elaboration of various hypotheses. Some laws become entrenched to an enormous degree, and we usually signify this distinction by terming the law a *principle*. An example of such a highly entrenched law in physics would be the law or principle of the conservation of momentum.

The notion of entrenchment can then help us to resolve the difficulty we encountered in our elaboration of E from the propositions L_1, P_1, and P_2. We can determine which of our three propositions from the preexisting body of scientific knowledge is disconfirmed by the falsity of E by determining which of these three is the least entrenched, for that is the one it is most practical to reject.

7.2.2 Explanation and prediction

Explanation, as we have described it, is related in a specific way to prediction. To say that we can now explain an event A implies that had we known the explanans prior to the occurrence of A we could have predicted A's occurrence. If we have a law and a set of initial conditions falling under the antecedent class of that law we can make predictions of events falling under the consequent class of the law. Further than that, it should be seen that every elaboration to a statement describing an observable event constitutes a prediction of the event, not from the law alone but from the law and other statements of the preexisting body of scientific knowledge. In short, we have seen that on our description of explanation if an event can be explained it can be predicted. The question of the converse of this assertion naturally arises, i.e., "Does the fact that we can predict an event mean that we have explained the event?"

Consider the case of the tossing of a coin ten times where in each case the coin turned up "heads." Anyone asked to bet on the next toss would surely, if rational, bet "heads." In making a prediction one uses all the relevant information at one's disposal. If we had known nothing of the previous tosses of the coin we would have had no basis for choice. Now though the tosses of a coin are said to be independent events in which one toss has no effect on the next toss the fact that ten heads were thrown in a row would seem to favor the prediction that the next toss will also be a "head." Evidently something is acting to make the very improbable string of "heads" occur, and it would be foolish to bet otherwise. All this is by way of saying that though we cannot explain the string of "heads" we can predict the next toss. Of course the fact that we are led to make the prediction is based on the assumption that there is some explanation for the improbable recurrence of tosses resulting in "heads," but we need not be able to give the explanation in order to feel confident in our prediction of the next toss. The situation is then that the fact that we have the explanation of the event A implies that we could have predicted the event A whereas that we are justified in predicting the event A does not imply that we in fact have the explanation of A.

7.3 THEORIES

In the foregoing sections we have seen how laws serve in the explanation and derivation of events. But as we shall see in this section we are sometimes interested in the explanation and derivation of laws themselves. It is perfectly legitimate to ask why all satellites travel in elliptical orbits, and this is a request for the explanation of a law rather than of an event. It will be our contention in this section that laws are explained by *theories*. We argued previously that all explanations are deductive in form and so the explanation of laws will consist in the deduction of a law from other statements. The question that arises is the nature of these "other statements" and the method of their establishment.

The simplest theory from which a given law might be explained is itself nothing more than several other laws. If, for instance, we wished to explain why the radii from satellite to focus of any satellite sweeps out equal areas in equal times we might do so by reference to two other laws, viz., that all satellites travel in elliptical orbits and that the radius of anything traveling in an elliptical orbit sweeps out equal areas in equal times. Thus we have an explanation of the form

$$\frac{(x)(Sx \supset Ex)}{(x)(Ex \supset Rx)} \quad \text{Explanans}$$
$$(x)(Sx \supset Rx) \quad \text{Explanandum}$$

where Sx means x is a satellite, Ex means x travels in an elliptical orbit, and Rx means that the radius between the satellite and the focus of its orbit sweeps out equal areas in equal times. First, it is to be noticed that our explanation has a valid deductive form, though this form is not the same as that in the explanation of events. Second, there is nothing in the explanans that corresponds to initial conditions as they appear in the explanation of events. To this point then the only characteristic of theories we have determined is that laws are validly deducible from them.

Theories arise from the need to explain laws. Every theory then has what might be termed a *historical base* which consists of some set of laws that the theory was constructed to explain. That the laws that constitute the historical base of a theory are deducible from that theory is hardly surprising since the theory was constructed for that purpose. For this reason the worth of a theory is not judged on the grounds of the deducibility of its historical base. The worth of a theory lies largely in its ability to yield new laws outside of the historical base. The historical base of Daniel Bernoulli's kinetic theory of gases, e.g., was Dalton's law of partial pressures[9] and Boyle's law.[10] That the statement of the laws is deducible from the kinetic theory of gases is a tribute to Bernoulli's inventiveness but not to the worth of his theory for a great many other theories are constructable from which the historical base is deducible. The attractiveness of the kinetic theory of gases lies in the fact that laws outside of its historical base are also deducible from it, an example being Avogadro's law that equal volumes of different gases at the same temperature and pressure contain the same number of molecules. That a given general statement (law candidate) deduced from a theory is a law is to be determined through the methods discussed previously in section 7.2.1. The establishment of theories thus involves the derivation of laws, the establishment of which, in turn, involves the prediction of events. In this way we can say, derivatively, that a given set of events establishes a given theory, understanding thereby that the events establish a new law which is deducible from the given theory.

We have seen that one of the features of explanations is that they make the unfamiliar familiar and remove the element of surprise. In the explanation of laws this is usually accomplished by constructing a theory from which the laws are deducible and which is analogous to an already

[9]Dalton's law of partial pressures is that the pressure exerted by a mixture of gases is equal to the sum of the separate pressures that each gas would exert if it alone occupied the whole volume.

[10]Boyle's law is that at a constant temperature the volume of a given quantity of any gas varies inversely as the pressure to which the gas is subjected.

337

understood portion of nature. For this reason theories usually contain, as an integral part of their structure, an *analogy* or *model*. The kinetic theory of gases asserts that gases consist of molecules that are like tiny billiard balls flying about in all directions. Just as a great many billiard balls impacting on a surface will impart their momentum to that wall and thus produce a pressure against it, the molecules hitting against the walls of a container that holds the gas produce a pressure against those walls. Thus in the kinetic theory of gases we have what might be called the billiard ball analogy. Under the billiard ball analogy we extend already established theories and laws to cover a new area. Thus Newtonian mechanics becomes applicable to molecules since molecules are like billiard balls and Newtonian mechanics applies to billiard balls. The term *molecule* is implicitly defined within the kinetic theory of gases as an object that is like a billiard ball but that is perfectly elastic—which is certainly unlike a billiard ball. Thus, there are respects in which the molecule is like a billiard ball and respects in which it is unlike a billiard ball. The aspects of the theoretical notions of a theory which correspond to the model or analogy we will call the *positive analogy* and any aspects of the theoretical notions that are not a part of the positive analogy we will call the *negative analogy*.

A term such as *molecule,* which is implicitly defined within the theory in such a way that we have no way of observing its referent or that no way of observing its referent is indicated by the theory, will be called a *theoretical term.* On the other hand, a term which designates an observable entity or property is said to be an *observation term.* There exist clear-cut criteria for the identification of entities designated by observation terms within a theory whereas no such clear-cut criteria are available for the hypothetical entities referred to by theoretical terms.

A theory is perhaps best described as a set of sentences of various kinds. The sentences can be divided into two groups, those that constitute the *body* of the theory and those that constitute the *dictionary* of the theory. The sentences of the body of the theory can be further subdivided into two groups, those that contain one or more theoretical terms which we will call *postulates* and those that contain only observation terms (aside from logical connectives, etc.) which we will call *propositions.*

From the above there emerges the problem of how the postulates of a theory can be used in the deduction of a law. Laws, being statements about the observable world, contain observation terms. If laws are deducible from the postulates of a theory, some account must be given of what happens to the theoretical terms that appear in the postulates but that do not appear in the laws deduced from them. This is accomplished by introducing the notion of a *correspondence rule,* which states a connection between the theoretical terms and those things observationally determinable. The sentences expressing the correspondence rules constitute what we have called the dictionary of the theory. It is the positive analogy that determines the appropriate correspondence rules. In the kinetic theory of gases the positive analogy indicates that the transfer of the momentum of the molecules to the walls of the container is directly connected to the observable pressure on those walls. Through a correspondence rule a postulate can be seen as implying a statement making assertions about observable entities only.

We have seen then that the positive analogy plays several roles in a theory; that of making the unfamiliar familiar; that of allowing for the extension of already attained knowledge and technique to the new problems the theory encounters; and that of indicating the relevant correspondence rules that make the deduction of laws from the body of the theory possible.

It is crucially important, however, to recognize the role of the negative analogy. The negative analogy as we have defined it refers not only to the specific aspects of the theoretical notions of the theory that do not correspond to the model or analogy, but also to those aspects that are left undetermined with respect to the model or analogy. In the case of the theoretical notion of molecule in the kinetic theory of gases, e.g., we have the perfect elasticity of the molecules as a part of the negative analogy on the first ground, i.e., a specific aspect of a theoretical notion of the theory that does not correspond to the billiard ball model. Another part of the negative analogy, however, is the color of molecules, which is left undetermined with respect to the model in the sense that though billiard balls are colored, whether molecules correspond to them in this respect is irrelevant to the kinetic theory of gases and thus left undetermined by it. The existence of a negative analogy in a given theory thus represents an area of possible growth of the theory.

This potential of the negative analogy is perhaps better understood by an example again drawn from the kinetic theory of gases. Not long after Bernoulli formulated his theory it was discovered that Boyle's law failed when applied to gases confined to very small volumes. Since Boyle's law in its original form was deducible from the theory and it now seemed that Boyle's law was incorrect, or at least incorrect in extreme cases, it seemed to follow that this constituted a failure of the theory. The situation was remedied, however, through a slightly more specific formulation of the properties of molecules, in particular by noting that whereas in large volumes it was admissible to consider the size of molecules infinitesimal, in small volumes this amounted to a gross oversimplification. For molecules, it was now said, have a very small size which is irrelevant to the derivation of Boyle's law as applied to large volumes, but where the volumes are extremely small the size of the molecules in relation to that volume become relevant and have to be considered. The possibility of making such changes in a theory without thereby destroying it, is owing to the fact that what is being changed is not crucial to the theory; as it previously was in that part of the negative analogy consisting of properties left undetermined by the theory.

As a theory develops in such a way as to allow for the derivation of changes in its historical base and so as to allow for the derivation of new laws, there is a general refinement of the theoretical notions of the theory leading to fewer and fewer irrelevant parts of the negative analogy. Eventually there comes a point when a theoretical notion becomes so refined and explicitly defined that clear-cut criteria of identification for the notion are available. The notion has then become such that it can become the subject of further inquiry. We can, e.g., ask why molecules have the properties that they have. The explanation of these properties is accomplished by the creation of another theory for which these statements of the molecule's properties function as the historical base and in which some new theoretical term is introduced to enable one to deduce those properties. It is the atomic theory that explains the properties of molecules and in which we find the new theoretical term *atom* introduced, by means of which the properties of molecules are explained. The atomic theory can then be called a "higher" theory than the molecular theory since the postulates and propositions of the molecular theory are deducible from those of the atomic theory.

The situation as we have described it consists of first the world and its constituent events which are explained on what might be called the first level of explanation by reference to laws. The laws, in turn, are explained on the next level of explanation by theories. The postulates and propositions of these theories may be explained at a still higher level of explanation by other theories, and so on to still higher levels of explanation.

7.3.1 Reduction and theories

The fact that the postulates and propositions of one theory may be deduced from another has led to the consideration of the possibility of all the assertions of a given area of science being deducible from another area of science. In particular there is a generally held view that the entire science of biology can be deduced from chemistry and physics, or as it is generally asserted that biology is reducible to chemistry and physics. It is also often claimed that chemistry is reducible to physics.

In order to facilitate a discussion of such claims it is useful to think of a given science as being a large set of sentences of varying kinds. We have already discussed what kinds of sentences these are, i.e., descriptions, laws, postulates, propositions, correspondence rules, etc. Let us now consider two sciences, A and B, whose sentences are represented by

$$a_1, a_2, a_3, a_4, \ldots$$

and

$$b_1, b_2, b_3, b_4, \ldots$$

respectively. Since there are most likely terms in B that are not in A and vice versa, the sentences of A are neither directly deducible from those of B nor vice versa. The claim that the science B is reducible to the science A then amounts to the following two claims: First, that every term of B is replaceable without loss of meaning by a term or group of terms of A—this might be termed the translation thesis; second, that after every sentence of B has been translated so that they contain only the terms of A, yielding say

$$b_1^q, b_2^q, b_3^q, b_4^q, \ldots$$

that all these sentences are then deducible from the sentences of A.

Given these conditions for the reduction of one theory to another it should be clear that the only way that one could know that a reduction could be carried out would be to, in fact, carry it out, and this is, to say the least, an extremely formidable task. It is, of course, possible to reduce specific parts of one science to parts of another and this has been done, e.g., in the case of the reduction of the biological description of digestion to physical and chemical processes. Large-scale reducibility claims like the ones mentioned at the beginning of this section, however, are to be taken not as claims that the reduction has been carried out but rather as claims that so far no one has seen any reason in principle why the reduction could not be carried out.

7.4 CAUSATION

Scientists are often pictured as seeking the cause of some specific event. As we have presented science this amounts to seeking the relevant initial conditions. Though it is true that scientists, when successful, do find these relevant initial conditions or causes, we have seen that it is not these that they seek. Scientists, or at least natural scientists, are not interested in the particular cause of a particular event that occurred, say, at time t_1. Indeed, it is the fact that there is a general law that relates events like the cause with events like the effect that allows us to identify some particular event as the cause of some other particular event. It was precisely this that was reflected in the fact that the relevant initial conditions were determined through the establishment of a law.

None of this, of course, is meant to preclude the talk of causes among scientists. Scientists do speak of the cause of a specific event, e.g., whenever they do an experiment. What is important, however, is to see how this talk of particular causes fits into the general features of science, and this is what we have tried to make clear. Since scientists do speak of causes it is useful to see in what different ways they do so. First we will distinguish between what is usually meant by "a cause" and "the cause." Some phenomena can be produced by various causes. Fever, e.g., can be caused by many different diseases. Each disease might be termed *a* cause of fever. Each such disease, or cause, constitutes a sufficient condition for fever, i.e., a condition that, if met, assures fever, but no such single disease would constitute a necessary condition for fever, i.e., a condition that must be met for fever to occur.

Some phenomena are produced by only one cause. Such a cause can be termed *the* cause. Evidently *the* cause is both a necessary and sufficient condition for the effect.

So far the things we have called causes were either necessary and sufficient conditions for their effects or sufficient but not necessary conditions for their effects. These, however, are not the only possibilities. We sometimes use the word "cause" of something that is a necessary but not sufficient condition for a given event. There are three necessary conditions for fire: oxygen, combustible material, and heat. None of these necessary conditions is a sufficient condition for fire. though all three jointly are both necessary and sufficient. Consider a situation in which it is known that there is a combustible material and oxygen present and a fire ensues. It would not be at all unusual in such a case to speak of some source of heat as being the cause of the fire. One can imagine a case where great heat and combustible material are normally present and oxygen is specifically excluded in order to avoid fire, in which case it may be said that the presence of oxygen caused the fire. In both these cases then we have causes that are necessary but not sufficient conditions for their effects. It is to be noted, however, that in all these cases the thing designated as the cause was sufficient *within the context* to bring about the effect. Surely heat by itself is not a sufficient condition but if we already have a combustible material and oxygen the addition of heat does constitute a sufficient condition for fire. So far then all our uses of "cause" share the fact that the thing designated as the cause is a sufficient condition at least within the context of the situation.

In the light of the foregoing it would not be surprising if we could find an example of a cause that was neither a necessary nor a sufficient condition for its effect. Let us consider two possible causes of sneezing. One may sneeze because one has a viral infection or because one has an allergy and an allergen is present. Neither one of these situations is a necessary condition for sneezing, for either one can produce it. Now whereas, an allergy plus an allergen is a sufficient condition for sneezing, the allergy alone is not. Therefore, an allergy is neither a sufficient nor a necessary condition for sneezing. Yet under the appropriate conditions it is perfectly all right to say that his allergy caused his sneezing.

It should be noted that all of our talk about causes as sufficient conditions is context bound. Whenever we claim that A causes B it is under the assumption that none of the things that can keep A from producing B will intervene. We are never in a position to state the entire set of conditions that together would constitute the sufficient condition (without qualification) for the effect. The reader should not take the foregoing as having been a complete discussion of the criteria of "cause." The fact that someone is a bachelor is surely a sufficient condition for his being an unmarried man, but one would not, after all, want to say that his being a bachelor caused him to be an unmarried man.

The question of the criteria of causal relationships is an enormously complicated one, which is largely beyond the scope of this short chapter. But it should be indicated that the most important attempt at formulating these criteria was made by David Hume (1711-1776). Hume gave the following three criteria for a causal relationship, say, between A and B: (1) A and B must be constantly conjoined, i.e., they must be found to always occur together; (2) A and B must be contiguous in time and space, i.e., they must be spatially and temporally "near" each other, and (3) A and B must be temporally ordered, i.e., one of them (the cause) must always precede the other (the effect). The Humean position is, however, better characterized by pointing out a condition omitted from the list of criteria than by giving those that are included. The quite purposely omitted condition is that of a necessary connection between the cause and the effect. Since, according to Hume, no such necessary connection is discoverable through observation of the world it can play no role in our decision that two events, say A and B, are causally related.

The Humean view of causation has been the dominant view in the philosophy of science and is quite consistent with the general model of science found in this chapter. It should be noted, however, that the Humean view has not gone undisputed and many philosophers of science today are non-Humean in their approach to causation.

7.5   MATHEMATICS AND SCIENCE

The great advance of the natural sciences over the social sciences is often attributed to the large-scale use of mathematics that occurs in the natural sciences and not in the social sciences. The same reason is usually given for the dominance of physics over the rest of the natural sciences. We turn now to a consideration of how mathematics is utilitzed by the sciences.

In the natural sciences we often find laws, postulates, propositions, and even more frequently correspondence rules formulated in mathematical terms. For instance, one of the correspondence rules of the kinetic theory of gases, which relates the operationally defined notion of temperature with the theoretical notion of the kinetic energy of molecules is expressed by the mathematical relation

$$T \sim mn\overline{c^2}$$

in which T is the temperature of the gas, m is the mass of the molecules comprising the gas, n is the number of such molecules, and $\overline{c^2}$ is the mean square velocity of the molecules. On the basis of the billiard ball analogy the expression $\frac{1}{2} mn\overline{c^2}$ is taken to be the total kinetic energy of the molecules. Thus the formula says that the temperature of the gas is directly proportional to the total kinetic energy of the molecules that comprise the gas.

Given these uses of mathematics we would like to be able to specify what conditions must be met by a given subject matter in order that we be able to apply mathematics to it. We will proceed in our attempt to specify these conditions by starting with the simpler applications of mathematics and working toward the more complex.

The most primitive use of mathematics in the sciences is, of course, *counting.* In counting *n* things what we do is establish a one-to-one correspondence between the things counted and the first *n* natural numbers. But matters are not quite so simple. There is a logical point to the question "How do you count rabbits?" and the humorous answer, "Quickly!" In order to count one must establish a technique for picking out the things to be counted, i.e., one must have a rule of individuation.

Another rather primitive use of mathematics is *ordering.* In establishing an ordering one must find some property of the entities to be ordered such that each entity becomes related by that property to at least one and at most one natural number. In addition one must define a relation between the entities regarding that property such that the relation is irreflexive, asymmetrical, and transitive. A simple example of an ordering is Mohs' scale of hardness. The entities here being ordered are perhaps best termed materials. The property that the entities share and in terms of which they are being ordered is hardness. The ordering is accomplished by relating the following materials to the following numbers:

Talc 1
Gypsum 2
Calcite 3
Fluorite 4
Apatite 5
Feldspar 6
Quartz 7
Topaz 8
Corundum 9
Diamond 10

The relation indicated in the ordering is "harder than." Any material bearing a higher number than another material is harder than that other material. It is to be noted that "harder than" is an irreflexive, asymmetrical, transitive relation. This is to say that no material is harder than itself, that for any two materials x and y if x is harder than y then y is not harder than x, and that for any three materials x, y, and z if x is harder than y and y is harder than z then x is harder than z. The relation x is harder than y is operationally defined as x scratches y. Thus a material of any given number on Mohs' scale can scratch any materials of a lower number on the scale and can be scratched by any material of a higher number on the scale. The place of a new material in the ordering is determined by what materials already on the scale it scratches and which materials already on the scale will scratch it.

The most important thing to note regarding orderings is that no mathematical operations can be performed upon them. It makes no sense at all to assert on the basis of Mohs' scale that fluorite is twice as hard as gypsum and half as hard as topaz. The numbers in the scale introduce an order, not a measure. Though mathematical operations like addition, subtraction, multiplication, etc. cannot be carried out on orderings they are amenable to statistical treatment. One can, for instance, speak of the number of materials of hardness 3 as compared with the number of materials of hardness 5.

The conditions that must be met for an application of mathematics that does allow operations like addition, subtraction, etc. are considerably more stringent than those required for an ordering. In order to apply mathematics of this sort to the entities designated by a term of science, it is necessary that the entities have a property, i.e., a quality, that can be measured by a specified procedure. Such a specified procedure is termed an *operational definition* of the quality being measured. For example, "temperature" can be defined by means of such instruments as thermometers and thermocouples, just as "length" can be defined by yardsticks. Through these procedures numbers can be associated with the qualities being measured. In order to apply, say, the operation of addition to these numbers and thus to the quality being measured, say lengths, we must give an operational definition of addition for this operation such that the result of carrying out the operation is a length. This resultant length will, on measurement in accordance with the specified procedure, correspond to a number that is the sum of the numbers corresponding to the other two lengths. Let us consider the case of what we mean then when we say that two yards plus three yards is five yards. First we mean that an object two yards in length plus an object three yards in length constitutes an object five yards in length. This, no doubt, will sound a bit peculiar until we see what we mean by "plus" in this context. We are saying that if you have an object two yards in length and place an object three yards in length against it so that the two measured lengths lie along the same direction, and then measure the resultant object by the same procedure that you used to measure each individual object the result will be five yards.

It should be noted that the application of higher mathematics, e.g., differential and integral calculus, must satisfy the same general conditions, though the operators and their operational definitions will, of course differ from case to case.

On this view the application of mathematics to the sciences amounts to giving an interpretation, in the technical sense of Chapter 5, to a given area of mathematics viewed as an uninterpreted syntactical system.[11]

7.6 THE PROBLEMS OF THE SOCIAL SCIENCES

Having completed our outline of the central concepts in the logical enterprise known as science, we will now consider an issue of both current interest and philosophical significance. This is the problem of the social sciences. Although we will not be able to resolve the problems in this area we will be able to indicate the various approaches employed, and we would certainly like to discuss these without the misunderstandings which so often abound in these areas.

First, why is there a problem with the social sciences? Most often, people believe that social scientific problems are basically problems in technique, sophistication, etc. Thus, it is felt that a discipline such as sociology is problematic because it has not developed the research techniques of a natural science and certainly has produced very few indisputable explanations. This may be true but we are not going to be concerned with the practical problems of the social sciences. Instead, we will consider the problem of the social sciences to be the question "Are the social sciences analogous to the natural sciences or are they fundamentally different?" Or, more compactly, "Are explanations in such fields as psychology and sociology of the same type as explanations in chemistry and physics?" A "yes" answer to these questions would result in our having to deal with certain philosophic issues, which in turn might require us to reinterpret our understanding of human activity, whereas a "no" answer would result in a number of problems not the least of which would be the admission that explanation was not the distinct activity it appears to be.

The second aspect of the "problem of the social sciences" which we will consider is whether the social sciences can be reduced to the natural sciences.

[11] Section 5. 1 is particularly relevant to this discussion and should be considered in conjunction with it.

Clearly, a "no" answer to our first question will result in a "no" answer to the second, but this need not mean that a "yes" for the first would mean a "yes" for the second. In our discussion of this attempted reduction we will, of course, appeal to the criteria of reduction as developed in section 7.3.1.

Finally, we will conclude this section by a consideration of certain specific issues that exist within the framework of the social sciences, namely, whether history is a social science or is reducible to one and to what extent psychology is the most "fundamental" social science.

7.6.1 Explanation in the social sciences

In the previous sections we have sketched a picture of explanation in the natural sciences as basically a deductive enterprise. That is, our model of explanation was the deduction of the explanandum from an explanans which was "true" or, at least, highly confirmed—the explanans containing a law or theory. Now, in the social sciences the explanandums consist of certain facts or descriptions of human behavior (whether in groups, or individually) and if the model of explanation of sections 7.1-7.5 is to apply here, we should be able to present examples of laws and/or theories in, say, sociology that can function as explanans. However, even a superficial knowledge of the social sciences would reveal certain problems here. First, there are few if any genuine laws of human behavior and second, any generalizations that do exist are *statistical.* That is, the social sciences usually present their results in the form of statistical generalizations (sometimes with numerical data and sometimes without). Thus, one would not be surprised to see a pattern of explanation in sociology which appears as follows:

People tend to do what the structure of their situation rewards and avoid doing what the structure penalizes.	Explanans
∴ government placement of workers in three differently structured situations (i.e., with different levels of job security, supervision, seniority, etc.) produced sharply different quantities and qualities of work.[12]	Explanandum

In this case the explanans points out a "tendency" or a probability but does not claim that this is a universal generalization as did the typical general

[12] This example is taken from a study of government workers by Peter Blau, "Competition and Cooperation in a Bureaucracy," *American Journal of Sociology,* 1954, 59: 530-535.

statement amongst the explanans as seen in section 7.2. Using the fragment of probability logic which we have discussed in section 3.11.2 we might present the following pattern of statistical explanation:

> In situation A, there is a .75 probability that persons will do b.
> John was in a situation A.
> ∴ John's doing b is explained.

Two points should be recognized here. First, the above pattern is quite unacceptable without clarification. This is so because, as it stands, it does not do what it purports to do. It is not clear whether what this pattern of explanation explains is that John did b or that the probability of his doing b was .75. Certainly, John's not doing b in situation A is perfectly consistent with the generalization that people tend to do b in situation A with probability .75.[13] Second, the use of the logic of probability presents us with the whole panoply of issues as to the correct interpretation of numerical probability statements. Further, even though we have presented the deductive model of explanation, it is clear that many explanations in the natural sciences are couched in statistical terms (e.g., statistical mechanics and quantum mechanics). The upshot of our discussion, then, is this: The social sciences do employ statistical and quasi-statistical explanations but, in spite of the inherent difficulties with such explanations, they are also found in the natural sciences, and thus their presence in the social sciences cannot be taken as indicative of a fundamental difference in their nature. However, there are arguments relevant to the possibility of reducing the social sciences to the natural sciences that, if sound, would support the essential incompatibility of the social and natural sciences.

7.6.2 The reduction of the social sciences to the natural sciences

Before beginning our discussion of this issue we remind the reader that any question of reduction can only be settled by the proper completion of the reduction. However, we will be considering arguments that would render such reduction, in principle, impossible and though there are good counter-

[13] For more on the many complex issues surrounding the statistical vs. the deductive model of explanation see Carl G. Hempel, "Deductive-Nomological vs. Statistical Explanation," in H. Feigl and G. Maxwell, eds., *Minnesota Studies in the Philosophy of Science* (Minneapolis: University of Minnesota Press, 1962).

arguments to these objections these latter arguments do not result in the reduction.

First, we must be aware of the reasons why anyone would want to attempt or could believe that such an attempted reduction would work. Human behavior—the object of study for the social sciences—can be seen as the exceedingly complex behavior of physical systems. Most biological processes of the human being are, at present, studied by chemical and physical means, and there is the feeling that once the neural mechanisms of human behavior are understood, the whole range of human behavior will be explainable solely in terms of chemical and physical theories.[14] However, since such reductive explanation is, at present, beyond the realm of practicality, it is of great importance to carefully consider any objections that might be raised to the possibility of such reduction.

If the reader will recall, a successful reduction would require (1) the proper translation of terms in one science to terms in the other and (2) the deductive explanation of facts of the "reduced" science in the framework of the "reducing" science. Most in principle objections to the reduction of the social to the natural sciences are claims to the effect that the translation of terms cannot be carried out properly. In general, they claim that human behavior, and the sciences needed to explain it, contain concepts that cannot be translated into the physicalistic contexts of the natural sciences. Thus, it is often claimed that the explanation of human behavior necessarily involves some sort of empathetic description (often called *Verstehen*) which cannot be translated into natural science terminology. Also, there are great problems with the proper interpretation of the free will question. It is often argued that humans can behave in ways characterizable as "free" whereas chemicals and atoms are nonfree or determined in their behavior. If such a distinction could be clearly drawn then there most certainly would be problems for the reduction hypothesis. However, as the reader can find out by reference to items in Selected Readings, the role of the free will issue in the reduction problem is very complex and cannot be dealt with adequately here.

In sum, there are a number of interesting objections to the reduction, but there are many arguments that undermine each of the objections though the

---

[14] Of course, it may never be practical to carry out such involved explanations for individual human action. Still, it is the *possibility* of such explanation which supports the possible reduction of the social to the natural sciences.

only possibility of resolving the question would be the successful completion
of the reduction.

7.6.3   History as a social science and the interrelationships of the social sciences

A very significant problem in any account of the social sciences is the
status of history and historical explanation. During recent years and
coincident with the development of social scientific investigation, historians
have often appealed to these sciences to explain important historical events.
Large-scale occurrences such as the French Revolution have been put in the
framework of economics, sociology, and even psychoanalysis,[15] and this has
led to the question of whether history is nothing but (i.e., is reducible to) the
specific use of social (and natural) science. As with the larger reduction
hypothesis considered previously there are a number of objections to this
possibility. It is sometimes felt that historical explanation is intrinsically
different from any sort of scientific explanation owing to the fact that the
material of history is unique and not subject to experiment or repeat-
ability.[16] Also, it is clear the historians almost never make any attempt to
formulate historical laws or generalizations as do the other sciences. Finally,
it is often argued that history necessarily contains judgments as to the value
of various occurrences and since such references are lacking in both the
natural and social sciences any reduction is ruled out immediately. As with
the arguments against the reduction of the natural sciences to the social
sciences, the arguments here can and have been countered by many other
good arguments and no general agreement has been reached.

The last point we will raise concerns the special problems that arise among
the social sciences. In particular there is a thesis generally known as
psychologism which claims that sociology, anthropology, and, to some
extent, economics can be reduced to psychology. The basis of this claim is
that the behavior of groups ought to be, in principle, explainable by reference
to the behavior of the individuals that make them up; since psychology is the
attempt to explain individual behavior, it is the most fundamental of the

[15] For more on the use of psychoanalytic approaches to history see Bruce Mazlish,
Psycho-analysis and History (New York: Harper & Row, 1964).

[16] Of course, the study of geological origins of the earth suffers from some of these
disadvantages, but is nonetheless part of natural science.

social sciences. Aside from the fact that psychology is not now in a position to fully explain even the behavior of individuals, much less groups, there are objections to the psychologistic thesis. It is not clear that group or social behavior is merely a simple function of individual behavior and, importantly, it is not easy to specify what sort of thing "the individual" that allegedly makes up a group is, since the concept of an "individual" is a theoretical term of a fairly high degree of abstraction. Thus, this and other problems relating to the social sciences are, as yet, unresolved though the logic of social scientific explanation certainly belongs in any discussion of the overall logical structure known as science.

8

philosophical arguments

8.1 PHILOSOPHICAL REASONING

Up to this point we have discussed basically two types of reasoning often, though sometimes misleadingly, known as deduction and induction. There can be no question that there are wide divergencies between scientific and formal logical reasoning, but our analysis has tried to make clear the key role of deductive methods in science and thus undermine any simplistic conception of logic and science as "opposites." Having done all of this, the reader may wonder at our inclusion of a separate chapter on philosophical reasoning. Many have thought and continue to think that philosophy as a discipline contains no peculiar or unique form of reasoning and that philosophical arguments consist in the subtle blending of formal and informal logic with factual claims and is—as a type of reasoning—reducible to logic and science. This claim—itself a philosophic one—may be warranted, but we felt that the form and basis of many philosophical arguments was sufficiently unique to include a chapter on them.

To this end we have gathered several specific arguments from the philosophic literature and we include them here with brief discussions of their context and intention. They do not represent the only kinds of arguments used in philosophy, but they are fairly typical and in one form or another recur over and again in philosophic writing. Whether they represent a unique

353

type of reasoning or just very abstract deductive and inductive arguments we leave as an open question. We will make no attempt to evaluate or discuss them in any detail as this will be left to the reader. In each case, however, we will include enough of the surrounding material to allow the reader to better carry out this evaluation.

8.2 DILEMMA

The first sort of argument we will consider is the *dilemma*. The reader will recognize that elements of the disjunctive syllogism are present in both examples below but it is clear that in each case there are special considerations that make the dilemma different from the elementary valid argument form. The most obvious source of this difference is the rejection of both (or at least the apparent rejection of both) disjuncts. To this extent the dilemma can be said to resemble the paradoxes discussed in section 6.2.4.

The initial example of dilemma comes from the Platonic dialogue known as the *Euthyphro*. The dialogues of Plato usually center around some concept (e.g., justice, friendship, knowledge, etc.) and contain Socrates as the main character with other characters representing various positions which Plato (and presumably Socrates) sought to question. In this particular dialogue, Euthyphro is a rather well-known and prominent citizen of Athens and his discussion with Socrates takes place in the vicinity of the Athenian court of law. The subject of this discussion is "piety" which is perhaps better translated as "righteousness" in general. The discussion arises as a result of the rather special circumstances in which Socrates finds Euthyphro. Socrates, himself, is on his way to the court to begin his own trial for impiety and corruption of the young and he discovers that Euthyphro is trying his own father for murder—an act that was extraordinary in view of the Greek attitude to the family and fathers in particular. Socrates feels that Euthyphro must certainly know what righteousness is, in view of the certainness with which he is willing to fly in the face of tradition. Further, Euthyphro's father did not murder another citizen but indirectly caused the death of a man who was himself a murderer. As the discussion of morality goes on it eventually reaches the issue of the gods' place in human ethical choices. The particular dilemma that Socrates then presents to Euthyphro is not an idle one because it can be generalized to apply to any ethical theory, such as Euthyphro's, that bases its conclusions on some part of god's will. Since this selection is rather extended we have italicized the most precise formulation of the dilemma as it occurs. However, the material that both precedes and follows this formulation is quite essential to a full understanding of the argument.

EUTH.   Yes, I should say that what all the gods love is pious and holy, and the opposite which they all hate, impious.

SOC.   Ought we to inquire into the truth of this, Euthyphro, or simply to accept it on our own authority and that of others—echoing mere assertions? What do you say?

EUTH.   We should inquire; and I believe that the statement will stand the test of inquiry.

SOC.   We will soon be better able to say, my good friend. *The point which I should first wish to understand is whether the pious or holy is beloved by the gods because it is holy, or holy because it is beloved of the gods.*

EUTH.   I do not understand your meaning, Socrates.

SOC.   I will endeavour to explain: we speak of carrying and we speak of being carried, of leading and being led, seeing and being seen. You know that in all such cases there is a difference, and you know also in what the difference lies?

EUTH.   I think that I understand.

SOC.   And is not that which is beloved distinct from that which loves?

EUTH.   Certainly.

SOC.   Well; and now tell me, is that which is carried in this state of carrying because it is carried, or for some other reason?

EUTH.   No; that is the reason.

SOC.   And the same is true of what is led and of what is seen?

EUTH.   True.

SOC.   And a thing is not seen because it is visible, but conversely, visible because it is seen; nor is a thing led because it is in the state of being led, or carried because it is in the state of being carried, but the converse of this. And now I think, Euthyphro, that my meaning will be intelligible; and my meaning is, that any state of action or passion implies previous action or passion. It does not become because it is becoming, but it is in a state of becoming because it becomes; neither does it suffer because it is in a state of suffering, but it is in a state of suffering because it suffers. Do you not agree?

EUTH.   Yes.

SOC.   Is not that which is loved in some state either of becoming or suffering?

EUTH.   Yes.

SOC.   And the same holds as in the previous instances; the state of being loved follows the act of being loved, and not the act the state.

EUTH.   Certainly.

SOC.   And what do you say of piety, Euthyphro: is not piety, according to your definition, loved by all the gods?

EUTH.   Yes.

SOC.   Because it is pious or holy, or for some other reason?

EUTH.   No, that is the reason.

SOC.   It is loved because it is holy, not holy because it is loved?

EUTH.   Apparently.

SOC.   And it is the object of the gods' love, and is dear to them, because it is loved of them?

EUTH.   Certainly.

SOC.   Then that which is dear to the gods, Euthyphro, is not holy, nor is that which is holy dear to the gods, as you affirm; but they are two different things.

EUTH.   How do you mean, Socrates?

SOC.   I mean to say that the holy has been acknowledged by us to be loved because it is holy, not to be holy because it is loved.

EUTH.   Yes.

SOC.   But that which is dear to the gods is dear to them because it is loved by them, not loved by them because it is dear to them.

EUTH.   True.

SOC.   But, friend Euthyphro, if that which is holy were the same with that which is dear to the gods, and were loved because it is holy, then that which is dear to the gods would be loved as being dear to them; but if that which is dear to them were dear to them because loved by them, then that which is holy would be holy because loved by them. But now you see that the reverse is the case, and that the two things are quite different from one another. For one is of a kind to be loved because it is loved, and the other is loved because it is of a kind to be loved. Thus you appear to me, Euthyphro, when I ask you what is the nature of holiness, to offer an attribute only, and not the essence—the attribute of being loved by all the gods. But you still do not explain to me the nature of holiness. And therefore, if you please, I will ask you not to hide your treasure, but to start again, and tell me frankly what holiness or piety really is, whether dear to the gods or not (for that is a matter about which we will not quarrel); and what is impiety?

The second example of dilemma comes from a considerably more recent source, the *Critique of Pure Reason* by Immanuel Kant (1724-1804). This work is a highly intricate one in which the particular selection below represents one, relatively minor, part. In it Kant is arguing for the general absurdity of treating the issues of space and time in the traditional ways. His attack on this traditional viewpoint involves first setting up the dilemma and then showing that both choices are equally convincing and equally supportable. Since, however, both choices are mutually exclusive, Kant feels that he has reduced the original positions (each of which is represented by one "horn" or disjunct) to absurdity. *Antinomies* is the special name that Kant gave to this use of the dilemma. The reader should be aware that this selection actually involves two dilemmas, as Kant argues both for the absurdity of considering the universe as either limited (or unlimited) in time or space. In what follows below the reader can identify the dilemma by disjoining the "thesis" and the "antithesis" which are Kant's terms for the two horns of the dilemma.

THESIS

The world has a beginning in time, and is also limited as regards space.

PROOF

If we assume that the world has no beginning in time, then up to every given moment an eternity has elapsed, and there has passed away in the world an infinite series of successive states of things. Now the infinity of a series consists in the fact that it can never be completed through successive synthesis. It thus follows that it is impossible for an infinite world-series to have passed away, and that a beginning of the world is therefore a necessary condition of the world's existence. This was the first point that called for proof.

As regards the second point, let us again assume the opposite, namely, that the world is an infinite given whole of co-existing things. Now the magnitude of a quantum which is not given in intuition as within certain limits, can be thought only through the synthesis of its parts, and the totality of such a quantum only through a synthesis that is brought to completion through repeated addition of unit to unit. In order, therefore, to think, as a whole, the world which fills all spaces, the successive synthesis of the parts of an infinite world must be viewed as completed, that is, an infinite time must be viewed as having elapsed in the enumeration of all co-existing things. This, however, is impossible. An infinite aggregate of actual things cannot therefore be viewed as a given whole, nor consequently as simultaneously given. The world is, therefore, as regards extension in space, not infinite, but is enclosed within limits. This was the second point in dispute.

The world has no beginning, and no limits in space; it is infinite as regards both time and space.

PROOF

For let us assume that it has a beginning. Since the beginning is an existence which is preceded by a time in which the thing is not, there must have been a preceding time in which the world was not, *i.e.* an empty time. Now no coming to be of a thing is possible in an empty time, because no part of such a time possesses, as compared with any other, a distinguishing condition of existence rather than of non-existence; and this applies whether the thing is supposed to arise of itself or through some other cause. In the world many series of things can, indeed, begin; but the world itself cannot have a beginning, and is therefore infinite in respect of past time.

As regards the second point, let us start by assuming the opposite, namely, that the world in space is finite and limited, and consequently exists in an empty space which is unlimited. Things will therefore not only be related *in space* but also related *to space*. Now since the world is an absolute whole beyond which there is no object of intuition, and therefore no correlate with which the world stands in relation, the relation of the world to empty space would be a relation of it to no *object.* But such a relation, and consequently the limitation of the world by empty space, is nothing. The world cannot, therefore, be limited in space; that is, it is infinite in respect of extension.*

8.3 INFINITE REGRESS

The second type of philosophical argument to be discussed is the *infinite regress argument.* In this argument, which is itself a variation on the *reductio ad absurdum,* a position is shown to be unacceptable because it leads to an indefinite series of higher generality arguments which are themselves never resolved. The main source of dispute as to the validity of this procedure centers around the rejection of any argument that leads to such an infinite series. It is not obviously absurd for an argument to lead to such a series and yet in most cases in which the regress argument is employed the infinite series is taken as sufficient reason to reject the argument which led to it.

Our first example comes from the area of the philosophy of religion. Among the various attempts to prove the existence of God there is the famous cosmological argument first used in a different context by Aristotle and then applied

*Reprinted from Immanuel Kant, *Critique of Pure Reason,* pp. 396-398, by permission of St. Martin's Press, Inc., New York, and Macmillan & Company, Limited, London.

more directly to religion by St. Thomas Aquinas. We have included two forms of this argument as found in the *Summa Theologica* of St. Thomas Aquinas. Both forms employ the argument of infinite regress, but they do so in slightly different ways and the reader should attempt to understand these differences.

The existence of God can be proved in five ways.

The first and more manifest way is the argument from motion. It is certain, and evident to our senses, that in the world some things are in motion. Now whatever is moved is moved by another, for nothing can be moved except as it is in potentiality to that towards which it is moved; whereas a thing moves inasmuch as it is in act. For motion is nothing else than the reduction of something from potentiality to actuality. But nothing can be reduced from potentiality to actuality, except by something in a state of actuality. Thus that which is actually hot, as fire, makes wood, which is potentially hot, to be actually hot, and thereby moves and changes it. Now it is not possible that the same thing should be at once in actuality and potentiality in the same respect, but only in different respects. For what is actually hot cannot simultaneously be potentially hot; but it is simultaneously potentially cold. It is therefore impossible that in the same respect and in the same way a thing should be both mover and moved, i.e., that it should move itself. Therefore, whatever is moved must be moved by another. If that by which it is moved be itself moved, then this also must needs be moved by another, and that by another again. But this cannot go on to infinity, because then there would be no first mover, and consequently, no other mover, seeing that subsequent movers move only inasmuch as they are moved by the first mover; as the staff moves only because it is moved by the hand. Therefore it is necessary to arrive at a first mover, moved by no other; and this everyone understands to be God.

The second way is from the nature of efficient cause. In the world of sensible things we find there is an order of efficient causes. There is no case known (neither is it, indeed, possible) in which a thing is found to be the efficient cause of itself; for so it would be prior to itself, which is impossible. Now in efficient causes it is not possible to go on to infinity, because in all efficient causes following in order, the first is the cause of the intermediate cause and the intermediate is the cause of the ultimate cause, whether the intermediate cause be several, or one only. Now to take away the cause is to take away the effect. Therefore, if there be no first cause among efficient causes, there will be no ultimate, nor any intermediate cause. But if in efficient causes it is possible to go on to infinity, there will be no first efficient cause, neither will there be an ultimate effect, nor any intermediate efficient causes; all of which is plainly false. Therefore it is necessary to admit a first efficient cause, to which everyone gives the name of God.

The second specimen of infinite regress argument comes from Zeno of

Elea, the pre-Socratic philosopher of the fifth century B.C. The argument is employed as an attempt to prove the fundamental absurdity of motion, a problem which was of paramount importance to the pre-Socratic philosophers such as Parmenides. Xenophanes, and Heracleitus. The text of this version of the argument comes from the *Physics* of Aristotle since we have no extant edition of Zeno's original works. Zeno's arguments (or "paradoxes" as they are more commonly known) have had a fascinating history in philosophy and mathematical theory and have only been properly dealt with during the early twentieth century by employing the theory of infinite sets.

> Zeno's arguments about motion, which cause so much disquietude to those who try to solve the problems they present, are four in number. The first asserts the nonexistence of motion on the grounds that that which is in locomotion must arrive at the halfway stage before it arrives at the goal.
>
> The second is the so-called "Achilles" and it amounts to this, that in a race in which the slower runner is given a head start the quickest runner can never overtake the slowest, since the pursuer must first reach the point whence the pursued started, so that the slower must always hold a lead. This argument is the same in principle as the former which depended on bisection, though it differs from it in that the space with which we successively have to deal is not divided into halves. The result of the argument is that the slower is not overtaken: but it proceeds along the same lines as the bisection argument (for in both a division of the space in a certain way leads to the result that the goal is not reached, though the "Achilles" goes further in that it affirms that even the quickest runner in legendary tradition must fail in his pursuit of the slowest), so that the solution must be the same.

In essence, the first two arguments of Zeno can be put as follows:

1. In order for a person to get from one point to another (say A to B) he must first reach the midpoint. However, he must also be able to reach the midpoint of the distance from the midpoint of A-B to B. Since his trip will take him through an infinite number of such midpoints, he will never be able to reach B in a finite amount of time and so motion from A to B is impossible.

2. In this argument one is to imagine Achilles and a slower runner set to run a race in which the slower runner is given a lead. Now, after a certain amount of time Achilles will reach the point at which the slower runner started; however, in this time the slower runner will have run some small distance farther and will still have a lead. Achilles will then run this smaller distance and will again be at the point where the slower runner was after the first

interval but again the slower runner will have run some distance further on and will have a lead. Since this division goes on infinitely Achilles will never catch the slower runner at all.

8.4 ANALOGY

The last of our samples of philosophic arguments is, perhaps, the most common and yet the most difficult to analyze and evaluate. Often, philosophers make assertions which seem unsupportable by ordinary evidence. In many of these instances the philosopher appeals to an *argument from analogy* to support his position (or in some cases, to simply clarify his position). There has been considerable discussion as to whether the use of analogy or metaphor in metaphysical writing is argumentative at all, but it seems to us that the use of analogical arguments is so common that it is necessary to include examples in any catalogue of philosophical arguments. Whether they are indeed arguments or just explanatory devices or both we leave to the reader. However, when an argument based on analogy is presented in philosophic contexts it presents certain special problems for evaluation and we will briefly consider them.

First, it is clear that analogical arguments are inductive arguments in that the premises of the argument support but do not necessitate the conclusion. However, in most uses of analogy in philosophical arguments the conclusion of the argument goes far beyond the usual inductive range of support. To see this let us consider two uses of analogical arguments as inductive arguments. In the case of inductive arguments from a sample of a population to the whole population the argument would appear as follows:

All the members of the population sample have property M.
∴ The entire population has the property M.

In this case the whole population is considered as analogous to the sample and this can be verified or refuted. In fact, while this argument may be helpful to establish certain conclusions it is such that it can be completely unpacked and checked. We can always, in theory, check the whole population for property M. (The reader should refer to the sections in Chapter 7 that deal with the confirmation of laws in science for a fuller discussion of the problems associated with arguments such as the one above but our only point here is that such arguments can be checked though perhaps not with certitude.)

In the second example this sort of checking is less possible but still can be performed. The argument can be written as follows (it should be familiar to those who have read Chapter 3):

> The flow of water in pipes is analogous to the flow of electricity in circuits.
> ∴ Given that the flow of water in pipes has property M the flow of electricity in a circuit will have property M.

In this case the analogy is checkable by reference to certain features of the two physical systems with respect to the propositional logic as presented in Chapter 3. It is clear that the similarity of the two systems is not completely accurate but the point at which the two diverge is quite easily ascertainable and the argument presents no great riddle.

However, in the case of the two analogical arguments reprinted below, one cannot test for accuracy or adequacy in that the philosopher never intended the argument to be used in either of the above ways. In our examples the analogy is used both to explain and support a certain view of philosophical issues and in both cases it would be missing the point to attempt the sort of evaluation which is usually performed on the inductive uses of analogical reasoning.

The first of our arguments from analogy comes from *Republic* of Plato. In Book VII of this work Plato uses an extended analogy to convince the reader of his particular position with respect to reality. Briefly, it is his concern to prove that the world of sensual, empirical belief is not the actual or real world and that there is indeed a reality which underlies or supports the mere appearance with which human beings come in contact in their daily lives. Now, this is certainly not an easy conclusion to prove and the well-known allegory of the cave can be seen as an argument to support it.

> And now, I said, let me show in a figure how far our nature is enlightened or unenlightened:—Behold! human beings living in an underground den, which has a mouth open towards the light and reaching all along the den; here they have been from their childhood, and have their legs and necks chained so that they cannot move, and can only see before them, being prevented by the chains from turning round their heads. Above and behind them a fire is blazing at a distance, and between the fire and the prisoners there is a raised way;

and you will see, if you look, a low wall built along the way, like the screen which marionette players have in front of them, over which they show the puppets.

I see.

And do you see, I said, men passing along the wall carrying all sorts of vessels, and statues and figures of animals made of wood and stone and various materials, which appear over the wall? Some of them are talking, others silent.

You have shown me a strange image, and they are strange prisoners.

Like ourselves, I replied; and they see only their own shadows, or the shadows of one another, which the fire throws on the opposite wall of the cave?

True, he said; how could they see anything but the shadows if they were never allowed to move their heads?

And of the objects which are being carried in like manner they would only see the shadows?

Yes, he said.

And if they were able to converse with one another, would they not suppose that they were naming what was actually before them?

Very true.

And suppose further that the prison had an echo which came from the other side, would they not be sure to fancy when one of the passers-by spoke that the voice which they heard came from the passing shadow?

No question, he replied.

To them, I said, the truth would be literally nothing but the shadows of the images.

That is certain.

And now look again, and see what will naturally follow if the prisoners are released and disabused of their error. At first, when any of them is liberated and compelled suddenly to stand up and turn his neck round and walk and look towards the light, he will suffer sharp pains; the glare will distress him, and he will be unable to see the realities of which in his former state he had seen the shadows; and then conceive someone saying to him, that what he saw before was an illusion, but that now, when he is approaching nearer to being and his eye is turned towards more real existence, he has a clearer vision,—what will be his reply? And you may further imagine that his instructor is pointing to the objects as they pass and requiring him to name them,—will he not be perplexed? Will he not fancy that the shadows which he formerly saw are truer than the objects which are now shown to him?

Far truer.

And if he is compelled to look straight at the light, will he not have a pain in his eyes which will make him turn away to take refuge in the objects of vision which he can see, and which he will conceive to be in reality clearer than the things which are now being shown to him?

True, he said.

And suppose once more, that he is reluctantly dragged up a steep and rugged ascent, and held fast until he is forced into the presence of the sun himself, is he not likely to be pained and irritated? When he approaches the light his eyes will be dazzled, and he will not be able to see anything at all of what are now called realities.

Not all in a moment, he said.

He will require to grow accustomed to the sight of the upper world. And first he will see the shadows best, next the reflections of men and other objects in the water, and then the objects themselves; then he will gaze upon the light of the moon and the stars and the spangled heaven; and he will see the sky and the stars by night better than the sun or the light of the sun by day?

Certainly.

Last of all he will be able to see the sun, and not mere reflections of him in the water, but he will see him in his own proper place, and not in another; and he will contemplate him as he is.

Certainly.

He will then proceed to argue that this is he who gives the season and the years, and is the guardian of all that is in the visible world, and in a certain way the cause of all things which he and his fellows have been accustomed to behold?

Clearly, he said, he would first see the sun and then reason about him.

And when he remembered his old habitation, and the wisdom of the den and his fellow-prisoners, do you not suppose that he would felicitate himself on the change, and pity them?

Certainly, he would.

And if they were in the habit of conferring honours among themselves on those who were quickest to observe the passing shadows and to remark which of them went before, and which followed after, and which were together; and who were therefore best able to draw conclusions as to the future, do you think that he would care for such honours and glories, or envy the possessors of them? Would he not say with Homer, "Better to be the poor servant of a poor master," and to endure anything, rather than think as they do and live after their manner?

Yes, he said, I think that he would rather suffer anything than entertain these false notions and live in this miserable manner.

Imagine once more, I said, such an one coming suddenly out of the sun to be replaced in his old situation; would he not be certain to have his eyes full of darkness?

To be sure, he said.

And if there were a contest, and he had to compete in measuring the shadows with the prisoners who had never moved out of the den, while his sight was still weak, and before his eyes had become steady (and the time which would be needed to acquire this new habit of sight might be very considerable), would he not be ridiculous? Men would say of him that up he went and down he came without his eyes; and that it was better not even to think of ascending; and if any one tried to loose another and lead him up to the light, let them only catch the offender, and they would put him to death.

No question, he said.

This entire allegory, I said, you may now append, dear Glaucon, to the previous argument; the prison-house is the world of sight, the light of the fire is the sun, and you will not misapprehend me if you interpret the journey upwards to be the ascent of the soul into the intellectual world according to my poor belief, which, at your desire, I have expressed—whether rightly or wrongly God knows. But, whether true or false, my opinion is that in the world of knowledge the idea of good appears last of all, and is seen only with an effort; and, when seen, is also inferred to be the universal author of all things beautiful and right, parent of light and of the lord of light in this visible world, and the immediate source of reason and truth in the intellectual; and that this is the power upon which he who would act rationally either in public or private life must have his eye fixed.

The second analogical argument comes from the Introduction to the *Nouveaux Essais* (*New Essays Concerning Human Understanding*) by G. W. Leibniz, the seventeenth-century German mathematician and philosopher. The work is intended as a rebuttal to the position of John Locke and the analogy we have chosen is central to the understanding of the Leibnizian criticism of Locke. It was Locke's position that the human mind is like a blank tablet (*tabula rasa*) at birth and that all of our knowledge comes to us through one or more of the senses. Leibniz is not in complete disagreement with this but his position is that the mind is not a passive or empty receptacle of knowledge but is in some way responsible for the structure of the knowledge which we do get from the senses. Leibniz attempts to argue for this position by countering the tabula rasa image of Locke with his own analogy of a block of marble.

Perhaps our able author will not differ entirely from my opinion. For after having employed the whole of his first book in rejecting innate knowledge (lumieres), taken in a certain sense, he nevertheless admits at the beginning of the second and in what follows, that the ideas which do not originate in sensation come from reflection. Now reflection is nothing else than attention to what is in us, and the senses do not give us that which we already carry with us. This being so, can it be denied that there is much that is innate in our mind, since we are innate, so to say, in ourselves, and since there is in ourselves, being, unity, substance, duration, change, action, perception, pleasure and a thousand other objects of our intellectual ideas? And these objects being immediate to our understanding and always present (although they cannot be always perceived on account of our distractions and wants), why be astonished that we say that these ideas, with all which depends on them, are innate in us? I have made use also of the comparison of a block of marble which has veins, rather than of a block of marble wholly even, or of blank tablets, that is to say, of what is called among philosophers *tabula rasa.* For if the soul resembled these blank tablets, truths would be in us as the figure of Hercules is in marble when the marble is entirely indifferent toward receiving this figure or some other. But if there were veins in the block which should mark out the figure of Hercules rather than other figures, the block would be more determined thereto, and Hercules would be in it as in some sort innate, although it would be necessary to labor in order to discover these veins and to cleanse them by polishing and by cutting away that which prevents them from appearing. It is thus that ideas and truths are innate in us, as inclinations, dispositions, habits, or natural capacities, and not as actions; although these capacities are always accompanied by some actions, often insensible, which correspond to them.

In concluding, we remind the reader that the philosophic arguments presented here are by no means uncontroversial and that they raise the following issues:

1. Are philosophical arguments unique as arguments or are they merely complex uses of logical and scientific arguments?

2. Are these arguments valid, and whether they are or are not valid, are there any special techniques of evaluation required?

Though such questions are certainly significant, we can only raise them as special issues in the pragmatic aspect of logic.

alternate symbols and notational devices

In this book we have employed the symbols used by B. Russell and A. N. Whitehead in their *Principia Mathematica* (1910-1913). However, we include this appendix so that the reader can better deal with the variant conventions that he might find in his reading of other works on logic. The notation we have used is the most widely employed, but each of the following may be encountered:

I.   Variant forms of propositional connectives and quantifiers:

Our Symbols	Variants
$\sim P$	$\overline{P}, \neg P, -P$
$P \,\&\, Q$	$PQ, P \wedge Q, P \cdot Q$
$P \vee Q$	
$P \supset Q$	$P \rightarrow Q$
$P \equiv Q$	$P \leftrightarrow Q$
(x)	$\forall x, \Pi x$
$(\exists x)$	$(\mathsf{E}x), \Sigma x$

Each of the variants can be used within the basic system of parenthetical and bracketing conventions as employed in this book.

II.   Devices for eliminating some or all occurrences of parentheses.

A. Order of precedence: By assigning varying orders of precedence to each of our connectives we can leave out a large number of our parenthetical devices while still retaining clarity. The order of precedence is as follows:

$$\equiv \supset v \, \& \sim$$

What this means is that there is greater degree of scope as one moves from right to left in the sequence. Thus, the formula, $P \supset Q \, v \, R$ is to be understood as, $P \supset (Q \, v \, R)$ in our full parenthetical notation. As an exercise that will allow the reader to become more familiar with this notational convention, write the full parenthetical form of each of the following formulas using the above order of precedence:

1. $P \equiv Q \, v \, R \, \& \, S$
2. $P \supset Q \equiv R \, \& \, S$
3. $N \, v \sim P \supset S$

Of course, this order of precedence will not eliminate *all* occurrences of parentheses (and/or brackets) since we will have problems of ambiguity with formulas that have more than one occurrence of the same proposition connective. Thus, our order of precedence will be of no use in the writing the following formula clearly:

$$P \supset Q \supset R \, \& \, S$$

In such cases, then, we will have to use some of our former conventions governing parentheses which would result in

$$(P \supset Q) \supset R \, \& \, S$$

B. The use of dots as parentheses and brackets: A method of dispensing with parentheses is provided by the notational convention involving dots in the following sorts of configurations:

$$., \quad :, \quad .:, \quad ::$$

The use of the dots is based on a certain obvious fact about the use of parentheses and brackets. The reader has probably realized that parentheses are not needed in pairs in order to carry out their function since elimination of ambiguity can be accomplished with only a "one-sided" device. Thus in the formula:

$$P \equiv [Q \,\&\, (R \vee S)]$$

we could eliminate a number of parentheses by placing them around the appropriate connective as below:

$$P \equiv [Q \,\&\, (R \vee S$$

However, it is clear that we still would require some additional conventions as far as the scope of these one-sided parentheses was concerned and the use of dots instead of parentheses (or, sometimes, in conjunction with parentheses) fills that need. The dots are placed next to the connectives and they have a scope that goes until the end of the formula (moving away from the connective) or until they are superseded by dots of a higher power. Two dots supersedes one dot, three supersedes two, etc. Below we have written three formulas with parentheses on the right and with dots on the left and these should serve as models for any future use of dots:

1. $P \equiv : Q \,\&\, . \, R \vee S$ $\qquad$ $P \equiv [Q \,\&\, (R \vee S)]$
2. $P \supset . \, Q \supset R$ $\qquad$ $P \supset (Q \supset R)$
3. $P \,\&\, : Q \supset . \, R \vee S$ $\qquad$ $P \,\&\, [Q \supset (R \vee S)]$

III   The Polish notation. So far we have considered various changes that can be made in the notational conventions; these have usually served either to simplify or were used because of their historical connections. However, the Polish notation (so-called because of its use by certain Polish logicians) involves major changes both in the writing of connectives and in the writing of formulas. The only aspect of this notation that does not significantly change is the use of letters such as p, q, r for propositions. Perhaps the best way to introduce this system is to begin with the monadic and diadic connectives in their simplest form. The following is a list of these connectives with their translation into the notation we have used on the right.

Np $\qquad$ $\sim\!P$
Kpq $\qquad$ $P \,\&\, Q$
Apq $\qquad$ $P \vee Q$
Cpq $\qquad$ $P \supset Q$

In this notation there is no need for parentheses as the left-most letter will indicate the scope of the connective; that is, in a formula with two connective letters such as $CCpqr$, we interpret the inner C as $P \supset Q$ and the outer C as $(P \supset Q) \supset R$. In this way the Polish notation avoids the need for parentheses.

definite descriptions

In Chapter 4 we introduced the use of individual constants to designate particular individuals. The examples of their use in that chapter, in connection with the symbolization of propositions, always involved the occurrence of proper names. There is another context, however, which seems to naturally present itself as one that would require the use of an individual constant for adequate symbolization.

The context we are speaking about is that of the use of descriptions that are meant to pick out a single individual or, to put it another way, that are meant to specify conditions that only a single thing could meet. Some examples of this sort of description, which is called a *definite description*, are

The author of Waverly
The tallest boy in the class
The current President of the United States

Since, on the face of it, these definite descriptions seem to do the job of proper names, i.e., they seem to designate particular individuals, we may be led into simply replacing such a description by an individual constant when symbolizing a proposition containing such a description. The point of this appendix is to show that however natural this use of the individual constant may seem it can lead to insuperable problems. After establishing this, we will present a method of symbolizing definite descriptions developed by Bertrand Russell which escapes these difficulties.

Let us consider the proposition,

1. The tallest boy in the class is Harvey.

Proposition 1 can be false for various reasons. One possibility is that the tallest boy in the class is not Harvey; say John is. Another possibility is that there is no tallest boy in the class. There are two ways in which this might occur. It is possible that there are no boys in the class and so no tallest one, or it may be the case that there are two or more boys of the same height that are taller than all the other boys.

In summary, 1 may be false if no one satisfies the definite description it contains or if more than one person satisfies it. In light of the foregoing it should be clear that the use of an individual constant to symbolize the definite description will not do. If we symbolize proposition 1 as

2. $a = h$

where a designates the individual who is the tallest boy in the class and h designates Harvey, we have a formula whose truth conditions are very different from those of 1. Of course 2 will suffice as a symbolization of 1 where we have the additional information that there is indeed one and only one tallest boy in the class. But as we have seen elsewhere we wish to make as small an existential assumption in our logic as possible, and the assumption that every definite description does in fact designate is a very strong assumption indeed. It is far better, then, to symbolize 1 in such a way that no assumption is made as to whether or not the definite description does in fact designate an individual.

We have seen that proposition 1 is true if and only if there is at least one and at most one tallest boy in the class and that boy is Harvey. In section 4.5.2 we developed a technique of symbolizing expressions that predicated properties of at least one and at most one individual. Utilizing that technique we get

3. $(\exists x) [(Tx \,\&\, (y) (Ty \supset (y = x))) \,\&\, (x = h)]$

which says that there exists something, say x, which is the tallest boy in the class, and if anything is the tallest boy in the class then that thing is x, and x is Harvey. Which can also be read, there is at least one thing and at most one thing that is the tallest boy in the class and that thing is Harvey. An examination of 3 will show that it has exactly the same truth conditions that we found for 1 and is thus a suitable symbolization of it.

In general then when we encounter a proposition of the form

The so-and-so is such-and-such.

we translate it as

$(\exists x) \{[\emptyset x \,\&\, (y) (\emptyset y \supset (y = x))] \,\&\, \psi x\}$

and not as ψa.[1]

---

[1] Although it is generally agreed that we should not symbolize "The so-and-so has property Ψ" as Ψa, not everyone agrees that it should be symbolized as we have above, à la Russell. It is argued that it is very curious to call a statement like "The present King of France is bald" false, since to do so would indicate that the present King of France, has hair on his head and not that there does not exist a present King of France. On the other hand a statement like "The golden mountain is golden" which seems like a truth is a falsehood on Russell's interpretation since there is no golden mountain. In this connection see P. F. Strawson, *Introduction to Logical Theory* (New York: Wiley, 1952) and Rudolf Carnap, *Meaning and Necessity* (Chicago: University of Chicago Press, 1947).

selected readings

The reader will find below the additional reading materials to which we have referred throughout the text. They are arranged by topic and the consultation of the items in each area should provide the student both with supplementary information and further bibliographic suggestions. There is no intention that this list be exhaustive, so much as introductory to further study.

I. GENERAL WORKS

The following three books are more advanced treatments of formal logic.

Church, Alonzo. *Introduction to Mathematical Logic*. Princeton: Princeton University Press, 1956.

Kleene, S. C. *Mathematical Logic*. New York: Wiley, 1967.

Mendelsohn, Elliot. *Introduction to Mathematical Logic*. New York: Van Nostrand, 1964.

II. SYLLOGISTIC

Bird, Otto. *Syllogistic and Its Extensions*. Englewood Cliffs, N. J.: Prentice-Hall, 1964.

Lukasiewicz, J. *Aristotle's Syllogistic*. Oxford: Clarendon Press, 1959.

III. PROPOSITIONAL LOGIC

The reader will find much advanced material in the general works listed above.

On truth trees

Beth E. W. *Formal Methods.* Dordrecht, Holland: D. Reidel, 1962.

Jeffrey, R. C. *Logic: Its Scope and Limits.* New York: McGraw-Hill, 1967.

Smullyan, R. M. *Theory of Formal Systems.* Princeton, N. J.: Princeton University Press, 1961.

On modal logic

Feys, R. *Modal Logics.* Paris: Gauthier-Villars, 1965.

Lewis, C. I. and Langford, C. H. *Symbolic Logic.* New York: Dover, 1951.

Von Wright, G. H. *An Essay in Modal Logic.* Amsterdam: North-Holland, 1951.

On many-valued logics

Rescher, N. *Many-Valued Logic.* New York: McGraw-Hill, 1970.

On the logic of probability

Carnap, R. *Logical Foundations of Probability.* Chicago: University of Chicago Press, 1962.

Nagel, Ernst. *Principles of The Theory of Probability.* Chicago: University of Chicago Press, 1939.

Von Wright, G. H. *Treatise on Induction and Probability.* New York: Littlefield Adams, 1960.

On the historical background of logic the reader should refer to

Kneale, W., and Kneale, M. *The Development of Logic.* Oxford: Oxford University Press, 1962.

IV. PREDICATE LOGIC

No special references are needed here. The general works above are sufficient.

V. FORMAL SYSTEMS

Again in this area the general works are very useful. In addition, however, consult:

Hilbert, D., and Ackerman, W. *Principles of Mathematical Logic*. New York: Chelsea, 1950.

Smullyan, R. M. *Theory of Formal Systems*. Princeton, N. J.: Princeton University Press, 1961.

VI. LOGIC AND LANGUAGE

Fodor, J., and Katz, J. *The Structure of Language*. Englewood Cliffs, N.J.: Prentice-Hall, 1964.

Ogden, C. K., and Richards, I. A. *The Meaning of Meaning*. New York: Harcourt, Brace & World, 1923.

Quine, W. V. O. *From a Logical Point of View*. Cambridge: Harvard University Press, 1953.

Robinson, R. *Definition*. Oxford: Oxford University Press, 1950.

Wittgenstein, L. *Philosophical Investigations*. New York: Macmillan, 1953.

VII. LOGIC OF SCIENCE

Feigl, H., and Brodbeck, M. *Readings in the Philosophy of Science*. New York: Appleton-Century-Crofts, 1953.

Nagel, Ernst. *The Structure of Science*. New York: Harcourt, Brace & World, 1961.

VIII. PHILOSOPHICAL ARGUMENTS

Passmore, J. *Philosophical Reasoning.* New York: Scribner, 1961.

Ryle, G. *Dilemmas.* Cambridge, Eng.: Cambridge University Press, 1954.

index